Peace Movements and Political Cultures

Peace Movements and Political Cultures

EDITED BY

CHARLES CHATFIELD

AND PETER VAN DEN DUNGEN

THE UNIVERSITY OF TENNESSEE PRESS / KNOXVILLE

LIBRARY OF CONGRESS CATALOGING-IN-PUBLICATION DATA

Peace movements and political cultures / edited by Charles Chatfield
and Peter van den Dungen.— 1st ed.
    p. cm.
    Results of a conference held at Bad Tatzmannsdorf and
Stadtschlaining, Austria, in Aug. 1986; sponsored by the Council on
Peace Research in History (United States).
    Includes bibliographies and index.
    ISBN 0-87049-576-3 (alk. paper)
    1. Peace — History — Congresses. 2. Peace — Research — History —
Congresses. I. Chatfield, Charles, 1934- . II. Van den Dungen,
Peter. III. Council on Peace Research in History.
JX1931 1986a   88-1902
327.1'72'09—dc19   CIP

JX
1931
1986a

Copy 1

FOR OUR COLLEAGUE
CHARLES DEBENEDETTI
(1943–1987)

Contents

Preface

THIS VOLUME IS THE RESULT of a conference held at Bad Tatzmannsdorf and Stadtschlaining, Austria, in August 1986, at which leading scholars from Europe, North America, and Australia compared peace advocacy in various nations and periods.

Hosted by the Austrian Institute for Peace Research and partially supported by the Berghof Stiftung für Konfliktforschung of the Federal Republic of Germany, the conference grew out of two decades of increasing scholarship in the history of organized peace movements and, also, of increasing concern among historians about issues of war and peace. It was the result of growing contacts between European and North American historians and of several years of planning. Indeed, the conference was sponsored and organized by the Council on Peace Research in History (United States)* and an informal group of European scholars.

One result of the conference was agreement to develop closer transatlantic cooperation. Moreover, the European delegates agreed to develop further an informal regional network which might expand professional contacts, stimulate historical research, and, eventually, evolve into a more formal structure.**

A second result of the conference was to refine the import of peace research in history. Although the study of organized peace movements had been of primary focus for some time, many participants sought a wider context for that study and others sought to broaden the field itself. After extended discussion, the field was understood to include *the study of the historic causes and consequences*

---

*Prior to November 1986, the Conference on Peace Research in History (CPRH)
**Regarding the CPRH and the European Working Group on Peace Research in History, see the organizational notes in this volume.

of violent international conflict and of the historic search for alternatives to the violent resolution of international conflict.

The present volume is a third result of the conference. The quality and originality of the scholarly papers presented there merited publication. Moreover, the participants found themselves discussing variations on strikingly similar themes although the subject matter of their presentations had been only loosely prescribed. Their deliberation is reflected in the introduction to this volume.

The anthology is dedicated to Charles DeBenedetti, a former president of the Council on Peace Research in History and a distinguished historian whose works include, in addition to many articles, *Origins of the Modern American Peace Movement, 1915–1929* (1978), and *The Peace Reform in American History* (1980). It was typical of his generosity that he edited on behalf of the CPRH a book published in the year of the Stadtschlaining conference, *Peace Heroes in Twentieth-Century America,* in the process taking time from his work on the protest movement in the Vietnam era. At the conference Professor DeBenedetti presented his assessment of the American peace movement from 1945 to 1985. Shortly thereafter he was disabled by a brain tumor. This volume, which includes his last writing, is dedicated to him as an expression of appreciation by colleagues who have benefited from his scholarly leadership and personal friendship.

CHARLES CHATFIELD
AND PETER VAN DEN DUNGEN

Introduction

PEACE MOVEMENTS AND POLITICAL CULTURES

PEACE MOVEMENTS. Can people do anything together to contain war and advance peace? The question echoes through public debate, as nations ratchet up the technology of war one deadly round after another, losing meaningful connections with political goals and distorting the economic and social priorities of the globe. It is impossible either to glorify warfare, as men did scarcely a hundred years ago, or to be sanguine about achieving peace.

International conflict is primarily the province of governments, and so the question can be sharpened. Can the organized effort of private citizens affect the policies of governments toward one another? Believing that they could make a difference, individuals have promoted peace in public fora for over a hundred and fifty years. In the twentieth century — and despite rising nationalism and recurrent war — they achieved a significant stage of organization. They formed voluntary societies and, collectively, peace movements. They sought to change foreign policy and learned to mobilize public support for that purpose. Some of them opposed specific wars. Some refused to participate in them. Most promoted world order and international conciliation.

Peace advocates did play a role in changing the international system. They advocated international law and conferences, arbitration, and even regional and global organizations before such programs were accepted by governments. They contributed to the proliferation of international nongovernmental agencies. They promoted arms control and disarmament. The legitimacy of war no longer can be taken for granted, and that in some measure reflects their vision and effort.

It is difficult to assess their influence. The sources of official policy are often obscure and the impact of public advocacy is largely indirect. Moreover, one generation's solutions often do not address the next generation's problems. The innovative quality of the League of Nations is overshadowed, for instance, by the war it did not prevent. Finally, peace advocates are caught up in the conflicts they try to suppress, the cultures they seek to change.

Certainly, governments and intergovernmental agencies act as though citizen opinion and efforts are important. In recent years public initiatives and protests have become notable features of the nuclear arms debate, constraining political leaders to manage or respond to public pressure. Clearly, it is widely assumed in the literature of political science that the public plays a role in foreign policy. Indeed, there is a body of scholarship which views this role as increasing in significance.[1] The criteria of effectiveness are not well formulated, however. In some measure this is because of specialization within the social sciences and the limits of available data. Studies of public opinion are not well related to analyses of public pressure groups and governmental responses to them, and there is a dearth of comparative studies of various societies.[2] Perhaps most important, present peace efforts are not well related to historical experience, although, as Gregory Flynn and Hans Rattinger have remarked, "many security-related attitudes currently being marketed as novel are really not that different from those observed in earlier years."[3]

Since the mid-1960s historians have made peace movements the subject of a growing and now substantial body of scholarship.[4] The literature encompasses the period from the first organized peace societies (1815) to the present. It is narrative, biographical, and interpretive. Within its purview are not only citizen peace efforts but, also, diplomatic history and foreign relations. It includes studies of organizations and trends together with analyses of specific historical periods and crises. In some cases peace movements have been related to feminism and programs for social change. In others the concept of peace advocacy has been expanded from antiwar activism to internationalism and alternative approaches to national security.

American scholars have extended their studies of peace efforts to European history, and a comparable historical literature has developed in Europe, particularly in England, Germany, and the Netherlands.[5] Accordingly, there is now a scholarly basis for collaborative studies of peace advocacy. Indeed, in 1985 an international network of historians cooperated to produce a comprehensive *Biographical Dictionary of Modern Peace Leaders.*[6]

The historiography of peace movements has reached a point where comparative study is possible, taking into account the contexts of the various political cultures. Historians have quite naturally described the social characteristics of peace advocates. The essays in this volume go a step further and reflect on the relationship between peace movements and their political cultures.

POLITICAL CULTURE.   The concept of political culture refers to the collective beliefs, values, and symbols which define the meaning of political choices.[7] In the words of Lucien Pye, it "suggests that the traditions of a society, the spirit of its public institutions, the passions and the collective reasoning of its citizenry, and the style and operating codes of its leaders . . . fit together as a part of a meaningful whole . . . [which] encompasses both the political ideals and the operating norms of a polity."[8]

Groups which seek to change national polity or, in this case, foreign policy reflect the political culture in which they seek change. Their orientation—indeed, their very appreciation of it—affects their public strategy and effectiveness. In this volume, the relationship between peace movements and national political cultures is explored in terms of late–nineteenth–century Austria and Germany, Britain in the era of World War I, France and Germany in the interwar period, Australia in the nuclear age, and the United States throughout the period.

In a real sense, a dominant political culture also pervades the international system. Accordingly, as advocates of peace endeavored to organize internationally, they were influenced by political culture on that level. In this volume, aspects of the relationship between peace movements and international political cultures are explored in terms of the organization of Freemasonry, the International Peace Bureau up to World War I, feminist perspectives in that time, the peace education movement in the interwar period, and the movement to check competition in nuclear arms since World War II. Moreover, several authors explore the relationship between national political cultures and internationalist commitment and organization, notably in the United States and Australia.

Taken together, the essays in this volume offer a fresh basis for understanding peace efforts against the background of national political cultures compared in any given era or of international cultures compared by period.

PACIFISTS AND PEACE ADVOCATES

The word *pacifism* originally was created to refer to all advocates of peace — peace-seekers. During World War I its usage often was narrowed to advocates of peace who opposed war altogether, and, especially in the United States, the word thereafter denoted this sense of *absolute pacifism*. In Europe today it retains its original reference to anyone working for peace, but it carries some ambiguity.

In this volume *pacifism* or *pacifist* is used in the original, broad sense and is interchangeable with *peace advocacy* or *peace advocate*. Even the most convinced advocate of military security today portrays himself as a peacemaker, but in these essays peace advocacy implies challenging military approaches to security and developing alternatives such as negotiation, problem solving, nonviolent action, and international organization. When absolute pacifism is intended, the word *pacifism* will be used with an adjective (in French parlance this is conveyed by *integral pacifism*).

HISTORIANS AND PEACE ADVOCATES

The authors of these essays are professional historians. Some have value commitments which affect their interest in and sympathy for peace advocates, but all attempt to distinguish between their own views and those of their subjects. Nonetheless, they raise common interpretive questions which, it becomes clear, have been shared by peace advocates. These questions form underlying, often unstated themes in the volume. They are noted here in order to alert the reader to the contemporary and analytical significance of these historical inquiries.

PACIFISTS AS DISSENTERS FROM AND PRISONERS OF THEIR POLITICAL CULTURES.   While peace advocates favored policy changes in their societies, they also shared the social values and assumptions which underlay established policies. As pacifists they shared some values, beliefs, and roles which they consciously forged for themselves; they had others, however, which were imparted to them through the culture in which they were socialized. Their choice of goals and strategy reflected not only their assessment of their societies but, as well, their subjective and often culturally given assumptions.

Although a social movement may be understood as a collective bearer of an alternative identity (as Roger Chickering proposes), it also shares important aspects of the prevailing national identity. This certainly was the case for peace groups. Sometimes clouding self-understanding, this condition also raises problems for political strategy: would it be most effective to pursue alternative foreign policies by challenging or by working with the dominant symbols and assumptions of a society? This quandary is evident, although it was not then explicitly perceived, in the cases of Wilhelmine Germany and Habsburg Austria. Similarly, the liberal and bourgeois character of most peace advocates in the late nineteenth and early twentieth centuries biased their vision of peace and their programs. A comparable problem faced internationalists in the United States, perhaps making them vulnerable to a hegemonic version of world leadership, and it has challenged opponents of nuclear arms internationally.

There are other examples of the problem of challenging selective aspects of an accepted political culture. The cosmopolitan aspirations of Freemasonry paled before division over both fraternal issues and nationalistic conflict. There was sometimes poignant conflict between individual roles and social loyalties in the international peace education movement and French pacifism between the world wars, and among the exiled German pacifists in the 1930s.

The extent to which socialization defined women's roles was recognized by the women who first forged a link between feminism and pacifism. Their perception was sharpened by World War I (or the Boer War in the case of Olive Schreiner), and was applied to the general process by which women were socialized into accepting a national security system based on military power. Their heightened consciousness led some women to take alternative roles and to promote other values.

In some respects, peace advocates in all periods might have been more effective if they had related their efforts more explicitly to the dominant cultural symbols and centers of power. In other respects, their failure to distance themselves from establishments appears to have led to their co-optation. This raises a question of contemporary as well as historical significance: what is the relationship between pacifist strategy and political culture as an explanation for success and failure in achieving concrete foreign policy goals?

In any case, appreciating the constraints of cultural milieu can help in the assessment of peace efforts. Even the meager record of

---

nineteenth-century pacifists was a measure of the force of nationalism, imperialism, Social Darwinism, and the presumed legitimacy and moral virtue of war. The historic significance of peace advocacy must be weighed against the force of contemporaneous currents.

PEACE ADVOCATES AS AGENTS OF SOCIAL CHANGE.   A second and related theme is the question of appropriate goals and strategies for change. Thus, peace advocacy evinces a tension between the ideal of transforming society and the strategy of reforming it incrementally. To some extent this tension reflects the weight of political culture. To a large extent it reflects choices of political approach which, most recently in the antinuclear campaigns, have divided peace advocates among themselves. The tension is expressed also in terms of alternative social philosophies. Often the limited goal of preventing the outbreak of war accompanies a disposition to reform existing institutions, whereas the larger goal of eliminating the occasion for conflict is associated with a commitment to transform society.

Variously expressed and often implicit, this choice of emphases separated liberal from socialist peace advocates prior to World War I. During that conflict, especially in the English-speaking world, it separated prowar internationalists from those absolute pacifists who nourished a deep concern for justice and concluded that violent responses to conflict ultimately reinforce injustice. The tension between alternative philosophies and strategies of social change characterized each period of peace advocacy discussed in this volume. It underlay the travail of Romain Rolland, and it was raised poignantly in the history of internationalism in the United States and in recent antinuclear arms campaigns.

Peace advocates must be interpreted—and must interpret themselves—in their roles as agents of social change on national and international levels. How has the effectiveness of peace advocates been influenced by the tension between peace understood respectively as social order and as social transformation? To what extent have pacifists been motivated by unexamined cultural assumptions, conscious choices in the light of political reality, or alternative philosophies? How does their experience parallel that of other reform and revolutionary groups? The essays which follow at least implicitly address these and similar questions.

PEACE MOVEMENTS AS POLITICAL ORGANIZATIONS. A third theme is suggested by the divisions and conflicts between various elements of peace movements and by their relationship to the public and governing elites. Several authors distinguish bourgeois/liberal from worker/socialist pacifists; but these descriptive words — bourgeois, socialist — are troublesome. Sociologically, pacifist constituencies have varied from nation to nation and from time to time. Moreover, peace advocacy has been further divided between male and female perspectives, as well as by national and ideological loyalties (thus, absolute pacifists have organized independently of peace advocates who could accept selective warfare). Clearly, organized peace effort has been a heterogeneous endeavor, often accompanied by complex conflicts of interest and perspective.

In some cases quite different pacifist constituencies have clustered around a single issue, notably the issue of nuclear arms with which this volume concludes. This leaves a peace movement quite vulnerable, since the *raison d'être* for a coalition vanishes when public interest shifts, as it may do when a program is defeated (as in the case of the arbitration campaign in the nineteenth century), or even when a campaign succeeds (as in the case of American withdrawal from Vietnam).

In any case, no constituent element has represented organized pacifism as a whole, and each movement has reflected the division of society at large. What, then, is a peace movement? Is it a cohesive social force or a series of ephemeral coalitions? How do relationships among constituencies affect overall efficacy? Have tensions among peace-seeking constituencies been more destructive or more creative for their cause? There are difficult methodological questions as well. How can mass opinion be assessed when it is largely inarticulate? Is elite opinion, which is articulate, representative of historic forces?

There is a substantial body of scholarship on the sociology of social protest, but peace movements do not figure much in it. In fact, the politics of peace advocacy may constitute a special case in social change. In order to address immediate threats to peace, pacifists must influence the foreign policy establishment, the point in governmental structure perhaps most removed from public influence. In order to address long-range issues, pacifists must obtain changes in the international system, changes which require governmental initiative but which seem removed from contemporary issues. Not surprisingly, peace advocates have been led by their various priorities to different, sometimes competing political strategies.

At the heart of the problem is the question of what William A. Gamson has called "the permeability of the political arena" — the degree to which the structures of political power can be influenced for change.[9] Since power is structured quite differently in the different societies which make up the international system, peace necessarily has been advocated quite differently in various contexts. The study of peace movements involves the assessment of organizations and positions in relation to their distinctive political cultures.

WAR, PEACE, AND INTENTIONALITY. Peace movements would not be worth assessing if they could have done nothing to prevent war. Thus, a fourth theme and pervasive concern of the authors of these essays is the question: can any organized effort alter the course of history? More precisely, in the context of this volume: to what extent can the organized effort of private citizens contribute to peace?

The answer given probably will reflect one's political culture more than historical analysis. The question is germane here because the authors bring their own concern for the future to their study of past peace efforts. The issue is put differently in each chapter of the volume: often it is not explicitly raised, nowhere is it answered, but implicitly it links each of these studies to the others, and links them all to the central concerns of our time.

NOTES

1. See Gregory Flynn and Hans Rattinger, *The Public and Atlantic Defense* (London: Rowman & Allenheld, 1985); Michael Howard, "Deterrence, Consensus and Reassurance in the Defense of Europe," in *Defense and Consensus: The Domestic Aspects of Western Security,* Adelphi Paper no. 184 (London: IISS, 1983), 17–27; David Greenwood, "The Defense Policy of the United Kingdom," in Douglas J. Murry and Paul Viotti, eds., *The Defense Policies of Nations: A Comparative Study* (Baltimore: Johns Hopkins Univ. Press, 1982); William Wallace, "Old States and New Circumstances: The International Predicament of Britain, France and Germany," in W. E. Peterson, ed., *Foreign Policymaking in Western Europe: A Comparative Approach* (New York: Praeger, 1978).

2. Thus Peter Schmide analyzed "Public Opinion and Security Policy in the Federal Republic of Germany," in *Orbis* 29 (Winter 1985): 719–42, without considering the organized sources of opinion shift or the mechanisms of translating it into policy, and the authors in Flynn and Rattinger's collection eschewed the vagaries of peace activism in favor of empirical opinion data. Two notable exceptions are Richard Flickinger's comparative analysis of public opinion formation and national policy in "Public Opinion, The Peace Movement and NATO Missile Deployment," *Peace and Change* 9, no. 1 (Spring 1983): 17–30, and the nation study of Jolyon Howorth and Patricia Chilton, *Defence and Dissent in Contemporary France* (New York: St. Martin's, 1984), some chapters of which develop the relationship between movement and opinion within a political culture. Ferdinand Müller-Rommel remarks on the general lack of comparative studies in "Peace Movements in Western Europe" (paper for the meeting of the Southern Political Science Association, 1984), 1–2.

Transnational networks of citizens in voluntary activity have been studied especially by Chadwick F. Alger of the Mershon Center at Ohio State University and his students, of whom Welling Hall's work is most relevant to this volume. Note her "Church-State Relations in Czechoslovakia, Hungary, East Germany, and the Rise of an Independent Peace Movement," a paper presented at Ohio State University, Winter 1984.

3. Flynn and Rattinger, 381.

4. For an overview oriented to American history, see especially the section on "Peace Historiography" in Charles F. Howlett and Glenn Zeitzer, *The American Peace Movement: History and Historiography* (Washington: American Historical Association, 1985), and Charles DeBenedetti, "Peace History, in the American Manner," in *The History Teacher* 18, no. 1 (Nov. 1984): 75–110.

5. The literature on and in England is well established, and that on the Netherlands is pursued in a combined historical and political science approach characteristic of Philip Everts, *Public Opinion, The Churches and Foreign Policy: Studies of Domestic Factors in the Making of Dutch Foreign Policy* (Leiden: Univ. of Leiden, 1983). The maturity of peace research in history in Germany was signaled by the publication of Helmut Donat and Karl Holl's encyclopedic *Die Friedensbewegung: Organisierter Pazifismus in Deutschland, Österreich und in der Schweiz* (Düsseldorf: ECON Taschenbuch Verlag/Hermes Handlexikon, 1983). A new literature is evolving in the Soviet Union and Eastern Europe, where scholars are reevaluating the League of Nations, the concept of peaceful coexistence, and the legacy of peace thought in that area. Notable in this respect is the work of Ruzann Ilukhina on the League in relation to pacifist mobilization of public opinion.

6. Harold Josephson, ed. (Westport, CT: Greenwood, 1985).

7. Sidney Verba, "Comparative Political Culture," in Lucian W. Pye and Sidney Verba, eds., *Political Culture and Political Development* (Princeton: Princeton Univ. Press, 1965), 513. The concept is especially well established in the field of comparative politics.

8. Lucian Pye, "Introduction," ibid., 7–8.

9. *The Strategy of Social Protest* (Homewood, IL: Dorsey, 1975), 1–13.

CENTRAL EUROPE TO 1914

ROGER CHICKERING

War, Peace, and Social Mobilization in Imperial Germany: Patriotic Societies, the Peace Movement, and Socialist Labor

THE CONCEPT OF SOCIAL MOBILIZATION figures large in controversies that have recently raged over the history of the German Empire. In one view, defended most forcefully by Hans-Ulrich Wehler,
the mobilization of social groups during the Imperial epoch was engineered to a great degree by the country's aristocratic and industrial
elites, who adopted strategies of manipulating the popular expression of political opinion in order to protect their own positions atop
the structure of social and political power from the challenges of
democracy and socialism.[1] This position has been attacked by a group
of historians who argue that the mobilization of social forces proceeded independently of the control of the country's elites and that
the effect of this mobilization was to destabilize rather than to so-
lidify the structure of power.[2] The implications of this debate extend
into many facets of the Empire's history, but the focus in much of
the exchange has been the question of war and peace. Wehler's critics have insisted that the spread of popular sentiment in favor of war
was due to the mobilization of opinion by organizations such as the
German Navy League and the Pan-German League, and that these
organizations resisted the attempts of the country's political leaders
to manipulate or control their activities.[3]

Both sides have undertaken the debate with great energy and rhetorical flourish, but they have obscured an important question. It
has to do with what one might call the cultural dimension of social
mobilization, and it is inescapable if social mobilization involved
the issue of war and peace. The question relates to the manner in
which social mobilization affected or grew out of a conflict over the
German Empire's central images.

One might, with Anthony Obershall, define social mobilization
as "the process of forming crowds, groups, associations, and organi-

zations for the pursuit of collective goals."[4] The critical elements in the definition are "organization" and "collective goals." Obershall's own work has provided confirmation and theoretical backing for the conclusions of the many historians who have argued that mobilization is an arduous process, which involves the forging of alliances and networks among myriads of already existing groups. The success of the process depends on how effectively broad issues, or collective goals, can be related to the immediate and mundane concerns, aspirations, and anxieties of the groups that are to be mobilized. In other words, social mobilization is rooted in the experience of social groups as collective entities. It is surely a truism, but political action in the name of abstract goals like national security or world peace has not succeeded (nor even taken place) unless large groups of participants have been convinced that the achievement of these goals affects them in direct and palpable ways. As one of David Lodge's modern English Catholic women puts it, upon joining an organization to mobilize opposition to the Church's position on birth control, "I wouldn't care about the population explosion if only it wasn't happening in our house."[5]

It is also a truism that collective goals are cultural phenomena. They are inextricably related to the symbols and images with which social groups define themselves and interpret their collective experience. In those frequent instances when social mobilization has been an aspect of conflict among social groups, the issue has been conflicting definitions of collective identity, and the conflict has pertained to definitions of the social system as a whole as well as of the groups in conflict. The groups mobilized into social movements have defined themselves collectively in a manner that clashes with other, usually hegemonic definitions of collective identity. In this sense, Alain Tourain is convincing when he writes that social conflicts are cultural conflicts, in which the ultimate stakes are control of "the production of symbolic goods, that is, the information and images, of culture itself."[6]

That the German Empire was plagued by social conflict is not in dispute. Even in the recent scholarly controversy, the issue has been the success of elite groups in managing conflict, not the existence of it. The pertinent question, though, is the extent to which issues of war and peace figured in the mobilization of conflicting social groups. The focus in the essay that follows is not the debates in Germany over war and peace as aspects or possible consequences of specific foreign policies, but, rather, the broader popular images of Germany's relationship to other countries, on orientations toward the outside world, as components of conflicting definitions of collective identity. The problem posed here is a comprehensive one, and its resolution can only be outlined. Under whose auspices did mobilization take place in connection with issues of war and peace in Imperial Germany? How effective was it? Which social groups were prone to this mobilization, and why? What was its cultural significance?

Whatever one might think of Wehler's broader analysis of the Imperial German political system, it is difficult to quarrel with his conclusion that public institutions of socialization were geared to support an authoritarian political culture: their purpose was to inculcate political attitudes and orientations consistent with a structure of power which was in significant respects authoritarian.[7] Orientations toward the outside world made up a crucial dimension of these attitudes, as did a set of images of Germany's place among the nations of the world.

Two public institutions of socialization, the school system and the army, were of particular importance in the development of these images and orientations. The impact of these institutions was so wide that virtually all Germans, regardless of social or religious background, underwent the experience of exposure to a common set of images at an impressionable age and in situations calculated to leave a lasting impression. Attitudes conveyed to children on the authority of teachers and textbooks laid the foundation for the subsequent assimilation of images by young male adults in their years of service in the regular army, in the levies of the reserves, and in the network of veterans' societies which comprised, with its more than three million members in 1914, far and away the largest genre of voluntary association in Imperial Germany.[8]

Studies of textbooks and curricula in use in German schools and of the political education conducted as an integral part of military training have documented the character of the images of international relations to which young Germans were exposed.[9] The prevalent images were those of a proud and virtuous country surrounded by a hostile outside world where aggressive enemies, envious of German accomplishments, awaited only the moment when the country's defenses slackened to attack. Violent conflict inhered in relations among sovereign states whose interests and ambitions were inevitably antagonistic and could ultimately be resolved only by force of arms. Accordingly, the absence of conflict could never be more than an interlude, whose end was a constant likelihood.

Several features of these images deserve emphasis. The first is the manner in which they comported with the thinking of professional soldiers on the subject of international relations.[10] In fact, the systematic spread of these "military attitudes" into the civilian populace was a principal aspect of the celebrated phenomenon of German militarism (at least in its traditional form);[11] the effect was to popularize collective images of Germany as a beleaguered fortress and images of war as an inevitable if not desirable aspect of international affairs. These images were in turn invested into the entire network of the Empire's national symbolism; in addition to the most immediately relevant symbols (the army and navy), the flag, the monarchy, colonial empire, and the German cultural heritage all carried connotations of military power, validation through conflict, and German resolve amidst a hostile world.

A second important feature of these images is that their connotations were authoritarian. They placed a premium on domestic unity, the suppression of internal debate, and the disciplined acceptance of higher authority, in a civilian as well as a military context. Custodianship of the national symbols, responsibility for tending the national security and for determining the occasion for resort to arms, resided properly with the men who stood atop the structure of power and authority—the emperor and his appointed advisors. This responsibility lay, by clear implication, beyond the competence of the popular representatives who sat in the Reichstag, an institution more suited, in the dominant imagery, to expressing the lamentable extent of the country's internal antagonisms than to providing firm leadership in the hour of collective need.

In the imagery officially propagated, the issues of war and peace were beyond the legitimate purview of political debate in Imperial Germany. This conviction was manifest not only in the care with which the Reichstag's voice was restricted in matters of foreign and military policy, but also in the suspicion among Germany's leaders of any independent attempt to mobilize opinion on questions that touched on the nature of international relations. These leaders recognized that the integrity of an authoritarian system at home rested on specific images of the collective identity and that social mobilization could threaten these images if it were engineered outside the public institutions that undergirded a process that amounted to official mobilization.

In an era in which questions of war and peace affect immediately the life of every human being on the planet, it is easy to forget how remote these issues were for most Germans in the era before the First World War. For all their emphasis on military attitudes and values, the patterns of public socialization paradoxically encouraged this sense of remoteness by lending currency to the proposition that active concern for the country's collective destiny and security was the business of the leaders who, by virtue of their background, training, and experience, were uniquely qualified and authorized to worry about such things. The most significant challenge to this proposition came with the mobilization of a social group whose collective experience was peculiarly conducive to thinking about war and peace.

Two developments at the end of the nineteenth century focused the attention of some groups in Germany on questions of the country's relationship with the rest of the world. Growing rivalries with other imperial powers was one such development, once the German government established protectorates over African territories in the 1880s and then, at the end of the next decade, launched a campaign to construct a battle fleet. The other major development was the growth of tensions, within Germany itself and throughout central and eastern Europe, between Germans and other ethnic groups. In response to both developments, several patriotic societies were founded whose goal was to mobilize popular opinion and financial resources in order to support the German cause in these struggles. Altogether, about a half-dozen of these organizations took shape during the last two decades of the nineteenth century, the most prominent of which were the German Colonial Society, the German School Association, the Eastern Marches Society, the German Navy League, and the Pan-German League.[12]

In most respects, the portrayal of world politics in the programmatic literature of these organizations was consonant with the imagery being purveyed by public agencies in Imperial Germany. The dominant images were those of virtuous Germans surrounded by aggressive enemies whose motives were uniformly sinister and sprang from envy of everything German, particularly of German culture.[13] Upon closer examination, the images propagated by these societies proved to be an anxiety-laden extension of the official imagery, in some cases almost to the point of caricature. The position of Germans throughout the world was perilous: the nation's enemies were united in a conspiracy, the threat they posed was imminent, and its remedy called for the most ruthless and aggressive policies.

The consonance between this imagery and the official one was deceptive, however, and the mobilization of patriotic sentiment in these organizations presented a challenge to the established structure of power, at first implicitly, later directly. The patriotic societies claimed to serve the same national symbols as did the government, but their activities were founded on the assumption that the public had a vital role to play in promoting national security. The radical imagery of these organizations, particularly that of the Pan-German League, carried the implication that the government was not sufficiently alive to the perils the nation faced and that it was unprepared to undertake the necessary countermeasures—in building up armaments on land and sea, in encouraging colonial expansion, in supporting ethnic Germans fighting for cultural survival around the world, and in combating subversion at home. This patriotic criticism of the government and its policies rested on assumptions better described as populist than democratic; the patriots had little faith in the Reichstag but claimed for themselves the role of articulating and embodying the will of the nation—a role which, they contended (especially after the embarrassments of the *Daily Telegraph* affair in 1908), the monarch and his advisors were incompetent to perform.

Radical nationalism in the German Empire provided ideological cement for the mobilization of a distinct social group. Despite their pretensions to mobilize the entirety of the nation, the patriotic societies drew the bulk of their active membership from the educated male upper–middle class, the *Bildungsbürgertum*. The distinguishing features of this group were academic education and employment in public bureaucracies as higher officials of various descriptions and as teachers, usually in *Gymnasien*. These credentials conditioned the social experience of these men, by qualifying them for the prestigious roles of embodying and partaking in both culture (by virtue of their being *gebildet*) and authority (as representatives of the state).[14] The fact that issues of foreign policy intruded with such force into this group—that these men were particularly receptive to the anxious imagery of conspiracies among envious enemies—reflected the strains, both cultural and emotional, which they experienced in these roles.

The authority and cultural values that they represented were under attack in an era of rapid change, social conflict, and international tension. These men were, so to speak, culturally in the front line, where their images of themselves and their own roles were under stress. Their response was to translate challenges to the authority and values which they embodied into conspiracies among the enemies of German culture, authority, and power throughout the world.

The collective self-image of these patriots emphasized their own special roles as pioneers of the national cause. Because of their *Bildung,* they insisted they were themselves the true custodians of the national symbols, the men most fit to guide the nation in its conflicts with the rest of the world. In the years just prior to the war, they announced their aspirations to dismantle existing governmental bodies and the system of political parties in order to rule the country themselves. The most celebrated statement of the ambitions of this "national opposition" was the so-called *Kaiserbuch* of Heinrich Class, the chairman of the Pan-German League, who proposed that a body dominated by "virtuous men of character," distinguished in the first instance by their education, henceforth guide the nation's destiny.[15]

The sentiments of Class and other radical nationalists now resonated with special force, for by the eve of war and after long years of practice, these men had learned well the techniques of mobilization. Their influence extended throughout a broad network of voluntary associations which catered to an upper–middle-class constituency—in addition to the patriotic societies themselves (which were extensively interlocked), a host of other civic, cultural, and recreational societies. Beyond these stood a host of other organizations which had massive memberships and were available for mobilization in the name of national security—patriotic choral and gymnastic societies, shooting clubs, and veterans' associations.[16]

The German government was not unaware of the potential danger of patriotic sentiment mobilized independently in these organizations. The government's policy was to attempt to ensure the docility of the patriotic societies, but this policy was frustrated in the end, owing in part to the way officials also tried to exploit the force of popular patriotism. In order to guarantee that patriotic sentiment not conflict with officially sanctioned images of war and peace, officials built channels of influence into most of the patriotic societies. These usually took the form of bureaucratic support, as in the cases of the Navy League and the Eastern Marches Society, or the provi-

sion of lucrative public contracts and other financial favors, as in
the case of the Colonial Society.[17] At the same time, in order to bring
pressure on the Reichstag when budgets had to be approved, officials
encouraged the patriotic societies to present radical demands in public, but these officials were evidently insensitive to the danger of
breeding frustration among the patriotic activists should the government's own programs fail to fulfill expectations they encouraged.
The government's policies thus simultaneously purchased the docility of the leaderships of these organizations and nurtured the potential for opposition among the activists on the local level. The possibility that this frustration would be mobilized was enhanced as one
major organization, the Pan-German League, resisted official blan-
dishments and articulated, in increasingly radical form, a program
of patriotic opposition to the German government's policies.

Effective mobilization of patriotic opinion in opposition to the
German government came on the eve of the war, during a protracted
public debate over two massive army bills. The government's evident
mishandling of the Agadir crisis in the summer of 1911 combined
with the alarming gains of the Social Democrats in the Reichstag the
following year to provide impetus for an enormous popular coalition, which demanded a program of expansion and modernization
of the German army far beyond the extent thought wise by either
the civilian or military leadership—a program whose financing required, in addition, a significant enlargement of the fiscal powers of
the parliament.[18] The driving force behind this popular mobilization
was the German Defense League, an organization whose founding
the Pan-Germans oversaw, but whose dramatic growth was due to
the fact that it brought together, on the local level, chapters of the
other patriotic societies. It was a remarkable phenomenon, for the
premise on which the Defense League operated was that Germany's
established leadership was incompetent to judge the country's military needs and that the mobilization of national opinion was required to repair the situation.

Although the expansion of the army was legislated amidst an
orgy of patriotic rhetoric, the elements of conflict in the spectacle
were clear to observers on both sides. The slogans and accusations
which animated the mobilization of patriotic sentiment were in significant respects incompatible with the authoritarian tenets of militarism being officially propagated. The conflict had ultimately to do

with the power to define and interpret the collective identity of the German nation. During a debate ostensibly about the combat-readiness of the army, a fraction of the German upper–middle class signaled its own pretensions to displace the country's officially constituted leadership as the custodian of the national symbols.

The history of the middle-class peace movement in Imperial Germany presents a number of interesting points of comparison with the mobilization of opinion in the patriotic societies. The pacifists shared with the radical nationalists the belief that decisions about war and peace should reflect public sentiment and, like the patriots, the pacifists proposed to mobilize this sentiment. Their efforts met with virtually no success, however, for their campaign lacked any cultural foundation and the images they sought to popularize clashed frontally with images being promoted officially.

The middle-class German pacifists, who were to be found primarily in the sparse ranks of the German Peace Society, proceeded from assumptions about the nature of international relations that were fundamentally at odds with those of both the official militarism and the vision of the radical nationalists.[19] Whether from ethical or utilitarian considerations, the pacifists argued that harmony rather than conflict was the natural state of relations among sovereign states; however appropriate to earlier epochs, war had become, in the pacifists' view, a senseless, destructive anachronism in the modern era of growing financial and commercial interdependence and a growing sense of international moral community, which corresponded to the natural peace-loving instincts of all people. This emerging state of affairs was to be institutionalized in the form of an international political organization with the powers to arbitrate and adjudicate international disputes on the basis of a comprehensive code of international law, as well as in democratic reforms to render the foreign policies of all states responsive to the pacifistic inclinations of their citizens.

Advocacy of these views subjected the pacifists in Germany to every form of attack on their realism, patriotism, and even their sanity. Their realism is not at issue here (although it must be said on their behalf that the war that broke out in 1914 emphatically vindicated their beliefs), but the common charges were groundless that pacifists were unpatriotic. Patriotic considerations were in fact para-

mount in the vision of these men and women who calculated that
any future war in Europe would be ruinous for their own country
and that a stable system of international law would ensure German
preponderance on the European continent and validate German claims
to a more extensive overseas empire.

In interpreting international affairs, the pacifists thus appealed to
much of the same symbolism as did the radical nationalists. The
power, pride, and integrity of the German nation were never in question, nor was the superiority of German culture nor even German
claims to colonial empire. In the credo of the pacifists, however, this
symbolism took on different connotations and suggested a different
collective image of the German nation. As they played down the mo-
tif of conflict in international politics or displaced it into nonmilitary spheres such as commercial competition, the pacifists removed
from the national symbolism the anxious connotations of beleaguerment and isolation in a world of enemies. The fulfillment of the national destiny, the documentation of German cultural superiority,
was to come as the country led the civilized states of the world toward
international order and law.

The difficulty was that investing the national symbols with these
connotations undermined the official interpretation in the most basic
way. To assume that order and harmony rather than violent conflict
represented the natural state of international relations robbed the national symbols of their authoritarian color and threatened to rein-
vest them with democratic connotations. The pacifists' enthusiasm
for the German monarch was outspoken, but they regarded him not
so much as the symbol of authority and military power as a symbol
of peace, the *Friedenskaiser* whose role was to serve as executor of
the popular desire for a world without war.[20] It was clear to most
of the German pacifists, however, that the full translation of this
popular will into policy was going to demand the democratic reform
of significant features of the German constitutional system, most
centrally increasing the power of the Reichstag in the areas of foreign and military policy.[21]

In German pacifism the interpretation of the national symbolism
thus conflicted in significant respects with the images propagated
both by public institutions of socialization and in the campaigns of
the patriotic societies. The pertinent question is whether this alternative imagery reflected the experience of any significant social group

in Imperial Germany or lay at the root of any significant social conflict over issues of war and peace — in other words, whether pacifism
provided the symbols and slogans for any kind of social mobilization.

The most prominent figures in the German peace movement came
from an extraordinary diversity of social backgrounds. They included
an Austrian noblewoman, a renegade academic historian, a Protestant clergyman, an Austrian Jewish journalist, an industrialist with
a modest fortune in gold- and silver-processing, and one of the city
fathers of Frankfurt am Main.[22] In no sense, however, did they represent any broader social groups or experiences broadly shared. Even
the ranks of the German pacifists (to the extent that one can speak
of ranks) do not make generalizations easy about common social
experience. The most typical categories represented were *petit bourgeois* — primary-school teachers, subaltern officials in local bureaucracies, and small businessmen, all of whom were most frequently
to be found in the west and south, particularly in the state of Würt-
temberg, where regional resistance to the costs and authoritarian values of large armies might have figured in creating a certain popular
sympathy for pacifism.[23] In all events, the men and women in the
peace society were far less likely to display the academic credentials
and bureaucratic rank which were hallmarks of the social experience
that encouraged radical nationalists to embrace a vision of world
politics so rife with conflict and anxiety.

The number of active pacifists was very small, so small in fact
that the term mobilization seems inappropriate to describe their activities. The peace society itself, nominally some ten thousand members strong, surely comprised no more than a few dozen activists.
Nor could the peace society plug into the kinds of broad organizational networks that were available as auxiliaries to the patriotic
societies. The local branches of the Left-Liberal political parties
(whose tradition was the most cordial to pacifism) cooperated occasionally with chapters of the peace society, as did a few masonic
lodges, free-thinkers' associations, feminist organizations, and assorted other reform groups, most of which were commonly regarded
as eccentric.[24]

The social and cultural terrain on which the German peace movement operated was extremely narrow. To this movement fell in fact
not the role of mobilizing any substantial body of opinion on the
issue of war and peace, but, rather, of documenting how pervasively

the national symbolism in Imperial Germany connoted a vision which was diametrically at odds with the pacifists' belief that peace rather than war was the natural state of international affairs.

The middle-class peace movement was defined by the issue of war and peace; but the pathos of the movement raises the question of whether mobilization is an appropriate term with which to analyze its history. The history of the socialist labor movement in Imperial Germany raises the opposite question. The extent, organization, and self-consciousness of the movement, and the degree to which it clashed with prevailing norms and institutions, made it into an almost classic case of successful social mobilization. It is much less clear, though, whether the issue of war and peace had much to do with the mobilization of this social group.

The dominant ideological position in the Social Democratic party admittedly embraced a number of propositions on this issue. The socialists were a self-avowed party of international proletarian unity, peace, conciliation, and opposition to the arms race and militarism. The assumptions which underlay these propositions, however, reflected an analysis of international relations which partook curiously of elements of both middle-class pacifism and radical nationalism. The party's ideologues reasoned that the definitive elimination of warfare from human affairs, the establishment of peace as the natural condition of relations among the nations of the world, awaited the triumph of socialism. Until the revolutionary transformation of social relations, the interaction of capitalist states was destined to be characterized by conflict. The analysis of the radical nationalists was thus a more accurate description of the current state of affairs than was that of the middle-class pacifists, whom the Social Democrats persistently derided for the naiveté of their expectations.[25]

The thinking of the party's leadership with regard to international relations has been subjected to intensive scrutiny and has perhaps been ascribed more significance than it deserves.[26] The subject was of comparatively minor importance to the party until shortly before the outbreak of war, when the threat of internal strife no less than the growth of international tension provoked more extended interest and debate. And it is by no means self-evident that the men and women who discussed issues of foreign policy in the party's leadership were representative of the rank and file.

This last problem has direct bearing on the question of social mobilization, a phenomenon which by its very definition relates to the attitudes and experiences of the rank and file and the organization of these attitudes into an effective political force. The focus in the analysis of mobilization of needs begins at the grass-roots level, with those so-called "base-processes" in which immediate concerns translate into political practice.[27] At issue is thus the culture of the labor movement, the manner in which German socialist workers interpreted and symbolized their own experiences and endowed these with political content—and whether the subject of international relations figured much in the process.

The growth of interest in recent years in workers' culture has made possible some tentative answers to the question of what workers actually thought about war and peace and the extent to which these issues affected the cultural values and collective self-images nurtured within the socialist labor movement. It seems clear that a cohesive set of values and images did emerge in considerable tension with the dominant culture. The extensive network of cultural and recreational organizations supported, arguably more than did the workers' political clubs, what scholars have come to call a socialist subculture; it was, in the description of one author, "a home, a party-fatherland, a counter-fatherland of the worker, opposed to the Wilhelmine fatherland from which he [or she] was excluded."[28] This sociocultural milieu of the German labor movement was structured around the countersymbols of class conflict, of working-class power and integrity within a hostile society and culture. These symbols thus lent meaning to the experience of a large group of men and women who were denied access to power and cultural legitimacy by dominant social and cultural institutions. The fostering of counter-symbols and collective counterimages involved, among other things, a more or less systematic campaign to frustrate the socialization being conducted by the state in schools and the army.

As Vernon Lidtke has recently pointed out, the concept of a socialist subculture and the integrationist sociological theory that underlies much of the analysis of this phenomenon have tended to deemphasize the elements of conflict between subculture and dominant culture.[29] The theory would have made little sense to Imperial Germany's leading soldiers, who were haunted by the specter of masses of workers both immunized against the militarist values of the dominant culture and determined to subvert these values within the army and without.[30]

The little evidence that survives and has been collected about workers' attitudes toward war and peace suggests that these apprehensions were exaggerated. The fact that the evidence is so scant is itself telling: most workers did not devote much thought to the subject of war and peace, for they had difficulty linking international affairs to the kinds of issues and problems that related immediately to them and exercised them sufficiently to turn to collective action.[31] Foreign relations were, in the words of one contemporary observer, "an area remote from the daily practice of the labor movement."[32] Several studies have documented the intrusion of themes that bore on world politics into workers' festivals and other cultural activities, but this intrusion typically took the form of ritual condemnations of militarism and affirmations of international proletarian unity. Much of this rhetoric had an almost millennial ring to it and produced, as Gottfried Korff has noted in connection with May Day demonstrations, "a diffuse and ideologically desensitizing effect."[33] In this respect, the recollections of the worker Adam Scharrer no doubt point to a widespread tendency. At one May Day celebration in Hamburg, Scharrer recalled, the speaker began by dwelling on the significance of the international celebration of labor: he "spoke for a long time about abstract things until heckles from the audience forced him to talk about conditions in the shipyards."[34]

A tendency to regard world politics as something remote and abstract was an indication of how little these issues figured in the social experience of German workers. This tendency might well have reflected also the fact that the socialization of German workers was not free of contradictions. All working-class children received a substantial exposure to the dominant values, symbols, and images in their public education; and many (although it is impossible to guess how many) of the men who became active in the socialist labor movement had that exposure intensified during service in the regular army, the reserves, and even in veterans' associations (despite the concerted attempts of authorities to keep socialists out of all these institutions). If this experience did not lead workers to push their thinking about war and peace into the safe and distant confines of rhetorical abstraction, it resulted in the kind of confusion which Paul Göhre encountered in the factories of Chemnitz. There, among avowed Social Democrats, he discovered men who took pride in their military units and uniforms, who remembered fondly their service in the colors, and who regarded the emperor — that central symbol of the dominant culture and its military values — as a "thoroughly sympathetic and popular [*volksthümlich*] figure."[35] Significantly too, Göhre discovered among these champions of international working-class solidarity a great deal of resentment against foreign workers who threatened their jobs.[36]

The place of attitudes toward war and peace in workers' culture is a subject that would reward far more thorough and systematic study than it has received here. These attitudes appear to represent one area in which some of the values and orientations of the dominant culture lived on in the cultural milieu of the German labor movement. This observation is not to suggest the militarization of the labor movement, but, rather, the pervasiveness of military values in the dominant culture and a variety of avenues through which these values could be imported into the cultural world of German workers.

The massive antiwar demonstrations in which the German labor movement participated during the last years of peace might seem to challenge this observation and to indicate that socialist workers had by this time been mobilized for peace.[37] To interpret these demonstrations only from this perspective, however, would be misleading. The German labor movement became actively concerned with questions of war and peace only on the eve of the First World War, and then in part because radicals had precipitated an ideological crisis in the Social Democratic party by linking these questions to the debate over revolutionary tactics. By this time there were also ample indications, beyond the pronouncements of Gustav Noske in the Reichstag or of revisionist ideologues in the press, that both the party leadership and many in the rank and file had accepted perhaps the most basic tenet of the dominant culture — the proposition that the symbols of the nation were valid, vulnerable, and worth defending by force of arms.[38]

The mobilization of the German public in favor of war in August 1914 revealed just how broadly this tenet was accepted. Public proclamations of support for the war effort came from patriotic societies, peace societies, and socialist groups; moreover, these proclamations conveyed a unanimity of attitude which few observers would have thought possible only weeks before.[39] The scenes of August 1914 documented graphically the limits of social conflict in Imperial Germany when the issue of war and peace became actual. These scenes also revealed how effectively the state had established the cultural limits within which popular discussion of this issue took place in Imperial Germany.

Public institutions of socialization propagated an interpretation of the national symbolism that emphasized images of German vulnerability and beleaguerment in a hostile world. The only effective mobilization of popular sentiment on questions of foreign or military policy to take place independently of official agencies was the one presided over by the patriotic societies on the eve of the war, but this mobilization occurred in the name of a set of symbols and collective images similar in fundamental respects to those being officially promoted. The attempt to inculcate a fundamentally different set of images was left to the outsiders in this culture. The middle-class pacifists failed utterly in their attempt to revise dominant orientations toward the outside world, while the challenge issued to the dominant culture by the socialist labor movement involved questions of war and peace only peripherally. And when the test arrived, in the form of a war almost universally regarded as defensive, socialist workers and middle-class pacifists demonstrated the extent to which their thinking too had been conditioned to accept the use of armed force to repel aggressive enemies.

The recent controversies over the German Empire have obscured the significance of this point, perhaps because in the debate both sides are in some respects right. Mobilization of opinion did take place outside government control, and it was evidence of conflict which the government found increasingly difficult to manage. At the same time, however, this conflict took place within a cultural framework and conceptual vocabulary which agencies of the state had promoted in order to buttress an authoritarian order. And in the end, the symbols and images that composed this vocabulary proved vigorous enough to unite Germans of all social groups until the enduring strains of war pulled them apart.

NOTES

1. Hans Ulrich Wehler, *Das Deutsche Kaiserreich 1871–1918* (Göttingen: Vandenhoeck & Ruprecht, 1973).

2. Richard J. Evans, ed., *Society and Politics in Wilhelmine Germany* (London and New York: Barnes & Noble, 1978); David Blackbourn and

Geoff Eley, *The Peculiarities of German History: Bourgeois Society and Politics in Nineteenth-Century Germany* (Oxford and New York: Oxford Univ. Press, 1984).

3. Geoff Eley, *Reshaping the German Right: Radical Nationalism and Political Change after Bismarck* (New Haven and London: Yale Univ. Press, 1980). Cf. Wolfgang Mock, "'Manipulation von oben' oder Selbstorganisation an der Basis? Einige neuere Ansätze in der englischen Historiographie zur Geschichte des deutschen Kaiserreiches," *Historische Zeitschrift* 223 (1981): 358–75; David Blackbourn, "The Politics of Demagogy in Imperial Germany," *Past and Present,* no. 113 (Nov. 1985): 152–84.

4. Anthony Obershall, *Social Conflict and Social Movements* (Englewood Cliffs, NJ: Prentice-Hall, 1973), 102.

5. David Lodge, *Souls and Bodies* (New York: Morrow, 1982), 123.

6. Alain Touraine, "An Introduction to the Study of Social Movements," *Social Research* 52 (1985): 774. Cf. Obershall, *Social Conflict and Social Movements,* 187.

7. Wehler, *Das Deutsche Kaiserreich,* 122–31.

8. Reinhard Höhn, *Die Armee als Erziehungsschule der Nation* (Bad Harzburg: Verlag für Wissenschaft und Technik, 1963). On the veterans' associations, see Dieter Düding, "Die Kriegervereine im wilhelminischen Reich und ihr Beitrag zur Militarisierung der deutschen Gesellschaft," in Karl Holl and Jost Dülffer, eds., *Bereit zum Krieg: Kriegsmentalität im wilhelminischen Deutschland 1890–1914. Beiträge zur historischen Friedensforschung* (Göttingen: Vandenhoeck & Ruprecht, 1986), 99–121.

9. Horst Schallenberger, *Untersuchungen zum Geschichtsbild der Wilhelminischen Aera und der Weimarer Zeit: Eine vergleichende Schulbuchanalyse deutscher Schulgeschichtsbücher aus der Zeit von 1888 bis 1933* (Ratingen: Henn, 1964); Folkert Meyer, "Volksschule und Politik in Preussen. Untersuchungen zur sozialen Situation und politischen Funktion der preussischen Volksschullehrer in der zweiten Hälfte des 19. Jarhhunderts" (Ph.D. diss., University of Freiburg, 1975).

10. See Samuel P. Huntington, *The Soldier and the State: The Theory and Politics of Civil-Military Relations* (Cambridge: The Belknap Press of Harvard Univ. Press, 1957); Morris Janowitz, *The Professional Soldier: A Social and Political Portrait* (New York: Free Press, 1960).

11. See Stig Förster, *Der Doppelte Militarismus: Die deutsche Heeresrüstungspolitik zwischen Status-quo-Sicherung und Aggression 1890–1913* (Wiesbaden: Steiner, 1982); V. R. Berghahn, *Militarism: The History of an International Debate* (New York: St. Martin's, 1982).

12. For the literature on these organizations, see Roger Chickering, *We Men Who Feel Most German: A Cultural Study of the Pan-German League, 1886–1914* (London: Allen & Unwin, 1984).

13. Ibid., 74–101, 185–97.

14. Ibid., 102–21.

15. Daniel Frymann [Heinrich Class], *Wenn ich der Kaiser wär': Politische Wahrheiten und Notwendigkeiten* (Leipzig: Dieterich, 1912), 134–35.

16. Chickering, *We Men,* 183–212.

17. Roger Chickering, "Patriotic Societies and German Foreign Policy, 1890–1914," *International History Review* 1 (1979): 470–89.

18. Roger Chickering, "Der 'Deutsche Wehrverein' und die Reform der Deutschen Armee," *Militärgeschichtliche Mitteilungen* no. 1 (1979), 7–33.

19. Roger Chickering, *Imperial Germany and a World Without War: The Peace Movement and German Society, 1892–1914* (Princeton, NJ: Princeton Univ. Press, 1975); Friedrich-Karl Scheer, *Die Deutsche Friedensgesellschaft (1892–1933): Organisation, Ideologie, politische Ziele. Ein Beitrag zur Geschichte des Pazifismus in Deutschland* (Frankfurt a. M.: Haag & Herchen, 1981): Wilfried Eisenbeiss, *Die bürgerliche Friedensbewegung in Deutschland während des Ersten Weltkrieges: Organisation, Selbstverständnis und politische Praxis 1913/14–1919* (Frankfurt a. M., Berne, and New York: Lang, 1980); Dieter Riesenberger, *Geschichte der Friedensbewegung in Deutschland: Von den Anfängen bis 1933* (Göttingen: Vandenhoeck & Ruprecht, 1985).

20. Alfred H. Fried, *The German Emperor and the Peace of the World* (London: Hodder & Stoughton, 1912).

21. Chickering, *Imperial Germany,* 122–62.

22. Ibid., 72–88.

23. Scheer, 114–24; Chickering, *We Men,* 315–16.

24. Chickering, *Imperial Germany,* 122–62.

25. Ibid., 259–85.

26. I find it difficult to understand the observation of Roger Fletcher that "there has been very little serious study of German socialist foreign-policy views in the pre-1914 era," in Fletcher, *Revisionism and Empire: Socialist Imperialism in Germany, 1897–1914* (London: Allen & Unwin, 1984), 2. See, for example, Dieter Groh, *Negative Integration und revolutionärer Attentismus: Die deutsche Sozialdemokratie am Vorabend des Ersten Weltkrieges* (Frankfurt a. M.: Propylaen, 1973); Walter Wittwer, *Streit um Schicksalsfragen: Die deutsche Sozialdemokratie zu Krieg und Vaterlandsverteidigung 1907–1914* (Berlin: Akademie Verlag, 1964); Hans-Christoph Schröder, *Sozialismus und Imperialismus: Die Auseinandersetzung der deutschen Sozialdemokratie mit dem Imperialismusproblem und der "Weltpolitik" vor 1914* (Hannover: Verlag für Literatur & Zeitgeschehen, 1968); Wolfram Wette, *Kriegstheorien deutscher Sozialisten — Marx, Engels, Lassalle, Bernstein, Kautsky, Luxemburg. Ein Beitrag zur Friedensforschung* (Stuttgart: Kohlhammer, 1971); Ina Hermes, *Gegen Imperialismus und Krieg: Gewerkschaften in der II. Internationale 1889–1914* (Cologne: Pahl-Rugenstein,

1979), 34–46, 83–95, 174–87; and Friedhelm Boll, *Frieden ohne Revolution? Friedensstrategien der deutschen Sozialdemokratie vom Erfurter Programm bis zur Revolution 1918* (Bonn: Verlag Neue Gesellschaft, 1980).

27. Dieter Groh, "Base-Processes and the Problem of Organisation: Outline of a Social-history Research Project," *Social History* 4 (1979): 265–83.

28. Quoted in Adelheid von Saldern, "Wilhelminische Gesellschaft und Arbeiterklasse: Emanzipations- und Integrationsprozesse im kulturellen und sozialen Bereich," *Internationale wissenschaftliche Korrespondenz zur Geschichte der Arbeiterbewegung* 13 (1977): 484. Cf. Guenther Roth, *The Social Democrats in Imperial Germany: A Study in Working-Class Isolation and National Integration* (Totowa, NJ: Bedminster, 1963); Vernon Lidtke, *The Alternative Culture: Socialist Labor in Imperial Germany* (Oxford and New York: Oxford Univ. Press, 1985); Dieter Langewiesche, "The Impact of the German Labor Movement on Workers' Culture," *Journal of Modern History* 59 (1987): 506–23.

29. Ibid., 6–7. Cf. Gerhard A. Rigger, "Workers' Culture in Imperial Germany: Problems and Points of Departure for Research," *Journal of Contemporary History* 13 (1978): 180.

30. Reinhard Höhn, *Sozialismus und Heer*, vol. 3, *Der Kampf des Heeres gegen die Sozialdemokratie* (Bad Harzburg: Gehlen, 1969).

31. Dick Geary, "Identifying Militancy: The Assessment of Working-Class Attitudes toward State and Society," in Richard J. Evans, ed., *The German Working Class, 1888–1932* (London and New York: Barnes & Noble, 1982), 237.

32. Quoted in Bruno Hübner and Jürgen Lampe, "Die Haltung der revolutionären deutschen Sozialdemokratie zum Italienisch-Türkischen Krieg 1911/12," *Militär-Geschichte* 23 (1985): 430.

33. Gottfried Korff, "Volkskultur und Arbeiterkultur: Ueberlegungen am Beispiel der sozialistischen Maifesttradition," *Geschichte und Gesellschaft* 5 (1979): 99.

34. Wolfgang Emmerich, ed., *Proletarische Lebensläufe: Autobiographische Dokumente zur Entstehung der Zweiten Kultur in Deutschland* 2 vols. (Reinbeck: Rowohlt, 1974–75), vol. 1, 360.

35. Paul Göhre, *Drei Monate Fabrikarbeiter und Handwerksbursche: Eine praktische Studie* (Leipzig: Grunon, 1891), 108–42. Cf. Werner Blessing, "The Cult of the Monarchy, Political Loyalty and the Workers' Movement in Imperial Germany," *Journal of Contemporary History* 13 (1978): 361–71.

36. Göhre, 129.

37. See Dieter Groh, "The 'Unpatriotic Socialists' and the State," *Journal of Contemporary History* 1 (1966): 162, and *Negative Integration*, 356.

38. Groh, "'Unpatriotic Socialists,'" 155–61, and Fletcher, *Revisionism*

and Empire, passim. Cf. Hans-Christoph Schröder, *Gustav Noske und die Kolonialpolitik des deutschen Kaiserreiches* (Berlin and Bonn: Dietz, 1979).

39. Susanne Miller, *Burgfrieden und Klassenkampf: Die deutsche Sozialdemokratie im Ersten Weltkrieg* (Düsseldorf: Droste, 1974), 31–74; Chickering, *We Men,* 290–91; Chickering, *Imperial Germany,* 317–26.

JOST DÜLFFER

Citizens and Diplomats: The Debate on the First Hague Conference (1899) in Germany

THE HAGUE PEACE CONFERENCE formed a challenge to the existing international system, to governments and diplomats, and to peace movements.[1] The first of these conferences convened in 1899 after the Russian Tsar had taken the initiative; the second one took place in 1907 in a completely different international setting. Although it is true that the international peace movement had some influence on the issuing of the Tsarist manifesto of 24 August 1898, its publication was intended to be and indeed came as a great surprise everywhere. Especially its wording seemed to offer prospects for the creation of a new international order because it was based on the diagnosis of a pathology in world politics, especially in regard to the armaments race.[2] If things were really as bad as Tsar Nicholas II announced in an official diplomatic note, something had to be done.

Although national reactions varied greatly from country to country, they can in general be seen as an expression of different political cultures. It is possible to distinguish among four lines of German response to the Hague proposals: those of diplomatic and military officials, political liberals, socialists, and the small minority of pacifists.

THE OFFICIAL POSITION

Emperor William asked in his congratulatory telegram to the Tsar:

> Could we for instance figure to ourselves a Monarch holding personal command of his Army, dissolving his regiments sacred with a hundred years of history and relegating their glorious colors to the walls of the armories and museums (and handing over his towns to Anarchists and Democracy).[3]

From the beginning therefore it was clear that if only because of domestic reasons the army as a potential instrument for civil war could not be a subject of international limitations. At the conference itself the German military delegate, Colonel Gross von Schwarzhoff, argued that German armaments were proof of the superiority of German domestic and economic strength and efficiency in comparison to other countries:

> As far as Germany is concerned, I can reassure her friends completely and dissipate all benevolent anxiety regarding her. The German people are not crushed beneath the weight of expenditures and taxes . . . ; they are not hastening towards exhaustion and ruin. Quite the contrary; public and private wealth is growing, the general welfare, the standard of life are rising from year to year. As for compulsory military service, which is intimately associated with these questions, the German does not regard it as a heavy burden but as a sacred and patriotic duty, to the performance of which he owes his existence, his prosperity, his future.[4]

German diplomats were no more willing to support arbitration, which would have implied the acceptance of new obligations in international politics. Three principles were of paramount importance to the government. First, the international order was dominated by the great powers. The implementation of the principle of "one state — one vote" at the conference could undermine this order as could also the additional rights of an arbitration scheme. In the official instructions for the German delegation it was observed:

> Small uninterested states as subjects, small questions as objects of arbitration are conceivable; great states and great problems are not. That is because the state in growing analogy to its importance regards itself as a means in itself, not as an instrument for the achievement of higher external aims.[5]

In the Kaiser's words: "The Netherlands or Denmark or Sweden submit to arbitration, because they cannot fight for their claims, a great power would not."[6] The danger of an "ochlocracy of states" had to be avoided at all costs.

Second, the unlimited sovereignty of the national state had to be safeguarded. Baron von Holstein — the senior counselor and most influential person behind German foreign policy at that time — wrote in his official instructions for the German delegates to the conference:

> For the state there is no aim superior to the protection of its interests. . . . In the case of great powers these will not necessarily be identical with the maintenance of peace, but rather with the violation of the enemy and competitor by an appropriately combined group of stronger states.[7]

The principle of arbitation was therefore undesirable, the instructions suggested. "Arbitration without a guarantee of impartiality is nothing other than ordinary intervention, . . . a new disease of the world order, a greater danger to peace." It should be made clear from the outset that Germany's wish for "a place in the sun" in the sunrise of world politics was not to be hampered by international obligations.

Third, this demonstration of strength was accompanied by a somewhat pessimistic view of the inner status of German society. This was alluded to in the Kaiser's telegram to the Tsar. In this context the chief legal advisor to the foreign office argued, looking to the future, that in case the other powers succeeded in establishing a permanent court of arbitration, "the force of circumstance, the pressure of erroneous public opinion and the conceivable assumption that there was weak government in Germany" might make it difficult for Germany to resist pressure to accept such a court.[8]

That the German government did cooperate to a certain extent in the Hague conference despite severe reservations and even contempt for all peace moves had to do with an awareness of the Reich's actual weakness. Germany could hardly afford to isolate itself completely in international politics.[9] It had to preserve the *Dreibund,* maintain good relations with Great Britain and prevent further French attempts to abandon its isolation. Above all it had to keep open the "line to Russia" (*Draht nach Russland*). The initiator of the peace conference, William's cousin Nicholas II, had to be allowed to save face. Therefore the German position at the Hague conference from the outset could have nothing to do with a reform of international politics but was really based on traditional diplomatic assessment to preserve its international status and prestige among the great powers. "I agree to this nonsense," noted the Emperor with regard to the Hague arbitration court, "in order that the Tsar won't be disgraced before Europe! But in practice I should continue to rely on God and my sharp sword! I shit on all the resolutions."[10]

The Liberal Case

In the Reichstag debates on the budget and the military bill (Quinquennat) from December 1898 to February 1899, only among the liberals and socialists was hope voiced for positive results from the peace conference. Friedrich Naumann, the founder of the *Nationalsozialer Verein* (National Social Association), which merged with the left liberal *Freisinnige Vereinigung* (Free-thinking Union) in 1903, gave a lecture entitled "Tsar and World Peace" (10 February 1899).[11] He differentiated between small countries which were bound to the status quo and the two world powers, Great Britain and Russia, which could be content with their present status. In a third category were states such as Germany, which were dynamic: "this ascending Germany, with its powerful trade, its expanding industrial development and its modern financial life is, taken as a whole, indeed strong enough to pay for its defense." Arbitration, congresses, and similar diplomatic devices were to be regarded positively, but they were not fit to determine questions of life and death.

Naumann continued his analysis by arguing,

> In the history of mankind there is . . . a struggle for existence between nations in which some rise, some fall. A struggle which can be mitigated by reason, diplomacy and moderation, but which is per se existent in nature and which therefore has to penetrate to the surface. The struggle between rising and falling nations is linked, on the other hand, to the struggle for the economic possession of the globe. . . . How could mankind advance on the path to peace? Certainly not by dissolving the guarantees of peace, that is, the agglomeration of power, but only by the growth of the large-scale power concerns [*Grossbetriebe*].

Naumann could accept the conference to the extent that it would create this new grouping, resulting in a continental league between France, Russia, and the German Empire. Such a combination of powers would indeed provide some guarantee of peace, but by rather different means than those making up the eight proposals of the conference agenda.

Another of the liberal critics of Wilhelmine politics was Hans Delbrück. In his first reaction to the Tsarist manifesto, one month after its publication, he assessed it as "a diplomatic masterstroke."[12] It derived from domestic difficulties in a system of serfdom and was aimed at western liberal opinion. "What we want is free space for a natural development of our nation; what the Russians want is domination, they hope for world domination." The masterstroke of Russian diplomacy "seems to have the tendency to backfire, that is, if the peace conference fails and nations realize as a consequence that they cannot just sit back idly, but are in a highly dangerous situation." Some months later, after having read Jean de Bloch's books, he wrote in a more thorough dissertation entitled *War of the future and peace of the future*: "Economic damages will not prevent the war of the future, but on the contrary, it will be an intensive means of warfare."[13] Power was the only thing which mattered in international politics, and by that instrument the European powers had partitioned Africa in the last twenty-five years; "in the next century they will partition Asia — by what right? What could arbitration do, where there is no right?" Disarmament would increase the probability of war because the assessment of power would be more complicated. He feared that the peace movement might bring about the opposite of what it was striving for.

> If the peace movement limited itself to an agitation for international arbitration tribunals it would probably be rather harmless. But to the more or less theoretical demand for courts of arbitration was immediately linked that for practical disarmament and in this combination, in this illusion that disarmament means peace, lies the danger.[14]

Pleading for imperialist expansion of all states and especially the German Reich he concluded: "without war, if it is possible, but it [the partition of the world] is something which will not be bought too dear by any amount of blood."

Peace as far as possible, but war if it should be necessary — so the attitude of Naumann and Delbrück can be summarized. If these were somewhat liberal expressions of the dominant political culture of the Kaiserreich, the question of the socialist and pacifist alternatives should be raised in this context.

SOCIALIST ATTITUDES

In socialist thought two strategies against war were formulated which may be called preventive and curative.[15] True peace could only exist, of course, after a fundamental change in productive relations had come about, involving the abolition of class rule and the introduction of socialism. The resolution of the first congress of the Second International, held in 1889, proclaimed: "war, the sad product of the present economic conditions [will] only disappear, when the capitalist system of production has been replaced by the emancipation of labor and the international triumph of socialism."[16] In the long run that view could not be the only guideline for action, however, and thus a preventive strategy gained more and more influence. In 1880, August Bebel had created the link between future expectations and actual politics: "In a war of defense we do not defend our enemies and their institutions, but ourselves and the country, the institutions of which we want to transform according to our own ideas, [the country] which alone is our field of action."[17] And Friedrich Engels brought the ambivalence to a head in 1895, arguing:

> Peace assures the victory of the German social democratic party in about ten years. War will bring her either victory in two or three years or complete ruin, at least for fifteen to twenty years. Faced with that, the German socialists would be mad to want a war, in which they would stake everything on one throw instead of awaiting the sure triumph of peace.[18]

Under these circumstances socialist reaction to the Tsar's proposal was that it was the right thing coming from the wrong man. But William II was not completely correct in fearing that it was a "brilliant weapon of agitation" for them.[19] In a resolution of the 1898 party rally, the social democrats welcomed the manifesto as "fully affirming and justifying the resolute opposition of social democracy of all countries to the almost insane military armaments."[20] But they advised the Tsar to begin with reforms in his own country:

> It is the opinion of the party rally that nations preserve their "holiest goods" best when they join social democratic efforts for a peace of nations, freedom of nations and welfare of nations by a strong support of social progress. That means a suspension of class conflict and an advancement of knowledge and education in all fields.

Standing armies should be abolished and international disputes settled in the same way that civilized nations resolved their internal disputes, that is, through legal proceedings.

In the Reichstag debate on the military budget, Bebel found in the wording of the Tsar's manifesto a strong argument against a further increase of military personnel. When he termed the government draft of the military budget a "mockery" of disarmament plans, he was called out of order. He warned that "if the fifteen million trained soldiers should line up for the great general march in Europe to begin the mutual war of annihilation, . . . this would strike the last hour of bourgeois society." Bebel believed that the terrible devastation which would occur

> would inevitably raise in the minds in all nations the question whether this is a state of affairs which is in accord with human dignity . . . or whether those, who had so far cherished and protected this state of affairs and used all their might to maintain it, should not once and for all be prevented from preserving such a system any longer.[21]

On the whole, therefore, it was not surprising that Social Democrats expected little from and found nothing in the results of the 1899 conference. An international meeting of socialists in Amsterdam on 22 May 1899 confirmed this just at the beginning of the Hague gathering.[22] The German deputy, Hermann Molkenbuhr, underlined the unavoidable necessity for the ruling class to unleash another war (and therefore to require armies) in order to secure the export of surplus production to countries overseas. The socialist antidote had to be the solidarity of the international proletariat. It should be clear that in Germany there was no contact between the socialists and the bourgeois peace advocates. Indeed, a well-known socialist present at a Stuttgart demonstration was the only one to vote against a resolution in support of the conference passed by his bourgeois friends.[23]

THE ATTITUDE OF THE PEACE MOVEMENT

At the turn of the century the organized German peace movement numbered about 5,000 persons, organized in some 56 local groups.[24] Roger Chickering's "educated guess" counts no more than 200–300 persons active in the movement.[25] Through the Tsarist manifesto, however, they received a fresh impulse. Had not their position outside the popular mainstream suddenly become officially acknowledged? Could not the pariahs of German society now claim respectable support for some aspects of their diagnosis as well as their therapy of international politics?

The spring of 1899, before the beginning of the Hague conference, was the only time in the Kaiserreich that the peace movement
held mass meetings in several large cities.[26] In Munich a "committee
for demonstrating for the peace conference" was founded and held
its first meeting on 28 January 1899 with several thousand participants.[27] On 8 March 1899 another meeting took place under the
chairmanship of Professor Lipps at which Dr. Ludwig Quidde, among
others, spoke; 1,500 persons were said to have attended.[28] At those
meetings there was a tendency to compare the German Emperor's
attitude toward peace with that of the Russian Tsar, in a manner un-
friendly to the former.

The movement spread from Munich to other cities, especially in
southern Germany. Assemblies in Frankfurt (10 April), Mannheim
(11 April), Stuttgart (9 May), and Esslingen/Neckar were reported.
Speeches were delivered mostly by the same persons. Their party affiliations ranged from National Liberals to the south German *Volks-
partei* (People's Party). Women were especially active in this movement. The fact that they also made speeches and joined in passing
the resolutions elicited derision for the assemblies from official circles. The number of persons attending and adhering by acclamation
to the resolutions cannot be ascertained with precision. But, apart
from the assemblies, signatures were collected and sent to the petition committee of the Reichstag and the Bundesrat, both of which
passed them on to the government for further consideration.[29]

The Munich resolution bore 37,700 signatures, and a similar text
was signed at Königsberg by 2,350 persons. A bound volume of signatures supporting a declaration of sympathy for disarmament contained 7,650 names. In Berlin, Alfred Hermann Fried organized a
committee which, according to his own testimony, delivered 100,000
copies of the Munich resolution on the opening day of the peace conference.[30] In Munich, Leonore Selenka, a professor's wife and until
then known only as a feminist, began a world-wide campaign by
women for the success of the coming conference. A list, which was
said to have one million signatures, was handed over to the president
of the Hague conference on 15 March 1899.

The peace movement seemed to be developing into a mass movement, transcending the circles of ridiculed and sectarian pacifists.
But the conference itself and, more so, the ensuing Boer war dealt
a severe blow to that awakening. Afterwards it fell back to its old

size and influence. But its apparent proximity to official acknowledgement was bought to a large extent by partial acceptance of the official standpoint, as the following extract from the above-mentioned declaration of sympathy makes clear:

> We do not want Germany to disarm, as long as the world around us bristles with bayonets. We do not want to diminish our position in the world or refrain from any advantage which we can get from a peaceful contest of nations. We do not want Germany to be weakened by even a tiny fraction of its strength in relation to other nations if it should at any time be forced, despite its love for peace, to defend its national independence in a war forced upon it. But we want, by international agreements, to use every honorable means to prevent the outbreak of wars.[31]

"We do not want to interfere with the tasks of statesmen and politicians" was the underlying assumption of this resolution. It was conceived as a petition to the authorities, and it was exactly in this limited stance that the peace movement achieved its greatest success (in attracting supporters). Indeed, when shortly after the publication of the Tsarist manifesto a Krefeld citizen criticized German Sedan celebrations in a letter to the editor of a French newspaper, he was placed under police surveillance.[32]

The main arguments made by the German peace movement for a better international order in combination with the Hague plans can be gauged by referring to the views of some of its leaders. Eugen Schlief, a National Liberal professor of law from Strasbourg and a main speaker at the Stuttgart peace rally, warned against rousing moral disgust against war among the masses.[33] That would be as dangerous and wrong as idealizing war. Beginning with the formal acceptance of the international territorial status quo, a state of law could be created to take the place of the present anarchy. Eduard Löwenthal, one of the pioneers of the peace movement since the 1860s, but now an outsider without much contact with the Peace Society, criticized the peace movement as "childish" because it approved facultative arbitration as resolved at the Hague.[34] That only a compulsory international system of justice could be a guarantee of peace had been his *ceterum censeo* for decades.

In a lecture based on Bloch's perspective of a future war, Pastor Otto Umfrid, vice president of the *Deutsche Friedensgesellschaft* (German Peace Society) since 1900, nevertheless argued,

> A nation has the right to claim as much soil, but also as much
> freedom of movement, as is necessary for it not to be hindered in
> the formation of its character, of the development of its national
> life and the unfolding of its power.[35]

But this right should no longer be realized by force but come about
as a natural right by justice, and arbitration was the first step in the
right direction.

Alfred Hermann Fried, the most prolific of all German and Austrian pacifists, was, as always, concerned to be realistic and to distance himself from anything that could be considered utopian.[36]
Peace was a question of reason, especially a calculation of material
loss and gain. For this theory he claimed a scientific approach as a
new science of peace. In practice, this could lead to a policy of "at-
tentism": truth would be victorious; it was only necessary to wait.
Proceeding from these assumptions, he warned in his February 1899
pamphlet, *What can the St. Petersburg peace conference achieve?*,
against overoptimistic hopes for perpetual peace or complete disarmament. "The position of these heavily armored states is quite
different from the position citizens have in civilized nations." One
had to assume the attitude of statesmen and diplomats who proceeded gradually. Armaments were, in fact, only the consequence of
the anarchic system, not the cause. Therefore legal relations first had
to be established — and they could only be developed gradually:

> Indeed the present times do not offer an assurance that arbitra-
> tion courts could gain validity in really great legal issues. . . .
> Those who are of the opinion that the first move towards the pa-
> cification of Europe could be made by the implementation of an
> arbitration court are as misguided as those who want to create the
> basis for justice through disarmament.[37]

But what could be done? Fried himself made a remarkable proposal connecting cultural progress, imperialism and peace, on the
grounds that a certain standard of civilization was needed in order
to replace the sword by law.

> The peace movement is of the opinion that up to a certain level
> of civilization war is a cultural factor which must therefore still
> be regarded as a bitter necessity. But at a certain level of develop-
> ment it [war] will take an about turn and will become an impedi-
> ment to civilization.

War between European states on European soil was already now almost impossible. The only possible scene of conflagrancies was on and about colonial territory. He believed that "the wars of the twentieth century will contribute to the consolidation of the world state federation."

In order to prevent these wars, diplomats at the coming conference in St. Petersburg should find out the common interests of their states and establish a "European colonial alliance."

> We are satisfied with the United States of Europe for a particular purpose, i.e. a real business contract, a society with limited liability for the opening up of China, of Africa and of God knows for what other yet underdeveloped lands. Profits will be divided according to the amount of income, costs of management will be considerably reduced, material profits for all states will be gigantically increased. . . . Common world politics will create a common world law.[38]

Although Fried was a convinced pacifist who devoted his life to the promotion of peace, he was not opposed to all wars. His main idea was that rational analysis would lead states to prefer peaceful methods in the future. In Bloch's tradition he saw the new century as one of science, enlightenment, and progress. As is well known, nothing at all came of this at the Hague. Nevertheless, in 1900, Fried relentlessly propagated the conventions and resolutions.[39] As a born optimist he tried to convince the German public that the Hague conference of 1899 had been a turning point, quoting Goethe's words after the battle of Valmy (1792): "Here and now a new epoch of world history has begun and you can say you were witnesses." Elsewhere in the same book about the results of the Hague conference he wrote, "A new era in world history has begun. After the days of the Hague a new calendar will be created: the era of the hejira of war."

CONCLUSION

Roger Chickering has recently developed a framework for the analysis of the political culture of Wilhelmine Germany as a whole. He proceeds from the assumption that emotions, prejudices, and anxieties, and not rational analysis of interests are most important for people's orientations. They are formalized in symbols and rites which are developed and protected by men and organizations of the prevailing political spectrum.[40] Chickering convincingly shows that in Imperial Germany the Pan-German radical right and many of the patriotic societies moved from support of governmental efforts for the concrete implementation of these symbols at the turn of the century to massive criticism of Reich policies in the conviction that they themselves were the only ones who could advance national honor and greatness. With regard to pacifists, therefore, his assessment is clear: "The pacifists' program was so hopelessly out of touch with political reality that it might be more appropriate to ask why they found any sympathy at all."[41]

For analytical purposes it may be useful, nevertheless, to break up such a cluster and to differentiate between various parameters in such a value system so that the position of individuals, social groups, or political parties may be measured on a number of scales related to the main features of our topic. One of the parameters may be the emotional basis of a position, which can be either anxious or excessively self-confident. As to the aims of politics in international affairs, a scale can be constructed from status quo to unlimited growth and expansion; regarding domestic politics, the possible attitudes would range from self-determination of the individual to obedience; regarding political organization, from democracy to authoritarian rule. In these three respects the social methods to be employed may be classified as ranging from peaceful compromise to aggressiveness and war, and here again we can differentiate between methods of first choice and ultimate means. What follows if we employ these parameters, not for a diagnosis of the whole Empire, but only for a snapshot of attitudes towards the 1899 conference?

In official circles pride and self-confidence prevailed. But they were derived mainly from the prospect of Germany's continuing rise as a world power, while on the domestic side fear of social upheaval resulted in a certain pessimistic undertone: the prerogatives of the crown in the semiconstitutional system had to be protected. For the question of peace and war, the official mind found it necessary to leave open the expectation of warlike solutions, of Germany pursuing aggressive policies.

Liberal critics such as Naumann, and to a certain degree also Delbrück, seemed largely to share this attitude, especially the view that war might be a necessity in the future if expansion should encounter difficulties. They differed from officialdom most in their assessment of domestic structures and to a lesser extent also in the methods of actual foreign policy which they promoted.

By comparison, the Social Democrats' official proclamation represented clear alternatives. Their self-confidence was based primarily on their belief in the power of the working-class, and only secondarily on the nation. They opted for peaceful solutions of international conflicts, but they doubted the ability of capitalist national states to achieve them. Therefore individual as well as collective liberation was required to change the existing domestic (especially economic) system, and in this regard force or revolution was an ultimate possibility. Of course, these attitudes may characterize only a mainstream of thought and not the collective mentality of the Social Democratic rank and file.[42]

It cannot be doubted that the tiny peace movement was in an outsider position because it preferred peaceful methods for the solution of conflicts even if, as was the case with Fried, it might see war as an ultimate necessity. That was its main challenge to the value system of the Empire and the reason for its marginal position. Of course, the party affiliations and inclinations of peace movement members indicated that they supported individual self-determination or political democracy, which contributed to their isolation. What should be stressed is that most of them attached considerable importance to national greatness and expansion and that hardly any of them was content with the status quo of the German Empire in world politics. Although they were self-confident and optimistic, in some respects they were also naive. They were loyal citizens, as their attempt to petition the government in the spring of 1899 shows, but many of them did not see that far-reaching national aims could be interpreted by other nations as a threat. That was the point which elicited criticism, derision, or contempt from established circles.

Thus, in many respects the German pacifists at the turn of the century were also part of the accepted value system and held the same convictions as the ruling elite. *German World Politics and No War,* the title of a liberal and not pacifist pamphlet by Hans Plehn, published in 1913, could also have been a slogan expressing the pacifists' attitude towards the Hague peace conference of 1899.[43] Whether it was realistic may be open to debate. It was at least optimistic, and

pacifists remained optimistic in spite of all setbacks. When World
War I started, Fried commented, "The work of peace will continue!
Carrying Clausewitz further, we can say: war is the continuation of
the work of peace, but with other means."[44]

NOTES

1. The First Hague Peace Conference took place from 18 May to 29
July 1899, the Second from 15 June to 18 Oct. 1907. Cf. Calvin D.
Davis, *The United States and the First Hague Peace Conference* (Ithaca, N.Y.: Cornell Univ. Press, 1962) and *The United States and the Second Hague Peace Conference. American Diplomacy and International Organization (1899–1914)* (Durham, N.C.: Duke Univ. Press, 1975); Jost Dülffer, *Regeln gegen den Krieg. Die Haager Friedenskonferenzen 1899 und 1907 in der internationalen Politik* (Frankfurt, Berlin, and Vienna: Ullstein, 1981). Ralph Uhlig's forthcoming study on the Interparliamentary Union will be especially helpful.

2. *Foreign Relations of the United States, 1898* (Washington: U.S. Government Printing Office, 1899), 541.

3. *Die Grosse Politik der europäischen Kabinette,* ed. Johannes Lepsius et al. (Berlin: Deutsche Verlagsgesellschaft für Politik und Geschichte, 1922–1927) vol. 15, doc. 4222 (29 Aug. 1898). Hereinafter cited as GP (English original by William II).

4. James Brown Scott, ed., *The Proceedings of the Hague Peace Conferences: The Conference of 1899,* transl. of the official texts (New York: Oxford Univ. Press, 1920), 308ff. Cf. GP, 15, 4259.

5. GP, 15, 4255 (9 May 1899) and 4256 (12 May 1899).

6. Note by Emperor William on a report by the German minister Stockholm, *Politisches Archiv des Auswärtigen Amtes Bonn,* IAAa 37, no. 1, vol. 5. Hereinafter cited as PA/AA.

7. GP, 15, 4255 (9 May 1899) and 4256 (12 May 1899).

8. GP, 15, 4300 (10 June 1899).

9. Peter Winzen, *Bülows Weltmachtkonzept. Untersuchungen zur Frühphase seiner Aussenpolitik, 1897–1901* (Boppard: Boldt, 1977), and "Der Krieg in Bülows Kalkül: Katastrophe der Diplomatie oder Chance zur Machtexpansion," in Jost Dülffer and Karl Holl, eds., *Bereit zum Krieg. Kriegsmentalität im wilhelminischen Deutschland 1890–1914* (Göttingen: Vandenhoeck & Ruprecht, 1986), 161–93.

10. GP, 15, 4320 (21 June 1899), p. 306 (final handwritten comment by the Emperor).

11. Friedrich Naumann, *Zar und Weltfrieden. Öffentlicher Vortrag* (Berlin: Die Hilfe, 1899), 8, 11, 15. Regarding Naumann, see: Dieter Düding,

Der Nationalsoziale Verein 1896–1903. Der gescheiterte Versuch einer partei-politischen Synthese von Nationalismus, Sozialismus und Liberalismus (Munich: Oldenbourg, 1972); Peter Theiner, *Sozialer Liberalismus und deutsche Weltpolitik. Friedrich Naumann im wilhelminischen Deutschland (1866–1919)* (Berlin and Baden-Baden: Nomos, 1983), 73ff.; contributions by Holl and Albertin in Karl Holl and Günther List, eds., *Liberalismus und imperialistischer Staat. Der Imperialismus als Problem liberaler Parteien in Deutschland 1890–1914* (Göttingen: Vandenhoeck & Ruprecht, 1975).

12. Hans Delbrück, "Politische Korrespondenz," *Preussische Jahrbücher* 94 (25 Sept., 1898): 188; Annelise Thimme, *Hans Delbrück als Kritiker der wilhelminischen Epoche* (Düsseldorf: Droste, 1955); Arden Bucholz, *Hans Delbrück and the German Military Establishment* (Iowa City: Univ. of Iowa Press, 1985); Gordon A. Craig, "Delbrück: The Military Historian," in Peter Paret, ed., *Makers of Modern Strategy* (Oxford: Clarendon Press, 1986), 326–53.

13. Ivan S. Bliokh, *Budushchaia voina v teknicheskom, ekonomisches-kom i politicheskom otnosheniakh,* 6 vols. (St. Petersburg: Efron, 1898). There were full translations in French, German, and Polish. Cf. Peter van den Dungen, *The Making of Peace. Jean de Bloch and the First Hague Peace Conference* (Los Angeles: Center for the Study of Armament and Disarmament, Occasional Papers, no. 12, 1983) and *A Bibliography of the Pacifist Writings of Jean de Bloch* (London: Housmans, 1977); Hans Delbrück, "Zukunftskrieg und Zukunftsfrieden," *Preussische Jahrbücher* 96 (1899): 218, 220, 221, 229.

14. Delbrück, "Zukunftskrieg," 221.

15. Friedhelm Boll, *Frieden ohne Revolution? Friedensstrategien der deutschen Sozialdemokratie vom Erfurter Programm 1891 bis zur Revolution 1918* (Bonn: Neue Gesellschaft, 1980), 9–14; Hans-Josef Steinberg, *Internationaler Sozialismus und deutsche Sozialdemokratie. Zur Ideologie der Partei vor dem Ersten Weltkrieg* (Bonn: Neue Gesellschaft, 1967); Wolfram Wette, *Kriegstheorien deutscher Sozialisten – Marx, Engels, Lassalle, Kautsky, Bernstein, Luxemburg* (Stuttgart: Kohlhammer, 1971).

16. Quoted in Boll, *Frieden,* 75.

17. Werner Jung, *August Bebel. Deutscher Patriot und internationaler Sozialist* (Pfaffenweiler: Centaurus, 1986), 35.

18. "Der Sozialismus in Deutschland" in Karl Marx and Friedrich Engels, *Werke* (Berlin: Dietz, 1963), 22, 256.

19. GP, 15, 4216 (marginal note).

20. *Protokoll über die Verhandlungen des Parteitags der Sozialdemokratischen Partei Deutschlands* (Berlin, 1898; reprint Berlin and Bonn: Dietz, 1979), 65, cf. 220ff. (Bebel).

21. *Stenographische Berichte über die Verhandlungen des deutschen Reichstages 1890–1914* (Berlin: Verlag der Buchdruckerei der Norddeutschen

Zeitung, 1899), 165, col. 211 D; Stig Förster, *Der doppelte Militarismus. Die deutsche Heeresrüstungspolitik zwischen Status-quo-Sicherung und Aggression 1890–1913* (Wiesbaden: Steiner, 1985), 91–108.

22. Report of the French minister, The Hague, 24 May 2899, *Ministère des Affaires Etrangères, Paris*, NS Russie 25; German minister, The Hague, 26 May 1899, PA/AA, IAAa 37, no. 1, vol. 11; cf. *Kölnische Zeitung*, 25 May 1899.

23. *Der Beobachter*, 10 May 1899 (the opposing vote was cast by a Social Democratic writer named Stern).

24. Roger Chickering, *Imperial Germany and a World without War. The Peace Movement and German Society, 1892–1914* (Princeton, NJ: Princeton Univ. Press, 1975); Friedrich-Karl Scheer, *Die deutsche Friedensgesellschaft (1892–1933): Organisation, Ideologie, politische Ziele. Ein Beitrag zur Geschichte des Pazifismus in Deutschland* (Frankfurt a. M.: Haag & Herchen, 1981); Dorothee Stiewe, "Die bürgerliche deutsche Friedensbewegung als soziale Bewegung bis zum Ende des Ersten Weltkrieges" (Inaugural dissertation, Freiburg i. Br., 1972).

25. Chickering, *Imperial Germany*, 66. In his chapter in this volume, "War, Peace, and Social Mobilization in Imperial Germany: Patriotic Societies, The Peace Movement, and Socialist Labor," Chickering reduces the number to a few dozen activists.

26. Chickering, *Imperial Germany*, 56.

27. *Berliner Neueste Nachrichten*, 29 Jan. 1899.

28. Report, Prussian Minister, Munich, 12 March 1899, PA/AA IAAa 37, no. 1, vol. 7.

29. Material in PA/AA IAAa 37, no. 2, vol. 5 and 6; *Zentrales Staatsarchiv der DDR, Potsdam*, Reichsamt des Inneren, no. 12971.

30. Scheer, *Friedensgesellschaft*, 89 (also for what follows).

31. *Berliner Neueste Nachrichten*, 29 Jan. 1899.

32. PA/AA IAAa 37, no. 1, vol. 2 (the man was an otherwise unknown Emile Breul from Düsseldorf).

33. *Der Beobachter*, 10 May 1899.

34. Eduard Löwenthal, *Weltpolitik und Weltjustiz. Oder: Die Kulturwidrigkeit des Nicht-Interventionsprinzips im Völkerrecht* (Berlin: Selbstverlag, 1900).

35. Otto Umfrid, *Recht, Gewalt und Zukunftskrieg* (Esslingen: Langguth, 1901), 2.

36. For Fried see, besides the authors cited in note 24: Wilfried Eisenbeiss, *Die bürgerliche Friedensbewegung in Deutschland während des Ersten Weltkrieges. Organisation, Selbstverständnis und politische Praxis 1913/14–1919* (Frankfurt, Bern, and Cirencester: Lang, 1980), csp. 188–226; Brigitte Hamann, *Bertha von Suttner. Ein Leben für den Frieden* (Munich and Zurich: Piper, 1986); Scheer, *Friedensgesellschaft*, 39–49.

37. Alfred Hermann Fried, *Was kann die Petersburger Friedenskonferenz erreichen?* (Berlin: E. Pierson, 1899), 6, 13, 20, 22, 26ff.

38. When Fried was writing his article, it was still believed that the conference would take place in the Russian capital; cf. Dülffer, *Regeln gegen den Krieg,* 54–68.

39. Alfred Hermann Fried, *Die Haager Conferenz, ihre Bedeutung und ihre Ergebnisse* (Berlin: H. Bermühler, 1900), 28, 73.

40. Roger Chickering, *We Men Who Feel Most German: A Cultural Study of the Pan-German League 1886–1914* (London: Allen & Unwin, 1984), 16–18 and passim.

41. Chickering, *Imperial Germany,* 326.

42. Hans-Christoph Schröder, *Sozialismus und Imperialismus. Die Auseinandersetzung der deutschen Sozialdemokratie mit dem Imperialismusproblem und der Weltpolitik vor 1914* (Hannover: Verlag für Literatur und Zeitgeschehen, 1975); Wolfram Wette, *Gustav Noske* (Düsseldorf: Droste, 1987, forthcoming); Roger Fletcher, *Revisionism and Empire. Socialist Imperialism in Germany 1897–1914* (London: Allen & Unwin, 1984).

43. Hans Plehn, *Deutsche Weltpolitik und kein Krieg* (Berlin: Puttkammer & Mühlbrecht, 1913).

44. *Die Friedenswarte,* 1914, 281.

SOLOMON WANK

The Austrian Peace Movement and the Habsburg Ruling Elite, 1906–1914

EFFORTS TO ORIENT THE Habsburg Empire to peace in the decade prior to World War I illustrate Konrad Jarausch's observation that "since governments rather than individuals generally make war (at least between states) influencing their decisions is crucial for the success or failure of peace advocacy."[1] However, the experience of the Austrian peace movement, set against the deepening social and nationality conflicts after 1906, suggests also that the potential for influencing governments is limited by the political context and perceptions of peace advocates.

THE HABSBURG CONTEXT*

Imperial Austria was, in A. J. Mayer's provocative description, the last survivor of the "Old Regime" in Europe.[2] The efforts of the Austrian peace movement to influence the Habsburg ruling elite must be seen against the background of the authoritarian and militaristic values of an elite composed of high aristocrats, military officers, and imperial bureaucrats. In a time of rapid industrial change and challenges from new social groups and national elites, the effort to hold together the traditional form of sociopolitical integration that was non-national, hierarchical, and socially compartmentalized taxed the elite's political and psychological faculties. Frustration triggered a mood of pessimism about the empire's future.[3]

In fact, the multinational Habsburg Empire in 1906 was in a pe-

*As used in this essay, the name Austria refers to that half of the Austro Hungarian Empire legally known, after the Compromise of 1867, as "the kingdoms and countries represented in the Reichsrath [parliament]" but commonly referred to as Austria.

riod of stagnation. Striving for emancipation, the Czech and Hungarian national elites and the working class had called into question the old form of corporate social and political integration, along with the hegemonic position of the traditional ruling groups. Although the established system was challenged, no group or coalition proved capable of establishing a preponderant position and a new social order.[4] This contributed to the ennui and stagnation of the empire.

An attempt at a new democratic integration during the prime ministership of Baron Max von Beck, 1906–1908, quickly succumbed to strong tendencies to restore and secure the hegemony of the traditional ruling groups by means of state power and executive authority.[5] Internally, this involved an attempt to strengthen authoritarianism. The goal was a modernized form of late–eighteenth-century Habsburg absolutism with a centralized bureaucratic-military state oriented around the Germans in the empire. Externally, predominance by the elite predicated the militarization of foreign policy in the Balkan peninsula aimed at establishing Austro-Hungarian hegemony in the region. This policy, initiated in the crisis provoked by the annexation of Bosnia and Herzegovina in October 1908, became more aggressive and expansionist after Foreign Minister Alois von Aehrenthal's death in February 1912. At that time civilian and military leaders concluded that military measures alone could contend with what they perceived as the Serbian threat to the Habsburg Empire's existence.[6]

After the annexation crisis, the ruling elite took steps to eliminate the parliamentary system. Parliament was provoked into obstruction by the government's efforts to trim democratic reforms introduced in 1906–1908 and by its dilatory handling of nationality issues. The objective was to prove that Austria could not be ruled in a parliamentary fashion, and then to use the emergency powers granted to the executive by Paragraph 14 of the Austrian constitution to show that Austria could be ruled without a parliament. In March 1914, parliament was unexpectedly adjourned, and Count Karl Stürgkh, the Austrian prime minister, showed no inclination to recall it anytime soon.[7] The war which broke out on July 28, 1914, also appeared to be a suitable instrument to justify the efforts of the traditional elites to restore their hegemony, although this was by no means the sole cause of the First World War. The emergency measures enacted by the Austrian government, which were more drastic

than those of any other belligerent state, included suspension of the
constitution of 1867, military jurisdiction over all political "crimes,"
and censorship.[8]

THE PEACE MOVEMENT IN AUSTRIA

By 1906, the peace movement had established itself in the Austrian
half of the dual monarchy on a more-or-less firm footing, despite
the authoritarian and militaristic character of the official culture.[9]
However, its activities were hampered and constrained by police harassment and infiltration, and by the severe restrictions on rights of
association, assembly, and free speech that existed behind the liberal
facade of the Austrian constitution of 1867. These restrictions applied to all political organizations, but they were enforced with much
greater severity against pacifist and antimilitarist organizations.[10]

As elsewhere in Europe, there were really several peace movements
in Austria, but with respect to influence on the Habsburg ruling elite
only two of them counted: the bourgeois and the socialist peace
movements. Their strengths, strategies, and potentials for influence
differed in relation to their respective positions in the Austrian socioeconomic order.

Neither the bourgeois nor the socialist peace movement was pacifist in the strict sense of absolute renunciation of war or participation in it. Nor did either advocate civil disobedience and refusal of
military service as called for by nonviolent anarchists. There were
absolute pacifists and anarchists in Austria, but the peace movements
associated with absolute pacifism and anarchism were too weak and,
in the case of the anarchists, too divided between advocates of violence and nonviolence and too harassed by the police to be effective.[11] In any event, civil disobedience and refusal of military service
were not realistic public alternatives in pre-1914 Austria, where criticism of the laws pertaining to military service was dealt with harshly
and where conscientious objectors were treated as common criminals.

The bourgeois peace movement consisted of two wings which were
distinct organizationally but similar ideologically. The first was constituted of peace advocates who had a political base in the German-
Austrian Liberal party and worked within the established parliamentary system to change the domestic and international conditions
they saw as responsible for war and militarism. From the founding

of the Austrian constitutional-parliamentary regime in 1867 until the 1880s, the Liberals were antiabsolutist, antimilitarist, and opposed to large defense budgets and expansionist foreign policies. In the 1880s, the Liberals became increasingly unable to sustain themselves against the rising tide of non-German nationalism and antiliberal mass political parties. In order to preserve their political and social power and prestige, the Liberals formed a coalition with the traditional ruling groups. As that alliance became tighter after 1900, they shifted to support of military conscription and an active foreign policy in the Balkan peninsula to maintain the prestige of the Habsburg Empire as a Great Power. Liberal peace advocacy consequently became ambiguous but, nevertheless, the Liberals remained associated with the peace movement.[12] After the turn of the century, the Liberal peace advocates and their leading political spokesman, Ernst von Plener, were closely identified with the peace program of the Inter-Parliamentary Union, which promoted a general world arbitration treaty for matters not touching on the honor or vital interests of the signatory nations.[13]

Not surprisingly, the Liberal peace advocates were overwhelmingly male, middle-aged, and upper–middle-class. They included a disproportionate number of parliamentarians and lawyers but also a relatively large number of academics and businessmen. Many Liberals were members of the Austrian establishment; although they sought support for their proposals in parliament and in the liberal press, their preferred strategy was to persuade Habsburg decisionmakers to adopt a policy of international arbitration.[14]

The Austrian Peace Society (APS) constituted a second wing of the bourgeois peace movement. The APS, really a special grouping within the liberal peace tradition, was founded in 1891 by Bertha von Suttner with the help of Alfred H. Fried and was associated with the Universal Peace Congress.[15] Unlike the Liberal peace advocates, the Austrian Peace Society was apolitical. This policy not only allowed some members of the Habsburg elite to associate themselves on purely formal terms with the APS but also permitted non-Germans, such as the Czech intellectual and parliamentarian Thomás Masaryk, to join the society. Women were attracted by Suttner's emphasis on the nurturing role of women and on the emancipation of women as a condition for a peaceful society.[16] The number of young intellectuals, writers, and artists associated with the bourgeois peace movement was remarkably small. This dearth may be attributed, to a significant degree, to the *fin de siècle* crisis of liberal culture in Austria that discredited rationalist notions of peace and human nature underlying the peace movement.[17] In fact, although its membership was somewhat broader, the chief support of the APS came from the same upper–middle-class groups as the Liberals.

The APS sought to eliminate recourse to war by exerting moral and humanitarian pressure for democratic institutional reforms through means outside of politics, especially through education. Like the Liberals, it strongly advocated international arbitration. The APS sought to generate pressure from public opinion enlightened by the press, although APS leaders again were like the Liberals in relying on elite decision-makers to adopt their goals.[18] By 1906, Fried had replaced Suttner's ethical pacifism with liberal-oriented utilitarianism and scientific rationalism as the foundation of APS arguments for peace. Fried argued in a deterministic fashion that social and technological evolution and the development of economic and cultural interdependence were tending inexorably toward the peaceful adjudication of disputes and the creation of a stable international political order as the foundations for a lasting peace.[19] This vision of peace, similar to the one projected by Norman Angell's *The Great Illusion,* was shared by the Liberals.

Like the bourgeois peace movement, the socialist constituency was well-defined, but its working-class base was larger and better organized. The socialists saw capitalist imperialism as inevitably engendering war.[20] Accordingly, the public position of the Austrian socialists was similar to that proclaimed by the Second International at its 1891 congress in Brussels. The only way to guarantee permanent peace was through the establishment of a socialist society. The only real peace movement was therefore the Second International.[21] The failure of bourgeois pacifists to view capitalism as the cause of war ruled out cooperation between the two groups. Accordingly, the socialist press in Austria saw the Hague peace conference of 1899 as an exercise in cant and hypocrisy.[22]

Until 1906 the idea of war against war through war against capitalism served the socialists well enough as a peace policy. Their energies were concentrated chiefly on developing the Socialist party's organizational structure and on domestic reforms.[23] In fact, there was no urgency in regard to foreign affairs, since in the period from 1895 until 1906, Austria-Hungary pursued a generally passive foreign policy.[24]

The appointment of Count Alois von Aehrenthal as Austro-Hungarian foreign minister in 1906 signalled a change to a more active approach, culminating in the annexation of Bosnia and Herzegovina in October 1908. The annexation and the ensuing international crisis, however, threatened to embroil Austria-Hungary in the imperialist struggle of the great powers and thereby intensify the conflict among the nationalities within the empire and undercut reform by diverting financial resources to the military. Consequently, the socialists responded by formulating their own foreign policy which was, at the same time, a peace policy. Austria-Hungary's position as a Great Power had to be based on democratic institutions and national autonomy at home and avoiding involvement in conflicts of the great powers abroad. The best way to prevent the latter and to preserve peace was through maintaining the status quo in the Balkan peninsula. In essence, the socialist foreign policy called for Austria-Hungary to give up its great power pretensions and become a middling power. Espousing such a policy put the socialists at odds with the ruling elite, which saw its salvation in demonstrating the ability of Austria-Hungary to pursue the policy of a great power, especially in the Balkan peninsula.[25]

Some problematic elements in the foreign policy of Austrian socialism, however, corresponded in important ways to that of the elite. At the root of the socialist domestic and foreign policies were the views and sentiments of the party's largely German leadership, which considered Austria-Hungary an ideal territorial and economic unit within which to work for the achievement of socialism. The socialist leaders therefore supported the preservation of a German-led centralized Austrian state, albeit a more democratic one than that envisaged by the ruling elite. Their support of German centralism put them in conflict with the idea of national self-determination at home and abroad, especially where Serbia and the monarchy's South Slavs were concerned. The only sort of national autonomy for which the socialists called within Austria-Hungary would be limited to cultural matters. In addition, the socialist foreign policy supported the Triple Alliance as a bulwark against the spread westward of Tsarist absolutism.[26]

In practice, therefore, the peace policy of Austrian socialists was not too different from that of bourgeois peace advocates. Both groups accepted the continued existence of Austria-Hungary and its membership in the Triple Alliance. Both rejected the absolute pacifist position and recognized the legitimacy of a defensive war and military conscription, at least for the time being. Furthermore, ever since the Copenhagen congress of the Socialist International in 1910, the Austrian socialists were among those who opposed the general strike as a means of preventing war and openly doubted the effectiveness of any political means against war.[27] Increasingly, the socialists took a more positive attitude toward international arbitration and disarmament, and the Basel congress of the Second International of 1912 called for cooperation with the bourgeois peace movement, thereby retreating from the idea that peace required the overthrow of capitalism.[28]

Despite the fact that on a practical level the two peace movements had much in common and there were some contacts between revisionist socialists and bourgeois peace activists, direct cooperation between them was never established. On the one hand, both socialist criticism of the bourgeois failure to see the economic causes of war and armaments and differences in the assessment of concrete actions created barriers to frank support of the bourgeois peace movement. On the other hand, bourgeois peace advocates harbored reservations towards the socialists. Plener and upper–middle-class liberal pacifists had become part of the Austrian Establishment, which saw itself threatened by the socialists' domestic political and social reform program. The movement of the German-Austrian bourgeoisie closer to the Habsburg ruling elite strengthened class distinctions and biases among peace advocates.[29]

Bertha von Suttner and Alfred Fried were not entirely unsympathetic to the socialist peace movement, but they distanced themselves from it, at least in order to make the APS palatable to the upper classes. Fried stressed "the serious work of scientific and moderate pacifism as against socialist endeavors,"[30] while Suttner lamented in her diary in 1907 that "the [Hague] peace conferences move much too slowly—the Revolution will overtake them."[31] The tendency within the bourgeois peace movement was to use the socialists as bogeymen to frighten governing elites into accepting international arbitration and arms reductions.[32]

Failing to establish cooperation, let alone a common peace strategy, the two peace movements sought to influence Habsburg statesmen in their own ways: the bourgeois from within by using its access to decision-makers, the socialists from without by mass demonstrations such as those which proved successful in the campaign for universal manhood suffrage.

THE BOURGEOIS PEACE RECORD

The success of Bertha von Suttner's *Lay Down Your Arms!*, the peace publicity of the APS and the liberal press, together with the apprehension over domestic instability aroused by mass demonstrations for universal manhood suffrage, created in the minds of Habsburg decision-makers an image of a strong peace movement and of a public opinion that had to be appeased.[33] Kajetan von Mérey, the diplomat named to head the Austro-Hungarian delegation at the second Hague peace conference, admitted as much to the German ambassador at Vienna several months before the convening of the conference. In February 1907, Mérey told the German ambassador, whose government wanted to obviate the whole idea of compulsory arbitration, that in view of the strength of the peace movement in Austria, some kind of compulsory arbitration treaty was necessary.[34] For this reason, and under prodding by respected upper–middle-class peace advocates, flexible statesmen such as Aehrenthal could be persuaded to support a treaty proposal for universal compulsory arbitration which was restricted to what appeared to be relatively harmless cases, such as commercial and navigation treaties, sanitary conventions, agreements concerning diplomatic and consular immunity, and disputes over the interpretation and application of international treaties. As a further sop to the "peace apostles," Aehrenthal agreed to a proposal committing governments to examine seriously arms limitations leading to reductions in military budgets.[35]

Bourgeois peace advocates knew of the halfhearted attitudes of statesmen like Aehrenthal. After all, Heinrich Lammasch, an independent bourgeois peace advocate and a renowned expert on international arbitration, was legal adviser to the Austro-Hungarian delegation to the Hague peace conference and took part in internal foreign office discussions which drew up the instructions for the delegation.[36] Lammasch nonetheless accepted the reality of national sovereignty, although he envisaged imposing limitations on it as an incremental process.[37] Therefore, he and Plener were pleased when a large majority of states attending the conference voted for a universal compulsory arbitration treaty, but they were disappointed when the treaty failed to become international law because of the rule requiring the unanimous consent of the states for the adoption of resolutions brought before the conference. The fact that Austria-Hungary, initially disposed to approve the treaty, cast its vote against it under German pressures, added to their disappointment.[38]

Despite its defeat at the conference, the idea of a compulsory arbitration treaty did not die. The representatives voted to take up the matter again at a third conference to be held in 1915. Lammasch looked forward to its acceptance then. Hopes for the future notwithstanding, the failure to achieve a compulsory arbitration treaty at the peace conference ended the effectiveness of the liberal peace movement; it no longer had anything new or significant to contribute.[39] It became moribund after 1907 in part because it had tailored its proposals to get them adopted by the decision makers and also because the elimination of parliament undercut the APS strategy of putting public pressure on the government to enact democratic reforms. In a deeper sense, however, its demise was a result of the German-Austrian bourgeoisie's integration into the authoritarian sociopolitical conceptions and aggressive foreign policy of the Habsburg ruling elite.

THE SOCIALIST PEACE RECORD

As the bourgeois effort declined, the socialist peace movement gained strength and was tested in a series of conflicts in the Balkans and Near East. Ever since the annexation crisis of 1908–09, those areas had become the focal point of the imperialist conflicts of the European powers, any one of which it was feared might degenerate into a general war. Two of these conflicts involved Austria-Hungary, although not as a belligerent: the Italo-Turkish war, which broke out at the end of September 1911, and the Balkan wars of 1912–1913.

Austria-Hungary was affected by the Italo-Turkish war because Italy was a member of the Triple Alliance. On the one hand, the socialists pressured Habsburg decision-makers to do everything possible to keep the war localized. On the other hand, they sought to prevent the eruption of a war between Austria-Hungary and Italy, a possibility they confronted as a result of strident calls by the war-party in Vienna to take advantage of Italy's military engagement in Tripoli to conduct a preemptive war. The allegedly treacherous ally stood accused of threatening the existence of the Habsburg Empire by supporting anti-Habsburg nationalist movements in the Italian-inhabited regions of the empire and challenging Austro-Hungarian predominance in the western half of the Balkan peninsula.[40]

After the outbreak of Italo-Turkish war, the International Socialist Bureau (ISB) called for demonstrations condemning not only Italy's aggression but all imperialist policies. The ISB's position was accepted by both the executive committees of the socialist parties and the broad mass of organized labor. On November 5, the day on which the Italian government announced the annexation of Tripoli, large demonstrations took place in all European capitals, including Vienna. Afterwards European socialism put all of its energies into a peace offensive to promote a growing antiwar movement among workers. Even though they did not end the war immediately, the huge demonstrations reinforced the socialists' commitment to oppose war, despite a split within the Italian socialist party which led its moderate wing to support the war on nationalist grounds and in exchange for government promises of postwar social reforms and universal manhood suffrage.[41]

The expression of antiwar sentiments among workers in Austria, especially in Vienna, was very strong. Shortly before the outbreak of the Italo-Turkish war, workers were agitated by the sharp increase in the cost of living. Unrest led to large and angry protest demonstrations against the rise in prices, one of which, on 17 September, led to bloody street clashes with police. It seems likely that the radicalism of those demonstrations carried over into the antiwar campaign.[42] The strength of the workers' antiwar sentiments probably helped to discourage a preemptive war, which might well have unleashed a world conflict in 1911. It also seems likely that the demonstrations served to strengthen the moderating hand of Foreign Minister Aehrenthal who, seeing military action at that time as too dangerous, resisted pressure for a preventive strike and actively sought to localize the Italo-Turkish conflict.[43]

The Balkan wars of 1912–13 presented European and Austrian socialists with a much greater challenge. The socialists devoted their efforts to restricting the conflict to Turkey and the Balkan states. The Austrian socialists were immediately concerned because it was their country which threatened to widen the war. Victories in northern Albania brought the Serbs to the Adriatic coast. Habsburg statesmen announced their unalterable opposition to Serbia's gaining access to the sea, fearing that with the addition of territory Serbia would become stronger, more economically independent of Austria-Hungary, and more influential with South Slavs in the monarchy. By mid-November 1912, tension between Austria-Hungary and Serbia was running very high and militarists in Vienna were urging intervention, a policy which was supported by the foreign minister, Count Leopold Berchtold (Aehrenthal died the preceding February). When Russia mobilized troops along the Austro-Hungarian border, the possibility of a clash appeared real.[44]

In this threatening situation, Austrian socialists concentrated on the diplomatic maneuvers of their government. Realizing that a policy of maintaining the status quo was untenable, the socialists immediately proclaimed a policy of the "Balkans for the Balkan peoples" and, through meetings, rallies, and speeches in parliament, sought to prevent intervention. The Austrian socialists, especially their leader Victor Adler, also gave strong support to the peace initiative of the ISB at its meeting in Brussels on October 28. In an impressive show of unity, the ISB called upon workers in all countries to oppose the threat of a general war with mass action. The ensuing European-wide agitation by workers culminated in mass demonstrations in all of Europe on 17 November. In Austria, large protests took place not only in Vienna and Prague but also in the capital cities of all of the Austrian provinces.[45] This mobilized public opinion as never before, proving that the workers were determined to oppose a general war.[46]

To emphasize the urgency of the situation and to increase the pressure on the governing elites of the European great powers, the ISB called for a special congress of the Socialist International. Meeting at Basel on 24–25 November, the International adopted a peace manifesto which reflected the position of Adler and the Austrian socialists. It called for autonomy for the Albanians and a democratic federation of Balkan states. The Austrian socialists would oppose an attack on Serbia as well as all attempts to deprive it of its recent gains or to reduce it to a colony. The Austrian party would continue its efforts to transform the Habsburg monarchy so that the South Slavs could gain democratic self-rule within the Habsburg monarchy. The socialist parties of England, France, and Germany were charged to prevent their respective allies from abetting Russian or Austria-Hungarian intervention. Socialists were enjoined to cooperate with the middle classes and all pacifist groups to prevent the outbreak of a major war.[47] The manifesto ended with a warning to the ruling classes: "the very prospect of such an abomination as a world war would be enough to provoke the indignant hostility of the workers and drive them to revolt."[48]

The Basel peace manifesto provided the impetus for a further round of antiwar demonstrations by workers all over Europe in December 1912. Austria did not intervene, but Serbia did eventually evacuate the Albanian port of Durazzo under threat of war by Vienna in May 1913.[49] The Socialists again stepped up their antiwar campaign at the end of June 1913, when Austria-Hungary appeared on the verge of intervening to prevent Serbia from harvesting the territorial fruits of its victories in the second Balkan war.[50]

The European socialists' antiwar campaign in 1912 possessed a remarkable cohesion and unanimity. There is little doubt that the wave of mass antiwar demonstrations acted as a restraining influence on governing elites by serving notice that they would have to reckon with the resistance of the organized working class if it should come to a wider war.[51] Of course, the existing tensions between the government of the authoritarian Stürgkh and the parliament might have made the specter of internal disturbances arising out of socialist antiwar activity in the event of war appear more real to the Habsburg ruling elite.[52] Lammasch, who knew of the pending Basel congress of the International, mentioned its antiwar campaign as an argument against intervention in a memorandum to Franz Ferdinand.[53] The archduke, whose position with regard to intervention was ambiguous because of Austria-Hungary's internal weaknesses, became aware of the resolutions of the Basel congress and appears to have been impressed by the huge demonstration that took place on its opening day.[54] The socialists' antiwar campaign was effective enough that the Austrian government, having dissolved parliament in March 1914, took steps to deal with antiwar movements in the event of another diplomatic crisis.[55]

Additional factors operated to restrain the Habsburg elite. The German government, without whose support a military action in the Balkans was too risky because of the possibility of a clash with Russia, remained lukewarm in regard to an Austro-Hungarian intervention. "I find that you rattle too much — with my sword," Kaiser William is reported to have told Archduke Franz Ferdinand at a meeting held on 22–23 November 1912.[56] The significance of other factors

notwithstanding, one can agree with the historian Georges Haupt
that European socialism's 1912 campaign was "a powerful and impressive antiwar demonstration" which, in terms of the cohesion
and unity of those who organized it, must be considered a great
success.[57]

In that light, the absence of a similar campaign in July 1914 is
striking. Why did the ISB and the executive committees, the organizational arms of the International and the Austrian socialist party
respectively, make no preparations to act internally in anticipation
of sharpening international tensions, as they had done in 1912?
Among the standard explanations, the two most often cited factors
for socialist ineffectiveness in 1914 are internal disunity and nationalism. The successful antiwar campaign of 1912, it is claimed, only
blurred the fact that conflict between right and left wing factions at
Basel made it impossible to reach agreement on concrete means to
prevent war, that is, direct action such as a general strike, which the
majority of Austrian socialist leaders strongly rejected. In essence,
each national section of the International was left to decide the question of tactics for itself.[58] Hence there were no clear-cut and unified
organizational directives in 1914. The difficulty is that the success
of 1912 did not depend on direct action but, rather, on mass demonstrations, rallies, and antiwar speeches by socialist parliamentary
deputies.

The other hypothesis is that through the increasing integration of
workers into various states, nationalism overwhelmed socialist internationalism.[59] If it was a significant factor in 1914, however, why
was nationalism not equally significant in 1912? As Haupt suggests,
the question of why the socialists were ineffective in 1914 is a complex problem.

After the successful antiwar campaign of 1912 and the actions of
the great powers themselves to prevent the spread of the war, Austrian
socialist leaders, like their comrades in other European countries,
developed a confidence in the conventional conflict-regulating mechanisms of the great powers. Their confidence was based in turn on a
relatively optimistic assessment of the possibility of avoiding a war between the European great powers. Because clashes of the last years before 1914 had taken place on the peripheries of Europe, the danger
of a military conflict between the great powers arose only through
their being drawn into those peripheral conflicts. Victor Adler and
the majority of socialist leaders, including some left-wing ones such

as Karl Kautsky, thought along lines similar to Alfred Fried's "scientific pacifism" and concluded that the interests of the capitalist classes made it highly improbable that the imperialist states would go beyond military threats or a limited military engagement to a confrontation demanding all of their resources and threatening the existence of the international economy. In short, reason appeared to be triumphing.[60]

These short-term theories, however, distorted all long-term analysis of the growth of conflict between the great powers, leading to a weakening of the socialist peace campaign and antiwar propaganda among the workers. Accordingly, in 1914 socialist statesmen in Austria and other countries were politically and ideologically unprepared for war. Moreover, the antiwar stance of the International was already qualified by acceptance of the legitimacy of worker participation in a defensive war, and socialist leaders of the various national parties attributed defensive intentions to their own governments and aggressive intentions to other governments. This was especially true in France and England in regard to Germany and, to a lesser degree, Austria-Hungary. Several recent studies suggest that the weakness of the socialists' antiwar stance in 1914 also reflected the desire of party leaders and bureaucrats to protect their organizations from suppression by governing elites.[61]

The position of the Austrian socialists in 1914 reflected the general pattern of ideas and attitudes described above, but in a way specific to the Austrian situation. Party leaders operated on the assumption that Austria had been economically weakened by the costs of military mobilization during the Balkan Wars and that Russia was unprepared for war. Therefore, the assassination of Franz Ferdinand on 28 June 1914 aroused little concern among Austrian socialist leaders. Like the public in general, they did not expect it would lead to war. Most of the members of the party's executive committee were away from Vienna on vacation at the time of the presentation of the ultimatum to Serbia on 23 July and could not organize opposition to an escalation of the conflict. Later, as the crisis became more serious and war appeared a distinct possibility, there is evidence of antiwar stirrings among rank and file socialists and trade union workers. While protests broke out here and there on the local level, the majority waited for directives from the party leadership. These never came.[62]

The party leaders, even when they grasped that the Austro-Serbian dispute was more serious than they first thought, stressed its local

character and did not see it as leading to war. Even after the ultimatum to Serbia, when party leaders concluded that war was likely,
they refrained from calling for an antiwar campaign similar to the
one in 1912 because, among other reasons, they feared that demonstrations might encourage Serbian truculence. After the declaration
of war against Serbia, they appeared to be politically paralyzed.[63]
To a certain extent, they were caught in the contradictions of their
own foreign policy. On grounds of political strategy, Marxist economic theory, and pro-German cultural bias, Austrian socialist leaders were committed to preserving the Austro-Hungarian state. This
commitment also obliged them to oppose the strivings for independence of non-German ethnic groups — above all the South Slavs —
which threatened the destruction of the multinational empire. Hence
they shared with the Habsburg ruling elite an interest in preserving
the Habsburg Empire. Well aware that Tsarist absolutism was the
bête noire of the Austrian socialists, the ruling elite could appeal to
them by depicting Russia as the aggressor.[64]

On a psychological level and in a richly detailed study, Rudolf
Ardelt points to a cognitive dissonance as a major reason for the
party leaders' passivity in July 1914. On the one hand, they were
deeply convinced that the working class had to take determined action to preserve peace. The outbreak of war would signal a defeat
and reveal the real political weakness of the working-class movement. Even before the onset of the crisis, socialist political leaders,
whose entire political behavior was adapted to forms of parliamentary opposition, feared a direct confrontation with state power, even
though that was the only way to influence the government in a situation in which parliamentary government had been suspended. However, after Austria enacted "dictatorial" measures on 25 July, confrontation with state power risked the suppression of the Socialist
party, and with that the legitimacy and very existence of its leaders
as a political elite. As it was, the emergency measures permitted the
continued existence of the party's bureaucratic structure and newspapers — subject, of course, to heavy censorship — while robbing them
of their political and oppositional functions. Its leaders eliminated
the pain of cognitive dissonance by accepting the war as a defense
against the Tsarist enemy.[65]

What is particularly important about Haupt's and Ardelt's studies is that they call into question the traditional explanations for the
collapse of the socialist antiwar activity in 1914. If there was no repe-

tition of the excitement and waves of workers' protests that took place in Vienna in November and December 1912, the fault lay chiefly with the party leadership, not with the masses. Some evidence suggests that the masses were ready to take action similar to that in 1912. In July, initiatives for protests by workers and union officials appeared on the local level, but these received at best timid support from the leadership. In the absence of clear directives or support for local protests, internationalism and the antiwar spirit began to ebb. After the declaration of war, nationalism filled the ideological vacuum.

CONCLUSION

It is easy to conclude that the Austrian peace movement was a failure, always bearing in mind that it was the Habsburg ruling elite that ultimately committed the nation to war. Incapable of reconstructing Austrian society along democratic and national lines, the ruling elite fell prey to a self-destructive vision of political redemption through authoritarian and military means. Given that political context, the collapse of the peace movement was perhaps unavoidable. Still, there is enough evidence to show that the bourgeois and socialist peace movements at times exerted a moderating influence on the elite—the bourgeois from within and the socialist from without. Their influence could have been stronger if sociopolitical anxiety had not pushed the German-Austrian liberal bourgeoisie closer to the ruling elite and if the ideological perceptions of the liberals and the socialists had not blocked cooperation between them. It seems likely that the absence of mass demonstrations by the socialists in July 1914, comparable to those of 1912, encouraged the Habsburg ruling elite in their aggressive designs.

From the perspective of our own time, however, the failure of the bourgeois and socialist peace movements appears less complete. With regard to the bourgeois peace movement, peace researchers might consider softening their criticism of "respectable" peace advocates who were members of the establishment. For some historians, including this writer, the very fact that they were close to the governing elites vitiated their proposals. By accommodating their proposals to what they thought the rulers might accept, rather than calling for the immediate transcendence of the existing international system, bourgeois peace advocates allowed the ruling elites to use them for their own purposes. The decision-makers could thus appear to be in accord with the desires of pacifist public opinion when, in fact, they opposed those desires as unattainable and unrealistic.[66]

International arbitration often is cited as a case in point. At the 1907 Hague Peace Conference, most states agreed to a universal compulsory arbitration treaty that appeared to leave the existing international system and the idea of absolute national sovereignty untouched. (The creation of the Permanent Court of Arbitration at the Hague in 1899 was an earlier example of agreeing to a form without substance.) Yet as Jost Dülffer points out, the apparently harmless subjects agreed upon for arbitration at the conference — i.e., disputes over the interpretation and application of international treaties — are not so innocuous as the foreign ministers and diplomats imagined, and they did constitute some limitation of absolute national sovereignty.[67] Furthermore, the fact that a third conference was agreed upon bid fair to make the Hague meetings regular international gatherings and the subjects of disarmament and compulsory arbitration prominent agenda items.

Thus, while the proposals advanced by bourgeois peace advocates were acceptable to the ruling elite because they could be realized within the existing system, these same proposals were open to development along lines that had the potential to alter the international system in ways that offered better guarantees of peace. Confronted by the reality of state power and the likelihood that proposals adopted by the elite had a better chance of realization, the socialists who chose that strategy do not appear so self-deluding as once thought.

A similar balance sheet may be drawn up for the socialist peace movement. The weaknesses of its position in 1914 are well known but those existed in 1912. What characterized the early but not the later period was a movement that anticipated events, initiated an intensive campaign of propaganda, and acted across national boundaries to exert pressure on individual governments simultaneously.

Nigel Young may be correct in his criticism of the transnationalism of the pre-1914 bourgeois and socialist peace movements as a linkage of leaders and organizations rather than of peoples and communities.[68] On the basis of the 1912 antiwar campaign, however, one might argue that even that degree of peace education and transnational unity would be a significant achievement today. It would be worthwhile for historical peace research to launch a full-scale investigation into the 1912 antiwar campaign not only on the level of leaders and parties, but also on the local level of workers and trade-union branches. The latter is especially important, since most research on the pre–1914 peace movements in Austria and elsewhere focuses on peace elites and their organizations. An investigation of the lower echelons of the movements might illuminate the relative strengths of nationalism and internationalism in the consciousness of workers in Austria and how each was strengthened and/or weakened. In a more general way, such an examination might reveal something about the rise and fall of antiwar movements. Furthermore, most of the successes of the socialist peace movement before 1914 were related to the fact that the workers, the primary constituency of the parties, were capable of bringing economic pressure to bear on the system and the governing elite. Is the power of peace movements permanently restricted without such a force?

Despite its failure to prevent the outbreak of World War I, there are some lessons to be learned from the experience of the bourgeois and socialist peace movements in Austria before 1914. Peace research and peace movements have been and continue to be oriented toward two different definitions of peace: positive and negative. Positive peace, as defined by Francis Beer, is a broad conception that covers "various levels below international relations and contains specifications for substantive social justice or processes of political order based on previously articulated general laws."[69] Negative peace is defined more narrowly: the absence of "the direct violence between states," i.e., the absence of war.[70] While the two are not mutually exclusive (elements of both are present in the minds of many peace researchers and peace advocates), the heavy stress on positive peace in recent years has tended to include every social problem within peace research, and has led "peace research [to] become what a black hole is in astronomy."[71]

As a consequence, there is a danger of losing sight of the fact that, although demands for positive peace were not achieved in the past, elements of a negative peace have been created. Without at all abandoning the goal of social justice and order, it seems advisable to place a somewhat greater emphasis on discovering ways of minimizing violent conflicts between states, strengthening institutionalized methods of nonviolent conflict resolution, and developing policy alternatives within the existing international reality that could lead to altering it as well. Such internal alteration of the system was the common goal of the bourgeois and socialist peace movements in Austria and other countries before 1914. Ideological differences merely served to mask the similarity. Continuing on the path of early twentieth-century efforts to achieve negative peace may not be new or very bold, but if we are to stop oscillating "between radical proposals for reform [of international relations], which have no possibility of implementation and reassertion of the relevance of traditions [of diplomacy] which were obsolescent fifty years ago," peace research must seek some middle ground.[72]

NOTES

1. Konrad Jarausch, "Armageddon Revisited: Peace Research Perspectives on World War One," *Peace and Change* 7, nos. 1–2 (Winter 1981): 114.

2. Arno J. Mayer, *The Persistence of the Old Regime. Europe to the Great War* (New York: Pantheon, 1981), 109–19.

3. See Adam Wandruszka, "Finis Austriae? Reformpläne und Untergangsahnen in der Habsburgermonarchie," *Südostdeutsches Archiv* 11 (1968): 112–123; William Jannen, Jr., "The Austro-Hungarian Decision for War in July 1914," in Samuel R. Williamson, Jr. and Peter Pastor, eds., *Essays on World War I: Origins and Prisoners of War* (New York, Brooklyn College Press, 1983; distributed by Columbia Univ. Press), 55–81; Solomon Wank, "Varieties of Political Despair: Three Exchanges between Aehrenthal and Goluchowski, 1898–1906," in Stanley Winters and Joseph Held, eds., *Intellectual and Social Developments in the Habsburg Empire from Maria Theresa to World War I: Essays Dedicated to Robert A. Kann* (Boulder: East European Quarterly Press, 1975; distributed by Columbia Univ. Press), 203–40.

4. See Arthur J. May, *The Hapsburg Monarchy 1867–1914* (Cambridge, Harvard Univ. Press, 1952), 305–32.

5. Johann Christoph Allmayer-Beck, *Ministerpräsident Baron Beck* (Vienna: Verlag für Geschichte und Politik, 1956), 139–63.

6. See Wank, "Varieties of Political Despair"; Wank, "Political Versus Military Thinking in Austria-Hungary 1908–1912," *Peace and Change* 7, nos. 1–2 (Winter 1981): 1–15; Samuel R. Williamson, Jr., "Vienna and July 1914: The Origins of the War once More," in Williamson and Pastor, *Essays on World War I,* 10–35; Fritz Fellner, "Die 'Mission Hoyos'" in *Recueil des travaux aux Assises scientifiques internationales. Les grand puissances et la Serbie à la veille de la Première guerre mondiale* (Belgrade: Serbian Academy of Sciences, 1976), 387–418.

7. On internal politics in Austria from 1908 until 1914 see May, *The*

Hapsburg Monarchy, 425–438; Alois Czedik, *Zur Geschichte des k.k. öster-reichischen Ministerien 1861–1916,* 4 vols. (Teschen, Vienna, and Leipzig: Verlagsbuchhandlung Karl Prochaska, 1917–1920), vol. 4, 9–80, 342–78; Alexander Fussek, "Minister-Präsident Karl Graf Stürgkh und die parlamentarische Frage," *Mitteilungen des Österreichischen Staatsarchivs* 16–17 (1964–65): 337–58; Rudolf G. Ardelt, "Die Krise des Reformismus unter den Regierungen Bienerth und Stürgkh," in Helmut Konrad, ed., *Imperialismus und Arbeiterbewegung in Deutschland und Österreich* (Vienna: Europa Verlag, 1985), 65–87.

8. Christoph Fuhr, *Das K.u.K. Armeeoberkommando und die Innenpolitik in Österreich 1914–1917* (Graz: Hermann Böhlaus, 1958), and Felix Hoglinger, *Ministerpräsident Heinrich Graf Martinic* (Graz: Hermann Böhlaus, 1964).

9. The only monograph on the Austrian peace movement before 1914 of which this writer is aware is Richard R. Laurence, "The Problem of Peace and Austrian Society, 1889–1914: A Study in the Cultural Origins of the First World War" (Ph.D diss., Stanford University, 1968). The following are useful overviews: Richard R. Laurence, "The Peace Movement in Austria, 1867–1914," in Solomon Wank, ed., *Doves and Diplomats: Foreign Offices and Peace Movements in Europe and America in the Twentieth Century* (Westport, CT.: Greenwood, 1978), 21–41; and Albert Fuchs, *Geistige Strömungen in Österreich* (Vienna: Globus Verlag, 1949), 249–75. Valuable biographical and bibliographical information is in the entries on Austrian peace activists in Harold Josephson, ed., *Biographical Dictionary of Modern Peace Leaders* (Westport, CT.: Greenwood, 1985); see also the German counterpart: Helmut Donat and Karl Holl, eds., *Die Friedensbewegung: Organisierter Pazifismus in Deutschland, Österreich und in der Schweiz* (Düsseldorf: ECON Taschenbuch Verlag/Hermes Handlexicon, 1983).

10. Laurence, "The Peace Movement in Austria," 21–23.

11. On the Anarchist peace movement, see R. Laurence, "The Peace Movement in Austria," 26, and the entry on Rudolf Grossmann (Pierre Ramus) in Josephson, *Biographical Dictionary.* See also Gerfried Brandstetter, "Rudolph Grossman (Pierre Ramus). Ein österreichischer Anarchist," in Gerhard Botz, et al., eds., *Bewegung und Klasse. Studien zur österreichischer Arbeitergeschichte* (Vienna, Munich, and Zurich: Europa Verlag, 1978), 89–118.

12. On the Liberal peace movement, see Laurence, "The Peace Movement in Austria," 21–23, and Fuchs, *Geistige Strömungen in Österreich,* 249–258. On German-Austrian liberalism, see ibid., 5–39, and Robert A. Kann, *The Multinational Empire: Nationalism and National Reform in the Habsburg Monarchy 1848–1918,* 2 vols. (New York: Columbia Univ. Press, 1964), vol. 2, 89–97.

13. See Laurence, "The Peace Movement in Austria," 30, and his entry

on Plener in Josephson, *Biographical Dictionary*. For further information on Plener see Fuchs, *Geistige Strömungen in Österreich*, 14–17.

14. On the Liberal press and the peace movement see Richard R. Laurence, "The Viennese Press and the Peace Movement, 1899–1914," *Michigan Academician* 12, no. 2 (1980): 155–64.

15. On Suttner see: Laurence, "The Peace Movement in Austria," 26–28; Fuchs, *Geistige Strömungen in Österreich*, 258–61; Brigitte Hamann, *Bertha von Suttner: Ein Leben für den Frieden* (Munich and Zurich: Piper, 1986); and the entry on Bertha von Suttner in Josephson, *Biographical Dictionary*, 921–24. On Fried see: Laurence, "The Peace Movement in Austria," 33–34; Fuchs, *Geistige Strömungen in Österreich*, 261–64; and Roger Chickering, "Alfred Fried," in Josephson, *Biographical Dictionary*, 303–5.

16. For Suttner on women and peace, see Hanna Schnedl-Bubeniček, "Pazifistinnen: Ein Resümee zur theoretischen Ausführungen und literarischen Darstellungen Bertha von Suttners und Rosa Mayreders," in Gernot Heiss and Heinrich Lutz, eds., *Friedensbewegungen: Bedingungen und Wirkungen* (Vienna: Verlag für Geschichte und Politik, 1984), 96–113; and Brigitte Hamann, "Pazifismus in Wien um 1900," in Peter Berner, Emil Brix, and Wolfgang Mantl, eds., *Wien um 1900* (Vienna: Verlag für Geschichte und Politik, 1986), 226–31.

17. See Richard R. Laurence, "Viennese Literary Intellectuals and the Problem of War and Peace, 1889–1914," in Erika Nielsen, ed., *Focus on Vienna 1900: Change and Continuity in Literature, Music, Art and Intellectual History* (Munich: Wilhelm Fink Verlag, 1982), 12–22.

18. On the APS, see Laurence, "The Peace Movement in Austria," 26–30.

19. In addition to the works cited on Fried, see Roger Chickering, *Imperial Germany and a World Without War: The Peace Movement and German Society 1892–1914* (Princeton, NJ: Princeton Univ. Press, 1975), 94–109.

20. On the socialist peace movement in Austria in general, see Laurence, "The Peace Movement in Austria," 34–36, and references in Fuchs, *Geistige Strömungen in Österreich*, 85–129 ("Arbeiterbewegung"), and 251–75 ("Pazifismus"). References to Austrian socialist antiwar activity are scattered throughout Georges Haupt, *Socialism and the Great War: The Collapse of the Second International* (London: Oxford Univ. Press, 1972).

21. See ibid., 11–12.

22. Laurence, "The Viennese Press and the Peace Movement," 160.

23. Ludwig Brügel, *Geschichte der österreichischen Sozialdemokratie*, 4 vols. (Vienna: Verlag der Wiener Volksbuchhandlung, 1921–1925). Volume four covers the years 1889–1907.

24. See Francis R. Bridge, *From Sadowa to Sarajevo: The Foreign Policy of Austria-Hungary, 1866–1914* (Boston: Routledge and Kegan Paul, 1972), ch. 6.

25. Ruth D. Roebke-Berens, "Austrian Social Democratic Foreign Policy

and the Bosnian Crisis of 1908," *Austrian History Yearbook* 17–18 (1981–1982): 104–23, and Stefan Verosta, *Theorie und Realität von Bündnissen: Heinrich Lammasch, Karl Renner und der Zweibund (1897–1914)* (Vienna: Europa Verlag, 1971), 336–40, 594–622.

26. See Roebke-Berens, "Austrian Social Democratic Foreign Policy," 113, 117, 122–23, and "Austrian Social Democratic Peace Policy and the Balkan Crises of 1912–1913," *Peace and Change* 7, nos. 1–2 (1981): 20, 25.

27. Haupt, *Socialism and the Great War,* 31.

28. Ibid., 90–91, and Laurence, "The Austrian Peace Movement," 34–36.

29. On the failure of cooperation between Socialist and bourgeois peace advocates see: Fuchs, *Geistige Strömungen in Österreich,* 256–58; Fritz Klein, "Sozialistische und Pazifistische Friedenskonzeptionen vor 1914," in Isabella Ackerl et al., eds., *Politik und Gesellschaft im Alten und Neuen Österreich: Festschrift für Rudolf Neck zum 60. Geburtstag* (Vienna: Verlag für Geschichte und Politik, 1981), 324–27; Sandi E. Cooper, "Liberal Internationalists before World War I," *Peace and Change* 1, no. 2 (1973): 18; and Roger Chickering, *Imperial Germany and a World Without War,* 259–63, 278–85.

30. Quoted in Solomon Wank, "Introduction," in Wank, *Doves and Diplomats,* 9.

31. Quoted in Klein, "Sozialistische und Pazifistische Friedenskonzeptionen," 334.

32. Cooper, "Liberal Internationalists before World War I," 18.

33. Solomon Wank, "Diplomacy against the Peace Movement: The Austro-Hungarian Foreign Office and the Second Hague Peace Conference of 1907," in Wank, *Doves and Diplomats,* 55–62, 77.

34. Ibid., 70. See also Jost Dülffer, *Regeln gegen den Krieg? Die Haager Friedens-Konferenzen 1899 und 1907 in der internationalen Politik* (Frankfurt a. M., Berlin, and Vienna: Ullstein, 1981), 313.

35. Wank, "Diplomacy against the Peace Movement," 66–68.

36. Ibid.

37. On Lammasch, see Solomon Wank, "Heinrich Lammasch," in Warren F. Kuehl, ed., *Biographical Dictionary of Internationalists* (Westport, CT.: Greenwood, 1983), 412–15, and Laurence, "The Peace Movement in Austria," 30–32.

38. See Wank, "Diplomacy against the Peace Movement," 70–78, and the entry on Ernst von Plener in Josephson, *Biographical Dictionary.*

39. See Laurence, "The Austrian Peace Movement," 29–30.

40. Bridge, *From Sadowa to Sarajevo,* 335–37.

41. Haupt, *Socialism and the Great War,* 65; Sandi E. Cooper, *Patriotic Pacifism: The Political Vision of Italian Peace Movements, 1867–1915,* Center for the Study of Armament and Disarmament, Occasional Papers Series, no. 14 (Los Angeles: California State Univ., 1985), 24–28; and Janos

Jemnitz, *The Danger of War and the Second International in 1911* (Budapest, Hungarian Academy of Sciences, 1972), 92, 99.

42. On the unrest over higher prices see: May, *The Hapsburg Monarchy, 1867-1914*, 428; Ardelt, "Die Krise des Reformismus," 72-74; and Haupt, *Socialism and the Great War*, 142.

43. Wank, "Political Versus Military Thinking in Austria-Hungary," 8-9.

44. See Bridge, *From Sadowa to Sarajevo*, 346-48.

45. The demonstrations in Vienna and some other places in Austria took place on 10 November. See Fritz Klein, "Die Antikriegskundgebungen der II. Internationale am 17. November 1912," *Zeitschrift für Geschichtswissenschaft* 32 (1975): 1416.

46. On the antiwar campaign in general see ibid., 1411-23. For Austria see: Roebke-Berens, "Austrian Social Democratic Peace Policy," 17-28; Jan Havránek, "Der Tschechische Pazifismus und Antimilitarismus am Vorabend des ersten Weltkrieges," in Heiss and Lutz, eds., *Friedensbewegungen: Bedingungen und Wirkungen*, 134-35; and Brügel, *Geschichte der österreichischen Sozialdemokratie*, vol. 5, 119-20. On the role of the ISB see Haupt, *Socialism and the Great War*, 76-82.

47. On the Basel congress see: Roebke-Berens, "Austrian Social Democratic Peace Policy," 21-23; Brügel; *Geschichte der österreichischen Sozialdemokratie*, 121-26; and Haupt, *Socialism and the Great War*, 83-104.

48. Quoted in Roebke-Berens, "Austrian Social Democratic Peace Policy," 22.

49. Bridge, *Sadowa to Sarajevo*, 352-53.

50. Roebke-Berens, "Austrian Social Democratic Peace Policy," 24.

51. Ibid.; Haupt, *Socialism and the Great War*, 82, 91.

52. Verosta, *Theorie und Realität von Bündnissen*, 412-13.

53. Ibid., 416.

54. Brügel, *Geschichte der österreichischen Sozialdemokratie*, 169-70.

55. Verosta, *Theorie und Realität von Bündnissen*, 414. Perhaps a demonstration by 250,000 workers in Berlin influenced the German emperor's attitude (Haupt, *Socialism and the Great War*, 82).

56. Ibid., 91. See also 82.

57. Haupt, *Socialism and the Great War*, 83-91. On the Austrian position in regard to the general strike see ibid., 165. See also p. 10 and n. 28 above.

58. Haupt, *Socialism and the Great War*, 219, and Laurence, *The Austrian Peace Movement*, 36.

59. See Haupt, *Socialism and the Great War*, 107-10, 150-60, and Chickering, *Imperial Germany and a World Without War*, 272-78.

60. For a detailed study in the Austrian context see Rudolf Ardelt, "Die österreichische Sozialdemokratie und der Kriegsausbruch 1914: die Krise

einer politischen Elite," *Jahrbuch für Zeitgeschichte* (1979); 59–130. See also Haupt, *Socialism and the Great War,* 197, 241.

61. Haupt, *Socialism and the Great War,* 232–35, and Ardelt, "Die österreichische Sozialdemokratie und der Kriegsausbruch 1914," 62–85.

62. Ardelt, "Die österreichische Sozialdemokratie und der Kriegsausbruch 1914," 63–67.

63. Haupt, *Socialism and the Great War,* 237–39, 241.

64. Ardelt, "Die österreichische Sozialdemokratie und der Kriegsausbruch 1914," 67, 73–79, 85, 118–20.

65. For some suggestive comments, see *Socialism and the Great War,* 232–37.

66. Jarausch, "Armageddon Revisited," 111; Fuchs, *Geistige Strömungen in Österreich,* 257; and Wank, "Introduction," in Wank, *Doves and Diplomats,* 3, 9–10.

67. Dülffer, *Regeln gegen den Krieg?,* 313.

68. Young, "Why Peace Movements Fail: An Historical and Social Overview," *Social Alternatives* 4, no. 1 (1984): 14.

69. Francis Beer, *Peace against War: The Ecology of International Violence* (San Francisco: W. H. Freeman, 1981), 6.

70. Ibid.

71. Hylke Tromp, quoted in Hakan Wiberg, "The Peace Research Movement," in Heiss and Lutz, *Friedensbewegungen: Bedingungen und Wirkungen,* 183.

72. Robert Rothstein, "On the Costs of Realism," *Political Science Quarterly* 87, no. 3 (1972): 362.

INTERNATIONAL CONTEXTS

WERNER SIMON

The International Peace Bureau, 1892–1917: Clerk, Mediator, or Guide?

A HUMAN SOCIETY WHICH WAS totally unorganized on the international plane, abounding with rivalries: this is what pacifists attempted to overcome through the establishment of a world community tending towards the harmonization of particular interests.[1]
In their attempt they were fettered by the fact that most of them were
unable to free themselves from the shackles of social, political, and
cultural values prevalent within their national communities — values
impeding, even precluding a world community.

There often existed different national approaches to the problem
of peace and war. French and Italian friends of peace reflected on
it more in juridical terms, Germans and Austrians more in ethical
ones. Especially the French held that international peace was insepa-
rably connected with mankind's quest for political freedom and cultural self-expression. What counted for them was the reality of the
idea: peace built on justice and liberty. Many Germans, on the other
hand, believed that peace was feasible only if those striving for it
were prepared to accept the realities of the day. Justice and liberty
were goals that would eventually spring from what counted most for
these people — the creation of peaceful conditions in the world. Within
the international peace movement one comes across quite irreconcilable notions of the true meaning of peace. Accordingly, when the
protagonists of European pacifism decided in 1891 to set up an organization devoted to the coordination of efforts for world community, they were daringly entering "terram incognitam."

The birth and first years of the International Peace Bureau (IPB),
its internal structure, organs, and activities have been, one is tempted
to say, conclusively described by Irwin Abrams in "A History of
European Peace Societies, 1867–1899."[2] It is appropriate to ask, however, whether and to what extent the men responsible for running the

daily affairs of the IPB—Elie Ducommun, Albert Gobat, and Henri Golay—were able or willing to reconcile conflicting ideas among their fellow pacifists. The first twenty-five years of the organization provide two different settings in international relations, a period of calm and one of turmoil.

From the outset, indeed even before the IPB came into being, the role it was to play had been disputed.[3] Should it confine itself to mere administrative duties, should it act as mediator as circumstances might require, or was it to inspire and guide the organized peace movement—to formulate ideas?

To Hodgson Pratt, one of the spiritual fathers, the option was clear enough, in view of the alarming state in which he found the movement.[4] Pratt's critical attitude had become apparent in an article published in Bertha von Suttner's journal, *Die Waffen Nieder (Lay Down Your Arms)*.[5] What in his eyes characterized the situation more than anything else was complacency and lack of devotion. A handful of zealous fighters could hardly make up for the mass of more or less inactive bystanders who showed no readiness to sacrifice time or money for the advancement of the pacifist cause. Peace societies frequently consisted of only a president and a secretary; the proceedings of the Universal Peace Congresses and other peace propaganda, all neatly compiled and printed by the IPB, found little interest among the movement's adherents; the Congresses themselves, paling in intellectual appeal, had in recent years attracted fewer and fewer people. That Pratt's article had not just been written in a brief mood of uneasiness but, rather, reflected his general view becomes evident from a remark he addressed several months later to the IPB secretary, Elie Ducommun: "It appears to me that the peace friends do not criticize themselves sufficiently, and that they are by far too complacent."[6]

ELIE DUCOMMUN (1892–1906): A LIMITED MANDATE

For all his admiration for the great organizer and political analyst, Pratt occasionally made no secret of his profound disagreement with Ducommun on the role of the Bureau. The English pacifist would not accept the notion that the Bureau had to refrain strictly from making any public political statement or from acting in the interest of international peace as an evenhanded mediator between

conflicting parties. In his opinion, the seat of the IPB and the strong
Swiss element dominating its organs (a secretariat run by Swiss citizens and a Permanent Committee consisting exclusively of Swiss personalities) furnished excellent opportunities for the organization to
offer its good offices in times of international crisis.[7] Ducommun's
immediate reaction to this idea is not known, and it is questionable
whether he touched on its real substance when, in 1895, he suggested
to the General Assembly of the Peace Societies that it "authorize the
Bureau's Permanent Committee to accept a mandate to act in cases
of urgency on behalf of the Societies."[8] Commenting on his own initiative, Ducommun said that "the less one talks about the IPB the
more it will grow in authority."[9] For the secretary, anything that
might compel the Bureau to take a political position—impartial
though it might be, and no matter whether within the narrow confines of the organized peace movement or on a wider international
plane—would risk its very existence. To suggest that the Bureau
should publicly state an opinion on issues such as the Dreyfus Case
or the persecution of Jews in Russia: "horribile dictu."[10] The arguments which Ducommun deployed against taking action in such
cases could shift. He argued, for instance, that initiatives would be
premature because taking sides, as in the "affaire Dreyfus," would
jeopardize any mediatory role that the bureau might eventually be
asked to assume, or he simply denied that the issue at stake touched
questions of international peace at all, as in the case of the Russian
pogroms.[11]

It appears that Ducommun was justified in interpreting the Peace
Bureau's role, and his own as secretary, in a very restrictive way. The
statutes did not permit the IPB to take an active part in the political
opinion-making process. They spoke of technical and administrative functions only: informing members and member societies of
what was going on in the movement; making sure that Congresses
and other gatherings were properly prepared and completed; execut-
ing the resolutions of such gatherings; setting up and maintaining
a reliable documentation service and registry; preparing bibliogra-
phies on peace questions. It was Ducommun himself who in 1896
suggested that the Bureau be given more freedom of action, a suggestion which met with the opposition of a strong minority at the
Budapest Peace Congress and was accepted only after the secretary
had humbly offered to withdraw it altogether: "The Congress gives
the IPB full powers to take steps between any two Congresses and

in cases of urgency which will not allow of previous consultation
of the Peace Societies, by appealing to Governments and public
opinion, with a view of bringing about a peaceful solution of imminent conflicts, provided that such steps are restricted to the reaffirma-
tion and application of principles already adopted by the International Congresses."[12] In view of the event at Budapest, one is tempted
to appreciate Ducommun's attitude. To run an institution like the
IPB required much circumspection: controversial issues had to be
shelved, if not suppressed, in order to keep the ranks closed at least
outwardly.

It was only natural, however, that people who considered Alsace-
Lorraine an issue that should be discussed among pacifists would approach the Bureau to prepare the ground and act as mediator, if not
as arbiter. Ducommun had just set up his office at Berne and started
to think about the forthcoming Universal Congress, which was to
be held in the Swiss federal capital, when Pratt and the French peace
leader Frédéric Passy ventured the idea of holding during the Congress a special conference devoted solely to "problems which still
threaten the peace of Europe."[13] Ducommun was willing to address,
on behalf of the IPB, a circular to carefully selected outstanding personalities, inviting them to form a commission on Alsace-Lorraine
and to submit, after deliberations unmolested by public curiosity,
proposals to the governments of Germany and France for a solution
of the problem.[14] The secretary was quite willing, moreover, to back
the plan by discreetly sounding out the opinions of those who might
eventually sit on an international Alsace-Lorraine commission. However, Pratt and Passy had to understand that the Bureau could under no circumstances take an official initiative because "on different
sides one would not hesitate to blame us for an interference considered to be out of place and not falling within the limited mandate
conferred upon the Bureau."[15] Others whose names were closely associated with the Bureau, like Pratt himself, Albert Gobat, then secretary of the Interparliamentary Union, or even the IPB's Danish
president, Fredrik Bajer, might serve as initiators.

In fact, Ducommun endorsed the plan because it would not be
directly associated with the Congress itself.[16] Once the body of wise
men had quietly discussed the issue behind closed doors, one could
easily prevent the Congress participants from taking it up in public.
As it happened, the commission never saw the light of day, nor was

Alsace-Lorraine ever mentioned during the Congress. Ducommun could be satisfied.

Yet, to conclude from this that the chief of the IPB lacked political character and vision would be false. Although Ducommun's correspondence with other peace leaders rarely reflects frankness on a given controversy, this is understandable enough if one knows that the Bureau's papers always had to be kept open for inspection by the members of the IPB's Commission.[17] Among the rare sources from which one might judge Ducommun's political outlook are some letters addressed to the French pacifist Emile Arnaud, who himself was not a very talkative man yet really enjoyed the secretary's confidence. "You are the vanguard of the peace army's left wing," Ducommun once wrote to the president of the International League for Peace and Freedom, "whereas I am the element which rallies the different corps of that army. As vice-president of the International League I completely share your views. As secretary of the Bureau, however, I should not evince them or even impose on anyone my way of seeing things politically, religiously, or morally."[18] It should be noted that this comment was in reply to a letter in which Arnaud had drawn a clear distinction between his league's program and the brand of pacifism personified by Frédéric Passy and Bertha von Suttner, two people with whom Ducommun maintained exceptionally close and cordial relations, but who, according to Arnaud, failed to recognize that international peace logically called for political freedom.[19]

In the test case of Alsace-Lorraine, Ducommun — no doubt against his personal convictions — sided with those such as the Germans and Austrians (but including Passy) who refused to take up the question. Thus he did not share the views of Arnaud, Pratt, Gaston Moch, and Ernesto Teodoro Moneta, who stood for national self-determination in substance and for more outspokenness in style.[20]

Ducommun's success in maintaining and perhaps even enhancing the reputation of the small IPB is partly to be explained by his own personality. His intellectual and physical devotion to the cause of peace were unequalled, his competence and experience unquestioned, his diplomatic skills, sense of discretion, and patience admired, and his good nature seemingly magnetic.[21] Beyond the personal factor, however, lay something more important: during the first fifteen years of its existence, the Peace Bureau steered through relatively smooth waters. The movement was smaller and ideologically more coherent than it was to become. Although ability to find consensus on political issues was hardly much better developed than subsequently, there was a greater willingness to shelve them for the time being.

ALBERT GOBAT (1907–1914): THE BUREAU COMMITTED

In 1907 the helmsman had gone. His successor, Albert Gobat, who later assumed the title "director," was a person of deep-rooted pacifist principles and of good will. Otherwise he seems to have lacked all Ducommun's gifts. That he tended to speak out or write in plain and undiplomatic language what he deemed to be wrong probably won him few personal friends. On the other hand, he was respected for the very frankness with which he expressed his views. As chief of the IPB, Gobat never hesitated to take sides and, thereby, to shape opinions in one direction or another.

In his book, *Le Cauchemar de l'Europe* (*The Nightmare of Europe*), Gobat accused the Germans of having inflicted on France in 1871 a peace treaty that must inevitably call for vengeance. In fact, he foresaw a war between France and Germany into which the other nations would be drawn as well.[22] In order to prevent it, he urged the Germans to yield by granting Alsace-Lorraine full political autonomy within their Empire. Autonomy for the disputed territory could hardly be considered an excessive or novel demand. Most French pacifists were ready to accept it as a maximum concession, and among their German counterparts it had been seriously discussed for years. Nevertheless, Adolf Richter, president of the German Peace Society, could not hide his and his followers' suspicion, and he reproached the IPB director for a "French-chauvinist" bias.[23] By writing his book and by delivering public speeches at Strasbourg,[24] Gobat had done something unthinkable for his predecessor: he had committed the IPB. Surprisingly, its reputation did not suffer. Nor was it damaged when in 1912 he edited on behalf of the Bureau a documentation on the Tripoli war which infuriated those Italian peace advocates who had turned into chauvinists.[25]

After 1911 the day-to-day business of the Bureau was managed by Henri Golay, a former Swiss government official. Although he had no record to speak of as a pacifist, he loyally followed Gobat in his thinking and decisions. With Gobat being too deeply involved in political and social activities which lay outside the IPB's scope, Golay had sufficient room to develop his commitment to the cause of peace and, thus, to gain gradual acknowledgement within the movement. He had been chosen secretary in order to execute rather than to shape policy. His position therefore was not comparable with that which had been enjoyed by Ducommun who, though carrying the same title, had always been tacitly recognized as political chief of the office. When Gobat died in early 1914, Golay had no chance to fill his post. The directorship remained forever vacant, primarily because during the ensuing decades the IPB lacked the regular revenues to maintain it. Instead, after Gobat's departure, the Permanent Committee of Three exercised political control over the Bureau's affairs. Especially between 1914 and 1925, when this body was dominated by Georges Bovet, an influential and ambitious French-Swiss politician, journalist, and internationalist, the activities of Golay were closely scrutinized. On the other hand, as the years went by it was only natural that, notwithstanding his willingness to acquiesce, Golay's political influence grew with his acquisition of intimate knowledge about everything happening in the movement.

Such was the situation of the IPB when in July and August 1914 Austria's refusal to settle her dispute with Serbia on a peaceful basis and Germany's violation of Belgian neutrality shattered the foundation on which the European peace movement had been erected — the coexistence between French and German pacifism.

HENRI GOLAY (1911–1917):
THE BUREAU'S FIGHT FOR SURVIVAL IN WARTIME

During the war Golay never hesitated to show where he stood. The basic principle proclaimed for decades by the peace movement, the rule of law in international relations, now was defended by France. According to Golay, the Bureau had failed in its essential task already at the beginning of the hostilities. "A vigorous and unanimous protest of all the pacifists in the world would have been necessary," he wrote. "I fully know, my dear colleague, that it is IPB's first duty to be neutral. However, to protest against a flagrant violation of our principles, is this to mean that we deviate from our duty? I do not think so. If today we are not prepared to uphold our ideals, who will listen to us once peace has been concluded?"[26] The meeting of the IPB Council in January 1915 clearly aggravated the situation of the organization. Ludwig Quidde, Alfred H. Fried, and their Austrian-German followers, together with Dutch support, succeeded in preventing a condemnation of the Central Powers, and any chance of maintaining French interest in the Bureau seemed to evaporate. The French Council members — Arnaud, Moch, Charles Richet, and Théodore Ruyssen — probably were not much impressed by the degree of determination with which the secretary of the IPB defended their cause.

It fell to Golay to fight for the survival of his office. True, in his eyes it was futile to attempt to rally the pacifists of the nonbelligerent countries led by the Dutch, in order to hammer out acceptable peace proposals.[27] Nevertheless, the zealous activities of these pacifists worried him immensely: the risk that the IPB would lose control over the whole movement should not be overlooked, he observed. "I am deeply pained to note that the Bureau does not act, and I am afraid that the forthcoming manifestations will shift the peace societies and especially the Bureau into the background."[28] His fear that the Bureau would gradually fall into oblivion while new peace organizations emerged whose aims he despised led Golay to seek French support. Arguing in favor of participation by the IPB and the French pacifists in a "Study Conference" that had been convened for December 1915 at Berne, he wrote to a French correspondent, "I ask myself whether it would not have been in our interest to give a sign of life. The January meeting has been a fiasco because neither you nor the English were present. If both France and Great Britain had sent three or four delegates, Giretti's motion [condemning Germany and Austria] would have passed and, thus, to day we would stand on solid ground."[29]

That Golay even backed the idea of his Austrian adversary, Alfred Fried, to call an informal meeting on Swiss soil between German and French pacifists probably was motivated by the same fear.[30] In one respect Golay and Fried wholeheartedly concurred: the Bureau had to act.[31] For Fried it had to serve as a neutral mediator between the hostile peace camps, a role that the secretary was not willing to accept. If he were resolved to bring Germans and French together, then obviously it was with the intention of teaching the

Germans a lesson. In order to regain its old reputation as the true center of the international peace movement, the IPB had to be freed from the image of ineptness which it had suffered since January 1915. Golay's appeal to the French peace friends to stem the tide of neutral pacifism by vigorously joining the debate within the Swiss pacifist arena fell on deaf ears. For the French, genuine pacifists had but one duty, to work for victory against German militarism. There was no longer a place for an organization like the Peace Bureau to serve as a neutral mediator or even as a platform from which the Germans could be publicly censured. The status quo was satisfactory enough — a Bureau whose political activities had been suspended, but perhaps useful from time to time to provide the French with information on what was developing on the enemy's side. The IPB should maintain contacts with all peace groups regardless of whether they acted, overtly or not, in the interest of the Central Powers.[32]

Time and again Golay was faced with the reality that the attitude of the French Council members met with the approval of the majority within the Permanent Committee. Bovet and Henri Carrière, the second member, representing French-speaking Switzerland, held that the Bureau should stay aloof from any participation in peace initiatives and from attempts to pave the way for a Franco-German meeting, whether during a Council session or unofficially along the lines of Fried's proposal. The Committee's neutral policy from January 1915 had been correct, Bovet stated.[33] It was a strange situation indeed: Golay firmly shared Bovet's and Carrière's personal viewpoints as far as questions of war responsibility and future peace terms were concerned; but, on the other hand, he desperately struggled against their determination to keep the voice of the Bureau silent. In this regard he was warmly supported by the third Committee member, Franz Bucher-Heller, a German-Swiss pacifist who, despite his unquestionable commitment to Switzerland's neutrality, seems to have been somewhat receptive to German arguments.

In December 1916 the German government came up with a proposal for a negotiated peace settlement. Although this offer was at once rejected by Germany's opponents, it was quite favorably received in the neutral European countries, especially among the German-Swiss public.[34] A group of mainly German-Swiss members of the Federal Parliament asking to discuss, "in view of the present world situation," the position and tasks of the Bureau with the Permanent

Committee, must have considerably embarrassed Bovet and Carrière.[35] Easy as it might be to ignore appeals from pacifist circles,
a move by influential parliamentarians to mobilize the IPB in favor
of the German peace offer was not to be taken lightly. Talks took
place on 19 December between the councilors (Zuercher and others)
and the Committee, joined by Golay. Discussion revealed not only
the profound difference between German- and French-speaking Swiss
on peace and war but also the ambiguous situation of Golay. In a
meeting with Zuercher several days earlier, he had conveyed the impression of being an "isolated" and "abandoned" man. It is highly
doubtful that the councilor's views on the IPB's political role were
to the secretary's liking. Rather, Golay had sought support for a re-
activated Bureau whose task it would be to repel what he regarded
as mostly foreign-inspired tendencies in Switzerland to endorse peace
at any price, and to concentrate instead on a propaganda campaign
that would focus on the old French slogan, "Peace through Justice."
Obviously, Bovet, who chaired the meeting, was not amused by his
subordinate. He bluntly remarked, "The conversations led by M.
Golay [with councilor Zuercher] outside the special mission with
which he had been charged, do not bind the bureau. The latter has,
for the moment, no proposal to make."[36]

   In the Permanent Committee the rift was never so deep as during
the ensuing months. Bucher-Heller stubbornly defended the German-
Swiss view in order to utilize the Bureau for a peace campaign, whereas
Bovet and Carrière refused to move. Bucher-Heller's enthusiasm
faded away only with the news of the United States' entry into the
war.[37] This and the upheavals in Russia must have convinced him
that the chances of an immediate and negotiated peace had become
slim indeed. Both events indicated that the war was being fought for
democracy, for ideals which the French in particular had always defended. Bucher-Heller now was prepared to yield and join hands
with Bovet and Carrière.

   The French Council member Théodore Ruyssen suggested issuing on the Bureau's behalf a letter that not only greeted America's
action but even hailed the Russian revolution. The Committee hesitated. Such a step, Bovet argued, at least required prior consultation
of the German pacifists. In fact, he had already tried to sound out
Quidde, who had not even bothered to reply.[38] His silence seemed
understandable enough in view of the fact that somewhat earlier the
IPB had refused to convey to Russia a message of the German Peace

Society which had stated explicitly that the German pacifists were fighting for the same cause as the Russian revolutionaries, and which had culminated in the statement that "since the Russian people has liberated itself from the yoke of autocracy there can be no doubt that the idea of democracy will soon be victorious."[39]

Ruyssen's proposal was finally taken up, although neither the events that had animated him to make it nor the war parties were to be mentioned. For the first time during the war, the Peace Bureau openly and unequivocally declared what kind of peace it favored: "The Bureau's attitude maintained since the outbreak of the war, and the line of conduct to which it was bound by the decision of the Council in January 1915, have exposed us to the criticism of those who wanted it to associate itself with numerous endeavors to conclude an immediate peace. We continue to believe that we could not follow such an advice without breaking with our history." Only if certain ideas had finally gained the upper hand, the letter went on, a veritable peace, and not just a truce, would arrive. Clearly, "reconciliation" or "compromise" had become words of the past. When pacifists were reminded that "the society of nations comprises only democratic nations," there could be no doubt which nations the Bureau considered to be excluded. The letter concluded by stating that "there is no pacifism without democracy," and that "by fighting for democracy we fight for peace, a lasting peace founded on international justice and the liberty of nations."[40]

It had taken Georges Bovet three years to commit the IPB openly to the Allies. Personally he had never hidden his sympathies for their cause. Indirectly he had even supported it by thwarting the frequent attempts of the German pacifists and various peace groups in Holland and Switzerland to engage in campaigns for an immediate peace settlement. And yet, unlike Golay, who had insisted since August 1914 that the status and reputation of the IPB would be irretrievably lost if it did not take the Allies' position and who had even been willing to convene the Bureau's Council in order to transform it into a tribunal censuring German pacifists, Bovet had formally preserved the neutrality of the organization. Now this kind of neutrality could be given up. Recent events had showed that the tides of war were turning in favor of those forces whose goals were identical with principles formulated and postulated for decades by pacifists reared and acting in liberal and pluralist societies.

In the final event, the conceptions of Hodgson Pratt, Emile Arnaud, and Albert Gobat prevailed over those represented by Elie Ducommun. In order to be acknowledged inside and outside the international peace movement, the Peace Bureau had to take a stand.

NOTES

1. The term "unorganized international society" is used in Georg Schwarzenberger, *A Manual of International Law,* 5th ed. (London: Stevens, 1967), 8ff.

2. (Ph.D. diss., Harvard University, 1938).

3. For the discussions in the 1880s that led to the formation of the IPB, see ibid., 349ff.

4. Regarding Pratt, see the entry in Harold Josephson, ed., *Biographical Dictionary of Modern Peace Leaders* (Westport, CT: Greenwood, 1985).

5. Pratt, "Reveil Geblasen," in *Die Waffen Nieder* 6, no. 10 (1897): 353–57.

6. Pratt to Ducommun, 20 May 1898, Archives du Bureau International de la Paix, United Nations Library, Geneva (hereinafter cited as BIP/A), no. 162/11.

7. Pratt to Ducommun, 24 Oct. 1894, BIP/A, no. 162/11.

8. BIP, "Procès-verbal de la 3ᵐᵉ Assemblée générale" (1895), 6.

9. Ducommun to Teodoro Moneta, 24 Nov. 1895, BIP/A, no. 2/3.

10. Ducommun to Bertha von Suttner, 28 Jan. 1898, and to Moneta, 2 April 1901, BIP/A, nos. 169/5 and 164/9.

11. Ducommun to von Suttner, 28 Jan. 1898, and to Moneta, 2 April 1901, BIP/A, nos. 169/5 and 164/9.

12. *Bulletin officiel du 7ᵉ Congrès universel de la Paix* (Budapest: n.p., 1896), 139.

13. Ducommun to Passy, 6 Mar. 1892, BIP/A, no. 183/1.

14. Passy to Ducommun, 13 Mar. 1892, BIP/A, no. 183/1.

15. Ducommun to Passy, 28 Mar. 1892, BIP/A, no. 183/1.

16. Ducommun to Pratt, 6 April 1892, BIP/A, no. 183/1.

17. The Commission (since 1914 the Council) of the IPB consisted of 35 (since 1914 of 50) persons who played prominent roles in the organized peace movements of their respective countries. Meeting twice a year, this body was charged with the general political supervision of the Bureau.

18. Ducommun to Arnaud, 3 May 1892, BIP/A, no. 183/1.

19. Arnaud to Ducommun, 21 April 1892, BIP/A, no. 183/1.

20. For Passy's attitude, see Passy to Ducommun, 26 Nov. 1894, BIP/A, no. 183/2; for Moch's see *Almanach de la Paix* (1895), 40ff. and *La Paix*

par le Droit (1895), 42; for Pratt's views as modified, *La Paix par le Droit* (1895), 71ff.; and for Moneta's, ibid., 142ff.

21. A biographical sketch of Ducommun has been published by Victor Monnier, "Notes et Documents pour servir à la Biographie d'Elie Ducommun," in *Revue européene des Sciences sociales* 22, no. 67 (1984): 139–64.

22. (Strasbourg and Paris: Treuttel & Würtz, 1911), 20ff.

23. Richter to E. Montandon, 11 April 1911, BIP/A, no. 184/4.

24. Corr. A. Gobat–G. Kern, 1911; BIP/A, no. 184/4.

25. *In Rei Memoriam — Manifestations officielles du pacifisme contre la guerre déclarée par l'Italie contre la Turquie* (Bienne: W. Gassmann, 1912).

26. Golay to J. van Beek en Donk, 3 Dec. 1914, Pers. Corr. H. Golay, BIP/A. He referred in this passage to a "vigorous and unanimous protest" against Germany and Austria-Hungary.

27. Golay to Th. Ruyssen, 24 June 1915, Pers. Corr. H. Golay, BIP/A.

28. Golay to Fr. Bucher-Heller, 29 Sept. 1915, Pers. Corr. H. Golay, BIP/A. By "manifestations" he referred to a so-called "Study Conference" initiated and mainly to be organized by the Dutch "Anti-Oorlog-Raad."

29. Golay to a French pacifist, 29 Sept. 1915, Pers. Corr. H. Golay, BIP/A. In January 1915 a German-Austrian-Dutch majority had voted down the resolution of Italian Council member Eduardo Giretti.

30. Golay to a French pacifist (Théodore Ruyssen?), 7 July 1915, Pers. Corr. H. Golay, BIP/A.

31. Fried to Golay, 14 Oct. 1914 [*sic*]; Golay to Ruyssen, 19 Oct. 1915, Pers. Corr. H. Golay, BIP/A.

32. On Fried's suggestion to convene a Franco-German meeting and on the French reaction, see Comité Permanent, procès-verbaux, séance 7 Aug. 1915, BIP/A. The French pacifists' view of the role of the IPB is reflected in Golay's report on his journey to Paris in April/May 1916, ibid., séance 15 May 1916 (Annex).

33. Ibid.

34. See Wolfgang Steglich, *Bündnissicherung oder Verständigungsfrieden — Untersuchungen zu dem Friedensangebot der Mittelmächte vom 12. Dezember 1916* (Göttingen: Musterschmidt, 1958), and V. H. Rothwell, *British War Aims and Peace Diplomacy 1914–1918* (Oxford: Clarendon Press, 1971), 60. For the Swiss attitude see Jacob Ruchti, *Geschichte der Schweiz während des Weltkrieges, 1914–1919,* I (Bern: M. Drechsel, 1928), 307–13.

35. E. Zuercher, BIP/A, 15 Dec. 1916 [copy]; Comité Permanent, Procès-verbaux, séance 19 Dec. 1916.

36. Ibid. Among the parliamentarians the only French-Swiss representative, de Montenach, dissented from his colleagues' views.

37. Ibid., séance 12 May 1917.

38. Ibid., séance 11 Aug. 1917.

39. "An das Internationale Friedensbüro und ebenso an den Ständigen Ausschuss der Schwedischen Friedensvereine," 19 April 1917 (copy), file "Ludwig Quidde, 1914–1919," BIP⁄A.

40. "Aux Présidents et aux membres des Sociétés de la Paix," circular published in *Mouvement pacifiste,* no. 5/8 (1917).

NADINE LUBELSKI-BERNARD

Freemasonry and Peace in Europe, 1867–1914

SIDE BY SIDE WITH THE peace societies founded in the nineteenth century in the United States and Europe were associations which collaborated in working for peace. Among these societies, operating at national and international levels, was Freemasonry. In Europe, however, only a part of Freemasonry was involved in peace questions during the period between 1867 and 1914.[1] To understand why, it is necessary to distinguish among the three main currents then existing in Freemasonry: Anglo-Saxon Freemasonry, Latin Freemasonry, and the Germanic and Scandinavian Masonries.

But first of all, some Masonic organizational terms should be defined. A *lodge* is the basic organizational unit. An *obedience* is a federation of lodges for assuring the coordination of their work and their collective representation. If all the lodges practice the same rite, the obedience is called a *Grand Lodge;* if they practice several rites, they form a *Grand Orient.* A *Masonic Power* is a Masonic entity which exercises its authority over the boundaries of a territory and over men who recognize it.

Anglo-Saxon Freemasonry, grouped around the United Grand Lodge of England, was an institution of the Establishment, recruiting its members from the well-to-do, including the Court and the royal family. Especially concerned with philosophical research and philanthropic aid, it kept itself aloof from political debates and social movements. In addition to the lodges of Great Britain, the main ones were those of the United States, Canada, New Zealand, and India.

Latin Freemasonry, which included the lodges of France, Belgium, Luxembourg, Spain, Portugal, Italy, and Hungary, as well as those of the countries of Latin America and the colonies, was situated at the opposite pole. Separated from Anglo-Saxon Freemasonry by such factors as its broader social recruitment and its different philo-sophical and political orientation, Latin Freemasonry was a discreet, not to say, secretive institution. Moreover, it opened its doors to all sorts and conditions of men — young revolutionaries, craftsmen, workers[2] — and considered that calm political reflection and debate had an eminent place in Masonic work.

In the nineteenth century, the epoch of national and liberal revolu-tions in Latin countries — where the Catholic Church had absolute preeminence — Masonry evolved rapidly towards anticlericalism. This political orientation was due to the rigid and hostile attitude of the Church, which, in numerous encyclicals, condemned Masonry and threatened Masons with excommunication. However, the repeated attacks of the Catholic Church against Masonry must be seen in the historical context of the Church's fight against anticlerical parties which, in Italy, France, and Belgium, with the support of Masons, were fighting for the separation of Church and State and in favor of secularity.

These attacks led the Grand Orients of Belgium (in 1871) and France (in 1877) to abolish the obligation to invoke the Grand Archi-tect of the Universe and the presence of the open Bible during their work. The Universal Grand Lodge of England immediately broke off all relations with the Grand Orient of France. It went even fur-ther by forbidding any association with these obediences which it deemed to be irregular. As a result, the great Masonic powers of the Latin world were no longer recognized by the Anglo-Saxon and Ger-manic Grand Lodges.[3] The obediences of Latin America and Latin Europe, however, continued to maintain their relations with the Grand Orient of France. In fact, the revision of 1877 was only a pretext for the breach. French Masonry, and in particular the Grand Orient of France, had become suspect in the eyes of the English because of the rationalist trends and the democratic — and sometimes revolu-tionary — aspirations which were emerging there.

The Germanic and Scandinavian Masonries, however, were recog-nized by the Universal Grand Lodge of England.[4] They were reli-gious and traditionalist, rejecting any intrusion of politics in the Lodges and devoting themselves especially to symbolic and religious research. The regular obediences of the Netherlands and of Switzer-land performed the function of a hinge between the three groups and maintained good relations with all of them.[5]

Being politically oriented, the Lodges in the Latin Masonry were,

with those of the Netherlands and Switzerland, the only ones involved in the questions being debated by the peace societies.[6] Their
interest in these matters may be explained by various factors. Their
ideal and aims were very close to those of the peace societies: Latin
Freemasonry was a cosmopolitan institution, based on universal
brotherhood and contributing to the triumph of ideas of political
liberty, religious tolerance, and understanding between nations. It
considered that Masons should not only work towards the improvement of individuals but should also advance the progress of society.
It wished to fight against the chauvinistic politics which transformed
every foreign people into a natural enemy and to build a society of
nations in which war would be abolished.[7] Masonry always disapproved of war, and many Masons supported the idea of a lasting
peace.[8] By attempting to create between its members ties irrespective
of nationality, class, party, or religion, Freemasonry helped to develop pacific trends and to strengthen movements which tried to establish brotherhood and equity between nations. Moreover, peace
friends and Latin Masons were principally recruited from the same
political and social spheres: the liberal, laic middle-class of the cities.[9]

This closeness of aims and activities induced Latin Freemasonry
to support the ideas of peace and world understanding in the second
half of the nineteenth century. Latin Masons could not remain in-
different to this new movement and inside some Latin lodges peace
sections were founded. These were in contact with many peace societies and exchanged information with them; the Masonic press published news concerning peace.[10] In addition, Masons joined the peace
societies and actively participated in their work.[11] Questions such as
the abolition of standing armies, the causes of war, and the means
to prevent conflicts between nations were discussed not only by the
peace societies but also by the lodges. Two broad solutions were generally proposed: the reform of national and international society
and the reform of individuals. The first involved the development
of international law, the creation of a permanent court of arbitration, and the creation of the United States of Europe; the idea of
federation was seen as the best way of ensuring peace between peoples. The second set of reforms involved the generalization of compulsory schooling and, specifically, education for peace.[12]

THE FRANCO-PRUSSIAN WAR AND MASONIC DISUNITY

The lodges supported campaigns against wars and tried to alleviate the sufferings which they caused. Some lodges in Italy and Belgium not only protested against the Franco-Prussian War (1870) but made attempts to stop it.[13] The "Amis Philanthropes de Bruxelles" addressed a manifesto to the lodges of France and Germany, aimed at bringing about a rapid conclusion of peace.[14] The "Address to all of the Masons of France and Germany," an affirmation of civilization against barbarity, declared:

> Before this spectacle, there is no man without responsibility. . . .
> Europe cannot reflect without shame on the fact that after centuries of civilization, after a long practice of law and justice, nations refuse arbitration and prefer to rely on blind forces.

The Address recognized the legitimacy of defensive war and wars of liberation but put the nations on their guard against the limits of the right of defense since this right all too often transformed itself into aggressive designs and became lost in the retaliation following victory. Countries cannot use violence without danger because the use of force tends to corrupt. The Address asked the Germans not to invoke matters of race, nationality, or security as requiring the extension of their borders but rather to act in the manner recommended by Immanuel Kant—in accordance with a general rule for humanity. In addition, it pressured the French to establish a peace which would not be merely a postponement of the retaliation but would be instead a settlement without hate. Finally, it called upon France and Germany to come together and sign the first Treaty of Universal Peace.[15]

While the French Masons congratulated the Belgians for their manifesto, the German lodges, which were not allowed to deal with politics, reacted unfavorably. Because the Address infringed upon Masonic laws (which separated quarrels between peoples from the work of lodges), the three Prussian Grand Lodges asked the Supreme Council of Belgium—the highest Masonic authority—to censure "Les Amis Philanthropes."[16]

During the Commune of Paris (1871), part of French Masonry attempted to put an end to this fratricidal war. In April, more than 14,000 Masons marched in the streets of Paris and fixed their banners on the ramparts of the City, in the most dangerous places. By doing so they hoped to be able to stop the hostilities, but they had to be satisfied with a truce lasting only one day. French Masons also sent a manifesto to the Universal Masonry.[17] But the Italian, Belgian, and French appeals were all in vain. The German lodges applied to the letter the so-called Constitutions of Anderson (the fundamental Charter of universal speculative Masonry of 1723) which made fidelity to the sovereign and to the laws of the country a Masonic duty. Thus, accepting the Emperor's point of view, they endorsed the annexation of Alsace and Lorraine. The break in relations with the French Masons was total. The war of 1870 had opened a rift between the French and German Masonries which was never to be completely bridged again. The nationalism which prevailed on both sides of the Rhine swept away any difference between the initiated and the laity and rode roughshod over the universalism which Masonry had so often claimed for itself.

THE INTERNATIONAL MASONIC CONGRESSES
AND BUREAU OF MASONIC RELATIONS

In addition to the efforts made by lodges on the national level in favor of peace, there were initiatives taken on the international level. They were promulgated by the International Masonic Congresses, the International Bureau of Masonic Relations (IBMR), the International Masonic Manifestations for Peace, and the Universal League of Freemasons (ULF). Since the beginning of the nineteenth century, international Masonic congresses had regularly taken place in various European cities. Belgian Masons had asked for these meetings to be held periodically to find ways to establish true brotherhood between all men by eliminating the causes which presently stood in its path: racial conflicts, religious hatreds, political struggles, economic conflicts — "all lamentable sources of war and regression."[18] Nearly every meeting dealt with the maintenance of peace, and indeed some congresses, such as those in Antwerp (1894), The Hague (1896), Paris (1900), Geneva (1902), and Brussels (1904), were almost exclusively preoccupied with questions of universal peace, general disarmament, European federation, international law, propaganda in favor of international arbitration, and peace education.[19] In order to further these aims, international masonic meetings advocated not only the active participation of Masons in peace congresses and their support for peace societies but also the founding of sections of these societies in cities where they did not yet exist. Deputies and senators who were Masons were urged to join their country's section of the Interparliamentary Union and to cooperate in the extension of permanent international arbitration treaties. The meetings were also concerned with reestablishing friendly relations among all Masons, particularly between those in France and Germany.

All the measures advocated were accepted by the assemblies on the condition that Masons should act individually and that the Masonic Powers should remain independent.[20] This individualistic attitude, which never ceased to insist on the notion of autonomy — "the free Mason in a free Lodge" — was prejudicial to the strength of Freemasonry as an international association. Like other *internationales,* Freemasonry was concerned not to jeopardize its own existence on those occasions when no common attitude prevailed. The same difficulties occurred in some congresses when Masons tried to gain the adhesion of the assembly to oppose specific conflicts between nations. Such was the case at the Brussels Congress of 1904 when Lucien Le Foyer asked the Masonic Powers of the different countries to intervene with their respective governments to put an end to the Russo-Japanese war.[21] The assembly, however, shrank back from a direct approach, recalling with sadness the failure already met with during the Boer war.[22]

This example illustrates the paradoxical attitude displayed by international Freemasonry which declared, on the one hand, that it was ready to do anything for the benefit of humanity and for safeguarding peace but, on the other hand, rejected any joint action "to avoid any irritating political question."[23] Freemasonry in such situations feared to "tread the path of direct action, so strewn with pitfalls," because its principles required that "on the battlefield of life, Freemasons did not act as such, even less did they act as a separate party, but rather they acted as citizens in a completely free manner."[24]

However, since the beginning of the twentieth century, international Freemasonry had succeeded in putting in concrete form an idea nearly a century old: a universal Union of Masons.[25] To achieve this aim, Masons attempted to create international structures, ensuring technical cooperation in Masonic matters but also enabling better understanding between Masons in all countries. The International Masonic Congress of Paris (1900) created a standing committee composed of delegates from the Masonic Powers represented and asked

the Swiss Alpina Grand Lodge to implement this decision by establishing the permanent location of the Bureau in Switzerland. The International Bureau of Masonic Relations (IBMR), opened in Neuchâtel
in 1903, henceforth organized the International Masonic Congresses.
The office was also assigned the task of developing peace ideas.
Thus, at the Brussels Congress in 1904, the IBMR addressed

> an invitation to all the Grand Lodges and Supreme Councils to
> celebrate by a solemn gala order the date of the 18th May (open-
> ing of the First Hague Peace Conference) and in this way to as-
> sociate universal Masonry with the work of peace and of arbitra-
> tion between nations.[26]

In January 1905, the office acted on the invitation of the International Peace Bureau (IPB) to commit Masons of all lodges to send
petitions for achieving peace in the Far East. The relations between
the IPB, of which Elie Ducommun was the secretary (1892–1906),
and the Swiss Alpina Grand Lodge, of which he had become the
Grand Master (1905), facilitated this intervention in favor of peace.[27]

From this time onward, as a consequence of the refusal of most
of the Grand Lodges to bear their share of responsibility, the whole
burden of the IBMR rested on the shoulders of its representative,
Edmond Quartier-La-Tente.[28] He was, moreover, the only person responsible for its administration and its finances.[29] He tried to in-
form the Grand Lodges throughout the world of the Bureau and its
aims, but all in vain: more than nine-tenths of Masons maintained
complete silence.[30] Clearly, the IBMR, which wished to establish better and permanent relations between all Masons regardless of the
obedience or rite to which they belonged, failed. Before 1914, international Masonry had been incapable of organizing a truly international Bureau — unlike the peace friends, parliamentarians, and socialists. International Masonry had not succeeded in even laying the
groundwork for becoming, according to the wish expressed by *The
Freemason* in 1913, "the most powerful agent for the maintenance
of universal peace."[31] Indifference and intolerance among Freemasons — particularly the divergences, exclusions, and breaches between
Masonic Powers — reduced the IBMR to insignificance. It is not surprising that it did not survive the First World War.

INTERNATIONAL MASONRY AND THE APPROACH OF WAR

Besides the International Masonic Congresses and the IBMR, other masonic structures dealing with peace were the International Masonic Manifestations for Peace and the Universal League of Freemasons (ULF). It was obvious that one of the major weaknesses of international Masonry was the rivalry between France and Germany. Masons who wanted to work for the advancement of peace by reconciling these two countries — whose growing hostility threatened to degenerate into a conflict — organized the International Masonic Manifestations. Since 1870, all links had been severed between the Grand Orient of France and the German Masonic obediences. A first attempt at reconciliation took place in Luxembourg in 1900.[32] But it was not until 1907 that an official meeting between German and French Masons was held — at La Schlucht, in the Vosges, on French territory. During this event, the participants undertook to meet once a year whatever happened, and to cast their votes in all Masonic elections only for those of their brethren who shared their ideas. The annual meetings materialized and were attended by increasing numbers of participants from different countries.[33] These sessions, summoned "in the name of Peace and universal brotherhood," proclaimed that the abolition of war had always been one of the crucial points of the social program of Freemasonry, which had ceaselessly worked to propagate peace ideas, and repeated that universal harmony was not a chimera but an idea which was possible to achieve.[34]

On the eve of the First World War, Masons expounded the different ways in which they hoped to avert the danger of war. First of all, they urged lasting reconciliation between Germany and France. "Without this," they said, "all our efforts will be sterile, and we might even lose sight of the hope of one day witnessing the dawn of universal brotherhood."[35] They also counted on the impact of international meetings of Masons, which allowed for an exchange of views and the achievement of better mutual understanding. Since the aim of these events was also to conduct active propaganda for peace ideas, they recommended the same proposals as those adopted by the International Masonic Congresses.[36] They suggested that the Masonic Festival of Peace should be celebrated on 18 May, and that the example of the 34 Swiss lodges (and some in France) which had collectively joined the IPB at Berne should be followed. They also asked for help in the creation of lay groups which would promote peace by organizing popular conferences, educating young people, and participating in national and international events. Through schools and the press, and through private and public persuasion, they should bring about a true revolution of minds and modify the prejudices which were often so deeply rooted in public opinion. This was to be the triumph of Masonry in the supreme phase of its struggle for emancipation, in the pacification of peoples, called by the Austrian pacifist, Alfred H. Fried, "the first civilizing idea of our age."[37]

The means proposed for abolishing wars — education, propaganda, persuasion, development of international law and international arbitration — all required a long period of peace to be able actively to influence attitudes and mentalities. In the climate of militarism and intransigent nationalism which divided Europe in 1914, there were those who wondered whether this was not an illusion. Moreover, the movement of reconciliation came up against other difficulties within the world of Masonry itself. The German Grand Lodge (consisting of eight obediences, three of which were of the Prussian persuasion), refused to entertain relations of any sort with the Grand Orient of France, invoking the question of the Grand Architect and certain past political disagreements.[38] For their part, a number of French Freemasons regarded Franco-German rapprochement with a jaundiced eye. Matters were strained in particular at the Masonic Manifestation of Paris in 1911, in the middle of the Agadir crisis. The Council of the Order of the French Grand Orient, fearful of anti-German and anti-Masonic demonstrations, preferred not to open the doors of the Temple where the meeting was to have been held, forcing the participants to meet elsewhere.[39]

Mention should also be made of an autonomous association of Masons, acting individually, which was constituted at the first International Esperantist Congress at Boulogne-sur-Mer in 1905. Like some peace friends, the Masons present at this congress believed that a neutral international language would be an excellent means of improving international relations and intellectual understanding between Masons, and they decided to found the Esperanto Framasona (its activities turned out to be mostly theoretical).[40] Thus a new organization arose following the General Assembly of Berne in 1913: the Universala Framasona Ligo.[41] It sought to improve and develop relations between Masons all over the world and to call on them to fight for the triumph of a common ideal of brotherhood among them. Its first president was Dr. Sebastio de Magalhaes Lima, a Portuguese peace friend.[42] The 1914 war interrupted the nascent activities of the League, which could not resume its activities before the International Esperantist Congress of London in 1920.

The year 1914 toppled any remaining illusions. It showed up the fragility of the peace work accomplished by the lodges to bring people together and abolish war by strengthening universal brotherhood. What is more, the majority of Masons took a stand behind their particular government, whatever its responsibility in the conflict. As Albert Lantoine, the librarian of the Grande Loge de France wrote, the humanitarian proposals were shelved and international Masonry dressed up as the National Guard. The Masonic powers of the rival nations excommunicated one another, broke their fraternal links, and hurled themselves into the fray.[43]

CONCLUSION

International Freemasonry had been weakened not only by the divergences, exclusions, and breaches existing between the different Masonic Powers, and by the national antagonisms which were revived by the wars and crises which occurred in Europe before 1914, but also by its own doctrine and character. It proved extremely difficult to reconcile the need to avoid all irritating questions of a political nature and the wish to address subjects of vital interest to humanity.[44] How could it have been possible to advance towards "liberty, equality, fraternity, and peace" without immediately coming up against political realities which for certain people were "irritating"?[45] Here we are confronted with the illusory nature of the brotherhood and internationalism so often proclaimed in the lyrical declarations of the Congresses and Assemblies, which had never taken any account of the real play of political forces in the international context of these declarations. It is true that Freemasonry wished in this way to indicate the ideals to be attained and the path to be followed. It wanted to influence mentalities and to bring about perfection in the most diverse quarters, solely by the moral and intellectual effulgence of Freemasonry. But could Masons really act effectively to maintain peace unless their presence was seen? To put it another way, the secret character of the institution hampered its influence and propaganda, and made it more vulnerable to the criticisms and distortions of its enemies. Finally, events showed that the force of ideas expressed in a few years could not modify mentalities to such an extent as to defuse the force of arms.

NOTES

1. The chronological limits chosen coincide with the beginnings of the Masons' interest in the peace question and in the work of the peace societies, and with the event which stopped these activities.

2. J. Corneloup, *Universalisme et Franc-Maçonnerie, Hier-Aujourd'hui* (Paris: Vitiano, 1963), 77; D. Ligou, ed., *Histoire des Francs-Maçons en France* (Toulouse: Privat, 1981), 252.

3. See D. Ligou, *Dictionnaire Universel de la Franc-Maçonnerie*, vol. 2 (Paris: Navarre-Prisme, 1974), 1059.

4. It can be said schematically that there are in Germany three Prussian Grand Lodges which are the most traditionalist, six "Humanitarian" Grand Lodges, and the Symbolic Grand Lodge of Germany, all of them with affiliated lodges.

5. Regular obediences are those recognized by the United Grand Lodge of England.

6. See A. Miroir, "Franc-Maçonnerie et Politique en régime censitaire," in H. Hasquin, ed., *Visages de la franc-maçonnerie belge du XVIIIe au XXe siècle* (Brussels: Univ. of Brussels, 1983), 229–44.

7. E. Nys, "Idées modernes, Droit international et Franc-Maçonnerie," *Revue de Droit international et de Législation comparée* 9 (1907): 718–19.

8. E. Nys, *La Franc-Maçonnerie, son histoire, son action* (Brussels: E. Rossel, 1914), 59.

9. In Latin countries, Catholics were not interested in peace ideas and peace movements. Believers were influenced by the Church's attitude to war as being of divine origin. In addition, becoming a peace friend meant renouncing war as a solution to any kind of problem; for many Catholics this also meant renouncing the reinstatement of the pope on his temporal throne in the wars of Italian unification. These religious and political reasons combined with economic considerations: In the middle of the nineteenth century, the peace movement adhered to the doctrine of free trade. The Catholic electorate, however, mostly consisted of landowners who had a vested interest in protectionism and the maintenance of high prices for agricultural produce. Hence their lack of interest in peace initiatives (Nadine Lubelski-Bernard, "The Participation of Women in the Belgian Peace Movement (1830–1914)," in R. Roach Pierson, ed., *Women and Peace: Theoretical, Historical and Practical Perspectives* [London: Croom Helm, 1987], 76–89).

10. See: *Maçonniek Weekblad* (Utrecht) 7, no. 21 (25 May 1868): 1–2; no. 22 (1 June 1868): 1–2; and no. 23 (8 June 1868): 3–4; *L'Action Maçonnique, Journal de la Franc-Maçonnerie Universelle* (Paris) no. 8 (March 15, 1867); *Journal des initiés aux principes et à l'oeuvre de la Franc-Maçonnerie universelle* (Paris) 14 (July–Aug. 1868): 123; *La Chaîne d'Union de Paris, Journal de la Maçonnerie universelle* 10 (1 Sept. 1872): 509–10.

11. This explains why it is not surprising to find so many Masons in the peace societies; for instance, in *Austria*: A. Fried. See Harold Josephson, ed., *Biographical Dictionary of Modern Peace Leaders* (Westport, CT.: Greenwood, 1985); E. Krivanec, "La Franc-Maçonnerie en Autriche," in *Travaux de la Loge nationale de recherches Villard de Honnecourt,* vol. 2 (Neuilly-sur-Seine: Grande Loge nationale Française, 1980): 1, 115. In *Belgium*: A. Couvreur, E. Goblet d'Alviella, Ch. Houzeau de Lehaie, H. La Fontaine, Ch. Potvin. In *France*: E. Arnaud, F. Bastiat, L. Bourgeois, A. Briand, L. Le Foyer, Ch. Lemonnier, G. Moch, Ch. Richet. See entries for these peace leaders in Josephson, *Biographical Dictionary.*

12. *Le Chaîne d'Union de Paris* 9 (9 Aug. 1872): 463–67.

13. On 5 Sept. 1870, L. Frapolli, Grand Master of Italian Masonry and member of Parliament, sent, in the name of the Grand Orient of Italy, an address to his "Brothers of the democracy of France and of Germany," demanding of them a prompt and honorable peace. See *Records of the Grand Orient of Belgium,* no. 197, 17th day, 7th month, 5870.

14. See "L'Adresse à tous les Maçons de France et d'Allemagne," *Le Peuple* (Brussels), no. 287 (14 Oct. 1870): 1–2; G. De Roy, *Une page d'histoire pacifiste* (Tournai: Delcourt-Vasseur, 1906), 12–24.

15. *Le Peuple,* 2.

16. L. Lartigue, *Extraits des tracés du Livre d'Architecture de la Loge "Les Amis Philanthropes,"* 11 (Brussels, 10 April 1871), 5869–5875; *La Chaîne d'Union de Paris* 8, no. 4 (1 March 1872): 176 and 5 (1 April 1872): 226–27.

17. J. Mitterand, *La politique des Francs-Maçons* (Paris: Roblot, 1973), 76–78; *Histoire des Francs-Maçons en France,* 252–55.

18. Louis Frank, *Les Belges et la Paix* (Brussels: Lamertin, 1905), 70.

19. *Universal Masonic Conference of Antwerp from 21st–24th day, 5th month 1894* (Brussels: Weissenbruch, n.d.), 18–19 & 66; *International Masonic Congress at Geneva, 1902,* Swiss Alpina Grand Lodge, minutes of the Congress meetings on 5, 6 and 7 Sept. 1902 (Berne: Büchler, 1902), 64 & 78–79; *La Branche d'Acacia,* Bulletin de la loge "Les Amis Philanthropes," 1, nos. 1–2 (Brussels, March–April 1901) 10; *International Masonic Congress of Brussels 1904,* under the auspices of the Grand Orient and the Supreme Council of Belgium. Minutes of the meetings of the Congress on 27, 28, 29, and 30 Aug. 1904, publ. by the IBMR (Berne: Büchler, 1905), 98–113; *Bulletin du Grand Orient de Belgique* (Brussels), single installment (1904) 49, 59.

20. *Int. Mas. Cong. Brussels, 1904,* 108.

21. On L. Le Foyer see entry in Josephson, *Biographical Dictionary.*

22. *Int. Mas. Cong. Brussels, 1904,* 109–110.

23. *International Masonic Congress of 1904,* communication by P. Tempels on the theses he had formulated (n.pl., n.d.), 7–10.

24. "Extraordinary Congress of the International Masonic Association, meeting in Geneva, 1–4 Oct. 1925," *Bulletin du Grand Orient de Belgique* (Brussels: Secrétariat du Grand Orient, 1925), 176.

25. A. Lantoine, *Hiram au Jardin des Oliviers* (Paris: Gloton, 1928), 23–25. This is a collection of Masonic peace documents, published under the direction of Ed. de Plantagenet.

26. Ed. Quartier-La-Tente, *Le Bureau International de Relations Maçonniques. Son histoire, son but, ses difficultés, son avenir, 1902–1920* (Berne: Büchler, 1920), 28–29.

27. On E. Ducommun, see entry in Josephson, *Biographical Dictionary.*

28. Ed. Quartier-La-Tente was pastor at Fleurier, professor of theology at the University of Neuchâtel, Grand Master of the Swiss Alpina Grand Lodge (1900–1905), Representative of the IBMR (1905–1920), and Chancellor of the International Masonic Association (1921–1924). See D. Ligou, *Dictionnaire Universel,* vol. 2, 1066.

29. See "A propos du Bureau international de relations maçonniques," *Bulletin. Journal dévoué aux intérêts de la Maçonnerie universelle* (Neuchâtel: Bureau International de Relations maçonniques) 18, no. 55 (Oct. 1921): 173–83.

30. English Freemasonry (some 260,000 members) and the majority of the American Grand Lodges (some 2 million members) maintained complete silence in respect to the Bureau. Only a part of the Freemasonry of the Netherlands, France, Switzerland, Belgium, Italy, Luxembourg, Hungary, Spain, and Portugal (which represented some 90,000 members) supported the IBMR See Ed. Quartier-La-Tente, *Le Bureau International,* 51–52.

31. "If Masonry is united, fraternal and devoted, if it is true that its chain surrounds the universe, it will work for the suppression of conflicts between nations by international arbitration. It can succeed in this mission because it is free, cosmopolitan and universal and pursues the same goal everywhere. What influence could be exercised in the world by such an association if its members were able to act with perseverance and good will! Masonry can and should be the most powerful agent for the maintenance of universal peace." Quoted in *Bulletin. Journal dévoué aux intérêts de la Maçonnerie universelle* 18, no. 55 (Oct. 1921): 180.

32. The origin of these Manifestations goes back to a ceremony at the Luxembourg Lodge "Les Enfants de la Concorde Fortifiée." See P. Barral, "La Franc-Maçonnerie en Lorraine aux XIXe et XXe siècles," *Les Annales*

de l'Est I (Nancy, 1970): 32; *Historique des Manifestations maçonniques internationales 1907-1929* (Coblenz: Vereinsdrückerei, n.d.), 9-10.

33. Although at Luxembourg only eight nations had sent delegates, the following year at The Hague there were participants from 14 nations. See Ch. Bernardin, "Historique des Manifestations Maçonniques Internationales," *L'Acacia, Revue mensuelle d'études et d'action maçonniques et sociales* (April–May 1928): 48-49, 411.

34. See *Ve Manifestation Maçonnique Internationale de la Paix,* Luxembourg, 25-27 May 1912 (Berne: Büchler, 1912), 7-8.

35. Barral, "La Franc-Maçonnerie," 33.

36. *Ve Manifestation Luxembourg,* 1912, 10.

37. Ibid., 54-55.

38. Barral, "La Franc-Maçonnerie," 34.

39. 400 participants from Belgium, France, Germany, Luxembourg, and Switzerland attended the Fourth Masonic Manifestation in 1911. See *Historique des Manifestations Maçonniques Internationales 1907-1929,* 18-19.

40. The Esperantist Masons met only at the Universal Esperanto Congresses in Geneva (1906), Dresden (1908), and Antwerp (1911).

41. On the UFL see: *La Ligue Internationale des Franc-Maçons, son but et son activité* (Paris: Editions de la Ligue, 1930); Th. Marti, *Des hérésies maçonniques à la Ligue Universelle de Francs-Maçons* (Brussels: Lielens, 1978), 95ff.

42. S. De Magalhaes Lima (1851-1928), former Grand Master of the Lusitanian Grand Orient. See entry in Josephson, *Biographical Dictionary.*

43. Quoted by P. Chevalier, *Histoire de la Franc-Maçonnerie française (1877-1944)* (Paris: Fayard, 1975), 201.

44. "Extraordinary Congress, Geneva, 1925," 175.

45. Ibid., 184.

Feminist Pacifism

MARIA ANTONIETTA SARACINO

Woman, the Unwilling Victim of War:
The Legacy of Olive Schreiner (1855–1920)

THE LEGACY OF OLIVE SCHREINER is her effective use of both fiction and essay forms to identify women with classes oppressed and victimized by war. Acclaimed as a novelist and essay-writer, Schreiner was also a committed pacifist and an advocate of human rights. A child of two worlds, South Africa and England, she witnessed two wars: the Anglo-Boer war of 1899 and World War I—tragic events which left her physically unscathed but morally wounded. Those wars opened scars that had been etched on her youthful mind:

> When a child, not yet nine years old, I walked out one morning along the mountain tops on which my home stood. . . . My heart was heavy; my physical heart seemed to have a pain in it, as if small, sharp crystals were cutting into it. All the world seemed wrong to me. . . . I had grown up in a land where wars were common. From my earliest years I had heard of bloodshed and battles and hairbreadth escapes. . . . In my native country dark men were killed and their lands taken from them by white men armed with superior weapons. . . . I knew also how white men fought white men . . . and I had seen how white men used the dark as beasts of labour, often without any thought for their good or happiness.[1]

That recollection, published only a few months after Olive Schreiner's death, was her last and most personal form of pacifism.[2] Whereas in the face of impending war her tone had been polemic, in war's wake it became reflective. Her article anticipated a book which she planned as a spiritual testament for future generations. Schreiner's recollection continues:

> In my native land I have seen the horrors of a great war. Smoke has risen from burning homesteads; women and children by thou-

sands have been thrown into great camps to perish there; men whom I have known have been tied in chairs and executed for fighting against strangers in the land of their own birth. . . . I have not held a veil before my eyes, that I might profess that cruelty, injustice, and mental and physical anguish were not. . . . But, in the course of long years . . . something else has happened. That which was for the young child only a vision . . . has, in the course of a long life's experience, become a hope, which I think the cool reason can find grounds to justify, and which a growing knowledge of human nature and human life does endorse. *Somewhere, some time, some place—even on earth!*[3]

There were other voices for peace in Schreiner's England, of course, but hers stood out because of her distinctive personal and intellectual experience and because of her popularity as a novelist. Her views on war resonated through her popularity as an author, and she employed the language of fiction powerfully to convey her ideas on peace and the role of women to masses of people who never before had been interested in politics. She was also among the first to analyze the relationship between war and peace in terms of race, and this at a time when British imperialism had already laid claim to vast areas of the African continent.

In her time Olive Schreiner's efforts in favor of peace were well recognized in the reports of contemporary newspapers and in the writing of people who made her ideas their own. Unfortunately and incomprehensibly, her name slowly fell into oblivion, unmentioned in the majority of works on British imperialism. But more recently her writings have enjoyed a sort of second youth, and *The Story of an African Farm* (1883), *Woman and Labour* (1911), and *From Man to Man* (1926), have been reprinted, reread, and reevaluated. In spite of the present worldwide concern with themes of peace and war, however, Schreiner's political writings have been left largely in the shadow. It is time to recapture her testament on peace and war.

Born in 1855 in Basutoland, South Africa, of a German father (Gottlob Schreiner, a Wesleyan Minister sent to the Cape by the London Missionary Society) and an English mother (Rebecca Lyndall), Olive Schreiner was reared in the culture of the Bible. She liked to define herself as an English–South African, for she grew up with a firsthand experience of two cultures which at the turn of the century would come into dramatic contact through war.

In South Africa she witnessed oppression in a variety of forms.

She saw the Boers struggling against British imperialism, the African people of South Africa subjected to both Boers and Britons; she saw women subordinated to men, and black women forced to live in almost subhuman conditions. Endowed with a sharp, critical sensitivity to her surroundings, she did not accept the constraint of being a woman that might have been expected at the time. On the contrary, she created from her apparently disadvantaged position a kind of double vision, interpreting her society from the viewpoint of both the subordinated woman and the dominant white. "In her experience," write Schreiner's biographers Ruth First and Ann Scott, "Victorian society secluded and silenced women, colonial society even more so; but she moved from themes of women's subjection and powerlessness to those of national oppression and the struggles of subject races and classes."[4]

From the beginning, Schreiner's medium was her pen, her chosen ground the narrative form. The result was *The Story of an African Farm,* a novel composed when, barely out of her teens, she was earning her living in a Boer family as a governess (an experience common to an entire generation of female writers in the nineteenth century).[5] Set in South Africa, the novel centers upon the yearning for freedom and independence of a young woman, Lyndall, who ends up with a child born out of wedlock, but it also depicts the racial clashes and contradictions of the society from which it sprang. Schreiner carried the manuscript of the novel with her in 1881, when at the age of twenty-six she moved to her cultural home, England.

That was a necessary step also taken by other South African writers who likewise felt "a deep sense of deprivation that living in South Africa they were cut off from the world of ideas," as the novelist Nadine Gordimer puts it. "They went because the culture in which their writing could take place was not being created, a culture whose base would be the indigenous black culture interpenetrating with imported European cultural forms, of which literature was one; and because the works they had written . . . were solitary contradictions of the way in which that life was being conceptualized, politically, socially and morally."[6]

Within two years of Schreiner's cultural homecoming, *The Story of an African Farm* was published under the pseudonym of Ralph Iron. It met with tremendous success: in the first year of publication it had two editions, and by 1900 it had "overwhelmed the literate public of three continents and had sold a fantastic 100,000 copies."[7] It also stirred controversy. In London groups of infuriated ladies literally pulled the book off the shelves of public libraries and burned it,[8] while it became forbidden reading for many daughters of middle-class families.

The year of Olive Schreiner's arrival in London saw also the birth of the Democratic Federation, Britain's first Socialist Party. Three years later, in 1884, the first Socialist League was formed, bringing together people such as William Morris, Eleanor Marx, Edward Aveling, and Edward Carpenter. Aveling reviewed *The Story* in the September issue of *Progress,* a socialist paper, in an article entitled "A Notable Book" which explicitly placed the novel in a socialist perspective.[9] On this occasion Schreiner met Eleanor Marx, who remained her closest woman friend until Marx's suicide in 1898. The popularity of her book also led to Schreiner's lifelong friendship with the psychologist Havelock Ellis.

It was the novel, then, and the message it contained that originally attracted the interest of British militants who found mirrored in its literary form some of the issues central to socialist thought. But despite pressure from these people, Schreiner never took part in organized politics. A restive figure, perpetually torn between South Africa and England, she was perhaps too much of a free spirit to become tied to any group. Besides, her idea of politics went beyond the dichotomy between capital and labor to include racial oppression (the "Native Question," as it came to be phrased) and the subjection of women — white *and* black. Although Havelock Ellis brought her into contact with The Progressive Association (or The Fellowship of the New Life) and she contributed to the founding of the Men and Women's Club in 1885, she never played any specific role in either.[10] Nonetheless, in her association with socialist groups and their discussions, Schreiner found theoretical bases for ideas which she had intuitively drawn from her observation of South African reality and had expressed in her fiction.

The Anglo-Boer War at the turn of the century (1899–1902) pushed Olive Schreiner, by now an acclaimed and well-known writer, into active politics. She was back in South Africa at the time. There she witnessed two different faces of white rule, British and Boer, each armed against the other for the possession of the land of her birth. Her wholehearted sympathy went out to the Boers, who had been provoked, and in consequence she was regarded as a traitor by many of her British countrymen. Characteristically, she used fiction to get beyond polemics. In a beautiful short story called "Eighteen-ninety-nine" she exposed the devastating effects of war on the lives of two Boer women who witness the destruction of their entire family. When the story opens, a small child — later to be killed in the conflict — is questioning his grandmother:

> "Grandmother, did God make the English too?"
> She . . . waited for a while, then she said, "Yes, my child; He made all things."
> They were silent again, and there was no sound but of the rain falling and the fire cracking and the sloot rushing outside. Then he threw his head backwards on to his grandmother's knee and looking up into her face, said: "But, grandmother, why did He make them?"
> "Grandmother," he said suddenly, in a small, almost shrill voice, "do the English want *all* the lands of *all* the people?"
> The handle of his grandmother's knife as she cut clinked against the iron side of the basin. "All they can get," she said.[11]

Later, after the war has brought complete destruction, the two women are found dead inside their devastated house. Schreiner concludes:

> There is no stone and no name upon either grave to say who lies there . . . our unknown . . . our unnamed . . . our forgotten dead.[12]

Schreiner was face to face with war now and, although narrative remained her preferred form of expression, she concluded that she must write more directly against the violence she knew firsthand. In public speeches and newspaper articles, in long essays and personal correspondence, she insisted that war simply meant hell. She urged her English compatriots to withdraw their support of the Boer war and commit themselves to the cause of peace.

At the outset of the conflict she had written a long pamphlet called *An English–South African's View of the Situation,* full of passion for peace and love for the land of her birth:

> WHO GAINS BY WAR? Not England. She has a great nation's heart to lose. . . . She has treaties to violate. She has the great traditions of her past to part with. . . . WHO GAINS BY WAR? Not Africa! The great young nation, quickening to-day to its first consciousness of life to be torn and rent. . . . WHO GAINS BY WAR? Not the brave English soldier; there are no laurels for him here. . . . Go, gallant soldiers, and defend the shores of that small island that we love; there are no laurels for you here![13]

During the years of the Boer War and out of its devastation, Olive Schreiner concluded that women could make an especially significant contribution to the cause of peace. A powerful orator who knew how to touch the right chords, she had often devoted special attention to the women when she addressed large audiences at antiwar meetings. "To you, the women of South Africa," she said on one such occasion, "I would say one word before we part. . . . It is for you . . . to show that the heart of South Africa is unpurchasable by any gold from blood-stained hands. The heart of a womanhood of a nation is the treasure-house where its freedom is stored—a fearless, indomitable, unpurchasable womanhood; a fearless, indomitable, unpurchasable race."[14]

As time went by, what originally was only a persuasion took on a more and more coherent theoretical form. During the war years Olive Schreiner set out to complete a book on woman. The idea had been generated by her observation of the condition of native African women around her, and the writing already had occupied much of her time, but the first manuscript was destroyed when her house was looted at the outset of the war. Rewritten during the long house-confinement imposed by the conflict, in order "to force my thoughts at times from the horror of the world around,"[15] *Woman and Labour* appeared in 1911 and was an immediate best-seller.

Through the use of a language which intentionally appealed to the reader's emotions, *Woman and Labour* analyzed the social dynamics which in the course of centuries had led to the subjection of women. At the same time, the study offered support and historical grounds for the contemporaneous feminist demand for meaningful work. As a consequence of rapid technological innovations, Schreiner argued, material conditions of life have changed, and women have paid the highest price for this change. In the course of time they have slowly but steadily been robbed of their traditional work, roles which had always made them feel productive and had given them power within and over their extended family group. More generally, they have been robbed of their social role. Unlike their male counterparts, they have not gained any privileges in return for such dispossession; on the contrary, they have been pushed back into a condition of social parasites or reduced to their mere reproductive functions. Even this most vital role of theirs has continually been attacked: wars have repeatedly destroyed the human life which women repeatedly labored to create.

In a long chapter entitled "Woman and War," Schreiner offered a clear sense of the negative contribution of women to war:

> Men have made boomerangs, bows, swords, or guns with which to destroy one another; we have made the men who destroyed and were destroyed! We have in all ages produced, at an enormous cost, the primal munition of war, without which no other would exist. There is no battlefield on earth . . . which it has not cost the women of the race more in actual bloodshed and anguish to supply, than it has cost the men who lie there. *We pay the first cost on all human life.*[16]

As bearers of life, women carry in their bodies an amazing potential, and it is because of this potential that for centuries they have been exploited for war: "In nations continually at war, incessant and unbroken childbearing is by war imposed on all women if the state is to survive. . . . This throws upon woman as woman a war tax, compared with which all that the male expends in military preparations is comparatively light."[17] Schreiner concluded that the day had come for women to realize that of all people *they* can no longer contribute to the cause of human destruction. Knowing the history and cost of human flesh, she wrote, "no woman who is a woman says of a human body, 'It is nothing!'"[18]

The publication of *Woman and Labour* in the period of political unrest shortly before the outbreak of World War I caused a deep emotional stir among feminists and among women in general. It contributed to the rise of antiwar consciousness. The pacifist and social commentator Vera Brittain described the book as the "Bible of the Woman's Movement," which "sounded to the world of 1911 as insistent and inspiring as a trumpet-call summoning the faithful to a vital crusade."[19] By this time Schreiner had completely espoused the cause of pacifism and of conscientious objection on which, although seriously ill, she delivered several public speeches in England and South Africa. She also advocated a constitutional federation in South Africa so that her troubled homeland might avoid future wars, in this respect anticipating ideas which would later find spokesmen like Lord Lothian and other European federalists.

As a woman, a pacifist, and a feminist, Olive Schreiner suffered many disadvantages. She turned them into an important legacy, linking together many facets of women's experience and relating them to the struggle against war and oppression. Moreover, she showed that literature and politics did not necessarily represent two distant and separate fields, each endowed with a language of its own. On the contrary, and in her own writing the two fields often overlap and contribute to each other. Pacifists like Vera Brittain, journalists like the South African Ruth First, novelists like Virginia Woolf or — more recently — Doris Lessing and Nadine Gordimer: all in various ways and in their respective fields have taken up the legacy of Olive Schreiner and in their writings have acknowledged their debt to her.

On the theme of women's contribution to the cause of peace, her message was directly acquired by the novelist Virginia Woolf, who developed it into the unforgettable long essay, *Three Guineas*.[20] In this work Woolf argued that women have a fundamental role to play in preventing war, but she also insisted that the preliminary steps must be education and economic independence. This is the sense of the title: that everyone should invest three guineas in building more colleges for women.

Olive Schreiner, too, had recognized the importance of a free and independent education for women. In her will she provided that sums should be set aside for a scholarship for women at the South African College, Cape Town (the forerunner of the University of Cape Town), which would be administered by the University Council "without reference to race or colour or religion, poor women and girls to have preference."[21]

Education as a key way to combat racism and war: it was a path which Olive Schreiner opened up for women in her fiction, essays, and personal life.

NOTES

1. Olive Schreiner, "The Dawn of Civilization: Stray Thoughts on Peace and War. The Homely Personal Confession of a Believer in Human Unity." *The Nation and Athenaeum* [London] 26 March 1921, quoted in Cherry Clayton, ed., *Olive Schreiner* (Johannesburg: McGraw-Hill, 1983), 60; the full article is reprinted on pp. 60–64.

2. She died in South Africa on 10 Dec. 1920.

3. Schreiner, "The Dawn of Civilization," in Clayton, *Olive Schreiner,* 63–64 (my emphasis).

4. Ruth First and Ann Scott, *Olive Schreiner* (London: André Deutsch, 1980), 16–17. Ruth First was a South African university teacher and jour-

nalist and an active member of antiapartheid movements. She was assassinated by letter-bomb on 17 Sept. 1981 in Maputo, Mozambique.

5. Published under the pseudonym of Ralph Iron (London: Chapman & Hall, 1883; Penguin, 1971).

6. "The Prison-House of Colonialism: Review of Ruth First and Ann Scott's *Olive Schreiner*," *The Times Literary Supplement* [London]: 15 Aug. 1980, in Clayton, *Olive Schreiner*, 97; the full article is reprinted on pp. 95-98.

7. Paul Foot, "Introduction" to Olive Schreiner, *From Man to Man* (London: Virago, 1980), xi.

8. Edith Lees, "Olive Schreiner and her Relation to the Woman's Movement," *Book News Monthly* [New York] 33 (Feb. 1915) in Clayton, 46; the full article is reprinted on pp. 46-51.

9. Edward Aveling, "A Notable Book: Review of *The Story of an African Farm*," *Progress* [London], (Sept. 1883), in Clayton, *Olive Schreiner*, 67-69.

10. S. C. Cronwright-Schreiner, *The Life of Olive Schreiner* (London: Unwin, 1924).

11. Schreiner, "Eighteen-ninety-nine," *Stories, Dreams and Allegories* (London: Unwin, 1923), 33-34.

12. Ibid., 56.

13. *An English–South African's View of the Situation: Words in Season* (London: Hodder & Stoughton, 1899), 20-21.

14. "Speech on the Boer War at the Somerset East Women's Meeting," 12 Oct. 1900, in S. C. Cronwright-Schreiner, ed., *The Letters of Olive Schreiner, 1876-1920* (London: Unwin, 1924), 383-84.

15. "Introduction," *Woman and Labour* (1911; London: Virago, 1978), 19.

16. *Woman and Labour*, 169.

17. Ibid., 175-76.

18. Ibid., 170.

19. *Testament of Youth* (London: Victor Gollancz, 1933; Virago, 1987), 41.

20. (London: Hogarth Press, 1938; Penguin, 1977).

21. Schreiner's will, quoted in S. C. Cronwright-Schreiner, *The Life of Olive Schreiner*, 391-92.

JO VELLACOTT

Women, Peace and Internationalism, 1914–1920: "Finding New Words and Creating New Methods"[1]

WOMEN'S PEACE EFFORTS ARE OFTEN dismissed as simply part of the general softness of women's nature, or as part of their motherhood role, with no serious import for the public sphere. This patronizing view has not only made it possible to disregard the content of what peace women have said, but at times even succeeds in making peace a suspect cause among feminists. Many First World War feminists believed, however, that pacifism was not only a logical development from feminism, but an integral part of it. No matter what rhetoric of motherhood they used, the women who stood up to oppose the First World War (or any war) were stepping out of their assigned roles, and their actions must be located in the context of feminism.

In a culture which strongly enforces gender inequality and the widely differentiated traditional roles of men and women, where women are relegated to the private sphere, and where they are not organized to reclaim equality or push back the frontiers, women do not emerge as forceful opponents of war, demanding to be heard. They fulfill, instead, their assigned role in war as in peace, sacrificing their sons and lovers without complaint (mourning, yes, but complaining, no), keeping the home fires burning, loving soldiers, being sexually available, bearing and nurturing cannon-fodder for future wars, enduring hardships, taking on extra tasks for the duration and relinquishing them without a murmur when the men come home. This is the role of "our" women. The "enemy's" women also have a role: they are to be part of the bait, part of the prize; and humiliation through use and abuse of conquered women is part of the punishment to be inflicted on defeated warriors. Women are not expected to like all this, but the role allowed them in war has not included any mandate to resist it.[2]

In fact, the history of all women's peace movements may tend to show that those who challenge militarism are generally among the most advanced of feminists, with a good understanding of the scope and nature of patriarchy, and of what militarism means in terms of women's position. Feminist pacifism, accordingly, must be examined as a political statement.

ROOTS OF FEMINIST PACIFISM

The women's peace movement of the First World War had theoretical and practical connections with the prewar women's suffrage movement. These connections have been considerably obscured by the fact that the major suffrage organizations did not lend official support to antiwar activities. But most of the women who joined in the opposition to war had served an apprenticeship in the suffrage movement and saw arguments against war as an extension of their advocacy of suffrage.

Moreover, feminism and opposition to war both drew selectively on existing political traditions. Again the connections have been obscured, partly because of the prewar suffrage strategy of refusing to be identified with any one party position. The women for whom pacifism became part of feminism during the First World War drew especially on liberalism and some forms of socialism, but they drew the implications far beyond the traditional origins.

The contribution of liberal theory to the cause of women's equality is well known. John Stuart Mill's *Subjection of Women* (1869) became a textbook for women working in the suffrage cause in every western liberal democracy (although, as Catherine Marshall commented, it was not mandatory reading for young male liberals, even those who were brought up on Mill's other classical liberal texts).[3] What is less often remembered is that this book, like the women's suffrage petition of 1866, was not an isolated initiative of Mill or even of Mill and his wife Harriet Taylor Mill, but was part of a substantial stirring of awareness and activity among a group of middle-class feminist women, the Langham Place group. From 1867 on, the history of suffrage organizations was continuous, and Mill's liberal arguments remained in the forefront. Among the appropriately named "ruling class" there were really only two political parties until well into the twentieth century, and the middle-class feminist movement in the main supported the Liberal Party and drew on liberal theory, with its supportive beliefs in equality of opportunity, removal of discriminatory restrictions, representative government, and, above all, progress towards a rational and harmonious society. Liberalism's contribution to women's advancement was substantial, and clearly the vote had to be fought for and won. However, it can be argued that women gained admission to the male-dominated political system on men's terms, which were that the system itself remained unchanged.[4] In addition, the war was to shatter the liberal internationalist vision, which had been an important component of liberalism for many women and men.

Relevant themes existed also in radical socialist feminist traditions. The utopian or Owenite writings, speeches, and experimentation of the early nineteenth century were shot through with an extraordinary streak of powerful and uncompromising feminism, much of it written, preached, and practiced by both women and men, and addressing everything from sexual subordination to education to marriage laws to political inequality to limitation of job opportunities.[5] While by mid-century this feminist stream had been lost to view or suppressed, with the rise of a trade unionism hostile to female competition, the attraction of communitarian philosophy had not completely disappeared. Tenuous as are the links, the strength of the cooperative movement is a later manifestation of the same alternative style, with the Women's Co-operative Guild as a powerful female and largely feminist development inheriting a strong vision of a way forward to local, national, and global peace.[6]

The Syndicalism and Guild Socialism of the early twentieth century, emphasizing direct worker control and decentralization, also derived as much if not more from the communitarian socialist tradition as from the Marxist. Recent scholarship has shown the complexity of socialism and socialist feminism, as they survived and were revived in the early twentieth century. The common grass-roots emphasis on the humanitarian and ethical values of these traditions also emerges clearly.[7]

Both liberalism and socialism were important in the prewar nonmilitant suffrage movement and in the development of feminism itself, in theory, practice, and personnel. Feminists proved eclectic, taking what suited their cause from different traditions and not concerning themselves with minor inconsistencies. Such cross-fertilization and mutual nurture was healthy and allowed room for creative developments.

The two major British suffrage organizations were the Women's Social and Political Union (WSPU) and the National Union of Women's Suffrage Societies (NUWSS). The WSPU was the 1903 creature of the socialist Pankhurst family of Manchester. Reflecting frustration with slow progress in the struggle for the vote, the WSPU moved its headquarters to London in 1905 and mounted an increasingly aggressive campaign of harassment against the Liberal party, and of damage to public and personal property. The original tactic of disrupting meetings and of other nonviolent actions attracted needed attention. The escalating violence after 1910, although provoked by frequent delays and perceived bad faith, seems to have done the cause more harm than good. The leadership of Emmeline and Christabel Pankhurst became ever more autocratic, working-class and socialist connections were severed, leading dissenters were ousted, branches were largely left to their own devices, and the focus was increasingly on the inner circle of those planning and carrying out illegal actions and on repeated cycles of capture, hunger strike, release, and recapture of the most active militants.

The NUWSS was a far older organisation, able to trace its lineage back to the age of John Stuart Mill. Until recently, the lion's share of historical attention was given to the WSPU, but during the last few years the effectiveness of the nonmilitant organization has been increasingly recognized.[8] From the NUWSS came most of the leading women who moved into peace work, among them some of those directly responsible for building the prewar nonmilitant suffrage movement into a powerful force whose goal could not long have been denied.

In contrast to the WSPU, the prewar NUWSS made use of every legitimate means of political pressure, building up an extraordinary network of information, personal contact and publicity. The NUWSS, originally best known for its London drawing-room base, by 1907 included many of the impressive and numerically strong working-class suffrage organizations of the northern manufacturing areas. While Emmeline and Christabel Pankhurst had moved away from their socialist roots, the NUWSS had allied itself with the Labour Party. Official reasons for this were strictly strategic, in order to bring pressure to bear at parliamentary elections, but it had been an educative process for a number of leading suffrage women from a bourgeois liberal background. An equally important indicator of future (wartime) direction may have been the nature of decision-making within suffrage groups: while the Pankhurst leadership dealt ruthlessly with dissent, the NUWSS had steadily democratized itself in the prewar years and now had a highly responsive central and grass-roots organization.[9]

Although many suffragists did not look beyond the vote as a goal in itself, there were those who had begun to recognize that the political exclusion of women was only one facet of a system in need of radical change. Catherine Marshall is representative of those middle-class suffragists who had come from liberalism and the Liberal Party and had been driven, by the repeated refusal of the liberal government to enfranchise women, to question the system itself. The alliance with the Labour Party was far more than strategic for Marshall, and as an active speaker and organizer she worked closely with Labour men and women to bring over important Trade Union groups towards a firm declaration in support of women's suffrage. In the last few years before the war, in a Britain disturbed by labour troubles and by unrest in Ireland and in India, Marshall made profound connections between different kinds of oppression. In December 1913, in an interview with Sir Edward Grey, she spoke of the coming struggle between capital and labour, of the women's movement at home and abroad, and of a sense of "kinship with subject races." She applied her arguments concretely to the current British situation, and went on to claim:

> It matters enormously to the whole of civilisation whether these 3 great movements run on sound and healthy lines, or are driven into revolution. *The women will have great effect on both.*[10]

This kind of analysis takes the suffrage argument far beyond a mere request to be admitted to the liberal democratic system; implicit is a vision of the world where women's full participation will change some basic political values, and some of the criteria by which issues are judged.

Far from being a distraction or an aberration, then, the antiwar stance came as a logical development from the cause of women's suffrage. If the system was in ill-health because of the exclusion of half the race from decision-making in the public sphere, war had to be the most appalling manifestation of this malaise.

The progress of the British prewar suffrage movement had its counterpart in other western countries where the campaign for the vote was being actively pursued. The history of the struggle within each country, however, has tended to be written as if it existed in isolation rather than as a major movement all over the western world with a strong international consciousness and support network. Indeed, the international character of prewar suffragism facilitated the articulation of the widespread feminist rejection of war.

The International Women's Suffrage Alliance (IWSA) had been formed in 1904, emerging in part out of an older organization, the International Council of Women (ICW). The latter had built a widening and effective network on the basis of avoidance of issues perceived as controversial within the organization, and so was prevented from adopting women's suffrage, necessitating the formation of a separate organization. Interestingly, this caution had not barred the adoption by the ICW of its own peace committee, set up on the initiative of the Peace and Arbitration Committee of the American National Council of Women and chaired by May Wright Sewall.[11] These international organizations had provided the opportunity for an increasing number of women — mainly middle-class, but of a variety of backgrounds and occupations — to meet together, and to recognize common interests. The many faces presented by inequality brought for some a sober realization that gaining the vote would be only a first step.

Some practice of internationalism, then, had grown up in the prewar suffrage movement. By 1914, however, it still appeared far from being elevated to a principle. All the more interesting is the strength it showed in the face of the gross and hysterical hatreds between nations which were manifested and indeed fostered on both sides in late 1914.

PACIFISM DIVIDES THE SUFFRAGE MOVEMENT

Not all suffragists opposed the war, or sought alternatives to future conflict. War fever prevailed in late 1914. In Britain, opposition existed but coalesced slowly and painfully, and no major prewar organization was sufficiently united to give a clear lead. Individuals who rejected British intervention from the beginning were denied an effective forum because the liberal press immediately rallied to the support of the Liberal government. An almost universal belief that the war would be short also tended to hold open opposition in abeyance.[12]

War brought an immense amount to occupy the attention of the leading suffrage women. Emmeline and Christabel Pankhurst shelved not only suffrage agitation but, in effect, other feminist concerns as well, and stridently assisted the government's recruiting drive. The loose organization of the WSPU makes it impossible to form any clear impression of the position taken by the bulk of its members, but evidence is emerging that those who had not followed the Pankhurst leadership away from the WPSU's socialist origins, particularly in northern England and Scotland, included a number of quite radical opponents of the war.[13] Sylvia Pankhurst, disowned by her mother and sister and moving ever further to the left, divided her time between condemning the war and trying to protect the East London women she now lived among from the worst of its immediate effects.[14] Charlotte Despard, a deportee from the WSPU's central leadership and now leader of the Women's Freedom League (WFL), elected to continue suffrage agitation, seeing the war as the ultimate product of a society built on false principles.[15]

> So long as materialism — physical force — is the order of the day, so long as the spiritual consideration, which women and honest workers of both sexes would bring to the government, is absent, we shall have these epidemics of armed strife, this war hysteria. We must keep our own flag flying and emphasize our demand to have a voice in decision.[16]

Despard, too, was much occupied with the alleviation of the severe hardships caused by the disruptions of trade and employment to women who at the best of times lived a hand-to-mouth existence, and who had nothing to fall back on when they lost their jobs or when the army separation allowance failed to come through.

Another leading suffragist who took a stand against the war was Emmeline Pethick-Lawrence. Her association with the militant Pankhursts and their WSPU had come to an end in 1912 when she and her husband were ejected for questioning the policy promoted by Emmeline and Christabel Pankhurst. Emmeline Pethick-Lawrence's reaction to the war is of interest in clarifying the difference between feminist and militarist use of the rhetoric of motherhood. She recognized the false connotations of motherhood as a construct of a male-dominated society. During the war, as militarism on both sides became extraordinarily blatant in its demand that women become machines for producing cannon-fodder,[17] Emmeline Pethick-Lawrence, and many other feminists, did not respond by denying motherhood. What they saw as antifeminist was a militaristic approach, where bearing children became a service to a war machine. Opponents of the war reclaimed women's right to have babies, if they wished, but for life, not death. Nothing, perhaps, more vividly makes the link between militarism and women's subordination than this issue.

The long casualty lists rapidly brought home to women that a generation was being sacrificed: some were quick to sense that if things continued to be so mismanaged, babies then being born would be ripe to kill and be killed twenty to thirty years later. In the *Common Cause* for 4 December 1914, Emmeline Pethick-Lawrence responded to an article in the *Daily Mail,* in terms which now seem prophetic:

> The idea that this war is the last war and will end militarism is frankly flung aside. We are told that "we must see to it that the utmost care shall be given to the children who, twenty years hence, may have to repel another German attack. . . . Shells and machine guns are the principal munitions of the present war, but infants are the munitions of the future peace." We know how to translate that sentence. Shells and machine guns were said to be an insurance for peace before the war broke out, but today they are the munitions of war. The infants of today are destined to be the first and chief munitions of the war which the *Daily Mail* sees as a possibility twenty years hence.
>
> I call upon the collective motherhood of this nation and of the world to contemplate for one moment what this means. No war in the past has ever produced such casualty lists as the present war . . . but all this falls into insignificance in comparison with the possibilities presented by the next war. Let submarine craft, air craft, and bomb craft develop during the next twenty years as they have developed in our lifetime, and we can scarcely imagine the wholesale murder and massacre which will ensue. If this thing is to go on, the human race as we know it today will be wiped off the surface of the planet. This is the immediate menace to our children and to our children's children.[18]

From the day war broke out, the NUWSS, with its active headquarters and sophisticated country-wide network, responded to the emergency. Much that needed to be done was uncontroversial. Women were particularly hard hit by the dislocation in trade, exacerbated for garment workers by a sudden massive voluntary cutback in upper-class spending on clothes and luxuries. The men who rushed to enlist were whisked away by the Army, clothed and fed: provision for their families was often slow to come through or inadequate. Whatever suffragists could do to alleviate hardship, they did, in voluntary projects or in government-sponsored organizations; indeed, the government seems to have shown some belated respect for the skills and experience of these women and to have been glad to turn to them for help.[19]

The prewar NUWSS had had a feminist perspective covering a range of issues; while suffragists all saw the vote as an essential step in tackling these issues, they had not limited themselves to this single goal.[20] The prewar pages of the *Common Cause* show the scope of feminist research and the development of a feminist position on many topics, and as soon as the war began, members played an important role in looking after women's interests, exposing discriminatory regulations and making sure, as far as they could, that conditions in new jobs as they opened up would be beneficial rather than exploitative.

All this work was worthwhile, and there was enough of it to keep the suffragists busy and to enable them to sidestep the question of what war really meant to them, had they chosen to do so. Immediately following the outbreak of the war, acutely different opinions had surfaced in the NUWSS national executive. In common with many staunch Liberals, the President, Millicent Fawcett, hoped until the last minute for British neutrality in the conflict but accepted the inevitability of armed struggle as soon as war was declared. She felt that loyalty to the country and to the Liberal government demanded full support from women as from men.[21] For the more radical members, those who were now thinking in terms of major change, this would not do. Although they were as active as any in the relief of distress, for them the connection between war and a male-dominated society appeared clear. They were appalled by the German-baiting and Hun-hating climate which quickly developed, a climate they saw as inimical to women's interests as well as making impossible a reasonable, negotiated peace, satisfactory to both sides. Helena Swanwick wrote:

> A growth of militarist opinion, vindictive terms of peace, reprisals, uncritical and emotional yielding to any reports which may

discredit the enemy, and blindness to any faults which may be committed by ourselves: all these are dangers not only to civilisation, but, in particular, to the movement for the emancipation of women.[22]

When asked to speak on the subject of women and war, Catherine Marshall emphasized the role women might play in making the war into a turning point in international relations, and indeed in relations between people. "The task of the peacemakers," she declared in November 1914,

> will be helped or hindered by the kind of public opinion they have behind them, by the spirit in which each nation approaches the question of settlement. . . . We have got to live as friends with Germany when the war is over and must keep always uppermost in our minds the desire for lasting peace — not revenge or punishment. . . . When we think of our soldiers and sailors, we think of what they suffer. . . . But we should also think of the suffering we send them forth to inflict — not from choice of theirs, but because we have found no better way.[23]

Besides being moral and humanitarian (the qualities expected of women), this is psychologically and politically realistic, and in a tragic, negative way, it proved prophetic. Whatever evidence there is here of the influence on Marshall of liberal internationalism, socialist brotherhood, and ethical Christianity, she saw it rather as serving notice that feminism would and must be allowed to bring a new spirit into politics.

The first public outcome of the controversy within the NUWSS was that two leading members, Marshall and Kathleen D. Courtney, resigned their positions, but not their membership, in February 1915, over the issue of turning NUWSS resources towards education for peace, on which they felt that the Council meeting held that month had not given them a clear enough mandate.[24] Shortly afterwards, more than half the executive (including all the leading officers) followed them, judging that their differences with Millicent Fawcett and her closest followers were irreconcilable, and specifically, that there was no hope that the NUWSS would offer official support to a women's international conference.

PACIFISM AS INTEGRAL TO FEMINISM

The International Conference of Women for Permanent Peace, held at The Hague in April 1915, was planned and carried through by suffragists although, mainly out of political caution, few major suffrage groups in belligerent countries lent support. The IWSA had been scheduled to meet in June 1915, and when the invitation to meet in Germany was withdrawn Carrie Chapman Catt (USA), the President, cancelled the meeting altogether. Others felt that it should go ahead, although not simply as a suffrage meeting, and Dr. Aletta Jacobs of Holland convened a meeting in February 1915 to make plans. Forty years later, Catherine Marshall wrote:

> five of us from England, braving the U-boat menace in the channel, met four German and four Belgian women in Holland. . . .
> Germany and England were at war with one another and Belgium was under German military occupation, but we were all convinced that we who had worked together internationally for women's enfranchisement could work together even whilst our countries were at war, for the common objective of a just and lasting peace. Our faith was justified — it was a moving experience when we women from three belligerent countries met on the neutral soil of Holland.[25]

They met, they decided to call an international Congress, they fixed a date a mere eight weeks away, they agreed on general outlines, and they returned home to organize delegates. The British women met with overwhelming support from other women, mostly suffragists; within a few weeks there was a General Committee of at least one hundred and forty-four members, a central office, six local committees and more in process of formation. One hundred and eighty women committed themselves to attend, prepared to pay their way and cross the North Sea. But the British government cut down the number to twenty-five, and at the last moment the Admiralty closed the North Sea to shipping. Only three British women, who were fortunate enough to be already out of the country, were able to be present at this remarkable gathering. Over eleven hundred voting delegates were there from twelve countries, including Germany and Belgium, with over forty women from the United States.[26]

Gloomy predictions of bitter recriminations were not fulfilled. The organizers had required of participants a general agreement with the spirit (not necessarily the detail) of resolutions sent out in advance, and with admirable forethought had set out a rule of debate: "Discussions on the relative national responsibility for or conduct of the present war shall be outside the scope of the Congress."[27] With these precautions, with goodwill, and with Jane Addams presiding, the Congress debated earnestly and effectively. Resolutions were passed concerning principles of a peace settlement, war in its relation to women, and the need to change attitudes by the education of children and adults. The Congress adopted a "Plan for Continuous Mediation" by a committee of neutrals, drawn up by Julia Grace Wells, a Canadian working at the University of Wisconsin, and delegates carried this to governments throughout Europe and in the United States.[28] A second conference, it was decided, would meet when and where the postwar peace conference was held.

That remarkable Congress of 1915, taking place on the soil of Europe in the midst of a bitter war, was a landmark in feminist history. The women who planned, organized, and attended (or were prevented from attending) the Hague Congress knew that they were out of line. They had been told so by their governments, by the conservative press, and, more painfully, by the generally liberal and prosuffrage press, by some women in their own organizations, and doubtless in many instances by their families and friends. Many of their previous colleagues in suffrage work believed that they were being disloyal to their country and were delaying the advent of the franchise. What made them go forward in the face of all this? Why were they so sure that they were not giving up feminism for pacifism, but rather were taking feminism one essential step further?

One thing that stands out is their confidence, not necessarily in success in their ultimate aims, but in their sisters in the international suffrage movement, and in their obligation to do whatever they could. They had been demanding the vote for many years: they rightly believed themselves to be on the brink of success, and they had long been educating themselves to play a full part in public affairs. After saying for all these years that women must be heard, were they to sit back now in face of the enormity of war, and say nothing? They thought it their responsibility to speak out. They knew too that they could meet when men could not; and what is more, they were sure that they could meet amicably, where men might not have been able to.

The urgency felt by these women to play a part in developing alternatives to war was based on their belief that women's ability was equal to that of men, coupled with a rejection of the idea of sameness. It is not necessary to discuss at great length whether they believed gender difference to be attributable to nature or to nurture; essentially they were addressing the need to introduce into political affairs a whole set of values which had been relegated to women and hence excluded, along with the women, from public decision-making. Few women made any claim that these qualities were exclusively the property of women, but they saw little evidence of them in traditional international relations. The relatively few men who advocated talking in place of shooting were not being heard; the women must do what they could.

What was so important and so profoundly feminist about this peace initiative? What the women said at the Hague in 1915, in Zurich in 1919, and in Geneva throughout the long slide from 1919 to 1939, could have been said by men, and indeed much of it was, by a few men, at the same time. The key lies in that first conference at the Hague, where women who did not yet have the vote claimed the right to be heard in public. They were not given that right, but they went ahead and took it. They declared their views with courtesy and conviction, not merely on political issues seen to be within women's sphere, but on those most masculine of issues, international affairs and war. They urged that women should have a voice in the postwar peace settlement. They wanted admission to existing and future institutions not only because women were half of the human race and should have equality, but because they had something to bring that was lacking. They rejected the artificial dichotomy between male and female, public and private, but not on the grounds that women could be just like men if they moved into the public sphere; they were not interested in being just like men. They refused to sit back and wait for admission to male-dominated institutions, instead creating their own vehicle. Yet theirs was not, in modern terms, a "separatist" move; rather, it was an attempt to ensure the clarity of the message, the better to open a dialogue with the established male power. They sought and continued to seek opportunity to speak from inside, but they insisted on speaking. It is of central importance that they were not just demanding to be let into decision-making but, rather, were announcing that they would indeed speak in a different voice,[29] a voice which they said was desperately needed in international affairs and matters of war and peace.

The decision made at the Hague in 1915 to convene the next major international gathering at the time and place which should be chosen for the peace conference ran into a snag. In victory, the Allies prevented nationals of defeated countries from travelling to Paris, where, in any event, the peace terms were drawn up only by the victors. A flurry of telegrams ensued, and Zurich was chosen as the new venue; the Zurich conference of 1919, like its predecessor, became an object lesson in the manner of its holding, as well as in its decisions. Peace, for these women, was something which had to be negotiated by both sides in an atmosphere of reconciliation, mutual understanding and common humanity, so the women of the victorious countries refused to go to Paris and meet with each other. They went instead where they could meet with their defeated sisters, some of them emaciated by the effect of the Allied blockade.[30] Ironically, the French delegates were refused passports to travel to Zurich.[31]

The delegates gathered in the very week of the publication of the Treaty of Versailles. After a brief, intense study they cabled to the Allied statesmen of Versailles their unanimous strong criticism of the proposed terms of peace which, they believed, "seriously violate the principles upon which alone a just and lasting peace can be secured."[32]

The draft Covenant of the League of Nations had been available since February, and Helena Swanwick had an analysis already prepared for full discussion at Zürich.[33] Unlike the Treaty, which the delegates viewed as disastrous, the League gave grounds for hope, although some saw real danger in its imperfections. The temporary women's peace organization turned itself into a permanent one, the Women's International League for Peace and Freedom, and decided to set its headquarters wherever the League of Nations was established.

There followed many years of intense involvement in international issues centered in the Maison Internationale in Geneva. Leading members, among them Emily Balch, Catherine Marshall, and Madeleine Doty,[34] were already long-time students of economics and international affairs, and were soon very well informed on all the current issues. They refused to restrict their interests to so-called women's questions, and came up with a position on every major issue of the time. They urged that Germany be rehabilitated as soon as possible, rather than being further alienated. They questioned the economic wisdom of reparations, demanded an end to the blockade, and continued to seek ways in which peace could be founded on cooperation rather than competition. The policies they advocated were idealistic in one sense, in that they were firmly based on principle, but with rare exceptions they were also profoundly realistic.

Many feminist internationalists declared their adherence to socialist principles, but their experience had not shown them a socialism divested of militarism, which Marshall defined as "the desire to dominate rather than to co-operate, to vanquish and humiliate the enemy rather than to convert him into a friend."[35] They feared, too, the element in socialism which saw class warfare as inevitable or acceptable. Marshall asked,

> Can the solidarity of women be developed in such a way as to strengthen this movement towards internationalism, and at the same time to help find some other way than class war for bringing about the changes necessary in our social structure?[36]

The women wanted to put their own imprint on socialism, not simply to follow it blindly.

Again and again, in a variety of contexts, we are struck by the determination of these women to speak out in their own voice, to make the contribution they knew they could. This is what sets WILPF apart from other peace organizations. For at least the first decade after the war, it was a forum for women from all over the world, speaking out from a feminist perspective, urgently informed by a belief that, on the one hand, there was no place for women's equality or freedom in a militaristic society and that, on the other, women's insight and experience provided the greatest hope for a world in which the spirit of domination had to be replaced by new values. Although they never forgot the agony of women on all sides of the conflict in wartime, or in periods of severe dislocation, they did not stop with superficial reflections on nurturing qualities and women's capacity for love. Rather, they challenged the premises, methodology, and effectiveness of male statesmanship, and went far towards demonstrating by their example the alternative potential in which they believed. Shortly after the Zurich Congress, Emily Balch, reflecting on "the unanimity that prevailed among the women," wrote:

> It is evident that there was expressed a way of looking at life and its values that is valid and holds its own as truly as the deduction of mathematics, universally, and unaffected by differences of place, politics or any sort of particularism. . . .
>
> It was not only that there was throughout a complete absence of disagreeable "incidents", there was no temptation to oppose the

interests of one country to those of another: the most painful and difficult things could be discussed frankly because there was mutual trust and understanding. . . . Unanimity of purpose and feeling did not imply uniformity of opinion.[37]

Despite the knowledge, experience, and dedication of the feminist internationalists, and the active support of their numerically strong and enduring worldwide organization, they were unable to effect the changes they saw as essential if the world was to be saved from escalating disaster. An early nongovernmental organization in Geneva, with an extremely wide mandate, WILPF was respected and consulted, as were many of the members in their own countries. And yet they were powerless to prevent war.

Should we be looking at what these women did wrong, at what more they might have done to make themselves heard, or should we look at those who refused to listen? The women perhaps made one major error in that they overestimated the goodwill of the men who ruled, their readiness to hear. The women's approach was as conciliatory as they could make it; they wanted to engage in dialogue. They were clear that what they had to say, while not completely new, would yet be radically fresh in international relations, and they believed that it was desperately needed, because they foresaw — what did they foresee? Almost exactly what has now come to pass.

NOTES

1. Virginia Woolf, *Three Guineas* (1938; Harmondsworth: Penguin, 1977), 164. As a feminist historian, I made some use of the first person in the original version of this article, believing this to be consonant with a major theme of the paper, that of the urgent need of early twentieth-century feminists to speak "in a different voice" (see note 29) in metaphor and reality. The quotation used in the title bears on this. I agreed to rewrite or delete the passages where this usage occurred, in deference to the wish of the editors for conformity of style throughout the volume.

2. For discussion of women's role in war, see Jean Bethke Elshtain, "On Beautiful Souls, Just Warriors and Feminist Consciousness," and Nancy Huston, "Tales of War and Tears of Women," both in *Women's Studies International Forum* 5, nos. 3–4 (1982): 341–68, 271–82; Betty A. Reardon, *Sexism and the War System* (New York: Columbia Univ. Teachers College Press, 1985).

3. Marshall, ms. notes for speech to Keswick Liberal Club, 18 Nov. 1909, Catherine E. Marshall papers, Cumbria Record office (hereinafter cited as CEMP). Extensive material in this collection relates. I wish to acknowledge with appreciation the use of materials in this and a number of other collections, including the Fawcett Collection, City of London Polytechnic; papers of the Women's International League for Peace and Freedom at the University of Colorado, Swarthmore College Peace Collection, and the British Library of Political and Economic Science; Bertrand Russell Archives, McMaster University; private papers of Mrs. Barbara Halpern; private papers of Mr. Frank Marshall. For the Mills, see J. S. Mill and Harriet Taylor Mill, *Essays on Sex Equality,* edited and with an introduction by Alice S. Rossi (Chicago: Univ. of Chicago Press, 1970).

4. For a discussion of this, see Jo Vellacott, "Historical Reflections on Votes, Brooms and Guns. Admission to Political Structures—On Whose Terms?" *Atlantis* 12, no. 2 (Spring 1987): 36–39.

5. Barbara Taylor, *Eve and the New Jerusalem: Socialism and Feminism in the Nineteenth Century* (London: Virago, 1983); Jane Rendall, *The Origins of Modern Feminism: Women in Britain, France and the United States, 1760–1860* (London: Macmillan, 1985).

6. Jill Liddington, *The Life and Times of a Respectable Radical: Selina Cooper, 1864–1946* (London: Virago, 1984); Naomi Black, "The Mothers' International: The Women's Cooperative Guild and Feminist Pacifism," *Women's Studies International Forum* 7, no. 6 (1984): 467–76.

7. Sheila Rowbotham, *Friends of Alice Wheeldon* (London: Pluto Press, 1986), and see note 5.

8. Recent important work on the NUWSS includes Leslie Parker Hume, *The National Union of Women's Suffrage Societies, 1897–1914* (New York: Garland, 1982); Sandra Stanley Holton, *Feminism and Democracy: Women's Suffrage and Reform Politics in Britain, 1900–1918* (Cambridge: Cambridge Univ. Press, 1986); Les Garner, *Stepping Stones to Women's Liberty* (London: Heinemann, 1983); Jill Liddington and Jill Norris, *One Hand Tied Behind Us* (London: Virago, 1978). For the WSPU see Roger Fulford, *Votes for Women* (London: White Lion, 1957); Andrew Rosen, *Rise Up, Women!* (London: Routledge and Kegan Paul, 1974).

9. See Naomi Black, comment on Jo Vellacott, "Feminist Consciousness and the First World War," in Ruth Roach Pierson, ed., *Women and Peace: Theoretical, Historical, and Practical Perspectives* (London: Croom Helm, 1987), and also a revised version of the same article in *History Workshop Journal* 23 (Spring 1987).

10. Emphasis Marshall's. Ms. notes for interview with Sir Edward Grey, 15 Dec. 1913, in CEMP.

11. Sandi Cooper, "Women's Participation in European Peace Movements: the Struggle to Prevent World War I," in Pierson is of great interest

on the prewar period. See also Mary Sargant Florence, Catherine Marshall, and C.K. Ogden, in Margaret Kamester and Jo Vellacott, eds., *Militarism Versus Feminism: Writings on Women and War* (London: Virago, 1987), 5–6.

12. Charles Chatfield, "Concepts of Peace in History," *Peace and Change* 11, no. 2 (1986):13; Jo Vellacott, *Bertrand Russell and the Pacifists in the First World War* (London: Harvester, 1980), 7–27; Irene Cooper Willis, *England's Holy War: A Study of English Liberal Idealism during the Great War* (New York: Knopf, 1928; reprint, New York: Garland, 1972).

13. Rowbotham, passim.

14. Sylvia Pankhurst, *The Home Front* (London: Hutchinson [1932]); also *The Women's Dreadnought,* which S.P. edited. She formed and headed the East London Federation of Suffragettes.

15. Despard was ousted from the WSPU in 1907. Andro Linklater, *An Unhusbanded Life: Charlotte Despard, Suffragette, Socialist and Sinn Feiner* (London: Hutchinson, 1980).

16. Ibid., 177.

17. Kamester and Vellacott, 30–33, 127–30.

18. Quoted, ibid., 32.

19. Jo Vellacott Newberry, "Antiwar Suffragists," *History* [journal of The Historical Association, London] 62, no. 206 (Oct. 1977): 417; extensive material Aug.–Dec. 1914 in CEMP.

20. Margaret Kamester, "The Secondary Feminist Interests of the WSPU and NUWSS," unpublished (1982).

21. Ray Strachey, *Millicent Garrett Fawcett* (London: John Murray, 1931), 273–301.

22. H. M. Swanwick, "The Implications of the Women's Suffrage Movement — A Reply," *Englishwoman* 26 (May 1915): 176–77.

23. "Notes for Speeches. Cambridge, 3 November," (actually probably 5 Nov. 1914), ms. in CEMP.

24. Vellacott Newberry, "Antiwar Suffragists," 418, for more detail on Marshall's resignation and for a fuller account of the controversy.

25. "Forty Years Ago" [approx. 1955], ms. draft seen by courtesy of F. Marshall.

26. Gertrude Bussey and Margaret Tims, *Women's International League for Peace and Freedom* (London: Allen and Unwin, 1965) ch. 1; Emily G. Balch and Alice Hamilton, *Women at the Hague* (New York: Macmillan, 1915; reprint, New York: Garland, 1972); Mercedes Randall, *Improper Bostonian: Emily Greene Balch* (New York: Twayne, 1964), ch. 6; Lela B. Costin, "Feminism, Pacifism, Internationalism and the 1915 International Congress of Women," *Women's Studies International Forum* 5, nos. 3–4 (1982): 301–15; Anne Wiltsher, *Most Dangerous Women: Feminist Peace Campaigners of the Great War* (London: Pandora Press, 1985), chs. 1–6.

27. International Congress of Women, The Hague, April 1915: "Final programme," 1, WILPF papers, University of Colorado.

28. Bussey and Tims; Addams, Balch and Hamilton; Randall; Vellacott, "Anti-war Suffragists"; Wiltsher.

29. I am indebted for the term and the concept to Carol Gilligan, *In a Different Voice* (Cambridge: Harvard Univ. Press, 1982).

30. Jill Liddington, "The Women's Peace Crusade: The History of a Forgotten Campaign," in Dorothy Thompson, ed., *Over Our Dead Bodies: Women Against the Bomb* (London: Virago, 1983), 193; Randall, 261–70; Wiltsher, 200–11.

31. Randall, 262.

32. *Report on International Congress of Women* (Zurich: Women's International League for Peace and Freedom, 1919), 242–43, quoted in ibid., 267–68.

33. Ibid., 270.

34. Ibid., 297.

35. Marshall, "The Future of Women in Politics," in Kamester and Vellacott, 47.

36. Ibid., 51.

37. Randall, 269.

Interwar Europe

ELLY HERMON

The International Peace Education Movement, 1919–1939

> "The day when children will be taught to search for what is uniting people rather than for what is dividing them, that day we will not need to measure security anymore, peace will prevail among the nations."
>
> — Aristide Briand*

THE NOTION OF ORIENTING THE public to peace through formal education is a modern concept, although it evolved over some four hundred years.[1] Peace education became a truly international movement following World War I and, in the process, it left its prewar organizational base in pacifist societies. After an initial experiment with leadership from nongovernmental organizations, it was sponsored by the League of Nations. Concurrently, the original pacifist thrust of peace education was supplanted by an emphasis on international understanding which, however, was largely devoid of political content. In the thirties the nongovernmental sector asserted itself increasingly as the League's authority declined and political issues became of primary concern, first in the form of human rights and then in response to the international crisis. Shifts in the organization, constituency, and orientation of peace education in the interwar years took place in relation to changes in international organization and politics.

During the nineteenth century, educational programs were associated with evolving peace societies in many countries and with the emerging international pacifist movement. By the beginning of the twentieth century, the main focus of peace education was already

---

*Address at the League of Nations' General Assembly, 5 Sept. 1929, cited by Jacques Chabannes, *Aristide Briand* (Paris: Librairie Académique Perrein, 1973), 264 (author's translation).

well established as the revision of curricula and school textbooks in the interest of international understanding. It was assumed that education was a long-range strategy, challenging the acceptance of war and building attitudes for peace. This goal enlisted people from different social and professional groups, such as teachers' associations, student and youth organizations, women's groups, and religious bodies.[2] From various quarters came suggestions that an international center should be established to coordinate educational activities.[3] However, peace education activities were undertaken mostly by local and national peace organizations.[4] Thus, the dominating features of the prewar peace education movement were its close association with the peace movement and the absence of autonomous coordination centers, particularly on the international level.

This state of affairs changed radically after World War I with the establishment of autonomous coordinating centers, which gave a considerable impetus to the international development of peace education.

The first coordinating center to emerge after the First World War was the Union of International Associations (UIA). It had been founded in Brussels in 1910 by Paul Otlet and Henri La Fontaine to coordinate international nongovernmental organizations (NGOs) and to enable them to operate as a significant factor in international affairs. In the euphoria of rising expectations for the new international order following the war, the founders of the UIA attempted to ensure for their organization a leading role in the promotion of intellectual cooperation and international education.[5] Indeed, given the reluctance of the founders of the League of Nations to involve it in these areas, the UIA seemed to be a natural candidate for the role of coordinator. In their tireless promotion of international intellectual cooperation, Otlet and La Fontaine also pushed ahead their grandiose project of establishing an international university which would be based on cooperation between governments, international NGOs, and the League of Nations, and dedicated to the development of international understanding. The project gained the moral support of the League of Nations and a number of governments but failed due to lack of financial backing.[6]

For a short while it seemed that the nongovernmental sector would substitute for the intergovernmental one as the key actor coordinating and promoting the fields of international intellectual cooperation and education for international understanding, areas where national authorities were particularly sensitive to external influence. However, after some hesitation and under the combined pressure of some governments and of NGOs such as the International Federation of the League of Nations Societies and the American School Citizenship League, which strongly advocated international coordination of peace education, the League of Nations assumed leadership in this area.[7] The decision came in 1925 with a League General Assembly resolution inviting the League-sponsored International Committee on Intellectual Cooperation to establish a subcommittee of experts in order "to consider the best methods of coordinating all official and non-official efforts designed to familiarize young people throughout the world with the principles and work of the League of Nations and to train the younger generation to regard international co-operation as the normal method of conducting world affairs."[8] This step was of crucial importance as it reflected the convergence of the three main sectors of modern international life — the nongovernmental, the governmental, and the intergovernmental — in the emerging international peace education movement, previously confined to the nongovernmental sector.

A remarkable manifestation of the collaboration between these various sectors was the international conference, "Peace by the School." Held in 1927 in Prague under the auspices of the Czechoslovakian government, it assembled delegates of numerous national and international education societies, peace organizations, and League of Nations agencies.[9] The conference convened at the initiative of the International Bureau of Education which, since its foundation in 1926 in Geneva, played a very active role in the promotion of peace education, organizing international conferences and summer schools for educators interested in peace education and providing information about progress in the field in different countries.[10] The Bureau was instrumental in the promotion of school textbook revision and the reform of history teaching in the interest of peace. It can be considered as a coordination center of the interwar peace education movement, although after 1929, when its status changed from nongovernmental to intergovernmental, the international coordination of peace education received a lower priority.

PEACE EDUCATION AS MORAL DISARMAMENT

The term "moral disarmament" was widely used in the sense of a comprehensive program with a view to promoting peace and international understanding in the context of both formal education and information only in connection with and following the Disarmament Conference of 1932. However, it had been employed long before by people from different professional and ideological quarters and different perspectives. Accordingly, there was no unanimity concerning the origins of the concept or even its very object and scope, although there was a consensus relating moral disarmament to the elimination of the general psychological causes of war.

The conceptual dichotomy of pacifists and internationalists was particularly obvious in this respect. Whereas some internationalists related moral disarmament to the promotion of international organization and traced the origins of the concept to the League of Nations Covenant or to endeavors such as the 1928 Kellogg-Briand Pact intended to renounce war, others went further back to prewar resolutions of the International Peace Congresses.[11] Even more significant were the differences of views with respect to the definition of the object and scope of moral disarmament: transformation of human behavior or reformation of international organization. A general definition of moral disarmament from a pacifist viewpoint was provided in 1923 by C. E. Playne, Council member of the International Peace Bureau: "Moral disarmament is the transformation of the aggressive, vindictive and revengeful mentality into a conciliatory mentality. . . . , the sacrifice of national interests in favour of interests not less real of the large human family, . . . altruism substituted for egoism . . . , reason and equity applied instead of passion and injustice."[12] This approach implied the use of propagandistic methods and, indeed, Playne called for a worldwide campaign to change the value system of society.[13] The internationalist approach to moral disarmament was clearly expressed in Théodore Ruyssen's report to the Universal Peace Congress in Berlin (1924). Although he considered the pacifist approach sentimental and unrealistic, Ruyssen said that moral disarmament was a prerequisite to military disarmament. He outlined a comprehensive program of education for international understanding, including history teaching and textbook revision, the creation of an independent and impartial press agency, and elimination of warlike imagery from the media. Such a program could be successful, he said, only with the establishment of an international security system under a supranational authority.[14] Peace education thus was identified with internationalism.[15]

By the mid-twenties moral disarmament had some popular following, notably in feminist and educational circles. Thus, the International League of Moral Disarmament by Women was founded in France in 1925.[16] In the same year the issue was raised unsuccessfully at the League of Nations General Assembly. In a debate about convening a disarmament conference, the Australian delegate connected moral to military disarmament in general terms.[17] A Haitian draft resolution called for history textbook revision "with a view to moral disarmament" by reducing "the number of pages devoted to military events and especially those in which wars of conquest are justified and held up for admiration."[18] Even some high-ranking military officials became interested. In 1925 the German general von Deimberg observed that "the best defense of the Rhine" was "suppression of hatred and Franco-German rapprochement," and the French general A. Percin published *Moral Disarmament,* urging that the glorification of war should be suppressed and the teaching of peace efforts at school encouraged.[19] Indeed, in 1932 the French Ministry of Education claimed that without legislative pressure "to free State education from the usual chauvinistic character, a co-ordinated move on the part of the teachers has sufficed to remove throughout the French Republic those manuals and textbooks on all subjects that display aggressive feelings toward other people."[20]

Only with the 1932 Disarmament Conference did moral disarmament achieve recognition in the international community. In the previous year the Polish government submitted a proposal for an international convention.[21] This led to the establishment of a Moral Disarmament Committee in the Conference in order to frame an international convention on peace education and information so that international understanding would complement arms control. Conflicting national policies threatened the committee as they disrupted the Conference. The division between winners and losers in World War I was a serious obstacle. While winners such as Poland and France viewed peace education as an instrument for the respect of the status quo, losers such as Germany and Hungary regarded it with suspicion.[22]

Also divisive was the diversity of political systems represented in the committee. Countries with authoritarian political regimes or with centralized school systems favored tight control of education and the mass media, whereas liberal governments and those with decentralized school systems preferred voluntary programs for peace and international understanding. Accordingly, the Polish draft of a convention was revised to eliminate recommended censorship and repressive measures. Particularly effective in this regard was James T. Shotwell, president of the American National Committee on Intellectual Cooperation. Shotwell had campaigned hard in the United States on behalf of moral disarmament, and he reported that it had been endorsed by even the Department of Superintendents of Education, then the most important governing body in the American educational system and one which he described as a "very reactionary body, nationalist to the core."[23] Shotwell proposed an alternative draft of the convention which respected the Anglo-Saxon tradition of freedom of expression and autonomy of the school system, arguing that otherwise the convention would not receive American support.[24] His effort contributed considerably to the committee's consensus that voluntary measures should be considered as a minimum basis for a convention. Shotwell was, however, in favor of some positive measures to be taken by all governments. Accordingly, his draft convention included a special article under which examinations in subjects related to peaceful resolution of international conflicts were to be required from governmental officials, considering that "it should be as important to have the strategy of peace in the mind of our government officials as the strategy of war."[25] Under a compromise agreement, states were to promote moral disarmament with all means in their power, but only under their respective laws which implied greater responsibility for the more centralized governments.[26] The compromise did not lead to the expected convention, however, because of the failure of the Disarmament Conference. Nonetheless, the moral disarmament negotiations which took place in this context are historically significant for officially linking arms control to peace education, which consequently gained, if not a basis in international law, at least international respectability.

A central aspect of moral disarmament was the use of the press in the interest of peace and international understanding. This proved to be an even more serious challenge than formal education, although its importance was acknowledged by governments, the League of Nations, NGOs and individual press professionals. Cooperation among these sectors led to a series of consultations, such as the conference of press experts convened by the League in 1927, conferences of governmental press offices in Copenhagen (1932) and Madrid (1933), and to an international organization of press editors and directors.[27] Although these efforts encouraged cooperation among governmental press offices and information offices, they did not produce the expected international convention.

Multilateral efforts were complemented by some bilateral agreements. A convention concluded between Poland and Nazi Germany in 1934 by which each nation agreed to create "a climate favoring understanding between the two countries deserves special mention."[28] Clearly, this agreement had no force. Even so, it suggests that nations which are radically opposed may find moral disarmament useful as an instrument with which to reduce tension or as a test case with which to assess real intentions. This was probably the view of the Polish government, and it was expressed by Shotwell, who commented shortly after the Nazi seizure of power: "the proposal for moral disarmament seems now very useful in the light of Nazi conquest of Germany."[29]

The short-term results of interwar moral disarmament efforts were modest. However, they established precedents that subsequently would be recognized in the United Nations Universal Declaration of Human Rights (1948) and in Article 20 of the International Covenant on Civil and Political Rights (1966), under which states are required to pass laws prohibiting "propaganda for war" and "any advocacy of national, racial or religious hatred that constitutes incitement to discrimination, hostility or violence."[30]

THE LEAGUE OF NATIONS AND PEACE EDUCATION

Following World War I, the internationalist education inspired by the League of Nations' conceptions of peace and security became the mainstream of peace education. To be sure, there were various important movements in educational reform which acquired an international dimension, notably those of the New Education and of Maria Montessori.[31] However, private initiatives were constrained by comparison with those supported by international agencies and some governments. NGOs remained the most dynamic sources of initiative in this area, but even they were influenced by their relationship to intergovernmental organizations.

Nineteen twenty-five marked a turning point in the League of Nations' policy regarding education for peace and international understanding. The League acquired the instruments of leadership by setting up the International Institute of Intellectual Cooperation (IIIC) as the executive organ of the International Committee on Intellectual Cooperation (ICIC), which established a subcommittee of experts to deal with the international coordination of peace education endeavors.[32]

The IIIC was keenly interested in developing closer cooperation between NGOs and the League. By the end of 1925 it had helped to set up a Coordinating (subsequently Joint) Committee of the Major International Associations (CC) interested in peace education which would fill the vacuum left by the lack of UAI leadership and serve as an international liaison between the League and NGOs interested in peace education.[33] The dependence of the CC on a League of Nations agency (the IIIC provided the CC with office space and secretarial aid) underlined the coordinating role of the international body.

For a time, the League's central position in peace education had a decisive impact not only on organizational patterns but also on conceptual approaches. A greater emphasis came to be placed on the short-term political implications — conventions and the like — which even attracted limited cooperation from national and international agencies. Among these, the Casarès procedure for revising school textbooks, adopted by the League in 1926, was the first and perhaps best-known initiative, although it had only meager results.[34] More successful were regional efforts on both nongovernmental and intergovernmental levels. These produced some significant results, such as the multilateral convention adopted by the Inter-American Conference for Maintenance of Peace (Buenos Aires, 1936) which, besides school textbook revision, provided that the signatory powers would teach the principles of peaceful resolution of international conflicts in their respective schools.[35]

As the League's approach to peace education became predominant, the absolute pacifist approach was rejected to the extent that it was opposed to any use of military force in international affairs. The League, recognizing the right of legitimate self-defense and advocating international sanctions, could not approve of the application of the principle of nonviolence in all circumstances. Consequently, pacifism was discarded and NGOs committed to it were relegated to the margins of the movement.[36] The CC not only refused to admit organizations whose commitment was considered too radical but also disapproved of the use of the term "pacifism" in its declaration of principles, as some of its founding members had suggested.[37] The mainstream of international peace education thus became linked with the internationalist rather than with the pacifist movement. It was committed to the League of Nations' ideals and aimed at propagating teaching about the League and the idea of international cooperation as being precisely the objectives of peace education.

On the other hand, the movement should not be identified indiscriminately with the League. The League of Nations societies are a case in point. Active in numerous countries, they not only promoted the League but also inspired peace education. The International Federation of the League of Nations Societies was represented in the CC but by no means dominated it. Although closely related, the League of Nations movement and the international peace education movement were distinct, and this is particularly relevant on the organizational level. There even NGOs which appreciated League ideals sought to safeguard their autonomy. League officials were not always sensitive to that concern. Even the ICIC Sub-Committee of Experts for the Instruction of Youth in the Aims of the League of Nations, the League's own policy-making organ in peace education, was irritated by certain initiatives of the CC which it regarded as interference. The subcommittee preferred to confine the CC to the role of a technical consultant for strictly pedagogical matters, and until the early thirties the CC had to comply with this view of its role.[38]

THE GROWING ASSERTIVENESS OF THE NGOS COORDINATING COMMITTEE

From the early thirties, however, recurring international crises revealed the League's impotence in matters of international security and resulted in a sharp decline of its prestige. Consequently, the League became increasingly dependent on the support of NGOs in its endeavor to reverse the tide of public discontent. The CC thus was able to assert itself more easily. From 1931 it was given a voice in formulating policies of the League's specialized organs charged with coordinating peace education efforts. It was represented at their meetings and, generally speaking, its position became comparable with the formal consultative status granted by the United Nations to select NGOs and, more particularly, their coordinating committees. Accordingly, the role of the CC was reconsidered by the ICIC. No longer was it regarded merely as a technical consultant; rather it officially had the responsibility for coordinating NGO activities in peace education with those of the League's specialized agencies.[39]

Although this shift was intended to strengthen the links between the NGO community and the League, the CC managed to gain some political autonomy. Indeed, in some circumstances, the CC asserted, as it had not done before, views which did not reflect the League's political options. Most of the NGO delegates at the CC no longer accepted the view held by influential League officials, that the interests of peace education were to be subordinated to political considerations when they were in open conflict.

The new assertiveness of the CC was perhaps best illustrated by its stand on Nazi racist policy. The CC generally did not interfere with national authorities in the field of education and tried to avoid anything which could be construed as propaganda. However, after the Nazis came to power in Germany, propaganda hostile to the very spirit of peace education became intolerable. The CC could not refrain from taking a stand against it, despite the disavowal of League officials still hopeful of using intellectual cooperation to preserve ties with Germany after its resignation from the League.[40] Subsequently, the CC became more outspoken against propaganda and national policies incompatible with peace education goals. The stand taken by the CC in regard to Nazi racist policy highlighted a conceptual evolution in the definition of peace education to include, in addition to the promotion of international understanding and cooperation, the respect of human rights.

Despite its growing assertiveness in regard to its ideological commitment, the CC did not give up its traditional principle of neutrality. Organizations whose political commitment seemed to be incompatible with this guiding principle still were not admitted to the Committee, although it became more liberal in this respect. This was not merely a matter of conservatism, since the CC always had considered political neutrality to be a prerequisite of its universality. Organizations from different social, cultural, and religious backgrounds were welcomed provided that they did not engage in political activity which could prevent the Committee from presenting a united front of international NGOs. Even so, the CC was heterogeneous enough to accommodate considerable conceptual diversity. The very heated debate over the stand to be taken on racist propaganda in the education system was but one manifestation of this diversity.[41] Debate over the relative priority of international cooperation and the defense of human rights was another.[42] Still other emphases in the CC were intercultural, social, and economic issues, such as East-West understanding, youth unemployment, and the social repercussions of the world economic crisis. Admittedly, these concerns had less priority then than now, but their very articulation in the thirties links the interwar peace education movement to its multidimensional successor.[43]

PEACE EDUCATION AND THE POLITICAL CONTEXT

Thus, with the changing circumstances, the peace education movement reorganized, gained a measure of independence, and adapted to new threats of conflict. Whereas in the twenties, it had been dominated by its connection with the League, in the thirties the Coordination Committee represented a more autonomous NGO community. Whereas earlier it had focused attention on the formal education system, attempting to revise school programs and textbooks in the interest of better international understanding, its thrust shifted to informal education and public opinion. As the propaganda of repressive regimes intensified, the international peace education movement increasingly responded with propaganda of its own, legitimizing activities which previously had been considered incompatible with the political neutrality required in formal education. Even within the CC, previously so scrupulous in this respect, there was strong pressure in favor of propaganda for peace in the schools.[44] The failure of disarmament and international conciliation incited even the moderate advocates of peace education to become more militant in their attempt to influence public opinion.

The rapid deterioration of international relations thus led to a significant shift not only in peace education methods but in its contents and priorities as well. When it became evident that the League was doomed, the movement distinguished between the political institution which remained to be reformed and the ideals of permanent value for which it had stood.[45] Education of public opinion in international affairs and advocacy of collective security based on the

League's principles became the first priority of peace education when faced with the unscrupulous use of military force by ultranationalist and aggressive regimes. By the end of the decade it had become difficult to distinguish between peace education and peace propaganda.[46]

The most remarkable manifestation of this development was the International Peace Campaign (IPC), launched in the mid-thirties by Lord Robert Cecil, a resolute League supporter. The IPC organized huge congresses which drew numerous participants from all parts of the world, represented various NGOs, and included intellectual and political leaders. These gatherings were instrumental in mobilizing public opinion. They created a vast network of organizations (about fifty international NGOs in 1939, according to the organizers) and individuals, and these were federated in a worldwide movement with over forty national committees.[47] They formed special study groups and educational commissions which extended their activities to all sectors of society. In some countries, such as France, Britain, and the United States, the IPC drew support from government circles.[48]

In addition to information and the general education of public opinion on international affairs, the IPC emphasized propaganda. Accordingly, it strongly denounced violations of international law and aggression, as in the bombardment of civil populations in China and Spain, and sought help for the victims. For the promoters of the IPC, the distinction between education and propaganda was obsolete.[49] The movement thus accelerated the emphasis on nonformal peace education, which had been growing in the CC since the early thirties. Whereas the CC never departed formally from its traditional principle of political neutrality, the coordinators of the IPC regarded strict neutralism as a futile exercise. They did not care about the political background of NGOs: all of them — trade unions and left-wing groups included — were invited to join the peace campaign, provided only that their political commitments did not interfere with the objects of the coalition. As the movement became increasingly committed to the principle of military sanctions against aggressors, it was repudiated, however, by absolute pacifists, including some of its own founders.[50]

Robert Cecil's leadership symbolized the conceptual coherence of the international peace education movement which was related to the League of Nations and also the convergence of the main sectors of international life in this movement. Cecil had served in each sector: as a Cabinet member, as a delegate of his government to the League of Nations, as president of the British League of Nations Union, which made a significant contribution to the promotion of both formal and informal peace education in Britain, and, finally, as president of the IPC, which extended education to political action.[51] In his various assignments, Cecil demonstrated, within the limits of the political constraints of his official position, his commitment to international peace and security and his conviction that the education of public opinion was instrumental for its achievement.

With the emergence of the IPC, the evolution of the interwar peace education movement was completed on both conceptual and organizational levels. In the last stage of its development, this movement went far beyond its prewar predecessors. It was structured in relation to the new forms of international organization, and it reached out for world public opinion, urging emergency measures for the immediate crisis without neglecting long-term educational goals related to deeply rooted causes of conflict. This combination of short- and long-range objectives with a particular concern for international organization according to agreed principles of international law characterized the maturation of a worldwide peace education movement organized on the basis of cooperation among the governmental, intergovernmental, and nongovernmental sectors of international life.

NOTES

Research for this study of international peace education in the interwar period was conducted with assistance from the Social Sciences and Humanities Research Council of Canada.

1. Thomas Renna, "Peace Education: An Historical Overview," *Peace and Change* 6, nos. 1–2 (1980): 61.

2. Clinton Fink, "Peace Education and the Peace Movement Since 1815," *Peace and Change* 6, nos. 1–2 (1980): 67–69.

3. Pedro Rosello, *Les précurseurs du Bureau international d'Éducation* (Geneva: International Bureau of Education, 1943).

4. Spencer Stocker, *The Schools and International Understanding* (Chapel Hill: The University of North Carolina Press, 1933), xxvi.

5. Elly Hermon, "Regards sur les ONG dans le mouvement international de co-opération intellectuelle et d'éducation pour la paix pendant l'entre-deux-guerres: Le cas de l'Union des Associations Internationales," *Canadian Journal of History* 20, no. 3 (1985): 337–67.

6. Ibid., 347–49.

7. Archives of the League of Nations, United Nations Library, Geneva (hereinafter LON), A.10(a), 1925, XIIA, 25 Aug. 1925, Part III. See also Hermon, "Regards sur les ONG", 338–41, and Pierre Bovet, "L'idée d'un Bureau International d'Éducation," *Christianisme Social,* (April–May 1928).

8. LON, A.107(a), 1925 XIIA, 22 Sept. 1925.

9. Pierre Bovet, ed., *La paix par l'école* (Geneva: International Bureau of Education; Prague: Société Pédagogique Comenius, 1927).

10. Pierre Bovet, *La réforme morale de l'enseignement de l'histoire conçu dans un esprit international* (Geneva: International Bureau of Education, 1927); Bovet, *L'institut Jean-Jacques Rousseau de 1912 à 1932* (Neufchâtel: Niestlé; Paris: Delchaux, 1932), 171–77; Marie Butts, "L'activité du Bureau International d'Éducation," *Christianisme Social* (April–May, 1928).

11. Julien Luchaire, *Le désarmement moral* (Paris: Valois, 1932), 101, 84; Stanislas Stronski, "Le désarmement moral," *Recueil pédagogique* (Sept. 1932), 17; Ernest Bovet, "Le désarmement moral," *Völkerbund* (3 Aug. 1932), 9.

12. Author's translation, "Le désarmement moral," *Le Mouvement Pacifiste* (July 1923), 81.

13. Ibid., 83.

14. "Le désarmement moral," *La Paix par le Droit* (Sept. 1924), 326–31. Ruyssen became Secretary-General of the International Federation of the League of Nations Societies.

15. Alfred Zimmern, "Le désarmement moral," *Völkerbund* 15 (Apr. 1932), 3; Luchaire, *Le désarmement moral,* 174–75.

16. Regarding this organization, see *Bulletin de la Ligue Internationale du Désarmement Moral par les Femmes* (Dec. 1925).

17. Général [Alexandre] Percin, *Le désarmement moral,* 2nd ed. (Orléans: n.p., 1934), 12.

18. LON, A.107, 1925; XII A, 22 Sept. 1925.

19. Percin, *Le désarmement moral,* 81, 30.

20. Otto-Ernest Schüddekopf et al., *History Teaching and History Textbook Revision* (Strasbourg: Council of Cultural Co-operation of the Council of Europe, 1967), 20. Regarding educational reform see also International Institute of Intellectual Cooperation, *School Textbook Revision and International Understanding* (Paris: International Institute of Intellectual Cooperation, 1933), and Jean-Louis Claparède, *L'enseignement de l'histoire et de l'esprit international* (Paris: Les Presses Universitaires, 1931).

21. LON, Conf. D. 16, 23 Sept. 1931.

22. Oscar Halecki, "La Pologne et le désarmement moral," *Le désarmement et l'opinion internationale,* vol. 2 (Paris: The European Center of the Carnegie Endowment for International Peace, 1932), 405–24; "France and Moral Disarmament," *Educational Survey* 4 (1933): 109–15; Otto Hoetzch,

"Considérations sur le désarmement moral envisagé du point de vue allemand," *Recueil Pédagogique* 3 (1932): 33–40; Albert Apponyi, "Point de vue hongrois concernant le désarmement moral," ibid., 29–32, and note of René Cassin (French delegate to the Moral Disarmament Committee), 19 Jan. 1934, Archives of the French Foreign Ministry, Paris (hereinafter FFM), Series: SdN, vol. 902, 54–57.

23. Shotwell to Montenach (Secretary-General of the ICIC), 18 May 1933, LON, 7 A/652/652.

24. Shotwell to Montenach, 4 Nov.; 27 Dec., 1932, Archives of the IIIC, UNESCO, Paris (hereinafter IIIC), B.V. 9; LON, 7 A/652/652.

25. Shotwell to Bonnet, 23 Sept. 1932, IIIC, B.V. 9.

26. Montenach to Bonnet (Director of the IIIC), 18 Jan. 1932; Shotwell to Montenach, 26 Jan. 1933; Montenach to Shotwell, 20 June 1933, in LON, 7 A/652/652; Montenach to Bonnet, 2 June 1933, and annexes in IIIC, B.V. 9; LON, Documents of the Moral Disarmament Committee (hereinafter CMD), CMD 26, 29 May 1933; and CMD 36, 17 Nov. 1933.

27. "The Role of the Press in Moral Disarmament," note prepared by the League of Nations Information Section, Dec. 1933, LON, 7 A/80131/652.

28. François Poncet (French ambassador in Berlin) to the Quai d'Orsay, 26 Feb. 1934, FFM, Series SdN, Vol. 902, pp. 70–71.

29. Shotwell to Bonnet, 13 May 1933, IIIC, B.V. 9.

30. For the full text of Article 20 and details regarding its adoption, see United Nations General Assembly Official Records, Sixteenth Session, Third Committee, 93–124, and "Report of the Third Committee," General Assembly Official Records, Sixteenth Session, Annexes, Agenda, Item 35, 6–8.

31. A. Ehm, *L'éducation nouvelle, ses principes, son évolution historique, son expansion mondiale* (Paris, 1938), and Maria Montessori, *La paix et l'éducation* (Rome: Opera Montessori, 1949).

32. For a summary of its activities, see Institut International de Coopération Intellectuelle, *L'Institut International de Coopération Intellectuelle, 1919–1946* (Paris: Institut International de Coopération Intellectuelle, 1947).

33. Danicl Alfred Prescott, *Education and International Relations* (Cambridge: Harvard Univ. Press, 1930), 117–19.

34. *L'Institut International* (op. cit.), 174; UNESCO, *A Handbook for the Improvement of Textbooks and Teaching Materials as Aids to International Understanding* (Paris: UNESCO, 1949), 16–20.

35. UNESCO, *A Handbook* (op. cit.), chs. iv, ix.

36. The term "absolute pacifism" is employed here in the sense of A. C. F. Beales, who used "pacifism" to refer to "the radical rejection of organized war altogether, from whatever premises." Charles Chatfield, introduction to Beales, *The History of Peace* (1931; New York: Garland, 1971), 7.

37. LON, Documents of the Coordinating Committee of the Major International Associations (hereinafter CE), P.V. 3, 1926.

38. Note of Hallsten-Kallia, 2 Mar. 1933, LON, 5C/1175/699.

39. Montenach to Waltz, 19 Oct. 1934, LON, 5C/1175/699.

40. Montenach to Murray, 24 Oct. 1933, LON, 5C/6812/319; Montenach to Pilotti, 24 Oct. 1933, LON, 5C/1175/699.

41. Report of Hallsten-Kallia, 21 Nov. 1933, LON, 5C/1175/699.

42. CE, P.V. 40, 4–5 July 1938; CE 328, 28 Jan. 1939, LON, SC/1175/699. Regarding the conceptual diversity within the interwar peace education movement, see Hermon, "Approches conceptuelles de l'éducation en vue de la compréhension internationale dans l'entre-deux-guerres," *Canadian and International Education* 15, no. 2 (1986): 29–52.

43. Regarding the multidimensional character of the present-day peace education movement, see the special issue on peace education, *Gandhi Marg* (July–Aug. 1984), and Hermon, "Conceptual Approaches to Peace Education: Challenges and Pitfalls," in Paris Arnopoulos, ed., *Prospects for Peace* (Montreal: Gamma Institute Press, 1986), 69–74.

44. Report of Hallsten-Kallia on the CC meeting of 19 Nov. 1931, CE 97, 15 June 1932, LON, 5C/583/300.

45. Speech of Eugène Beaupin, President of the CC, at the CC meeting of 6–7 July 1936, LON, 5C/1175/699.

46. Numerous advocates of peace-oriented education in the school systems were, however, particularly sensitive to allegations identifying education with propaganda, and they argued that peace-oriented education was perfectly compatible with the scientific spirit. Hermon, "Éducation et vérité: Aspects de la réforme de l'enseignement de l'histoire pendant l'entre-deux-guerres," *Historical Reflections* 10, no. 2 (1983): 295–312, and "Approches conceptuelles."

47. International Peace Campaign, *The Growth and Importance of the International Peace Campaign* (London: International Peace Campaign, [1939]), i, ii.

48. Ibid., 1.

49. In a survey of its development, the IPC defined its activities as "peace education and propaganda." The subtitle of the survey emphasized the educational character of its program: "A survey of the activities of the Movement which has for the first time organized a system of education in international affairs among the ordinary people of forty countries as a constructive step towards world peace," ibid.

50. Louis Launey, ed., *Le pacifisme intégral et le Rassemblement Universel pour la Paix* (Paris: La Rafale, 1936).

51. Donald S. Birn, *The League of Nations Union, 1918–1945* (Oxford: Clarendon Press, 1971).

NORMAN INGRAM

Romain Rolland, Interwar Pacifism and the Problem of Peace

FAMOUS FOR HIS STUBBORN STAND "au-dessus de la mêlée" against the folly of the First World War, for which he earned nothing but the bitter opprobrium of both his native France and of the Germany he loved, Romain Rolland (1866–1944) had become by 1918 France's most renowned pacifist and the "Conscience of Europe."[1] Winner of the 1915 Nobel Prize in Literature for his ten-volume novel sequence *Jean-Christophe,* Rolland had already completed a good portion of his life's work by 1918. Indeed, in many respects he had become part of the "older" generation before the war began; neither by inclination nor outlook did he belong to the "generation of 1914" described in such fascinating detail by Robert Wohl.[2] Rolland incarnated the "intellectuel engagé" of the 1920s and 1930s long before Sartre ever popularized the phrase. As Wilhelm Herzog wrote in the 1926 special number of *Europe* dedicated to Rolland on the occasion of his sixtieth birthday, he was

> a man who does not simply want to "do" literature. Rather, [he is] a man who wishes to help in bettering this miserable world, to transform its anarchy into an order inspired by reason. . . . Certainly not a marxist. But a man who, nevertheless, adopts the critical conclusions and the categorical imperative of Karl Marx.[3]

Committed to social justice and the principles behind the Russian Revolution, Rolland nevertheless declared in 1927 that "Bolshevism had destroyed [high ideals] by its narrow sectarianism, its inept intransigeance, and its cult of violence. It has engendered fascism which is Bolshevism in reverse."[4] Yet, by the beginning of the thirties and to the surprise of many, Rolland had "sudden[ly] and inexplicabl[y] conver[ted] to the communist cause."[5] As David Caute says, "No other idealist writer leapt as abruptly into the arms of Bolshevism as did Rolland."[6] Clearly, Rolland, too, was susceptible to the "rhetoric of his time." But he was not alone. His remark in the Prologue to *Quinze Ans de Combat* (1935) that "the 'I' of which I recount the evolution is not me: it is the whole age to which we belong" rings very true.[7]

His first postwar fictional hero, Clérambault, in the novel of the same name (1919), became, in Rolland's own words, "the apostle and the martyr of those who refused to bend their spirit to the inevitability of the violence which was being let loose over the whole world. . . . [The novel] became the gospel, the rallying point for all French conscientious objectors who were still rather uncertain about their faith."[8] In response to a critique of his interwar novel sequence, *L'Ame enchantée* [1921-1933], Rolland wrote in 1935 that its theme "is the negation of war," and he went on to say that "this refusal is still, to this very day, the basis of all my social ideas, as well as of those of our Soviet friends."[9]

The fight against war was not an isolated one for Rolland, however. Intimately and irrevocably allied to it was the categorical imperative of social revolution to which Herzog referred. As the interwar period progressed, this second tenet of Rolland's credo assumed increasingly large proportions. But looking back in 1940 on the early thirties, as he wrote his spiritual testament,[10] Rolland insisted on the binary nature of what he called his "extraordinarily perilous task: to lead the opposition to war, which was a fundamental article of my code of social action, and the fight against international oppression."[11] In the crepuscular seclusion of Vézelay, with the dust of the Nazi invaders before him, he could write with some justification, "I have never separated the struggle against capitalist and militarist imperialism from that for the defence of international peace."[12]

It is the purpose of this essay to examine this "perilous task" of Rolland's, to follow the evolution of his political thought on the problems of peace and pacifism, and to see how it was translated into concrete action in his relations with pacifist and war resistance organizations during the interwar years. This evolution was one from individualism to collectivism, from one "above the battle" to one in its very thick, "du Rêve à l'Action." This process can be divided into three distinct periods: the first from the Great War to about 1924, the second from then until the early thirties, and the final period from about 1932 to the outbreak of war in 1939.[13]

THE REJECTION OF VIOLENCE (1914-1924)

Rolland's individualistic position as the defender of civilization and justice dominates the first period. He spent the war years in Switzerland where he happened to be in July 1914, and it was from his Swiss retreat that he issued the periodic articles which earned him the general hatred of all sides in the conflict. The most famous of these was also the first, entitled "*Au-dessus de la mêlée*" (Above the Battle) — a title he was to regret in later life. In it Rolland, the independent man of thought, declared that "for us, the artists and poets, priests and thinkers of all countries, remains another task. Even in time of war, it remains a crime for finer spirits to compromise the integrity of their thought."[14] He laid the blame for the great European bloodletting at the feet of the rulers, and declared that there was no fatality about war: "The only fatality is what we desire; and more often than not, what we do not desire enough."[15]

The war years show us a Rolland who was committed to individualism, independence of thought, and internationalism, and who rejected categorically the war and all forms of historical determinism. In the famous interview with the republican German journalist, Hermann Fernau in July 1918, shortly before the close of the war, Rolland stated:

> I belong to no political party. Before the war I was invited several times to join pacifist organizations. . . . I was unwilling because this official pacifism seemed childish to me, as long as it did not declare itself revolutionary and republican. — By profession an Historian, I am by nature in every sense an independent man of ideas.[16]

Rolland greeted the Russian Revolution gladly as "the first act of that universal liberation of humanity from the tyranny of the past," which was necessary if mankind was "to escape a repetition of the sufferings of the First World War."[17] He was, however, quickly disillusioned by reports of Bolshevik terror and the atrocities committed by both sides in the civil war.[18] But while Rolland may have entertained doubts about the methods used by the Bolsheviks, he did not for one moment question the need to support this great social experiment, which he saw as a unique effort to break away from the bondage of the past. One year previously, he had defined to Marcel Martinet his own, rather different, brand of internationalism as "one of Love and not of Hate. It is doubtless impractical and more religious than realistic. But to each his own role. Mine is necessary, too."[19]

With the cessation of hostilities and the advent of peace negotiations in Paris, Rolland remained "profoundly disturbed"; he thought that it would be the peoples who would continue to suffer, and he feared above all else the hatred which would insinuate itself into the peace treaties and thereby make another future war inevitable.[20] When the Versailles Treaty was finally signed in June of 1919, Rolland's feeling of doom was complete. His prophetic reaction is recorded in his journal: "Sad peace! Ridiculous intermission between two massacres of peoples. But who thinks of tomorrow?"[21]

Rolland faced the dawn of the postwar world with his idealistic faith in liberty, the individual and the free struggle of intellectuals for social justice intact. In the spring of 1919 he issued his famous *Déclaration d'Indépendance de l'Esprit,* which by 1921 had provoked Henri Barbusse to attack Rolland's detachment from the real world of political problems where more was needed than "independence of thought," where the revolution required a commitment to action and, if necessary, to violence.[22] Rolland took issue with the tendency of Barbusse and *Clarté* "to assimilate the enigma of human evolution to a problem in Euclidean geometry."[23] As he wrote retrospectively in 1934, "I could not throw away my gods, those who had enabled me to live — the god Humanity, and the god Liberty, in order to serve only the god Revolution."[24] He defended his right to be within the revolution and yet remain a free man.[25] And he adamantly refused to accept the need for violence. "Our common enemy," he wrote to Barbusse, "is the oppressive violence of human society as it exists at present. But against that violence, you arm an adverse violence. In my view . . . that method only leads to mutual destruction."[26]

The answer lay elsewhere for Rolland, and it is here that the first intimations of the development of his thought on the methods of pacifism in the twenties appear:

> there is another weapon, much more powerful and suited for all,
> to the humblest as well as to the most exalted: it has already
> proved its efficacy amongst other peoples, and it is astonishing
> that no one ever speaks of it in France: it is that employed amongst
> Anglo-Saxons by the thousands of "conscientious objectors", that
> by means of which Gandhi is now undermining the domination of

the British Empire in India—Civil Disobedience. I do not say passive resistance, for make no mistake, it is the supreme resistance.[27]

The question of means and ends, of violence and nonviolence, is essential to an understanding of European pacifism and Rolland's development in it during the interwar years. In this initial period up to 1924, Rolland's rejection of violence was absolute and applied to all parties. As he wrote in the epilogue to Marianne Rauze's book, *L'Antiguerre,* in November 1923, "You perform a high and humane task in trying to group together all those who are opposed to violence, wherever it may come from, whatever it may be."[28] Revealing already the influence of Gandhi, and prefiguring his later concerns about the lack of realism amongst pacifists, Rolland wrote that action must be firmly anchored in faith and in the soul and must be prepared for the ultimate sacrifice. The positive task of those opposing *la patrie* was to offer a new ideal,

and not to shy away from making it burn brightly in the hearts of the men of today, with all the flames of a new faith. . . . Whether the soul exists or not, . . . you will only conquer if you act as if it did exist, as if you were sure of eternity. Because in the fight which is beginning, you are not a majority of numbers or of righteousness against an immoral minority. You are an elite, a moral minority. . . . You mustn't delude yourselves, my friends. A new faith, like that which you represent—human fraternity, the Unity of the living—is never victorious before long trials, sacrifices and martyrdoms.[29]

The summer of 1924 began something of a political *prise de conscience* in Rolland which forced a reexamination, and then a gradual repudiation, of his slide into the *Rêve* of individualist, idealist independence. In *Le Périple,* he wrote that during that summer, "away from Paris, sick, alone, and trying to hide from Action, I took up again the happy chains of a new novel cycle. In order to escape better, I had submerged myself into the life of a woman, *'une Ame enchantée.'"[30] But escape he could not.

In these summer months of 1924, a series of stunning events brought me violently back to reality from my dreams in the shadow of the old walnut at Villeneuve. In Italy on the 10th of

June 1924, Matteotti was assassinated. On the 6th of April 1926, Amendola succumbed after months of suffering brought on by the most cowardly of attacks. These noble men, these pure consciences, both of them enemies of all violence . . . were both friends whom I admired. During all of 1925 I was besieged in my retreat by the cries of anguish of the oppressed of the world.[31]

Recognizing for better or worse that he was the "conscience of Europe," Rolland publicly declared in September 1925 that he was "with all the oppressed, against all of the oppressors,"[32] thus beginning the slow transition in his political thinking which would see his conversion to communism in the early 1930s. From 1924 until then, however, he became increasingly involved in the struggle for peace *and* social justice which he believed inseparable. Nineteen twenty-four marks the beginning of the end of his cherished "independence of thought" upon which the demands of action were beginning to impinge. As he wrote,

> once entered into these seven circles of sorrows, it was no longer possible for me to disengage myself. . . . The more I attached a price to the maintenance of my independence, the more the parties at battle attached a price to conquering it, or if they could not do that, to exploiting it, in availing themselves of my name as of a palladium of moral conscience.[33]

The Struggle for Peace and Social Justice (1924–1932)

For Rolland, the period from 1924 to the beginning of the thirties was a time of searching, during which he attempted to rationalize his intellectual position in politics. And, as he later wrote, "the great influence which dominated my spirit in those years was that of Gandhi."[34] *Action*, consistent with his idealistic beliefs and nonviolent disposition, became the key goal. And, as Rolland was wont to say, there could be no more heroic action than that of nonviolent resistance.

> I could never tolerate that Gandhi's thought should be confused with that of an enervated pacifism which bends its back and acquiesces bleatingly. I have always insisted on the "fighting character," the word "sword" which Gandhi repeats constantly — opposing it to the steel sword, blade against blade to characterize the

heroic weapon of self-sacrifice, individual and collective, in the cause of the Truth.[35]

William Thomas Starr writes that "Rolland brought to the [peace] movement two concepts: the army of the individual conscience (the rights and the cause of the conscientious objectors), and the army of the collective conscience (Gandhi's Non-Acceptance)."[36] In fact, by 1924, Rolland had begun to see these two concepts as two sides of the same coin: the collective conscience of Gandhian nonviolent resistance would succeed only if it were founded upon a multitude of individual consciences who were strong within themselves. Increasingly, after 1924, Rolland applied to the peace movement and tried to reconcile the seeming antitheses of nonviolence and social revolution. Whereas Clérambault rejected the "mechanical perfection of the ant-hill" in favor of the "individualistic ideal more productive for society,"[37] Rolland's young interwar hero, Marc, like his creator, wished to reconcile the experiments being conducted in the U.S.S.R. and India. Society had to be changed, and these were the only hopeful possibilities which presented themselves. As Marcelle Kempf writes,

> Historic fatality had made them enemies, and he wanted to reconcile, like his young hero Marc, the Non-Acceptance of India with organized revolutionary violence, the rights of the Individual and the social imperative, *"le Rêve et l'Action."*[38]

It was a task which he later acknowledged was like trying to wed fire and water.[39]

As Rolland later realized, the world had to *will* the success of the great experiment in nonviolence, and times were not propitious for such a concerted effort of collective self-will. "Our words must not be equivocal," wrote Rolland to Gandhi on 16 April 1928.

> In the coming crisis there must be no doubt about Gandhi's thought. . . . it is necessary to weigh all the consequences of the orders given, to weigh the forces of the men to whom they will be entrusted. The young men of Europe are aware of the trials waiting for them. They don't want to be duped about the imminence of the danger, which too many "pacifists" are trying not to see and to put out of their minds. They want to look it clearly in the face, and they ask: "To what extent is it *reasonable,* to what extent is it *human, not to accept*? Must the sacrifice be total, absolute, without exception, without any consideration either for our-

selves, or for the things which surround us, and depend on us? And in all honesty to ourselves, can we be sure that this total suffering will diminish the sum total of future human suffering — or does it not risk handing over man's destiny to a barbarity without counter-weight?[40]

This long quotation is important for a number of reasons. It shows Rolland's awareness that a disciplined and well-thought-out approach to the problem of nonviolent resistance in Europe was needed. Moreover, the criticism of the lack of realism in pacifist thinking is one which reappeared in the thirties in increasingly strident tones. Finally, there is in the last phrase of the paragraph an ominous presage of the trials which awaited European pacifists and nonviolent resisters in the years ahead. In a sense, the final phrase is the rock upon which much of European, secular, left-wing pacifism was to founder in the late thirties.

Bringing together his ideas on peace and social revolution, Rolland told Gandhi in 1931 that "the only really effective nonresistance would be in the factories and arsenals, that of the working proletariat."[41] Accordingly, the "official" pacifism of governments and the League of Nations did not interest Rolland. Nor could he come to terms with the "pacifistic imperialism" of Count Richard Coudenhove-Kalergi and his journal *Pan-Europa,* whose eurocentricity and avowed hatred of Soviet Russia and the social revolution were the antitheses of Rolland's own beliefs.[42]

Rolland took a much livelier interest in the work of the War Resisters' International (WRI), a federation of war resisters' organizations which numbered affiliated sections in twenty-one different countries in 1928.[43] While condemning violence, the WRI espoused a *positive* pacifism which strove for "the removal of all the causes of war."[44] In the words of a 1927 WRI resolution, "the first object of the War Resisters' International must be to prevent war," by, among other things, "working for the suppression of Capitalism and Imperialism by the establishment of a new social order and international order based on the principle of co-operation for the common good."[45] When Gandhi briefly contemplated a European tour early in 1928, it was the WRI which Rolland commended to him as an organization deserving of his support, containing men of "limpid faith calmly prepared for every sacrifice."[46]

In a letter of greeting to the WRI at its conference in July 1928

at Sonntagsberg, Austria, Rolland echoed the appeal of the Rumanian
pacifist, Eugen Relgis, for the creation of a pacifist international:
"Put aside all that separates us, all these little shades of political,
social, religious, and philosophical ideas."[47] The only point of disagreement Rolland expressed was the assumption of Relgis and Professor Nicolai of the imminent "disappearance of war through its
own elephantiasis."[48] This tendency on the part of pacifist groups
to view the world through rose-colored spectacles annoyed and worried Rolland — the common theme running through his correspondence with pacifists in the twenties and thirties is the need to look
at the world objectively and realistically. War, he proclaimed, "armed
with new and gigantic weapons, threatens not to disappear before
it has made humanity disappear."[49]

But Rolland's views were evolving slowly. In 1928-29, in a protracted correspondence with Relgis over the latter's proposals for a
pacifist international, Rolland advocated not an abstract revolution
but, rather, one whose potential for violence he defended.

> No, I do not condemn the Revolution. . . . I believe revolution, as
> much as evolution, to be a necessary and fatal form of human
> development. . . . Revolution is not necessarily a synonym for
> cruel brutality. It can be an explosion of enthusiasm and love.
> Such was, at the beginning, the Revolution of 1789. . . . Revolu-
> tion is an almost inevitable *tempo* of the symphony of history.
> And one must deny neither the grandeur nor the good of it.[50]

In a long counterresponse, Relgis argued that revolution without recourse to violence was a chimera, throwing back in Rolland's face
his earlier statements against violence.[51] Rolland's position here on
revolutionary violence shows how far his thought had progressed
since the 1922 debate with Barbusse over the ends and the means
of the revolution. Clearly, he was moving from a position of un-
daunted individualism to one of support for an idea regardless of
its immediate implications. From this point on, Rolland increasingly
beat the drum according to the "inevitable tempo" of history.

This gradual relinquishing of individual responsibility for the
course of history can be seen in another article, written by Rolland
in 1928 for Madeleine Vernet, who published a newspaper entitled
La Volonté de Paix, the organ of a new group of war resisters in
Paris of the same name. An affiliated section of the WRI, *La Volonté de Paix* had been represented at the 1928 Sonntagsberg confer-

ence and had been active in a peace letter campaign in France and Belgium that year.[52] In his article Rolland posed the question, "Do we all want the same peace?" It was not enough to want it; one also had to desire the conditions necessary for peace, and that meant knowing what they were.[53] Rolland wrote that the great crisis of the age was not so much political, economic, or social as it was a matter of conscience. Humanity, he said, found itself at a turning point where it had to choose between an ideal based on the past and one based on the future. The former had begun to die, and the latter was not yet ripe. Yet it was essential to choose between them. The dying ideal was that of *la Patrie nationale,* and the one to come was that of *la Patrie humaine.*[54] Rolland's appeal to the members of *La Volonté de Paix* contained nothing really new. He reiterated his call for cooperation among all peoples in the fight for peace, a peace which must include social justice. What is of particular note, however, is his use of the slogan "He who wants the Ends, desires also the Means."[55] In this article the slogan is not applied directly to a revolutionary situation (although certainly implied), but it is nevertheless revealing as an indication of the direction of Rolland's thought. Six years previously he had attacked Barbusse for using precisely the same argument!

Throughout 1930 and 1931, Rolland became increasingly concerned that antimilitarist and pacifist groups were beginning to look upon conscientious objection as a simple matter of refusal of military service, considering neither a more positive contribution to society nor what sort of ultimate self-sacrifice this conscientious objection might entail in time of war, nor even what type of war the next one might be.

This fuzzymindedness bothered him a great deal. Early in January 1930 he wrote a letter to a group of French antimilitarists and libertarians on behalf of Eugène Guillot, an imprisoned conscientious objector.[56] Rolland supported on principle Guillot's *right* to be a conscientious objector, but rejected the prisoner's grounds, that as a libertarian he merely did not want to sign up for military service. "I do not accept this consequence or this alternative," he wrote. "Whether one accepts the idea of the *Patrie* or not, a man is never alone, and he must take account of the community. His conscientious objection is of value not to him alone, but also to the community, and it is it which he defends in defending his own conscience."[57] Rolland held up the International Civil Service, organized by Pierre Cérésole, as an example of a positive act of service to the community. Only if there were a *social* side to conscientious objection could it have any value.[58]

But Rolland was perhaps even more worried by the foolish optimism of some leaders of the peace movement – the "criminal illusions by which certain leaders of the European nonresistance movement caressed and deluded young people."[59] Small wonder, then, that he should find himself in complete disagreement with the practical implications of Albert Einstein's famous "2% speech" before the New History Society in New York City in December 1930. In this speech Einstein made two essential points: first, he held that if only two percent of the world's population refused military service, or any activity related to war, international conflict would become an impossibility; second, he argued for the creation, by international legislation, of an alternative service for those who refused military duty. The "2% solution" was immediately taken up by the War Resisters' International. In response to a WRI questionnaire of very influential people, Rolland maintained that it was for him an obligation of conscience to refuse to participate in war, either directly or indirectly. But if one moved from the level of moral obligation to that of practical utility, Rolland wrote, Einstein's proposal was modest indeed. Warfare had evolved considerably since 1914, he argued, and would continue to do so. He foresaw the day when small armies of technicians would fight battles of a destructive nature as yet unconceived.[60]

> It must be said bluntly, without illusions. [There is] no other practical way to abolish war promptly than to abolish the present system of government and society which is the generator of wars! In effect, the revolutionaries are right: a social revolution is necessary.[61]

He felt that perhaps the greatest revolutionary tactic for this purpose was the principle of Gandhian nonviolent resistance. But war clouds could not be simply wished away. Mere refusal on the part of just two percent of the population would not stop the modern war machine. Massive organization was needed, and a realization that self-sacrifice might very well be demanded. Interestingly, just two months before the "2% speech," Rolland had written to Einstein about the terrible responsibility borne by the leaders of the European antiwar movements, and about the efficacy of Gandhian nonviolent resistance:

> You know that this is my conviction as well. I should merely like to be sure that we never forget, and we never let those who listen to us forget, that in our violent Europe, on the eve of a new attack of *delirium tremens,* this refusal has, or will have, self-sacrifice as a necessary consequence. Those over whom we have spiritual charge must not be allowed to form illusions on the strength of our words; they must realize that we are leading them to almost certain martyrdom. If they agree to this, then so do we. In our hard human life, martyrdom is almost always the necessary stage through which reason must pass in order to progress into the world of facts.[62]

By stating that such a small proportion of the population could have such a great effect on world politics, Einstein was contributing to a dangerous illusion. The War Resisters' International simply compounded the error. And so, wrote Rolland,

> I clearly separated myself from A. Einstein and the War Resisters' International which had adopted Einstein's declaration; I have condemned their illusions, characterized by a dangerously childish optimism about the effectiveness in the abolition of war of simple individual refusal without any risks.[63]

PRAGMATISM AND PEACE (1932–1939)

The period of Rolland's life from about 1932 to the outbreak of war in 1939 is dominated by two major facts: his sudden conversion to a more doctrinaire support of Soviet Russia and, of course, the Nazi *Machtergreifung* of January 1933. To his credit, Rolland never allowed his intellect to become completely submerged in the Third International. With the Nazi-Soviet Pact in 1939, with his spirited defence of conscientious objectors in the wake of the Amsterdam Congress, among other things, Rolland continued to affirm a certain degree of independence. As Caute remarks, there *is* a difference between faith and blind faith.[64]

The trend of Rolland's thought was revealed at the Amsterdam Congress of August 1932, of which he and Barbusse were cochairmen. In his opening address to the Congress, read for him in his absence, he proclaimed the need for a common front against war and the system that engenders it.[65] "Action is the end of thought," he declared, "all thought which does not lead to it is an abortion and treason. . . . Future wars are in the hands of the working class. It depends on them to snuff them out."[66] Here Rolland seemed to imply that the struggle for peace had become the moral preserve of the working class, although such a position apparently contradicts his repeated calls for people of all political hues to join the fight against war. The final manifesto of the Amsterdam Congress condemned conscientious objectors and Gandhian nonviolent resistance. As one British pacifist remarked at the time, "Lord, how the word 'pacifism' stinks in the nostrils of most delegates."[67] In a letter to Barbusse, Rolland vigorously defended the principle of conscientious objection and nonviolent resistance, differentiating between them and the "pusillanimous and only too often hypocritical exploiters of a comfortable and verbal pacifism without risks."[68] In a rather disturbing indication of how far he had come toward the support of violent revolution, Rolland wrote,

> Everything can and must serve the common struggle: violence and nonviolence (apparent nonviolence for energetic Non-Acceptance, vigorously directed is the equivalent of the most violent blockade). Refusal of service disorganizes bourgeois society, to which the violent action of the proletariat gives attack.[69]

Here, for the first time, nonviolence is defended as a tool — and as a preliminary, subordinate one at that — of violence.

During 1932, Rolland was Honorary President of the *Ligue Internationale des Combattants de la Paix,* a position which he resigned at the *Ligue*'s Easter Congress in 1933 because of its apparent inability to define its position clearly, and perhaps more because of its statement that pacifism had to be placed above all else. As Rolland said in his resignation message,

> *Pacifism* could not conceivably be "placed above all else" without a demoralizing abdication — above the desperate struggles of the exploited and the oppressed, it could not be neutral — there are no neutrals in the face of oppression. Either one is against it or one is for it, is an accomplice. It is necessary to choose. It is too simple to proclaim oneself "against all wars." You cannot put the oppressed and the oppressors in the same bag. . . . Affirm clearly

your line of action. For myself, I affirm mine. I place before all
else the defence of the oppressed by the social state, and their
efforts to realize a new society—the defence of the social revolution and of the exploited peoples, and I call to their aid the allied
forces of the organized nonviolent resisters, the conscientious objectors, and the armed proletariat.[70]

Rolland's view of peace and pacifism can perhaps be summed up in
the title of the book he published in 1935: *Par la Révolution, la Paix.*
It is perhaps ironic that he should choose to use "Par la Révolution,
la Paix" as the title of the concluding article in this book, for in
many respects it marks an epilogue to his thought and activity in
the period up to around 1935–36. In this article, he wrote that despite his disgust with the bourgeois democracies, despite his implac-
able opposition to the imperialism of the West, despite all of the
things he saw around him with which he did not agree, yet nevertheless, he had no wish to see Europe fall into the trap of war once
again. He saw the threat of Hitlerism looming large, believed a war
imminent if not quite inevitable, and, in a prescient statement, argued that "it is not war, but peace, which is fatal to Hitlerism (which
is) incapable of resolving by ordinary means the social and economic
difficulties which are throttling it."[71] This is the beginning of the final phase of Rolland's political approach to the problem of peace
and pacifism, a phase in which he came to terms with the reality of
the Nazi threat and the need for some sort of accommodation with
the bourgeois democracies in the struggle against the new tyranny.

By 1936, Rolland had rejected Gandhian nonviolent resistance as
the method which could save Europe from war. He realized that
time was running out and that it was impossible to implement such
a splendid philosophy in Europe where people had lost the required
spiritual faith in a Divinity, and where totalitarian regimes based on
violence would have no compunction about slaughtering innocent
resisters.[72] What then to put in its place?

In 1936, under the auspices of the World Committee against Fascism and War, Rolland published two essays. The first was his *Mes
sage to the Brussels Congress,* and the second was *How to Prevent
the War.*[73] Here Rolland's prescription for peace is reduced to a practical, immediate level not present in his earlier articles. Instead of
calling for nonviolent resistance as a prelude to social revolution,
Rolland directed his attention to the problem of what the present

bourgeois democracies could do to ensure that war would not break out. He argued that *all* the nations of Europe—including Nazi Germany and Fascist Italy—should be invited to join a collective security pact. Departing from his earlier position, he declared his support for a revivified League of Nations to confront the present crisis. He continued to see the world situation through Marxian eyes, but he left no doubt in his readers' minds that for the moment the greatest danger by far was the Third Reich—the imperialisms of Britain, France, and even Italy paled by comparison.[74] Rolland was convinced that Nazism could not withstand the onslaught of an organized, collective peace offensive.[75]

The end was now in sight, however. Rolland, perhaps in a gesture of solidarity with his country in its hour of need, reversed his action of twenty-five years before, and returned to his native Burgundy from Switzerland, moving into a hillside property at Vézelay. The Nazi-Soviet Pact of August 1939 stunned him. He immediately resigned his membership in the *Association Française des Amis de l'U.R.S.S.* On 3 September, Rolland wrote to Daladier to express his complete support for the French cause:

> In these decisive days in which the French Republic raises itself to block the path against the Hitlerian tyranny over Europe, permit an old fighter for peace who always denounced the barbarism, the perfidy, the frenetic ambition of the Third Reich, to express to you his entire devotion to the cause of the democracies, of France, and of the whole world which is in danger.[76]

Thus, with the coming of war in the autumn of 1939, ended the interwar period and with it Rolland's active role as a leading light of European pacifism. He remained in the seclusion of his home at Vézelay, unmolested by the occupying German armies, until his death on 30 December 1944.

CONCLUSION

Over the course of the interwar period, Rolland moved gradually from support of individualism to collectivism, from *Civilisation* to *Humanité,* from *Rêve* to *Action.* This commitment to action took three successive forms: first, the primarily Gandhian approach with its emphasis on nonviolent resistance on both the individual and collective levels; second, the essentially Marxian approach with its emphasis on revolution as a prerequisite to peace; and finally, the pragmatism of the final years with its tacit support of the bourgeois democracies. The *common* theme throughout the entire interwar period was his insistence on the pressing need for clear thought, foresight, and the necessary definition of tasks, options, and reactions to potential political situations in a minority movement such as pacifism.

Just how representative of interwar French pacifism was Romain Rolland? The answer is probably to see his pacifism as an eclectic mixture of ideas and influences coming from a variety of international sources. For example, his early pacifist mysticism is in some ways completely out of step with the *political* nature of French pacifism, as opposed to the strong undercurrent of religious thinking informing much of Anglo-American pacifism. This early mysticism, traces of which remained right up to the end, was accompanied by an essentially elitist, individualistic, and idealistic approach to the problem of peace. This was the early Romain Rolland who could enthuse to Pierre Cérésole in 1923 that "I should greatly encourage young people looking for a thesis topic in history to study the origins and development of conscientious objectors."[77] At this stage in his development, Rolland undoubtedly viewed conscientious objection through glasses very similar to those worn in the Anglo-Saxon world — that liberty of conscience must be protected at all costs.

But as the twenties rolled into the thirties, this early individualistic ideal became overlaid with the trappings of a more orthodox Marxist view of peace and pacifism. Peace would be achieved only through revolution, and he finally came round to a reluctant acceptance of the potential for violence in the furtherance of that goal. Conscientious objection must therefore have a social side, and one should object only to certain wars and certain types of violence. Rolland was not alone in this thinking. The rise to power of the Nazis in Germany, and perhaps even more the case of the Spanish Civil War, produced a hierarchy of neopacifist values in some pacifists' minds. Thus, by at least 1930, Rolland's ambiguous stand on conscientious objection places him neither in the French anarchist/libertarian camp nor in the mainstream of French pacifism, which was always very wary of objection in any case.

Certainly from 1932 onward, Rolland was increasingly out of step with the main stream of French integral (or absolute) pacifism, typified by the *Ligue Internationale des Combattants de la Paix*. For French integral pacifists, putting peace first meant incurring the wrath not only of a traditional and also a new protofascist Right in France, it also meant fighting a continual rearguard action against the attacks of *L'Humanité* and the *Parti Communiste*. Amsterdam-Pleyel only served to exacerbate this phenomenon; the protestations of the French National Committee to the contrary, local Amsterdam-Pleyel groups continued to be dominated by local communists who made anyone suspected of so-called bourgeois pacifism anathema. Clearly, the major international events of the period, especially the rise of Nazism and the Spanish Civil War, greatly affected and informed the French pacifist debate. But this was conducted largely within the confines of a peculiarly French political culture and environment. The attacks of the far left and the extreme right acted as an ideological pincer which retarded and deformed the French peace movement. One sees this even today, where in France to say that one is a pacifist immediately elicits the assumption that one is also a member of the French Communist party. But in the twenties and the thirties the PCF espoused a bastard form of pacifism, an antimilitarism based not on principle but on political opportunism. The PCF was not and is not a genuinely pacifist party. Like all political parties, it has other, more dominant concerns.

Undoubtedly, the role of a republican conscript army is important in an understanding of French pacifism, too. In a country proud of its revolutionary tradition, the concepts of the "nation in arms" and the *impôt du sang* were particularly difficult to dislodge.

Rolland's slide into Stalinism and then his support of collective security gradually left behind the French integral pacifists who had seen in him the father of European pacifism—as they, in their turn, became increasingly isolated from the rest of French political society. With the collapse of 1940, pacifism became equated with defeatism and collaborationism—rightly or wrongly, and there are examples on both sides of the coin. Only now, some forty years later, is the French political psyche gradually freeing itself from the spectre of Vichy to the point where a reasonable discussion of the French variant of a common international phenomenon called interwar pacifism can finally begin.

Rolland was accused of renouncing his pacifism and urging recourse to violence. This is perhaps to distort his position. In 1931 he protested to Jean Guéhenno that he "did not and never would approve of violence; but there are many things in this universe that must be accepted without approval — life and its mutual destruction as it has been imposed on us, for example."[78] Rolland would undoubtedly have agreed with Bertrand Russell, who wrote retrospectively that "the doctrine which Tolstoy preached with great persuasive force, that the holders of power could be morally regenerated if met by non-resistance, was obviously untrue in Germany after 1933."[79] As the abyss opened before him once more in 1939, Rolland did not shrink from it. His pacifism was neither absolute nor immutable. With a heart heavy with both resignation and hope for the future, Rolland faced the war he was not to survive. As he put it in the epigraph to *Mère et Fils,* taken from Spinoza: "Peace is not the absence of war, it is the virtue born of vigor of the soul."

NOTES

This study is derived from my M.A. major research essay at the University of Toronto, which was supervised by Professor John C. Cairns. I would like to thank Professor Cairns, Professor Maurice Larkin of Edinburgh University, and Professor R. W. F. Wilcocks of the University of Alberta for their comments, as well as the Social Sciences and Humanities Research Council of Canada and the Master and Fellows of Massey College in the University of Toronto for the scholarship and Junior Fellowship which made this work possible. I would also like to express my deep appreciation to the Commonwealth Scholarship Commission in the United Kingdom for the travel grant which made possible my attendance at the American-European Consultation on Peace Research in History at Stadtschlaining, Austria, in August 1986.

1. Romain Rolland, *Le Périple* (Paris: Editions Emile-Paul Frères, 1946), 148. Unless otherwise indicated, all translations from French and German are my own.

2. Robert Wohl, *The Generation of 1914* (London: Weidenfeld and Nicolson, 1980), 15.

3. Wilhelm Herzog, "Témoignages à Romain Rolland," in *Europe* (No. spécial consacré à Romain Rolland) 38 (15 février 1926): 165–66.

4. Cited in Maurice Nadeau, "Romain Rolland," *Journal of Contemporary History* 2, no. 2 (April 1967): 216.

5. Ibid.

6. David Caute, *Communism and the French Intellectuals 1914–1960* (London: André Deutsch, 1964), 105.

7. Rolland, *I Will Not Rest,* trans. K. S. Shelvankar (New York: Live-right, n.d.), 12.

8. "Panorama," in ibid., 22–23.

9. Ibid., 43.

10. Rolland, *Le Périple,* 11–23. The words are from the title of Maurice Betz's preface: "Le Testament Spirituel de Romain Rolland."

11. Ibid., 151.

12. Ibid., 152.

13. David James Fisher develops a different periodization of Rolland's pacifist activity from mine but provides an interesting analysis of the period up to 1925. See Fisher, "The Rolland-Barbusse Debate," *Survey. A Journal of East and West Studies* 20, nos. 2–3 (Spring/Summer 1974): 120–59; "Romain Rolland and the popularization of Gandhi: 1923–25," *Gandhi/Marg* (July 1974), 145–80; "Pacifism and the Intellectual: The Case of Romain Rolland," *Peace and Change* 7, nos. 1–2 (Winter 1982): 85–96.

14. Rolland, *Above the Battle,* trans. C. K. Ogden (Chicago: Open Court, 1916), 53.

15. Ibid., 42.

16. Hermann Fernau, "Romain Rolland und der Weltkrieg. Eine Unter-redung," *Wissen und Leben* 20 (1 April–15 Sept. 1918): 301.

17. Frank Field, *Three French Writers and the Great War: Studies in the Rise of Communism and Fascism* (Cambridge: Cambridge Univ. Press, 1975), 57.

18. Ibid.

19. Cited in Marcelle Kempf, *Romain Rolland et l'Allemagne* (Paris: Debresse, 1962), 276.

20. Ibid., 210.

21. Cited in ibid., 221–22.

22. Rolland, *I Will Not Rest,* 91–94. For the interesting correspondence between Rolland and G. B. Shaw about the Declaration, see Rolland, *Par la Révolution, la Paix* (Paris: Editions sociales internationales, 1935), 11–14. Cf. Nicole Racine, "The Clarté Movement in France, 1919–21," *Journal of Contemporary History* 2, no. 2 (April 1967): 195–208; Jean Albertini's introduction and notes in Rolland, *Textes Politiques, philosophiques, et sociaux choisis* (Paris: Editions sociales, 1970), 179–81; and Henri Barbusse, "L'autre moitié du devoir. A propos du Rollandisme," ibid., 193–94.

23. Rolland, *I Will Not Rest,* 128.

24. "Panorama," in ibid., 16.

25. Ibid., 133.

26. Ibid., 135.

27. Ibid.

28. Rolland, "Contre un pacifisme négatif" (lettre à Marianne Rauze, 23 novembre 1923), in *Par la Révolution, la Paix,* 93.

29. Ibid., 95–96.

30. Rolland, *Le Périple,* 147.

31. Ibid., 148–49.

32. Ibid., 150.

33. Ibid., 150, 153.

34. "Panorama," in Rolland, *I Will Not Rest,* 39.

35. Ibid., 40.

36. William T. Starr, *Romain Rolland and a World at War* (Evanston, IL: Northwestern Univ. Press, 1956), 83.

37. Kempf, *Romain Rolland et l'Allemagne,* 224.

38. Ibid., 250.

39. "Panorama," in Rolland, *I Will Not Rest,* 40.

40. *Romain Rolland and Gandhi Correspondence* (New Delhi: Ministry of Information and Broadcasting, 1966), no. 125, Rolland to Gandhi, 16 April 1928, pp. 112–13.

41. *Rolland and Gandhi Correspondence,* no. 193, extract from Rolland's Diary, Dec. 1931, p. 169.

42. The expression is Coudenhove-Kalergi's in "Das Pan-Europa Programm," *Pan-Europa* 1, no. 2 (May 1924): 3. See also Richard Coudenhove-Kalergi, *Pazifismus* (Vienna and Leipzig: Pan-Europa Verlag, 1924). For Rolland's reaction to a *Pan-Europa* survey of the attitude of selected European intellectuals and politicians to the idea of a United States of Europe, see "Rundfrage. II. Teil" in *Pan-Europa* 2, nos. 6–7 (1926). For Coudenhove-Kalergi's position on war and the revolution, see "Krieg und Revolution," in *Pan-Europa* 4, no. 9 (Nov. 1928): 1–9.

43. War Resisters' International, *War Resisters in Many Lands* (1928), reprinted in Charles Chatfield, ed., *International War Resistance Through World War II* (New York: Garland, 1975), 382–448. War Resisters International is hereinafter cited as WRI.

44. Ibid., 388–89.

45. Resolution passed at a meeting of the International Council of the WRI, 21–22 May 1927, WRI, *International Council Communications, nos. 1–217,* Swarthmore College Peace Collection, Swarthmore, Pennsylvania.

46. *Rolland and Gandhi Correspondence,* no. 109, Rolland to Madeleine Slade, 7 March 1928, p. 98.

47. Letter of 24 July 1928 contained in *War Resisters in Many Lands,* Chatfield, *International War Resistance,* 424.

48. Ibid.

49. Ibid.

50. Rolland in Eugen Relgis, *L'Internationale Pacifiste* (Paris: André Delpeuch, 1929), 28–29.

51. Ibid., 90 and 107–8.

52. *War Resisters in Many Lands*, 404.

53. "La Volonté de Paix," Rolland, *Par la Révolution, la Paix*, 100.

54. Ibid., 101.

55. Ibid., 103.

56. "L'Objection de Conscience doit être non individualiste et libertaire, mais sociale" (Lettre pour la libération de l'objecteur de conscience Eugène Guillot — 8 janvier 1930, Réponse à un groupement d'antimilitaristes et de libertaires français) in Rolland, *Par la Révolution, la Paix*, 91–92.

57. Ibid., 91.

58. Ibid., 92.

59. "Sur la Résistance Passive" (Lettre du 14 juillet 1930 à un des jeunes organisateurs français du "septième camp d'amitié internationale" à Chevreuse), ibid., 69, no. 1.

60. "Correspondance avec Runham Brown au sujet de la déclaration de A. Einstein sur le refus de service de guerre," Feb. 1931, in ibid., 65–66.

61. Ibid., 66–67.

62. *Rolland and Gandhi Correspondence*, no. 381, Rolland to Albert Einstein, 12 Oct. 1930, p. 425.

63. "Panorama," in Rolland, *I Will Not Rest*, 82.

64. Caute, *Communism and the French Intellectuals*, 130.

65. "Déclaration lue à la première Séance du Congrès mondial de tous les Partis contre la Guerre," Amsterdam, 27 Aug. 1932, in Rolland, *Par la Révolution, la Paix*, 44–49.

66. Ibid., 48–49.

67. Martin Ceadel, *Pacifism in Britain, 1914–1945. The Defining of a Faith* (Oxford: Clarendon Press, 1980), 114.

68. "Lettre à Henri Barbusse sur la place qui doit être faite aux Objecteurs de Conscience et aux Gandhistes dans le mouvement révolutionnaire issu du Congrès d'Amsterdam," 20 Dec. 1932, in Rolland, *Par la Révolution, la Paix*, 61–62.

69. Ibid., 62–63.

70. "Le Pacifisme et la Révolution" (adresse du 15 mars 1933 au Congrès National de Pâques de la Ligue Internationale des Combattants de la Paix), ibid., 121, 123.

71. "Par la Révolution, la Paix," in ibid., 170.

72. Starr, *World at War*, 84–85.

73. Rolland, *Botschaft an den Kongress von Brüssell* and *Wie kann man den Krieg verhindern?*, trans. Rudolf Leonhard (Paris: Editions du Carrefour, 1936).

74. Rolland, *Wie kann man*, 17.

75. Ibid., 42.

76. Cited in Kempf, *Romain Rolland et l'Allemagne*, 273.

77. *Rolland and Gandhi Correspondence,* no. 326, Rolland to Pierre Cérésole, 10 Oct. 1923, p. 381.

78. Cited in William T. Starr, *Romain Rolland. One Against All. A Biography* (The Hague and Paris: Mouton, 1971), 236.

79. Bertrand Russell, *The Autobiography of Bertrand Russell* (New York: Bantam, 1969), 275.

KARL HOLL

German Pacifists in Exile, 1933–1940

GERMAN PACIFISTS HAVE BEEN largely overlooked in studies of
the phenomenon of the exiles produced by the National Socialist seizure of power.[1] What follows is a report of some of the conclusions
of recent research into the situation of German pacifists in exile after
1933.[2] At this stage it is possible to talk only of provisional results,
the bases of which are to be found primarily in archives in West Germany, Switzerland, and the United States. In order to obtain a more
complete picture, further research is necessary in many other countries. In fact, if one wanted to follow the trail of individual German
pacifists into exile, one would have to go to Asia, the Near East,
Canada, and Latin America, as well as, naturally, the United States.
For the fate of exile overtook German pacifists virtually everywhere.

The broad extent of exile has compelled the author to restrict his
research concerning about one hundred individuals geographically
to Switzerland, Czechoslovakia, France, and the United States. The
chronology of the analysis also had to be restricted: It ends in 1940,
because after this date the expansion of the Second World War and
the armed presence of Hitler's Germany in most of Europe produced
so dramatic a deterioration of the conditions faced by refugees that
one must now speak of a whole new dimension of the exile experience.

Pacifists are defined as those individuals who during the Weimar
Republic were members of organizations that belonged to the so-
called German Peace Cartel: members of organizations such as the
German Peace Society, the German League for Human Rights, the
German branch of the Women's International League for Peace and
Freedom, and the Peace League of German Catholics.[3] In view of
the social and political structure of the Weimar Republic, it was natural that a large number of the pacifist refugees were also members
of republican parties.[4]

First, the situation faced by German pacifists towards the end of the Weimar Republic and the way they reacted to events after Hitler's seizure of power on 30 January 1933 will be commented on. Then consideration will be given to the form of persecution they encountered, their experiences and living conditions in exile, and their political activities abroad.

THE VULNERABILITY OF GERMAN PACIFISTS

The experience of German pacifists in the last years of the Weimar Republic was already extraordinarily depressing. The German Peace Society, the largest pacifist organization, was in decline, if not in collapse. New peace organizations like the German Peace League, under the leadership of the jurist Arnold Freymuth, had begun to develop independently, after a serious and far-reaching ideological disagreement had set in.[5] On the one hand, the more moderate pacifists, for whom the historian and left-liberal Ludwig Quidde—the corecipient of the 1927 Nobel Peace Prize—had been a source of inspiration for a long time, emphasized the concepts of international organization, arbitration, and arms limitation as the keys to lasting international peace. This position, however, had come under increasing attack from a more radical and eventually successful group, which insisted that the only effective ways to prevent war were draft resistance, conscientious objection, and, if necessary, mass strike. This ideological clash resulted in a loosening of the vital and indispensable ties between the German peace movement and the republican parties and trade unions. Indeed, in 1931, the Social Democratic party declared membership in the German Peace Society incompatible with party membership.

The clash was one between two political cultures within the organized pacifism of Weimar Germany: between those who were in favor of classical representative parliamentary democracy and of individual liberalism, like Quidde, and those like Fritz Küster who stood for a new political concept of mass mobilization against the threat from the right.[6] To make things worse, the legal persecution of pacifists for "journalistic high treason" had long been established as a juridical practice. The most notorious case was that of Carl von Ossietzky, the editor and publisher of the *Weltbühne,* who was convicted on the basis of publishing an article which revealed the illegal cooperation between the German and Red armies in the field of aircraft testing.[7]

The peace movement was thus under duress and in decline even before Hitler became chancellor. On the basis of their previous experiences it must have seemed to German pacifists that the new régime would not alter much the repressive policies already being applied against the peace movement. However, any such expectations were cruelly destroyed. Even if the peace movement during the Weimar Republic did not have enough members to impress the Nazis, it had nonetheless long attracted the special hatred of Hitler and his henchmen as a fundamental challenge to their ideology. The efforts of the German pacifists to bring about the peaceful restructuring of international relations, the idea of international reconciliation, the demand for general disarmament, the universal condemnation of war and of the use of any form of violence in international life, when added to the pacifists' outspoken support for the Republic, its institutions for democracy and individual freedom: all this was so contradictory to the ideology and program of National Socialism that in the eyes of the new régime coexistence was unthinkable. Indeed, the elimination of pacifism and the pacifists appeared to follow inevitably, despite Hitler's frequent professions of his peaceful intentions, which were all too readily accepted outside Germany.[8]

Immediately after 30 January 1933, it became clear that Hitler was not prepared to tolerate pacifist organizations, let alone grant pacifists the right to propagate their ideas. The first wave of arrests of prominent pacifists set in directly after the Reichstag fire on 27 February 1933. Fritz Küster, the leading figure of the radical wing of the German peace movement, was arrested on 6 March. He made his way through several concentration camps and was released from Buchenwald only in the summer of 1938. Gerhart Seger, the former general secretary of the Peace Society and a Social Democratic member of the Reichstag, was arrested on 12 March and in June was sent to the concentration camp in Oranienburg, from which he succeeded — a most unusual case — in escaping, at first to Prague.[10] Ossietzky was again imprisoned during the night of the Reichstag fire and began the ordeal that led to his martyrdom. These are only a few of the more prominent cases. Many pacifists were unable to escape, because they initially underestimated the danger or because they were determined to remain in the country.

Other German pacifists were overtaken by events while they were out of the country. Among these pacifists were a number who had emigrated before 1933, after they had found conditions in the Weimar Republic intolerable. The leader of the German League for Human Rights, the mathematician and statistician Emil Julius Gumbel, who had already lost his teaching position in the University of Heidelberg because of nationalist agitation, emigrated in 1932 to France, where he taught first in Paris, then in Lyon.[11] Later, in an extraordinary adventure, he succeeded in fleeing to the United States. Friedrich Wilhelm Foerster, professor of pedagogy and philosophy, had emigrated to France long before 1933 and escaped in 1940 to the United States.[12] The international legal scholar Walther Schücking also belongs in certain respects to this category. In 1928 he had been appointed to the International Court of Justice in the Hague. After the Nazi régime gained power, they demanded that he give up his office and return to Germany. However, Schücking defied the régime, insisting that he had been appointed to the court for life, and remained in the Netherlands until his death in 1935 (after which his position remained vacant for Germany).[13] Thanks to their professional position, these refugees did not have to suffer the material deprivations felt by many pacifists who were able to find security in exile only after the greatest efforts, under desperate conditions, and often at the last minute, their fate made worse in many cases when they were deprived of their German citizenship.

Ludwig Quidde, who lived in Munich, at first hid for several days in that city before he succeeded in fleeing to Switzerland, where he lived until his death in Geneva in 1941.[14] Hellmut von Gerlach, who had long been the editor and publisher of the pacifist journal *Die Welt am Montag* (and who was an associate of Ossietzky), received an anonymous telephone warning from police headquarters in Berlin and fled on 1 March by train to Munich, where he hoped to find some safety.[15] After hiding for several days on a farm in the Bavarian mountains, he made a daring escape by automobile across the Austrian border. (His escape was arranged by the friends of the Munich pacifist, Constanze Hallgarten, a Jew who soon thereafter herself had to flee to France and the United States, accompanied by her son, the historian George Wolfgang F. Hallgarten.[16]) Because Gerlach had escaped in a hurry, he arrived in Vienna with practically no clothes and thus found it necessary to wear a suit of the late Austrian sociologist and pacifist, Rudolf Goldscheid, whose widow he met in the Austrian capital. Another pacifist, Otto Lehmann-Russbüldt, the former general secretary of the German League for Human Rights, was released from protective custody in March 1933, whereupon he crossed the Dutch border disguised as a monk.[17]

THE CONDITIONS OF EXILE

The material deprivation of exiled pacifists was often very great. The reasons for their deprivation were quickly apparent in the main centres of the emigration: Paris, Strasbourg, Prague, and the Swiss cities Zurich, Berne, Basel, and Geneva. Quidde, who was a member of the council of the International Peace Bureau in Geneva and worked tirelessly for the relief of the exiled, pointed to the main sources of the problem: Of the three principal groups of refugees, namely socialists (i.e. social democrats and communists), Jews, and pacifists, the first two categories normally had some form of support. The social democrats and the communists could rely on the support-network of their parties' organizations in the country of exile. The Jews also had a support-network abroad. The pacifists, however, had no support unless they were socialists, communists, or Jews.[18]

Accordingly, for numerous pacifists, the exile experiences entailed a significant social decline. On the one hand, many of the pacifist refugees were educated and used to earning their living in literary and journalistic activities; on the other hand, many refugees were workers or clerks, who found themselves competing with similar workers in their host country (provided they had secured a work permit). A frequent problem was the inability to use the language of the country of exile. Only a few were able to live in conditions that even approximated those they had known in Germany before their flight. For example, once those who fled to France had laboriously secured the "permis de séjour en France"—a guarantee of work that was by no means certain and was in fact being constantly jeopardized anew—the struggle for existence had only really begun. Thus Ludwig Quidde arrived in Geneva 75 years old and broken. This man, who had been a respected scholar in Germany, was compelled to work in a print shop and as a gardener until he received support from the Norwegian Nobel Committee in Oslo. He nonetheless had well-situated Swiss friends, who organized a banquet and fund-raising campaign for him. Quidde used the money which was raised primarily to support other pacifist refugees.[19]

The case of Heinz Fett does not appear to be unusual either. According to an account that Quidde received from Fett's friend Gustav Mönch, Fett had left Germany in 1933 and gone first to the Saar, then to France. Charged with antimilitarist activities, he was expelled from France. Thus began an odyssey which led him through Switzerland, Austria, Czechoslovakia, Yugoslavia, and Spain before new political conditions under the French Popular Front finally allowed him to settle in France.[20] Unfortunately, his troubles were not over. A typesetter, he was unable to use his skills because he could not speak French. Instead, he began to raise and sell rabbits at his home in the south of France in order to support his young family.[21] It was the hopelessness of such a situation that drove the jurist Arnold Freymuth and his wife to commit suicide some weeks after they arrived in Paris in 1933.[22]

The numerous cases of exiles demanded systematic, reliable, continuous, material support. In particular, the normal loss of German citizenship required an international solution along the lines of the so-called Nansen passport. No satisfactory solution of this problem was provided. Although Ludwig Quidde very quickly drew the attention of the International Peace Bureau to the difficult situation of the pacifist refugees, the members of the Bureau's Council, whose ideas had been shaped before the First World War, found it difficult to comprehend the social and emotional sides of the phenomenon of exile.[23] When Gerhart Seger, for example, tried to find support within the International Peace Bureau, his request was turned down by its secretary general, Henri Golay.[24] This painful experience forced Seger (who had written a sensational book about his experiences in the concentration camp at Oranienburg) to travel on to the United States, where he attempted to convey the truth about Nazi Germany not only by editing a socialist newspaper, but also by making extensive lecture tours.[25] His wife and child were allowed to leave Germany to join him in England only after a spectacular action on the part of women Conservative members of the British House of Commons, who invaded the German embassy in London.[26]

The attempt to aid German pacifists in exile met with opposition or indifference even within pacifist circles abroad. In order to alleviate the problem of increasing financial need, Quidde undertook in 1937 quite literally a beggar's journey to England, from which he returned with only a modest amount of money.[27] The same year he requested support from Frederick J. Libby, the Executive Secretary of the American National Council for Prevention of War.[28] Libby, responding coolly that his organization would have first to pay off its own substantial deficit before it could even begin to think about a subsidy for exiled pacifists, explained that the willingness of wealthy Americans to donate funds had already significantly declined because of their discontent with Roosevelt's New Deal policies.[29] Gertrud Baer, the General Secretary of the International Women's League for Peace and Freedom, encountered similar experiences during her visit to the United States in 1937 and expressed the belief that only the dramatization of individual cases would bring American aid in even modest amounts.[30]

It was almost impossible to convince the free world of the acute need of individual emigrants. This situation spurred the indefatigable Ludwig Quidde to propose to the Nobel Committee of the Norwegian Parliament that his Geneva-based "comité de secours aux pacifistes exilés" should be awarded the Nobel Peace Prize.[31] His motive was clearly two-pronged: international opinion should be made aware of the ordeal of pacifist exile, and the prize money should flow into the treasury of his committee. In spite of extensive preparations, support for Quidde's plan in the press, and his personal ties to politicians in Norway, the Nobel Committee did not decide in his favor. Despite the failure of his plan, Geneva, the home of the League of Nations, remained at least until 1940 the most suitable place for organizing support actions of all kinds, owing to the presence of numerous international organizations.

In Paris the French League for Human Rights had become a central meeting point for German emigrants, including pacifists. As early as 14 April 1933, Victor Basch, its president, wrote to his German counterpart Kurt R. Grossmann:

> From everywhere people are knocking on our door. I personally receive letters from professors, lawyers, and writers every day. Since the exodus the work of our bureau has been completely interrupted and devoted to serving Germans who demand identity cards, visas, advice, and help.[32]

Soon the French League had some help: Hellmut von Gerlach arrived in late April and established the "service allemand" in the headquarters of the League, from which he organized (mainly with the help of Konrad Reisner and Milly Zirker) various support activities until his death in 1935.[33] He provided material aid, mediated disputes, gave advice, and provided simple comfort to the desperate.

In Prague, Kurt Grossmann rendered similar services under the auspices of the "Democratic Refugee Relief Organization" set up by the League of Human Rights in Czechoslovakia.[34] His organization not only provided material support but promoted emotional cohesion among the refugees. It combatted the ever-present danger of resignation, attempted to prevent, in Grossmann's words, "the spiritual decline" of the émigrés, facilitated communication with the Czechoslovakian authorities, and developed security measures against infiltration and physical threats by the Nazis. Moreover, Grossmann's organization encouraged the refugees to participate in educational activities, to attend the theater, and it made information available about recommended readings and radio programs. According to Grossmann's report, the number of Germans taking advantage of these services between 1933 and 1935 was about 65,000.[35] (Since only two to three thousand belonged to the category of "pacifists and democrats," pacifists in the strict sense of the word represented only a tiny proportion of the total number of those immigrants.)

Pacifists like Quidde and Grossmann, who had access to money and international connections, faced another, especially important task. Quidde's most frequent task was to provide the suspicious French authorities with confirmation that a refugee was a genuine and active pacifist, so that he or she might then receive the required "certificat de loyalisme envers la France." The French authorities in any event allowed only a few German emigrants to remain in the vicinity of the French-German border. And the situation deteriorated after 1934, with the assassination of the Yugoslav king and the French minister for Foreign Affairs, Louis Barthou, in Marseille. It became still worse when in 1938 a conservative government succeeded the Popular Front and regarded all Germans — first and foremost radical democratic pacifist Germans — with suspicion.

THE POLITICS OF EXILE

Understandably, political activities, to the extent that exile pacifists were capable of undertaking them at all, ranked in importance behind the relief of immediate material needs, and these activities could never completely drive out depression, resignation, and anxieties about relatives at home. In exile many pacifists withdrew from politics altogether — not surprising in view of the restrictions that authorities in the host countries placed on their political activities. Harry Count Kessler, for example, while living in Paris, strictly avoided any contact with German émigrés.[36] Indeed, one such émigré, Friedrich Wilhelm Foerster, was designated by the Swiss authorities a "dangerous pacifist," whose departure from Switzerland was to be encouraged.[37]

Mention must be made of the profound and only too justified anxiety that many pacifists felt about Hitler's Germany. Alfred Falk, for example, left Strasbourg in 1935, not only because the city was too expensive for him, but because it was too close to the German frontier.[38] Anxiety also drove Helene Stöcker, the courageous pacifist feminist, to exchange her Swiss exile for British exile because she feared the annexation of Switzerland by Hitler's Germany.[39] Anxiety also deeply affected the émigré German pacifists in Prague (and made them fear, for instance, that after the Munich Conference of September 1938 they would be unable to find seats on airplanes to England). One would be tempted to speak of the German pacifists' resignation had not their voices been among those of the Cassandras who early pointed to the great threat that National Socialism posed to Europe. Hatred, anger, and disillusionment over the position of the social democratic leadership in the last years of the Weimar Republic were also widespread among émigré socialist pacifists. And out of their ranks appeared plans to reform the social democratic party and to remove the incapable "old boys" from the party leadership.[40] In the eyes of other pacifists such as Hellmut von Gerlach, however, squabbling among the German refugees about matters of German domestic politics could only detract from the need to defeat Hitler, an effort which demanded cohesion among the émigrés.[41]

Many pacifists harbored no illusions about an imminent end to Hitler's dictatorship. As Alfred Falk wrote to a colleague,

Take heed of my well-intentioned advice. Withdraw from all activities. Things German can be written off. Germany does not want us. It wants . . . to rule Europe. We have been spit out. The German people is so completely contaminated that it will only be brought to its senses after the next catastrophe. One has to think in terms of epochs. I, who have smelled in every hole, leave the rascals to themselves. We will need our weak forces later.[42]

In another letter he wrote,

> The German people, which has been completely poisoned in the depth of its soul . . . does not like us. We must reconcile ourselves to this situation. We have only one goal, one program: the struggle from outside against the brutes.[43]

As in the Weimar Republic, Ludwig Quidde in exile was again the target of attacks by more radical pacifists who were provoked by his characteristic position with respect to Hitler's Germany. For a long time Quidde professed his trust in Hitler's declarations of peace. Quidde's views, as he himself intended, were registered in the German Foreign Office in Berlin, which hoped to use him for German propaganda and therefore shielded him from the Gestapo's attempts to deprive him of his German citizenship. While most critics in exile regarded Quidde's position as the expression of an apolitical naiveté, which they had earlier often attacked, there appear to have been compelling private reasons for his behavior. Quidde had left his sick wife, who was half-Jewish, and her handicapped sister in Munich; he must have feared that a resolute demonstration against Hitler would have made their circumstances precarious.[44] In addition, the loss of his citizenship would have threatened his legal status in Switzerland, and this in turn would have worked to the disadvantage of other émigré pacifists and of his companion, Charlotte Kleinschmidt, who had followed him into exile along with her daughter.[45]

The outrage among exiled German pacifists over Quidde's pronouncements was understandable, but it did little to bring peace to their ranks. Continuing dissension made life difficult for those who, like Hellmut von Gerlach, were attempting to unite all the exile forces in the struggle against Hitler. Gerlach and others sponsored the founding in exile of branches of the German League for Human Rights — in Paris (which became the leading section of the League), Strasbourg, Prague, and London. One of the most significant undertakings of the Parisian branch was the attempt to save Carl von Ossietzky through the campaign to have him awarded the Nobel Peace Prize. Among the participants in this campaign (which succeeded) were the young German émigré Willy Brandt in Oslo, Quidde in Geneva, and the Czechoslovakian statesman Thomás Masaryk.[46]

The construction in Paris of the German popular front in exile posed a problem for Hellmut von Gerlach. There is little evidence that he finally abandoned his reservations about working with the communists and the Soviet Union. Nonetheless, given his conviction that all efforts to unify Germans in exile against Hitler had to be supported, he seems to have been prepared to cooperate with communists once they had ceased publicly to equate bourgeois democracy and fascism, and once they had announced their readiness for an alliance with socialists and democrats. Gerlach wanted to be pragmatic even with respect to the Soviet Union. As he wrote to Quidde, in order to defeat Hitler he "would even accept the support of the devil and his grandmother." Shortly before his death, Gerlach appears to have been ready to join the preparatory committee for the formation of a German popular front, "provided that other personalities closer to the political middle are also prepared to join."[47]

To the exiled pacifists, the end of the first phase of the Second World War in 1940 meant essentially new waves of emigration after the incorporation of Austria and the annexation of Czechoslovakia. The actual outbreak of World War II and the conquest of Poland, the Netherlands, Belgium, Luxemburg, Denmark, and Norway meant even more enforced dislocation. These events raised new anxieties and lessened the uncertain hope that Switzerland would remain spared and that France and England would stand firm. The new situation also meant new restrictions on the conditions of life, increased material deprivation, and for many pacifists the panicked attempt to leave the European continent, normally in the direction of America.

Above all, there now appeared a question of principle for every individual male pacifist. Should he serve in the armed forces of his guest country in the fight against his own countrymen? The question was unavoidable in several countries of exile: in England, in the United States, and most acutely in France.[48] A few pacifists denied the fundamentals of their pacifism and, having succeeded in overcoming the distrust of the French authorities, joined the Foreign Legion or served in the regular French army. The French populace, however, was naturally outraged against all Germans and often made no distinction between Hitler's Germany and its refugees. Many German refugees also found the Belgian populace hostile, as memories persisted of the German occupation during the First World War.

There now began the new, indescribable ordeal of German refugees, among them many pacifists, in the French internment camps at Le Vernet, Les Milles, Gurs, Catus, St. Cyprien, and elsewhere.[49] Quidde, by now openly critical of the Nazi régime, attempted to help. He turned not only to various international support organizations, but to his friends and acquaintances in the French peace movement, though often without finding sympathy.[50] To one of these friends Quidde criticized the French practice of interning precisely the most bitter opponents of the Nazi régime. The German refugees were, he maintained,

> the best allies against National Socialist Germany, to the extent that they speak French and are otherwise suited for actions. They must be utilized in the propaganda to enlighten the German people about Hitlerism. To the extent that they are unsuited for this effort, they should be employed to fill the holes torn open in the factories. In England the German emigrants have been treated completely differently. The English look at each individual case. All my pacifist friends in London are free.[51]

Quidde then attempted to find relief through the Red Cross in Geneva.[52] He drew attention to the epidemics of typhoid and paratyphoid that raged in the internment camps, to the plagues of fleas and rats, to the lack of lamps, beds, tables, dry straw, clothing and medicine. In October 1940 he received an answer from the Red Cross that these conditions were known and that a delegation would be sent to investigate.[53]

The desperate cries for help that now reached Quidde from German pacifists revealed even grimmer ordeals after the invasion of France by German troops. These reports told of the breaking up of internment camps as German troops approached, of air attacks on the crowds of refugees moving south, and of the attempts of enraged Frenchmen to attack transport trains and to lynch the Germans in them.[54] A moving voice of humanity can be heard among the letters that reached Quidde. A French woman, the secretary to the mayor of Fréjus, reported to Quidde that her husband had been taken prisoner by the Germans but she knew not where. She asked him to find out the location of her husband's prison in Germany and the condition of his health. Quidde answered immediately that he had contacted the Red Cross in Geneva. In return, he asked the woman to convey a kindly gesture to a friend of his own who was interned in the camp at Les Milles, namely Alfred Falk.[55] Several months later Quidde died.

After the defeat of France, the ominous article 19 of the armistice treaty brought the culmination of the frightful fate of all German refugees in France, and the exiled pacifists also had to confront this new situation. They all feared that the Vichy régime would surrender them on demand to the German government. Therefore they concealed themselves in unoccupied France, and many took refuge in the port city of Marseille (which, however, had become a gigantic trap); here they waited for the uncertain possibility of crossing the Spanish frontier, then crossing Franco's Spain to Portugal, and from there finally escaping to freedom in an ocean liner. Gestapo agents immediately turned up in Marseille and in other cities in Vichy France in order to place under surveillance the émigrés in whom they were particularly interested — naturally not only Germans. The legal conditions for leaving the country became increasingly difficult. To an even greater extent than before, the flight to freedom now became contingent on financial resources and on the willingness of Frenchmen and of the United States administration to help.[56] It also depended on the compassion, mobilized in the last minute, of American citizens who were prepared to vouch for German refugees. Escape depended finally on individual imagination and ruthlessness, as well as on the physical stamina of each refugee.

The help given by the two Americans Frank Bohn and Varian Fry, as well as by their friends, deserves special recognition. They made possible the flight of thousands by providing forged passports, financial support, and advice. Fry assumed the responsibility of caring for intellectuals who were in danger; among those who were rescued by his "Emergency Rescue Committee" were Lion Feuchtwanger and his wife (in whose rescue the American consul Bingham also played an important role), Heinrich Mann and his wife, Thomas Mann's youngest son Golo, Leonhard Frank, and Franz and Alma Werfel.[57] Among prominent pacifists who escaped through the same network was Emil Julius Gumbel.[58] The Social Democratic leaders Rudolf Breitscheid and Rudolf Hilferding, however, were unable to escape and were handed over by the Vichy régime. Breitscheid wound up in the concentration camp at Buchenwald, and Hilferding committed suicide in Paris before he could be sent off to a concentration camp.

The murder of the pacifist philosopher Theodor Lessing by a Nazi gang in his Czechoslovakian exile in 1933, and the kidnapping of the pacifist journalist Berthold Jacob in Switzerland by Nazi agents who lured him over the border in 1935, had already demonstrated how insecure life had become for German pacifist émigrés due to the merciless persecution from Hitler's régime.[59] (After escaping from

the French internment camp of Le Vernet, Berthold Jacob managed
to flee via Marseille, Spain, and Portugal to Lisbon, where he was
once again discovered by Nazi agents. Kidnapped from a hotel in
Lisbon, he was taken to Berlin — probably by aircraft — and murdered in 1944.) What could be done under such circumstances in order to maintain the coherence of pacifist conceptualization, not to
speak of organizational efforts, had little in common with the relatively encouraging initial phase of the Weimar Republic. What survived after Denmark and Norway — which had been favorite exile
countries — had been invaded, was only a shadow of the former German peace movement. Scattered all over the world, with small groups
of German pacifists or pacifist individuals remaining only in Great
Britain, and neutral Switzerland and Sweden, the traces of German
pacifism had practically been extinguished in Europe.

From the damages inflicted upon German pacifism by National
Socialism, there was, in fact, no possibility of real recovery. By the
time Nazi Germany was finally defeated, a great many exiled German pacifists had died. Of those who could have returned to Germany, many had grown too old. Others hesitated to do so because
they had been treated badly by their fatherland, or because they had
meanwhile established a new existence in the United States or elsewhere. Although some of those pacifists who survived in Germany
tried to reorganize German pacifism immediately after World War
II, the catastrophic result of Hitler's régime for German pacifism explains to a certain extent the lack of continuity that exists between
the peace movement in West Germany today and that in the Weimar
Republic.

NOTES

1. Exceptions are W. A. Berendsohn, *Die humanistische Front. Einführ-
ung in die deutsche Emigranten-Literatur,* vol. 1: *Von 1933 bis zum Kriegsausbruch 1939* (Zurich: Oprecht, 1946), and vol. 2: *Vom Kriegsausbruch
1939 bis Ende 1946* (Worms: Georg Heintz, 1976); A. Kantorowicz, *Politik
und Literatur im Exil. Deutschsprachige Schriftsteller im Kampf gegen den
Nationalsozialismus* (Munich: Deutscher Taschenbuch Verlag, 1983), 89–95.

2. The author is preparing a book on the subject.

3. Reinhold Lütgemeier-Davin, *Pazifismus zwischen Kooperation und
Konfrontation. Das Deutsche Friedenskartell in der Weimarer Republik*

(Cologne: Pahl-Rugenstein, 1982); Dieter Riesenberger, *Geschichte der Friedensbewegung in Deutschland. Von den Anfängen bis 1933* (Göttingen: Vandenhoeck & Ruprecht, 1985), 143–236; Karl Holl and Wolfram Wette, eds., *Pazifismus in der Weimarer Republik. Beiträge zur historischen Friedensforschung* (Paderborn: Schöningh, 1981); Friedrich-Karl Scheer, *Die Deutsche Friedensgesellschaft (1892–1933). Organisation, Ideologie, politische Ziele. Ein Beitrag zur Geschichte des Pazifismus in Deutschland* (Frankfurt a. M.: Haag & Herchen, 1981); D. Riesenberger, *Die katholische Friedensbewegung in der Weimarer Republik* (Düsseldorf: Droste, 1976).

4. K. Holl, "Pazifismus oder liberaler Neu-Imperialismus? Zur Rolle der Pazifisten in der Deutschen Demokratischen Partei 1918–1930," in J. Radkau and I. Geiss, eds., *Imperialismus im 20. Jahrhundert. Gedenkschrift für George W. F. Hallgarten* (Munich: C. H. Beck, 1976), 171–95; K. Holl, "Die Deutsche Demokratische Partei im Spannungsverhältnis zwischen Wehrpolitik und Pazifismus," in Holl and Wette, *Pazifismus,* 135–48; W. Wette, "Sozialdemokratie und Pazifismus in der Weimarer Republik," *Archiv für Sozialgeschichte* 26 (1986): 281–300.

5. Otmar Jung, "Spaltung und Rekonstruktion des organisierten Pazifismus in der Spätzeit der Weimarer Republik," *Vierteljahreshefte für Zeitgeschichte* 35 (1986): 207–43.

6. Ibid., 232–37; B. Goldstein, "Ludwig Quidde and the Struggle for Democratic Pacifism in Germany, 1914–1930" (Ph.D. diss., New York University, 1984); Holl, "Ludwig Quidde," in Ch. Rajewski and D. Riesenberger, eds., *Wider den Krieg* (Munich: C. H. Beck, 1987); Helmut Donat, "Die radikalpazifistische Richtung in der Deutschen Friedensgesellschaft (1918–1933)," in Holl and Wette, *Pazifismus,* 27–45; entry for Fritz Küster in Harold Josephson, ed., *Biographical Dictionary of Modern Peace Leaders* (Westport, CT: Greenwood, 1985).

7. F. Baumer, *Carl von Ossietzky* (Berlin: Colloquium, 1984); Karol Fiedor, *Carl von Ossietzky und die Friedensbewegung. (Die deutschen Pazifisten im Kampf gegen Wiederaufrüstung und Kriegsgefahr)* (Wrocław: Wydawnictwo Universytetu Wrocławskiego, 1985); Fiedor, *Militaryzmowi i Faszyzmowi — Nie. Carl von Ossietzky Zycie i Walka* (Warsaw and Wrocław: Panstwowe Wydawnictwo Naukowe, 1986); K. R. Grossmann, *Ossietzky — Ein deutscher Patriot* (Munich: Kindler, 1963); R. Koplin, *Carl von Ossietzky als politischer Publizist* (Berlin and Frankfurt a. M.: Annedore Leber, 1964); U. Madrasch-Groschopp, *Die Weltbühne. Porträt einer Zeitschrift* (Berlin and Königstein i. Ts.: Der Morgen, Athenäum, 1983); I. Deak, *Weimar Left-Wing Intellectuals. A Political History of the Weltbühne and its Circle* (Berkeley and Los Angeles: Univ. of California Press, 1968), 49–61, 189–98; Heinz Jäger [Walther Kreiser], "Windiges aus der deutschen Luftfahrt," *Die Weltbühne* 25 (1929), 402–7.

8. Riesenberger, *Geschichte der Friedensbewegung,* 237–52.

9. H. Donat and L. Wieland, eds., *Das Andere Deutschland. Unabhängige Zeitung für entschiedene republikanische Politik. Eine Auswahl (1925–1933)* (Königstein i. Ts.: Autoren Edition, 1980), lviii.

10. Gerhart Seger, *Reisetagebuch eines deutschen Emigranten* (Zurich: Europa-Verlag, 1936), 5–6.

11. Emil J. Gumbel, *Verschwörer. Beiträge zur Geschichte und Soziologie der deutschen nationalistischen Geheimbünde 1918–1924* (Vienna: Malik, 1924; new ed., with a foreword by K. Buselmeier, Heidelberg: Das Wunderhorn, 1979); F. J. Lersch, "Politische Gewalt, politische Justiz und Pazifismus in der Weimarer Republik. Der Beitrag E. J. Gumbels für die deutsche Friedensbewegung," in Holl and Wette, *Pazifismus,* 113–34; W. Benz, "Emil Julius Gumbel. Die Karriere eines deutschen Pazifisten," in U. Walberer, ed., *10. Mai 1933. Bücherverbrennung in Deutschland und die Folgen* (Frankfurt a. M.: Fischer, 1983); Ch. Jansen, "Emil Julius Gumbel – Ein Statistiker des Antimilitarismus," in D. Harth, D. Schubert, and R. M. Schmidt, eds., *Pazifismus zwischen den Weltkriegen* (Heidelberg: HVA, 1985), 31–41.

12. Friedrich W. Foerster, *Erlebte Weltgeschichte 1869–1953* (Nuremberg: Glock & Lutz, 1953), 555–56.

13. D. Acker, *Walther Schücking (1875–1935)* (Münster i. W.: Aschendorffsche Verlagsbuchhandlung, 1970), 204–5.

14. L. Cassebohm [L. Quidde] to Wehberg, Munich, 14 March 1933, Nachlass (hereinafter abbreviated NL) H. Wehberg, 70, Bundesarchiv Koblenz (hereinafter cited as BA); Ludwig Quidde, *Der deutsche Pazifismus während des Weltkrieges 1914–1918,* ed. Karl Holl (Boppard a. Rh.: Boldt, 1979), intro., 24–28.

15. Milly Zirker to Grossmann, Mexico, 13 Oct. 1963, Kurt Grossmann Papers, 14, Hoover Institution Archives, Stanford University, Stanford, CA (hereinafter cited as HIA).

16. Constanze Hallgarten, *Als Pazifistin in Deutschland. Biographische Skizze* (Stuttgart: Conseil-Verlag, 1965), 109–10; Karl Holl and A. Wild, eds., *Ein Demokrat kommentiert Weimar. Die Berichte Hellmut von Gerlachs an die Carnegie Friedensstiftung in New York 1922–1933* (Bremen: Schünemann, 1973), intro., 37.

17. L. Wieland, "Otto Lehmann-Russbüldt," in Helmut Donat and Karl Holl, eds., *Die Friedensbewegung. Organisierter Pazifismus in Deutschland, Österreich und in der Schweiz* (Düsseldorf: ECON Taschenbuch Verlag/ Hermes Handlexicon, 1983), 249–50.

18. Entwurf III (n.d., 1934), NL L. Quidde, 114, BA.

19. L. Quidde to M. Quidde, Geneva, 27 March 1938 and 7 April 1938, Handschriftensammlung, NL M. Quidde, Stadtbibliothek Munich.

20. Mönch to Quidde, Toulouse, 23 Feb. and 10 March 1938, NL L. Quidde, 32, BA.

21. Fett to Quidde, Saint-Pey, 3 March 1938; Toulouse, 7 April 1938, NL L. Quidde, 30.

22. A biography of A. Freymuth will be published by O. Jung.

23. Procès-Verbal des Séances du Conseil tenues à Locarno les 1–7 Septembre 1934, Papiers Golay, Archives du Bureau International de la Paix, United Nations Library, Geneva (hereinafter cited as BIP/A); 27 July 1934 Action en Faveur des Réfugiés Allemands, in Geneva, BIP/A; Quidde to H. Golay, Geneva, 14 Oct. 1934, NL L. Quidde, 141, BA.

24. Seger to Golay, Prague, 10 Dec. 1933; Seger to Quidde, Prague, 19 Dec. 1933; Golay to Seger, Geneva, 25 Jan. 1934; Seger to Golay, Prague, 30 Jan. 1934, NL L. Quidde, 141, BA; Comité Directeur du 1er octobre 1933 au 31 mai 1934, Golay to Seger, Geneva, 18 Dec. 1933, BIP.

25. G. Seger, *Oranienburg. Erster authentischer Bericht eines aus dem Konzentrationslager Geflüchteten,* intro. Heinrich Mann (Karlsbad: Graphia, 1934); G. Seger, *Reisetagebuch,* 109–33; J. Radkau, *Die deutsche Emigration in den USA. Ihr Einfluß auf die amerikanische Europa-Politik 1933–1945* (Düsseldorf: Bertelsmann Universitätsverlag, 1971), 68. Cf. Politisches Archiv des Auswärtigen Amtes, Bonn, Inland II A/B, Ref. Dtschl., Bd. 285/3, Gerhard Seger.

26. Seger, *Reisetagebuch,* 34.

27. Quidde to the members of the "comité de secours aux pacifistes exilés," Geneva, 22 May 1937; minutes of the meeting of the "comité de secours," 14 Oct. 1937, NL L. Quidde, 141, BA.

28. Quidde to Libby, Geneva, 25 June 1937, NL L. Quidde, 32, BA.

29. Libby to Quidde, Washington, D.C., 27 July 1937, NL L. Quidde, 143, BA. See also Quidde Papers, Correspondence with Libby, Swarthmore College Peace Collection, Swarthmore, PA.

30. G. Baer to Quidde, USA, 25 May 1937, NL L. Quidde, 143, BA.

31. L. Quidde, "Hilfe für Friedenskämpfer," *Die Friedenswarte* 37 (1937), 118–26, and 38 (1938), Heft 3/4; Quidde to Nobel Committee of the Norwegian Storthing, Geneva, 22 Jan. 1937, and 21 Jan. 1938, NL L. Quidde, 144, BA; Ernst Arrenberg, "Der Friedensnobelpreis," *Neue Zürcher Zeitung,* 9 Dec. 1936.

32. Basch to Grossmann, Paris, 14 April 1933, Grossmann Papers, 41, HIA.

33. For the period between 15 and 25 April, see v. Gerlach to Grossmann, Zurich, 15 April 1933 and v. Gerlach to Grossmann, Paris, 25 April 1933, Grossmann Papers, 41, HIA.

34. Demokratische Flüchtlingsfürsorge, ed., *Fünf Jahre! Flucht, Not und Rettung* (Prague: Selbstverlag der Demokratischen Flüchtlingsfürsorge, 1938).

35. Institut für Zeitgeschichte, Munich, Archiv (hereinafter cited as IZG), ED 201, Bd. 4, Denkschriften zur Flüchtlingsfrage 1936–1945, 1–9, Memo-

randum du Comité National Tchécoslovaque pour les Réfugiés allemands. Die deutsche Emigration in der Tschechoslowakei, 1933–1935.

36. L. Quidde to Kessler, Geneva, 14 Sept. 1935, Bestand Harry Graf Kessler, Nr. 1, 546, Deutsches Literaturarchiv, Marbach.

37. IZG, ED 201, Bd. 4, Denkschriften zur Flüchtlingsfrage 1936–1945, 491–92, Der "gefährliche Pazifist" Friedrich Wilhelm Foerster; Foerster, *Erlebte Weltgeschichte,* 545–46.

38. Falk to Carl Paeschke, Fréjus, 14 Nov. 1935, IZG, ED 205, Bd. 2.

39. H. Stöcker to Rosika Schwimmer, London, 26 July 1939, Schwimmer Lloyd Collection, Manuscript and Archives Division, New York Public Library.

40. See e.g., Entschliessung, Strasbourg, 12 June 1933, Alfred Falk, IZG, ED 205, Bd. 2, 42.

41. See e.g., H. v. Gerlach to Grossmann, Paris, 16 Nov. 1934, Grossmann Papers, 41, HIA.

42. Falk to Paeschke, Strasbourg-Königshoffen, 25 May 1935, IZG, ED 205, Bd. 2.

43. Ibid., 25 Feb. 1935.

44. Quidde to Kessler, Geneva, 14 Sept. 1935, Bestand Harry Graf Kessler, Nr. 1, 546, Deutsches Literaturarchiv, Marbach. For details, see Karl Holl, ed., *Ludwig Quidde. Der deutsche Pazifismus während des Weltkrieges 1914–1918,* intro., 25.

45. Wehberg to Dr. R. M. Müller, Geneva, 23 June 1961, NL H. Wehberg, 71, BA.

46. Holl and Wild, *Ein Demokrat,* intro., 41–42.

47. Ibid., 41. Cf. U. Langkau-Alex, *Volksfront für Deutschland?,* vol. 1: *Vorgeschichte und Gründung des "Ausschusses zur Vorbereitung einer deutschen Volksfront," 1933–1936* (Frankfurt a.M.: Syndikat, 1977), 80–82.

48. In re the case of H. Fett, see H. and K. Fett to Quidde, Toulouse, 23 April 1939, and Quidde to Fett, Geneva, 25 April 1939, NL L. Quidde, 36; and in re Mönch, see Mönch to Quidde, Toulouse, 31 Oct. 1939, NL L Quidde, 37, BA.

49. Max Heimann to Quidde, St. Cyprien, 9 Sept. 1940, NL L. Quidde, 42, BA.

50. E.g. to the president of the French Peace Society, Lucien Le Foyer: see Quidde to Le Foyer, Geneva, 16 Nov. 1939, and Le Foyer to Quidde, Arcachon, 9 March 1940, NL L. Quidde, 37, BA.

51. Quidde to Théodore Ruyssen (president of the League "La Paix par le Droit"), Geneva, 12 Nov. 1939, NL L. Quidde, 38, BA.

52. Quidde to the International Committee of the Red Cross, Geneva, 29 Sept. 1940, NL L. Quidde, 42, BA.

53. F. Barbey (member of the International Committee of the Red Cross) to Quidde, Geneva, 4 Oct. 1940, NL L. Quidde, 42, BA.

54. Among the reports that Quidde received were: Fett to Quidde, Toulouse, 2 July, 13 July, 29 July, and 17 Aug. 1940, NL L. Quidde, 42, BA.

55. Madame Fabre to Quidde, Fréjus, 21 Oct. 1940; Quidde to Madame Fabre, Geneva, 25 Oct. 1940, NL L. Quidde, 42, BA.

56. D. S. Wyman, *Paper Walls. America and the Refugee Crisis 1938–1941* (Amherst: Univ. of Massachusetts Press, 1968; New York: Pantheon, 1985).

57. Varian Fry, *Surrender on Demand* (New York: Random House, 1945; German ed., W. E. Elfe and J. Hans, eds., *Auslieferung auf Verlangen. Die Rettung deutscher Emigranten in Marseille 1940/41* (Munich: Hanser, 1986); D. Bénédite, *La Filière Marseillaise. Un chemin vers la liberté sous l'occupation* (Paris: Clancier Guénaud, 1984); A. Heilbut, *Exiled in Paradise. German Refugee Artists and Intellectuals in America, from the 1930s to the Present* (New York: Viking, 1983), 40–42.

58. Fry (1986), *Auslieferung,* 46; Bénédite, *Filière,* 68; W. A. Neilson, ed., *We Escaped. Twelve Personal Narratives of the Flight to America* (New York: Macmillan, 1941), 28–57 ("The Professor from Heidelberg").

59. J. N. Willi, *Der Fall Jacob-Wesemann (1935/36). Ein Beitrag zur Geschichte der Schweiz in der Zwischenkriegszeit* (Bern and Frankfurt a. M.: Lang, 1972).

The United States

DAVID S. PATTERSON

Citizen Peace Initiatives and American Political Culture, 1865–1920

ONE OF THE FRUITS OF the growing interest in historical peace research over the past two decades has been the publication of serious studies of the American peace movement in the generation before the First World War. This scholarship has explored the major developments in the movement and provided interesting insights into its main leaders and their ideas and programs. These works have also shed some light on the relationship between the peace and domestic reform movements in the so-called progressive era from about 1900 to 1914.[1] Little has been written, however, on the relationship between beliefs and values of American peace reformers and the predominant Victorian culture in late–nineteenth-century America. This important relationship evolved subtly but perceptively from the Civil War era to the early twentieth century. There was a certain affinity between the peace workers' and middle-class Victorian reform attitudes, and new approaches to the international system in the peace movement paralleled some trends in the larger political culture. An understanding of this relationship should help to explain why the peace movement, seemingly so well organized and influential in the decade or so before 1914, became divided and paralyzed after the outbreak of the European war.

THE LATE NINETEENTH CENTURY

In nineteenth-century America citizens shared their peace concerns in local peace societies. As Alexis de Tocqueville commented more generally on voluntary associations in the United States, peace societies were one of the many kinds of informal forums for tempering citizens' individualistic, anti-institutional proclivities.[2] Perhaps because

Americans had no strong family lines, clearly defined class structure, and controlling traditions, they early found associational activity a source of socializing and psychological support. In any event, the pervasiveness of these voluntary associations was a uniquely American phenomenon.[3]

Peace groups formed the organizational units of a loosely structured peace movement in mid–nineteenth-century America. Though badly divided by the sectional conflict in the 1850s and 1860s, the American peace movement slowly recovered after the Civil War. Starting with a nucleus of a few modest peace societies in the Northeast – particularly the American Peace Society headquartered in Boston, the Philadelphia-based Universal Peace Union, and a few nonresistant religious sects such as the Peace Association of Friends – the movement grew gradually in the 1870s, 1880s, and 1890s.[4] The Peace and Arbitration Department of the Woman's Christian Temperance Union (WCTU), founded in 1887, and the annual conferences on international arbitration begun by the Quaker businessman Albert K. Smiley at his hotel resort on Lake Mohonk, New York, in 1895, for instance, helped to attract new recruits to the movement. These peace advocates, together with their British counterparts, promoted an Anglo-American arbitration agreement. An Atlantic reform movement had existed before the Civil War, and in the 1880s and 1890s the number of activists had expanded to form an impressive transatlantic community of like-minded international reformers. Their campaign had some effect in fostering their governments' negotiation of the Olney-Pauncefote treaty. Although a skeptical Senate emasculated and then defeated the accord in 1897, international arbitration continued thereafter to be a major goal of the American peace movement.[5]

Many of the pre-1900 leaders, influenced by Garrisonian nonresistance or sectarian pacifism, were liberal reformers. Emphasizing the free individual above organizational restraints, they developed highly personal and relatively simple blueprints for a peaceful world. Peace seekers brought to peace societies a broad view of reform, with peace as one important ideal inextricably linked with the larger goal of a morally pure society. The Universal Peace Union, for instance, eschewed sectarian identification, but the religious component, as derived principally from the Society of Friends, remained important. The title page of each issue of its monthly journal announced: "Blessed are the peacemakers, for they shall be called the children of God."[6]

Although the markedly pacifistic inclinations of the pre-1900 peace workers made them a distinct minority in an age of virulent nationalism, imperialism, and war, they were not alienated from the mainstream of American society. Apart from its pacifist strain, their religious heritage was very much a part of a larger value system which was essentially Victorian.[7] An analysis of their value system clearly reveals their reform interests. However, it also shows conservative elements in their thought which help to explain their tolerance for the conservative direction of the peace movement after the turn of the century.

Perhaps their main ideological commitment in the secular realm was free trade. Almost without exception they were devoted followers of British free-trade liberals Richard Cobden, John Bright, and William E. Gladstone. Like the British liberals who inspired them, they asserted (although often without any rigorous analysis of economic theory) that the voluntary international exchange of goods and services would lead to the triumph of anticolonialism, antiimperialism, internationalism, and pacifism over colonialism, imperialism, nationalism, and war. More fundamentally, however, they admired these British leaders because they were moralists who preached the brotherhood of man and the peaceful mission of the Anglo-Saxon race. They especially revered John Bright, a Quaker, because of the high standard of ethical principle he attempted to infuse into British political life. One American peace advocate called Bright "the greatest British statesman of the nineteenth century — a Christian statesman, free from taint,"[8] while another said he was "surely one of nature's noblemen, a man of sterling, uncompromising principle."[9] Andrew Carnegie, an early advocate of Anglo-American friendship, later recalled that Bright was "my favorite living hero in public life."[10]

Their humanitarian interests prompted peace advocates to become involved in numerous domestic causes in the late nineteenth century. Members of the American Peace Society, for instance, were involved in such causes as vegetarianism, humane treatment of animals, children's legal aid, and civil service and municipal reform, while those in the Universal Peace Union were particularly active promoters of the abolition of capital punishment and the arbitration of labor-capital disputes, both of which were related to their abhorrence of violence in any form, and also prison reform, Indian rights, temperance, women's rights, and purity reform, including censorship of "offensive" literature.[11]

Women's rights, temperance, and social purity were intimately related in late-nineteenth-century America. A dominant value in Victorian America was the cult of domesticity.[12] The home, a deeply conservative institution, represented order, security, and the training of youth in self-control, hard work, and moral principles, while the saloon, prostitution, and pornography epitomized a counterculture of disorder, vice, disease, crime, and urban political corruption. The *Angel of Peace,* a peace periodical for children published by the American Peace Society, was advertised as "devoted to peace, temperance, good morals and good manners" and as "free from overexciting, sensational reading."[13] Not surprisingly, women in particular tied peace issues to everyday domestic life. In her endorsement of the WCTU Peace and Arbitration Department, WCTU president Frances Willard easily linked war to the temperance movement: "nothing increases intemperance like war, and nothing tends toward war like intemperance."[14] The social purity movement was intimately related to this concern for the physical and moral well-being of the body politic, and several peace advocates also participated in the national campaign against prostitution and pornography.[15]

In a sense the idealization of domesticity tended to encourage the entrapment of women in the home, but some women also managed to promote traditional Victorian ideals outside the household in voluntary literary societies and reform organizations. Some even challenged the existing social order and sought legislative changes, as in prohibition and suffrage, in the name of traditional morality. May Wright Sewall, leader of the National Council of Women, exemplified this blend of reforming zeal and domesticity. She helped to develop a manual on peace for the National Council of Women which emphasized that arbitration was a procedure equally relevant for the family, school, business, and relations among nations.[16]

Women's active participation in the American peace movement supports this view of their place in American society. Except for women's rights questions, probably more women were active in peace movements than in other reform endeavors. Historians have debated whether the "maternal instinct," or females as the biologically "weaker sex," or social conditioning caused this commitment, but in any case the attachment of a major segment of the peace movement to other reform causes compatible with women's rights certainly encouraged their involvement.

Between 1895 and 1898, peace advocates petitioned Presidents Cleveland and McKinley and lobbied in Congress against the prospect of war between the United States and Spain over Cuba. Alfred Love and Belva Lockwood were particularly active in utilizing the Universal Peace Union and the International Peace Bureau in Berne, Switzerland, to urge third power mediation by the Pope or European powers of the Spanish-American dispute.

Although all peace efforts failed to prevent hostilities, the peace workers joined anti-imperialists after the war in resisting the decision of the McKinley administration to annex the Philippines to the United States. Like the anti-imperialist leaders, almost all of them were sixty years old or more. Moreover, they shared the anti-imperialists' elitism and Anglophilic biases. Unlike most anti-imperialist leaders, however, who were rather narrow, peevish, pessimistic, negative, even backward-looking to a simpler, more innocent America, many advocates of peace involved in the nationwide debate over imperialism (1898–1900) tended to be liberal, optimistic, affirmative, and adjustable to new conditions in both domestic and international life. Boston's Edwin D. Mead noted that a major weakness of the anti-imperialist movement was its underlying pessimism, but he did not allow himself to despair. The Unitarian minister Charles F. Dole perhaps best expressed the peace advocates' optimistic vision of the nation's peaceful mission: "We are not pessimists; we are not mere conservatives; we never despair of the Republic," he wrote in December 1898.[17]

Their attitude toward the leader of the Democratic party, William Jennings Bryan, suggests the differences between the peace and anti-imperialist movements. Though individuals in both causes objected to Bryan's curious arguments in favor of Senate consent to the treaty with Spain, which transferred sovereignty of the Philippines to the United States, and for the most part applauded his subsequent stand against imperialism and for the early independence of the islands, the position of the anti-imperialists and peace advocates differed in the election of 1900. Most anti-imperialists perceived Bryan's views on domestic questions as too radical to endorse him as the Democratic presidential nominee, but with a few exceptions — most notably David Starr Jordan and Andrew Carnegie — the peace leaders supported him.[18]

An affirmative outlook is perhaps to be expected of dedicated peace workers, and the war and the imperialistic aftermath did not dampen their commitment to the cause. Indeed, other international and domestic developments almost simultaneously rekindled their hopes for world peace. The relatively short duration of the Spanish war and the declining insurgency in the Philippines after 1900 undoubtedly saved them from prolonged anguish. Moreover, the convening of the First Hague Peace Conference (1899), which Tsar Nicholas II of Russia had initiated, and the conferees' agreement to establish a Permanent Court of Arbitration at The Hague (though it was hardly "permanent" or a "court," because the Hague convention allowed only for a panel of arbiters from which nations could voluntarily select their adjudicators) seemed harbingers of possible future cooperation among nation states.

The septuagenarian Boston minister Edward Everett Hale launched a virtual one-man nationwide speaking tour in promoting the conference, which he viewed as a first step in an inevitable process leading to the future political federation of Europe. Other Boston reformers used the Twentieth Century Club, a high-minded civic organization, to boost the Hague gathering and promote its modest beginnings in the development of international institutions.

THE RISE OF PEACE ADVOCACY AFTER 1900

The peace movement swelled much more rapidly after 1900. About 45 new peace groups were begun in the 1900–1914 interim. One of the most prominent of the new groups was the New York Peace Society, which clergymen, lawyers, editors, and especially college professors and professional educators from the area founded in 1906. Within a year the new group had 600 members, and more than 1,000 had joined by 1912. Several of the new organizations were founded outside the Northeast. Prominent liberals like Jane Addams, Emil Hirsch, and Jenkin Lloyd Jones joined with professional and business people in the Chicago area, for instance, in reorganizing and revitalizing the Chicago Peace Society in 1909, which grew rapidly thereafter.

In addition, the Boston textbook publisher Edwin Ginn founded the World Peace Foundation in 1910 with a gift of $50,000 a year and the promise of a bequest of $1 million upon his death. Edwin

Mead and David Starr Jordan, president of Stanford University, were the two most influential directors of the new organization.[19] Believing that a sound liberal education was essential to good citizenship, the World Peace Foundation provided financial and moral support to educational peace endeavors, such as the Association of Cosmopolitan Clubs (international friendship societies composed of American and foreign students at several universities) and the American School Peace League. The Cosmopolitan Clubs produced George W. Nasmyth and Louis P. Lochner as youthful American peace leaders, while Fannie Fern Andrews, a Boston educator, became the driving force in the American School Peace League.

Ginn's gift, along with the persistent proddings of influential internationalists such as Nicholas Murray Butler, Hamilton Holt, and Theodore Marburg, increasingly weakened Andrew Carnegie's hesitancy toward using his money for the creation of an even more munificent peace trust. When arbitration treaties with Britain and other nations (as well as greater coordination among the peace societies) were advocated by President Taft, whom Andrew Carnegie greatly admired, the former steelmaster was finally prompted to establish the Carnegie Endowment for International Peace with a fund of $10 million in December 1910. Almost overnight Ginn's and Carnegie's gifts provided the peace movement with greatly enhanced revenues. Using its financial leverage, the trustees of the Carnegie Endowment persuaded the American Peace Society to move its headquarters from Boston to Washington, D.C., and to reorganize itself as a more truly national peace organization. Then it provided subventions to the American Peace Society and the International Peace Bureau for distribution to their affiliated peace groups in the United States and Europe, respectively.[20]

Moreover, several lawyers, interested in promoting international law and a world court, founded the American Society of International Law (1905) and the American Society for Judicial Settlement of International Disputes (1910). The creation of the Peace and Arbitration Commission of the Federal Council of Churches of Christ in America in 1911 bolstered the religious phase of the peace movement, at least among the Protestant churches. In early 1914, Frederick Lynch prevailed upon Andrew Carnegie, who was apparently dissatisfied with the deliberate and conservative policies of the Carnegie Endowment trustees, to give $2 million for the establishment of the Church Peace Union. By that date a few internationalists had begun to advance bolder plans for world organization, ranging from a league of the great powers to enforce the peace to a more inclusive world federation.

PEACE ADVOCATES AND AMERICAN POLITICAL CULTURE

What were the reasons for the extraordinary growth of the American peace movement in the decade before 1914? Some factors which help to explain rising peace activity in other times and places were not present in this interim. Widespread popular malaise from the horrors of the First World War or a pervasive sense of injustice at American military involvement in the Vietnam War, for example, stimulated peace movements in those eras, but among the newcomers to the peace movement in the early 1900s there is no evidence of similar reactions to the Spanish-American War, which they along with most Americans accepted as a "splendid little war," or to the Filipino insurrection. Similarly, the new peace advocates did not seem to be influenced by negative reactions to the armaments race in Europe and the United States or to the devastating weaponry being developed. Indeed, unlike those involved in the movement in the late nineteenth century, almost all of whom criticized the large navy programs of the Roosevelt administration after 1900, the great majority of new recruits favored an "adequate" navy (although they never defined the concept) and in a few cases readily endorsed the Navy League's proponents of a large navy.

To be sure, there were certain similarities which provided a sense of continuity in the peace movement. The leadership of the American peace movement throughout the entire period from 1865 to 1914, for example, was drawn overwhelmingly from well-educated, Anglo-Saxon, and Protestant elites, although those entering the cause in the first decade of the twentieth century tended to be more conservative and professionally oriented than their predecessors. The newer converts utilized the existing organizational base of the movement, especially the American Peace Society and the Lake Mohonk Conferences, to expand in new directions. Moreover, they also shared an unquestioned faith in inevitable moral progress. They perceived militarism and interstate conflict, for example, as anachronistic survivals of an earlier, unenlightened era rather than endemic or growing evils of modern life.

Both domestic and foreign events affected the direction of the movement. The urban-industrial transformation increased the complexity of American society. American social thought shifted in emphasis from moral absolutes to specialized, utilitarian knowledge, from direct democracy to intervening bureaucratic forms, and from ethical purity to efficiency.[21] The change was very gradual, however, and the development of the progressive reform impulse after about 1900 resulted in several different approaches to peace reform.

Much as domestic reformers turned to the state to solve the problems of a complex, urban society, so the few liberals entering the peace movement began to contemplate the establishment of authoritative intergovernmental institutions for war prevention. The approach of almost all the new leaders was cautious. Unlike the earlier peace reformers, many of whom derived their faith in moral values and inevitable progress from ideals of Christian humanism and the Enlightenment, the newer peace advocates limited their faith in moral progress to the so-called "advanced" or "civilized" great powers. They assumed as given, or even as a positive good, the asymmetrical power relationships in both the domestic and international order. Most of them also had serious reservations about the establishment of an authoritative world organization.

The conservative direction of the peace cause in the same years that the nation experienced a widespread reform movement appears at first glance to be something of a paradox. Part of the explanation for the conservative trend lies with the domestic reformers' comparative disinterest in the peace movement after about 1900. This allowed other elements to predominate in it. The liberals' disinterest is understandable. The overwhelming majority of them were preoccupied with domestic issues; international reform seemed very remote by comparison. Moreover, most American reformers did not easily discard their isolationist biases, despite the emergence of the United States as a great power. Comfortable with their nation's "free security," they were at best superficially acquainted with European power rivalries, American and European imperialism, protectionism, and the armaments race, all of which might threaten the security they assumed. Many liberals who were to become peace leaders and internationalists during and after the First World War showed no interest in foreign affairs, let alone the peace movement, before 1914.

In a related sense, the leaders of domestic reform groups increasingly began to prefer institutional and professional associations to personal and voluntary ones. Local and individual protest efforts gave way to bureaucratic activity, which became a salient characteristic of the progressive reform movement after 1900. Organizations like the Anti-Saloon League and the National American Woman's Suffrage Association pursued bureaucratic reform with increasing success. Though most American peace groups adjusted to these changes and adopted more practical programs, they could not compete effectively for the attention of liberal reformers who were increasingly attracted to what they perceived to be more tangible, immediate issues such as women's suffrage and prohibition. At an extreme was the Universal Peace Union, which eschewed all compromise and change. Not surprisingly, it failed to attract new recruits to the society, and when Alfred Love, its principal founder and leader, died in 1913, the Universal Peace Union expired with him.

At the same time, more conservative and professional people were attracted to the peace movement. Lawyers, for example, responded to both domestic and international developments. Internationally, they gave new impetus to certain traditional aims of the peace movement, such as periodic international conferences and the codification of international law, and promoted new ones, particularly the creation of an international arbitral court, which the Second Hague Peace Conference (1907) tacitly endorsed.[22] Domestically, as part of an increasingly self-conscious legal profession, they used the peace movement as an important organizational vehicle to promote the specialty of international law.

The motivations of Protestant clergymen were similarly complex. The ethical dimensions of war/peace issues have always engaged the attention of the Protestant churches, but their clergy were for the most part rather tardy recruits to the peace cause in early–twentieth-century America. Several ordained clergymen — William H. Short, James J. Hall, James L. Tryon, Charles E. Beals, for example — had found church work unrewarding or stultifying and turned to the burgeoning peace movement as a new outlet for their social concerns. As Beals, field secretary of the American Peace Society and secretary of the Chicago Peace Society, later noted, "After fifteen years of conscientious work in the pastorate, I felt that too largely the activities of the churches were devoted to saving the churches instead of to serving society. . . . Hence I left the pastorate and never have regretted taking the step."[23]

Others who remained clergymen seem to have joined the peace movement in part because they perceived that the churches would lose further influence in an increasingly secular and materialistic society if they failed to participate actively in the growing peace cause. Frederick Lynch in particular chided the churches for their tardy interest in peace questions.[24] The involvement of Protestant clerics was not merely defensive, however, because they also saw the peace movement as an opportunity to expand ministerial power and influence. Organizationally, it served as the most appropriate forum for encouraging the nascent Protestant unity movement which could revitalize the churches. Some leaders in the Federal Council of Churches of Christ in America, founded between 1905 and 1908, perceived the peace movement as a cooperative activity that might help the church unity movement at the outset. The Commission on the Peace and Arbitration of the Federal Council and the Church Peace Union were, in part, efforts at such unity. "Both," Roland Marchand has written, "owed their existence as much to efforts to promote church unity as they did to the quest for world peace."[25] A primary aim of the Church Peace Union from the outset was the funding and administrative oversight for international conferences and exchange programs of church leaders to foster both church unity and peace. The trustees of the Church Peace Union even included a few Catholic prelates and Jewish rabbis to indicate its ecumenical orientation.

Still other newcomers to the peace movement without clearly liberal or professional interests perceived it as a socially respectable outlet for their mildly reformist inclinations. They found most domestic reformers too liberal or narrowly self-interested to support, but involvement in the peace movement offered the opportunity for high-minded moral uplift without challenging the existing social order.

THE ZENITH OF THE PREWAR PEACE MOVEMENT

Between 1910 and 1914 the peace movement promoted several peace issues. Peace advocates were especially active in the campaign for President Taft's arbitration treaties with Britain and France. Like the Olney-Pauncefote arbitration treaty earlier, Taft's treaties were weakened by amendments in the Senate and never ratified. Peace advocates also opposed the U.S. imposition of tolls on foreign commerce in the Panama Canal, which threatened Anglo-American understanding. Finally, they endorsed the conciliation treaties of William Jennings Bryan, Woodrow Wilson's pacifist Secretary of State, agitated for a third international peace conference at The Hague in 1915, and resisted, though without much effect, President Wilson's military incursion into Mexico following the Tampico incident in the spring of 1914.[26]

By 1914 the American peace movement was at its zenith in terms of number of organizations, active membership, and financial resources. In the early summer of that year, peace workers were busily engaged in preparations for a July conference in London sponsored by the British liberal internationalist Norman Angell, an ecumenical church peace conference at Constance in early August, and the Interparliamentary Union and Universal Peace Congresses in Stockholm and Vienna later in August and September.

THE IMPACT OF THE FIRST WORLD WAR

The onset of the World War not only forced the cancellation of the August and September conferences but also shattered the outward cohesion of the prewar movement. A period of confusion and divisions within almost all peace groups followed. Unable to develop coherent positions on military preparedness, mediation of the conflict, and the prospect of U.S. military intervention, many groups became paralyzed. Some local and state groups dissolved under these pressures; others were slowly transformed. The New York Peace Society, for example, failed to take vigorous positions on the issues of American neutrality. Hamilton Holt, William Short, and other leading internationalists in the New York Peace Society used the body as a forum for initiating discussions on the need for a permanent international body with broad powers to require nations to try to arbitrate future major conflicts before resorting to war, but their desire for a broader constituency led them to form the League to Enforce Peace in 1915, which became the leading lobbying group for the creation of an authoritative world organization. The New York Peace Society finally endorsed the League to Enforce Peace but at the cost of the defection of many members who wanted the society to promote other peace issues. By 1920 the New York group had dissolved altogether.

The American Peace Society, much to the discomfiture of pacifistic liberals in it, also took no positions on military preparedness and mediation and acquiesced in U.S. belligerency. It eventually supported the international lawyers' campaign for U.S. membership in a world court but refused to endorse the bolder collective security position of the League to Enforce Peace. The endowed peace organizations also avoided positions on the immediate problems of American neutrality and focused instead on aspects of postwar world organization. With only a few exceptions, the prewar peace leadership rallied behind President Wilson's decision for war in early 1917.

How could such a well organized and apparently influential peace movement before the World War become so divided after 1914 and ultimately support U.S. involvement in the conflict? The answer lies with the changing direction of the movement during the progressive era. By 1914 most of the pacifistic reformers who had entered the cause before the turn of the century were either dead or too old to exert much influence on the peace movement. The post–1900 recruits also believed in peace, but they were not so pacifistic and had no demonstrable roots in sectarian pacifism or nineteenth-century moral reforms. Moreover, while they were internationalists, they were solid nationalists as well. Thus they were prepared to support U.S. involvement in the war as the best opportunity to provide their nation's leaders with additional leverage at the peace settlement for the establishment of authoritative international institutions.

Not too much should be made of the differences between the pre and post–1900 peace leadership, which were as much matters of degree as substance. The earlier leaders, for example, had been unsuccessful in preventing war with Spain. There were simply not enough antiwar activists throughout this era to resist with any success the pervasive nationalism. Moreover, most peace advocates in the entire period were part of a well-educated, Anglo-Saxon, Protestant establishment; as members of elite social groups, they were not disposed to challenge the dominant political culture. The peace advocates also shared elitist attitudes. They assumed that literate people from the upper and middle classes could more easily understand the civilized quality of their movement than the unenlightened masses, and the movement increasingly shunned contacts with labor, moderate socialist, and ethnic groups.

The conservative trend in the peace movement was challenged after 1914. Just as proponents of world organization founded new internationalist groups, so did pacifistic Americans create new organizations. The Women's Peace Party, American Union Against Militarism, Neutral Conference for Continuous Mediation, American Neutral Conference Committee, Emergency Peace Federation, and Fellowship of Reconciliation, for example, were founded during American neutrality. These groups, as well as others founded during and immediately after the period of American belligerency, attracted not only peace seekers disenchanted with the timidity of the peace societies and endowed organizations but impelled many more pacifistic liberals and socialists into the cause for the first time. Many of these antiwar newcomers became absolute pacifists and boldly linked peace advocacy with social justice causes. This pacifist leadership would serve as the vanguard of a vibrant and influential peace movement in the 1920s and 1930s.

CONCLUSION

The American peace movement between 1865 and 1914 mirrored some larger trends in American social and political life. Particularly in the early years, its members drew upon and contributed to several domestic reform movements. In the early twentieth century the movement seemed to lose its association with other issues of social change. Bourgeois class and professional biases predominated. The movement became separated not only from the religious and humanitarian impulses of earlier movements but also from the growing labor and socialist movements.[27]

In retrospect, the most important lasting development of the peace movement in the half century before 1914 was its growing internationalist perspective. Although American internationalists had little direct impact on Woodrow Wilson in the development of the League of Nations after the war, they had begun to think carefully about the implications of international political institutions long before the World War. They were thus in a position to champion American membership and leadership in the new world organization and to attempt to remedy its imperfections.

NOTES

1. See, for example, Warren F. Kuehl, *Seeking World Order: The United States and International Organization to 1920* (Nashville, TN: Vanderbilt Univ. Press, 1969); Sondra R. Herman, *Eleven Against War: Studies in American Internationalist Thought, 1898–1921* (Stanford, CA: Hoover Institution Press, 1969); C. Roland Marchand, *The American Peace Movement and Social Reform, 1898–1918* (Princeton, NJ: Princeton Univ. Press, 1972); David S. Patterson, *Toward a Warless World: The Travail of the American Peace Movement, 1887–1914* (Bloomington: Indiana Univ. Press, 1976); and Charles DeBenedetti, *The Peace Reform in American History* (Bloomington: Indiana Univ. Press, 1980), chs. 4–5.

2. Alexis de Tocqueville, *Democracy in America,* 2 vols. (1835; New York: Knopf, 1945), especially vol. 2.

3. A recent historical treatment of this theme is Brian O'Connell, ed., *America's Voluntary Spirit: A Book of Readings* (New York: Foundation Center, 1983).

4. Peter Brock, *Pacifism in the United States: From the Colonial Era to the First World War* (Princeton, NJ: Princeton Univ. Press, 1968), part 5.

5. Patterson, *Toward a Warless World,* chs. 1–2. Much of the material not specifically cited in the following notes is derived from this book. The transatlantic dimension of late–nineteenth-century reform, including interrelationships between the various movements, deserves further study. Its importance for the temperance movement is explored in Ruth Bordin, *Frances Willard: a Biography* (Chapel Hill: Univ. of North Carolina Press, 1986), 196ff.

6. The journal began with the title *Bond of Peace* in 1868, changed its title to *Voice of Peace* in 1874, and finally to *The Peacemaker and Court of Arbitration* (hereafter cited as *Peacemaker*), in 1882.

7. See the essays in Daniel Walker Howe, ed., *Victorian America* (Philadelphia: Univ. of Pennsylvania Press, 1976).

8. *Peacemaker* 1 (June 1883): 185.

9. Ibid. 2 (Aug. 1883): 27.

10. *Autobiography of Andrew Carnegie* (Boston: Houghton Mifflin, 1920), 282–83.

11. Marchand, *American Peace Movement and Social Reform,* 12–16; David S. Patterson, Introduction to microfiche edition of *The Peacemaker and Court of Arbitration* (1882–1913), The Library of World Peace Studies, ed. Warren F. Kuehl (New York: Clearwater, 1979), 6–9.

12. For a few examples of the expanding literature on women's social roles, see Barbara Welter, "The Cult of True Womanhood, 1820–1860," *American Quarterly* 18 (Summer 1966): 151–74; Glenda Gates Riley, "The Subtle Subversion: Changes in the Traditionalist Image of the American

Woman," *The Historian* 32 (Feb. 1970): 210-27; Kathryn Kish Sklar, *Catharine Beecher: A Study in American Domesticity* (New Haven, CT: Yale Univ. Press, 1973); Ann Douglas, *The Feminization of American Culture* (New York: Knopf, 1977); and Barbara Leslie Epstein, *The Politics of Domesticity: Women, Evangelism, and Temperance in Nineteenth-Century America* (Middletown, CT: Wesleyan Univ. Press, 1981).

13. Quoted in Marchand, *American Peace Movement and Social Reform*, 13.

14. Quoted in Patterson, *Toward a Warless World*, 24.

15. Compare, for example, the list of the leadership of the American Purity Alliance in David J. Pivar, *Purity Crusade: Sexual Morality and Social Control, 1868-1900* (Westport, CT: Greenwood, 1973), 281-85, and the list of vice-presidents of the Universal Peace Union published in the inside cover of *The Peacemaker* 14 (July 1895). For the deep involvement of the women's temperance movement in the efforts to suppress prostitution and pornography, see especially Epstein, *Politics of Domesticity*, 125-37.

16. See Michael A. Lutzker's essay on Mrs. Sewall in Harold Josephson, ed., *Biographical Dictionary of Modern Peace Leaders* (Westport, CT: Greenwood, 1985), 875.

17. Quoted in Patterson, *Toward a Warless World*, 87.

18. Cf. Robert A. Beisner, *Twelve Against Empire: The Anti-Imperialists, 1898-1900* (New York: McGraw-Hill, 1968), 9-17, 69, 82, 154, 186, 196, 228-33, 290; E. Berkeley Tompkins, *Anti-Imperialism in the United States: The Great Debate, 1890-1920* (Philadelphia: Univ. of Pennsylvania Press, 1970), 140-60, 258-260, 295; Frederic Cople Jaher, *Doubters and Dissenters: Cataclysmic Thought in America, 1885-1918* (New York: Free Press, 1964), 75-78; and Patterson, *Toward a Warless World*, 83-91.

19. See the essays on the founding and early purposes of the World Peace Foundation by Ginn's private secretary, Arthur N. Holcombe, in his book, *A Strategy of Peace in a Changing World* (Cambridge, MA: Harvard Univ. Press, 1967), chs. 7-8; and Peter Filene, "The World Peace Foundation and Progressivism, 1910-1918," *New England Quarterly* 36 (Dec. 1963): 478-501.

20. The literature on the creation of the Carnegie Endowment for International Peace is extensive. See Joseph Frazier Wall, *Andrew Carnegie* (New York: Oxford Univ. Press, 1970), 88off.; David S. Patterson, "Andrew Carnegie's Quest for World Peace," *Proceedings of the American Philosophical Society* 114 (20 Oct. 1970): 371-83; Marchand, *American Peace Movement*, ch. 4; and Michael A. Lutzker, "The Formation of the Carnegie Endowment for International Peace: A Study of the Establishment-Centered Peace Movement, 1910-1914," in *Building the Organizational Society: Essays on Associational Activities in Modern America*, ed. Jerry Israel (New York: Free Press, 1972), 143-62. For a recent synthesis by the present secretary of the

Carnegie Endowment, complete with photographs and cartoons of the period, see Larry L. Fabian, *Andrew Carnegie's Peace Endowment: The Tycoon, The President, and Their Bargain of 1910* (Washington, DC: Carnegie Endowment for International Peace, 1985).

21. See especially Robert H. Wiebe, *The Search for Order, 1877–1920* (New York: Hill and Wang, 1967).

22. Regarding U.S. policy on the Hague gatherings, see Calvin DeArmond Davis' two books, *The United States and the First Hague Peace Conference* (Ithaca, NY: Cornell Univ. Press, 1962) and *The United States and the Second Hague Peace Conference: American Diplomacy and International Organization, 1899–1914* (Durham, NC: Duke Univ. Press, 1976). For the role of the peace movement, see Kuehl, *Seeking World Order.*

23. Quoted in Patterson, *Toward a Warless World,* 172.

24. See Frederick Lynch, *The Peace Problem: The Task of the Twentieth Century* (New York: Franklin H. Revell, 1911).

25. Marchand, *American Peace Movement and Social Reform,* 342.

26. See Michael Lutzker's essay, "Can the Peace Movement Prevent War? The U.S.–Mexican Crisis of April 1914," in *Doves and Diplomats: Foreign Offices and Peace Movements in Europe and America in the Twentieth Century,* ed. Solomon Wank (Westport, CT: Greenwood, 1978).

27. For further development of the relationship between peace and social and political change, see Solomon Wank's introduction, ibid., 3–20, and Charles Chatfield, "Concepts of Peace in History," *Peace and Change* 11, no. 2 (1986): 11–21.

HAROLD JOSEPHSON

The Search for Lasting Peace:
Internationalism and American Foreign Policy,
1920–1950

WORLD WAR I AND THE rejection of the League of Nations by
the United States convinced American peace activists of all persuasions that they had to redouble their efforts to find alternatives to
war. With renewed vigor and commitment, they helped forge the
most dynamic peace movement in the nation's history, arguing that
unless America altered its way of interacting with other nations, the
United States would surely face the ravages of another war. Raymond B. Fosdick, an indefatigable promoter of international organization, grieved over the failure of the United States to break the
stranglehold of nationalism. "Our generation in America," he declared, "has betrayed its own children and the blood of the next war
is on our hands."[1] John H. Clarke, a founder and first president of
the League of Nations Non-Partisan Association, expressed similar
sentiments, observing that if the United States remained out of the
League, "the next war will come as the last one did, without our having any opportunity to prevent it and with only the privilege of fighting our way out of it."[2]

Not all peace activists agreed with Fosdick and Clarke that the
League of Nations was the answer to the age-old search for an alternative to war. In fact, the basic assumptions and peace philosophies
of the various opponents of war showed as much diversity as the tactics they employed. Legalists, pacifists, feminists, antimilitarists, and
anti-interventionists, all promoted their individual approaches to
peace. Some advocated the substitution of law for war and pressed
for the codification of international law, treaties of arbitration, and
the cultivation of international knowledge and understanding. Others favored disarmament and a reduction in the militarization of
American life. Some pacifists rejected the use of all force, while
other peace activists believed that only the deterrent effect of collec-

tive security would prevent future armed conflicts. The diversity of the American peace movement was both its strength and its weakness. Peace activists could rarely agree on a common program, yet their varied approaches created an extraordinarily active movement.[3]

Of the various factions comprising the American peace movement, the internationalists became the most influential. But like the movement of which they were a part, internationalists often argued and divided over policy alternatives. Some favored collective security and international organization. Those of a more conservative persuasion put a greater faith in law, favoring arbitration, a world court, the codification of international law, or some combination of these. Still others promoted international education and the strengthening of transnational interests. Regardless of their particular approach, all internationalists advocated a more active role for the United States in world politics and all demanded that the U.S. assume greater responsibility for global order. Basically optimistic, they all believed that peace could be achieved through international cooperation of one sort or another.[4]

Although the United States rejected membership in the League of Nations and adopted few of their policy recommendations during the interwar period, internationalists had a greater impact upon public opinion and the policy-making process than any other group comprising the diverse American peace movement. Moreover, during World War II their ideas found expression in the rhetoric of American foreign policy and came very close to being implemented in the postwar peace settlement.

Internationalism did not capture American diplomacy, however. At the moment of its greatest triumph—the establishment of the United Nations Organization with American participation—internationalism began to lose ground. As the Cold War emerged out of the turbulence of World War II, the United States backed away from adopting internationalism as the operational basis for its foreign policy. By 1950 the nation was committed to a policy of unilateralism and interventionism. It had thrust itself into world affairs, but not in the manner advocated by most of the internationalists. Instead of perfecting the machinery for maintaining world order, developed in 1945, and building upon it, American policymakers used the rhetoric of internationalism but rejected the policies and approach of its interwar advocates. Instead of internationalism, Washington embraced a foreign policy committed to spreading American influence and power by challenging the Soviet Union and the forces of radicalism around the world.

Still, the internationalists came closer to harmonizing their ideas with the exercise of power than any other citizen peace group in the United States. How and why did they become the most influential group within the multifarious American peace movement? To what extent did their policy prescriptions conform to the central tenets of American ideology? Why did the internationalist dream fade before the spectre of the Cold War? To what extent was their failure to capture American foreign policy due to external conditions and to what extent was it due to internal contradictions within internationalism itself? The answer to these questions can shed much light on both the nature of internationalism and the dynamics of peace activism in the United States.

SOURCES OF INFLUENCE AND APPEAL

The influence gained by the internationalists can be explained partly by their social position in American life. To a very large extent, they were people who understood and appreciated American corporate capitalism. Coming from the fields of law, education, banking, business, and politics, they felt much more comfortable in the presence of senators and congressmen than with labor leaders and political radicals. A survey of the 279 United States internationalists listed in the *Biographical Dictionary of Internationalists* reveals that over 92 percent of them were male, that an even larger percentage had attended college, and that a significant number had attended Ivy League universities with Harvard, Yale, Princeton, Columbia, and Brown the institutions of choice.[5] They were a remarkably homogeneous group, most of whom lived in the Northeast. The main offices of the leading internationalist organizations, the League of Nations Association (formerly the League of Nations Non-Partisan Association), the Woodrow Wilson Foundation, the Foreign Policy Association, and the Council on Foreign Relations, were all located in New York City. Although these organizations established branch offices and memberships throughout the country, most of the action took place in New York and Washington.[6]

The internationalists courted those in power both in the United States and in Europe, and usually were received openly and warmly.

Nicholas Murray Butler and James T. Shotwell, two of the leading figures in the Carnegie Endowment for International Peace, had access to the foreign offices of Europe as though they themselves were government officials.[7] Their broad network of contacts gave them a hearing in Congress, in the State Department, in the business community, in the media, and sometimes even in the White House. They did not view themselves as outsiders, seeking to overcome an entrenched and antagonistic establishment, but rather as part of the establishment, albeit out of power and with a minority voice.

This attitude was both a strength and a weakness. In their search for political allies to promote the League, the World Court, or some other scheme of international peace, they understood how the system worked and how to maximize their position within a given Administration. On the other hand, their desire to court those in power and to maintain their respectability kept their activities limited and within confined bounds. They chose a staid image and informal influence, instead of the public demonstrations and mass rallies characteristic of more radical peace organizations, such as the National Council for Prevention of War, headed by Frederick J. Libby, the Women's International League for Peace and Freedom, headed by Jane Addams and Emily Balch, and the National Committee on the Cause and Cure of War, headed by Carrie Chapman Catt.

The major internationalist organizations not only had access to power, they also controlled the purse strings of the peace movement. By comparison with the Women's International League for Peace and Freedom and the Fellowship of Reconciliation, the World Peace Foundation and the Carnegie Endowment for International Peace had enormous financial resources. The Carnegie Endowment, started with a $10 million grant from Andrew Carnegie, had an annual operating budget of more than $600,000 during the late 1920s. It made its presence felt in both Europe and the United States by publishing educational materials, funding many other peace groups and institutions, and establishing a wide network of contacts in government, business, and academic circles.[8]

Although more conservative in demeanor and philosophy than pacifist and antiwar religious groups, internationalist organizations often exhibited a crusading zeal. Like their British counterparts, American internationalists viewed the League of Nations, the World Court, and other multilateral schemes as the wave of the future. They infused their peace proposals with historic and even transcendent drama. Believing that the world was at "a turning point of History," that war was "no longer a safe instrument for statesmanship" and "too dangerous to employ," they argued with passion and conviction that only a new age of international cooperation could save civilization from the terror of modern armed conflict.[9]

During the interwar period American internationalists often invoked this sense of transcendent drama in an effort to build a broad-based constituency and to convert American public opinion to the internationalist cause. Although the leadership was homogeneous and East Coast oriented, the internationalists worked hard to educate all Americans on the need for the United States to take greater responsibility for the preservation of peace. They published books, pamphlets, and journals, sponsored radio broadcasts, promoted teacher and student exchanges, created an international relations curriculum in the nation's colleges and universities, and successfully raised funds. In the process they pushed Americans towards what Nicholas Murray Butler called "those policies of international cooperation and international effort which are the one alternative to chaos and disaster."[10] The Carnegie Endowment's *International Conciliation* pamphlet series, the Foreign Policy Association's *Foreign Policy Bulletin* and *Headline* series, and the Council on Foreign Relations' *Foreign Affairs* and *Survey of American Foreign Relations* reached thousands of Americans and emphasized the importance of understanding international relations in the modern world.[11]

All of these efforts helped to prepare the American people for a more activist foreign policy. Although the various components of the internationalists' program did not become policy during the two decades following World War I, the League, the Court, arbitration, arms limitation, and international cooperation gained a wide hearing and were fully debated. When the United States found itself in the midst of another World War, just as John H. Clarke had predicted, internationalist ideas were familiar to both political leaders and informed citizens, making the task of successfully promoting them somewhat easier.

That the internationalists became the most influential force within the peace movement was less a result of their prestige, their access to funds, and their strong educational and outreach effort than of their offering the program that seemed least threatening to the American people. Although their call for a League, a Court, disarmament, treaties to outlaw war, and other internationalist schemes, went further than most Americans were willing to go during the 1920s and 1930s, the interwar internationalists never challenged fundamental precepts of American nationalism. In fact, they sought to internationalize American institutions and values, not to abandon or modify them. Many of those who favored League membership supported it precisely because they believed that it would serve as a vehicle for spreading American influence and power. They saw the League as fashioning a world order in which American values would become guiding precepts.

Beyond their differences, internationalists agreed on some fundamental principles. None of them called for the surrender of American sovereignty and few of them saw a contradiction between the new instrumentalities of international cooperation and nationalism. As Charles DeBenedetti pointed out, even progressive internationalists wished little more than to attach "liberal purpose to modern nationalism." They hoped to purify nationalism of its mindless militarism and control it through political democratization. Through the League they hoped to harness the power of nationalism to universal human needs "by organizing lines of continuing cooperation among nations under the supervision of international experts and consenting diplomats."[12]

The key architects of American internationalism saw little conflict between American national interests and the new world order they envisioned. For them war had become an anachronism; science and technology had seen to that. Wars were too devastating, too all-embracing. What was needed was a new international order in which the main tenets of traditional American diplomacy, including free trade, national self-determination, freedom of the seas, and constitutional democracy, would become universal principles benefiting all peoples.[13]

If their proposals for a modified nationalism went too far for most Americans, the internationalists' plea for a world open to free trade was especially well received. Progressive internationalists argued that economic expansion would bring domestic prosperity and peace. Not only the United States but all industrialized nations, including Germany, Italy, and Japan, would benefit in the long run. They maintained that a "guaranteed open door" would serve as a "means of relieving economic pressure and removing the excuse for conquest." Moreover, economic expansion would benefit underdeveloped areas as well as industrialized nations. Together with free trade, economic expansion would give the industrialized countries access to needed resources and markets, and at the same time it would hasten the development of backward nations and promote their economic growth. Most Wilsonians believed that in a world where science and technology had made the possibilities for progress unlimited, no one had to suffer and all could prosper together. Even the staunchest opponent of the League and the Court could join with the internationalists in supporting economic expansion and free trade.[14]

INTERNATIONALISM BETWEEN THE WARS

Although most internationalists could agree that the United States should take a more active role in world affairs, they often disagreed over specific policy guidelines. In fact, internationalists often quarreled as much among themselves as with pacifists and isolationists. Advocates of collective security and League membership, for instance, found little value in the policies enunciated by those favoring the Outlawry of War, which called upon nations to make war illegal, codify international law, and establish a new world court free of all League influence and modeled upon the U.S. Supreme Court.[15]

Despite these differences, internationalists did establish a policy agenda during the interwar period. Recognizing that efforts to enter the League of Nations would be blocked by the Senate's two-thirds rule for treaty ratification, they concentrated upon two alternative quests. First, they sought to work more closely with the League and its agencies. Second, they hoped to instill in the American people and their government a sense of collective responsibility for maintaining world order by cooperating with other nations in efforts to aid victims of aggression and to isolate countries that resorted to war.[16]

After a slow start, internationalists successfully convinced the U.S. government to cooperate with League agencies and commissions. They were less successful, however, in campaigning for American membership in the World Court, despite the fact that it had support from Presidents Coolidge, Hoover, and Roosevelt, and from both major political parties. The Senate frustrated attempts to join by imposing severe reservations or, as in 1935, by failing to muster the two-thirds majority required for ratification.

Internationalists found strong public support for their efforts to limit the arms race. They joined with pacifists and women's peace groups in convincing the Harding Administration to convene the Washington Naval Disarmament Conference in 1921-22. Here the major world powers agreed to a new security framework for the Pacific that opened the way for naval arms reductions and the halting of new naval construction. As Charles DeBenedetti pointed out, the agreements reached in Washington "signaled the finest achievement of positive citizen peace action in the interwar period."[17] Unfortunately, subsequent disarmament conferences in 1927, 1930, and 1932 accomplished far less and did little to prevent the massive arms buildup during the 1930s.

Some American internationalists, strongly supporting arbitration as an alternative to war, promoted the League's effort in 1924 to draft the Geneva Protocol, which called for its signers to settle their disputes peacefully. In fact, American internationalists, including James T. Shotwell, David Hunter Miller, General Tasker H. Bliss, John Bates Clark, Isaiah Bowman, and Joseph Chamberlain, unofficially worked on some of the more difficult aspects of the treaty, including the development of an acceptable definition of aggression and a system of voluntary nonmilitary sanctions.[18] Similarly, American internationalists not only supported but were instrumental in the negotiations that led to the Pact of Paris in 1928, a multilateral treaty calling upon each of its signatories to renounce war as an instrument of its national policy and to agree to settle all of its international disputes peacefully.[19]

During the 1930s, internationalists moved away from efforts to take the United States into the League. Instead they concentrated on instilling within the American people and their government a sense of collective responsibility to help maintain world order and to assist Europe in avoiding war. Some worked on revisions of the League Covenant that would make it easier for the United States to cooperate in efforts to isolate and sanction aggressors. Shotwell, for instance, called for "associated" membership in the League that would allow nations like the United States to voluntarily cooperate with League sanctions without committing itself to collective security. He also called for regional security arrangements in which those nations closest to international disturbances would be responsible for dealing with the problem rather than having all equally obligated to take action. Such revisions in the League's security system, he believed, would allow the United States to become involved without facing the much more difficult issue of membership.[20]

Similarly, internationalists sought to move America's neutrality policy in a direction that would give the president more discretion in supporting European collective security efforts and in assisting victims of aggression. Opposing mandatory legislation that would limit the president's hand, they wanted a Neutrality Act that would permit him to distinguish between acts of belligerency and actions taken on behalf of the League of Nations to stop aggression.[21]

During the mid-1930s internationalists sought to work with other factions within the peace movement, but these efforts were usually short-lived and extremely difficult. While pacifists and internationalists both wanted neutrality legislation, their motivations were quite different. Pacifists and isolationists hoped to use such legislation to tie the hands of the Roosevelt Administration and to prevent the president from taking any action that might involve the United States in armed conflicts in Europe or Asia. Internationalists also sought to avoid war but believed that this could be accomplished only by sending a signal to the rest of the world that the United States would not thwart the efforts of the League to impose sanctions. They wanted a flexible policy that would allow the president to use the power of American trade to assist those nations standing up to aggression.

The passage of the Neutrality Acts of 1935, 1936, and 1937, with their mandatory requirement that the president embargo arms to all belligerents in time of war, frustrated and angered American internationalists, who believed that American security was tied to the configuration of power in Europe. Neither pacifism nor neutrality, they argued, would be able to keep America out of a major European war. More than ever they wished to instill in American foreign policy a sense of responsibility for maintaining world peace. Shotwell, who had emerged as the most articulate champion of the internationalist cause, spoke eloquently for the need to recognize the interconnectedness of Europe and the United States. In a 1938 editorial in the *New York Times,* he declared that "No remoteness from the scene of potential European conflict can isolate the United States from the consequences of a major war. No Neutrality Act can prevent the American people from favoring their natural allies. In any ultimate test of strength between democracy and dictatorship, the good-will and the moral support — and in the long run more likely than not the physical power of the United States — will be found on the side of those nations defending a way of life which Americans believe to be worth living." If the United States would not assist League members resisting aggression, it should do nothing to weaken that effort. At a minimum, he argued, it should use its trade policies in such a way that the United States did not block sanctions adopted by League members.[22]

INTERNATIONALISM TRIUMPHANT: ILLUSION AND REALITY

The start of World War II in 1939 and the Japanese attack on Pearl Harbor two years later seemed to prove the validity of the internationalists' approach and to confirm their prediction that the United States could not avoid involvement in world crises for long. Their efforts during the 1920s and 1930s had created a small but significant coterie of individuals ready to take up the banner of collective security and to support American intervention in the war as a means of establishing through military victory new international machinery that would keep the peace.

At first internationalists, supporting the principle of aiding the allies with measures short of war, organized into the Non-Partisan Committee for Peace Through Revision of the Neutrality Act and the Committee to Defend America by Aiding the Allies. In 1943, however, the League of Nations Association reorganized as the United Nations Association and initiated a campaign for a new world organization. Joining this effort were the Commission to Study the Organization of Peace, led by Shotwell and Clark Eichelberger and funded by the Carnegie Endowment for International Peace, and the Commission of the Federal Council of Churches to Study the Bases of a Just and Durable Peace, led by John Foster Dulles. These commissions established study and discussion groups throughout the country and mobilized public opinion in support of a new international organization.

Internationalists agreed that America must become a full participant in any future world organization and that it had to assume its full responsibilities as a world power. Furthermore, they seconded Henry A. Wallace's contention that "there must be worked out an international order sufficiently strong to prevent the rise of aggressor nations."[23] Beyond this, however, they had no specific plan in the early years of the war. They were encouraged by the great public interest shown in Clarence Streit's *Union Now* (1939), which called for a federation of Western democracies, but few of the interwar internationalists joined the movement for world federalism. Instead, operating out of the Commission to Study the Organization of Peace and the Commission to Study the Bases of a Just and Durable Peace, they began to envision an international organization that would not challenge the sovereignty of its members. Declaring that the United States had a "second chance" to take its rightful place in international affairs and that the nations of the world had another opportunity to organize themselves for peace, the internationalists emphasized the need for international cooperation and good will among *all* peoples. This was the theme of Wendell Willkie's *One World,* which sold more than 500,000 copies during its first month of publication in 1943.[24]

As the war progressed, a convergence of ideas developed between the internationalist peace activists, public opinion, and U.S. policymakers. Public opinion polls revealed a strong movement towards the internationalists' position. In 1942, George Gallup reported that 59 percent of the American people favored joining a new league and only 22 percent opposed. By 1944, 70 percent favored the idea, and in April 1945, 81 percent agreed that the United States should join a "world organization with police power to maintain world peace."[25] Internationalists had come to represent a new national consensus on foreign policy. Most Americans now agreed with Henry A. Wallace that the time had finally come for the nations of the world "to erect a lasting structure of peace—a structure such as that which Woodrow Wilson sought to build but which crumbled away because the world was not yet ready."[26]

At the same time, the Roosevelt administration expressed its support for some type of world organization (although the president seemed to vacillate between the need for such a confederation and a peace structure built upon a big power alliance to police the world). As early as 1941 the State Department began to study the issue of a postwar settlement, and in 1943 Congress passed resolutions endorsing membership in a future international organization. In 1944 representatives of the Allied nations met in Washington at the Dumbarton Oaks Conference to draft provisions for a charter for a United Nations Organization, and in the spring of the following year delegates from fifty-five nations met in San Francisco to sign the Charter. Several prominent American internationalists, including Eichelberger, Shotwell, and Dulles, attended the San Francisco conference as "consultants" to the U.S. delegation. In July 1945 two decades of campaigning seemed to pay off when the Senate gave its stamp of approval to the UN by a vote of eighty-nine to two.

Few internationalists, however, believed that the new organization would be enough. Some took up the call for world government. Like many scientists, Albert Einstein believed that atomic energy had fundamentally changed the international environment, but he went further than most of his colleagues to conclude that the only viable approach to peace was a world government with sufficient power to enforce its will.[27] Many internationalists agreed with Einstein and supported the concept of world federalism. Others believed that world federation was an impractical idea that had no chance of success. Instead they called upon the governments of the world to strengthen the United Nations by giving it the authority necessary to regulate atomic weapons and the military power required to enforce peace.[28]

Regardless of what sort of reforms they preferred, all internationalists had to confront the changed environment of the postwar period. Not only had atomic weapons altered strategic calculations, but the emerging Cold War between the United States and the Soviet Union undermined all previous peace plans. United States participation in the UN and the clear-cut commitment by the Truman Administration to an activist foreign policy gave the impression that the U.S. had made internationalism the foundation stone of its diplomacy, but the reality was quite different.

By 1947, the President had made clear that the United States would not rely upon the United Nations in dealing with the Soviet Union. Containment, the Truman Doctrine, the Marshall Plan, and even the Point Four program undermined the world organization by committing the United States to a policy of unilateralism and globalism rather than internationalism. Taking advantage of Article 51 of the Charter, the United States preferred to develop a security system based upon American power and regional alliances rather than strengthening the UN. American leaders infused NATO and their other regional alliances with the terminology of collective security, but in fact they were little more than old-fashioned military pacts and a clear return to the balance of power.

Radical pacifists had long argued that a foreign policy based upon collective security and force would threaten rather than ensure peace.

They did not alter their opinion after World War II.[30] Most internationalists, however, concluded that force was a necessary concomitant of peace and applauded America's willingness to challenge Soviet expansion. Even Norman Thomas, the Socialist leader and former pacifist, advocated a world police force capable of resisting aggression, supported the Truman Doctrine and the establishment of the North Atlantic Treaty Organization, and endorsed American participation in the Korean War.[31]

During the 1950s, some internationalists, like Shotwell and Eichelberger, focused their attention on expanding the power of the United Nations Organization and strengthening its peace-keeping ability. Others, like Thomas and the journalist Norman Cousins, took a greater interest in disarmament and the control of atomic weapons. Both groups, however, supported the emergence of a more activist U.S. foreign policy. Although they did not succumb to the irrational and fervid anticommunism of the period, they did applaud the American effort to contain Soviet power abroad and to spread the principles of liberalism and democracy around the world.[32]

What internationalists like Thomas and Cousins only later realized, and what Shotwell and Eichelberger never fully comprehended, was that American policymakers from Truman to Richard Nixon used the rhetoric and symbols of pre–World War II internationalism *principally* to win support for the expansion of U.S. power and the promotion of universalism. In fact, a basic tenet of pre–World War II internationalism, the "doctrine of responsibility," seemed to support the efforts of the postwar administrations to spread U.S. values around the world.[33] In the minds of American leaders, these values were precisely what the world needed to maintain peace, establish democracy, and bring about prosperity.

DENOUEMENT

In the mid-1980s, Thomas Hughes, President of the Carnegie Endowment for International Peace, lamented the demise of internationalism in America. He argued that thirty years earlier "the internationalist ethos embraced American mainstream conservatives and liberals alike" and that most Republicans and most Democrats were convinced "that a world nurtured by responsible internationalism would enjoy both greater security and greater material well-being." By the 1980s, however, American internationalism had "fallen victim to resurgent nationalism and an inhospitable world environment."[34]

While it was true that American policymakers paid more lip service to internationalism during the Truman and Eisenhower administrations than under President Ronald Reagan, it was not true that internationalism, as understood by its interwar advocates, was the centerpiece of U.S. foreign policy at any time after World War II. The U.S. became the chief financial supporter of the United Nations and many of its subagencies. On matters relating to national security and political power, however, the UN was viewed only as a peripheral instrument that might promote American interests intermittently. Following Roosevelt's lead, U.S. officials never put much faith in the United Nations. From the outset they viewed regional agreements as necessary insurance policies in the likely event that the UN failed. Even before the San Francisco conference, the United States was working on regional cooperation with Latin America.[35]

The Cold War, not the Nixon or Reagan administrations, dashed the dreams of the interwar internationalists. Perhaps it was inevitable, for implicit in their world view was the notion that the better world was one that organized around American principles. Few internationalists had seen in the League or in the United Nations a mechanism for fundamentally altering nation-state relations by surrendering sovereignty. Instead they had conceived of international organization as a way for great powers to cooperate better and a way for the liberating principles of free trade, self-determination, and constitutional democracy to replace nineteenth-century imperialism and balance of power.

American foreign policy was clearly influenced by internationalism following World War II. Most American leaders accepted the concept of responsibility in world affairs and did not seek to retreat from active involvement in international politics as their predecessors had done after World War I. In fact, the tendency was quite the opposite. American leaders now assumed that the United States had vital interests everywhere instead of nowhere but at home. Under the banner of anticommunism, American military and economic power was pushed to its outer limits.

To a certain extent, American internationalism contained the seeds of its own destruction. Its interwar advocates had viewed internationalism as a way to promote American interests through the cooperation of industrialized powers. Assuming that what was best for

America was best for the world, they uncritically believed that a harmonious relationship existed between American nationalism and
world order. What they failed to perceive was that unless all major
nations accepted the American vision of a better life, internationalism could not succeed. The Cold War guaranteed that the American commitment to the United Nations and to the principles of
internationalism would be short-lived. The emergence of the Soviet
Union as America's greatest rival following World War II led the
United States to reject internationalism and to adopt a policy of
unilateralism and globalism as the best means to assure its interests
in the world. The outbreak of the Korean War in 1950 revealed that
internationalism would be little more than a cover for American
policymakers to pursue their regional and global interests. This was
not what Shotwell, Eichelberger, Fosdick, or Clarke had in mind
in the 1920s when they began positioning themselves to influence
American diplomacy, but it was the logical result of the policies they
articulated.

Internationalists clearly had a positive impact upon post–World
War II global politics and American foreign policy. Their call for
international cooperation in the area of economic and social development, their promotion of international law, and their advocacy
of international organization as a moral alternative to unlimited national sovereignty found an important place in international relations following the defeat of Germany and Japan. But the limited
nature of their global vision, combined with the external reality of
the Cold War, allowed political leaders from Truman to Reagan to
give lip service to internationalist principles while pursuing policies
that negated those very principles.

NOTES

   1. Raymond B. Fosdick, ed., *Letters on the League of Nations: From
the Files of Raymond B. Fosdick* (Princeton, NJ: Princeton Univ. Press,
1966), 123.
   2. *New York Times*, 11 Jan. 1923.
   3. Harold Josephson, *James T. Shotwell and the Rise of Internationalism in America* (Rutherford, NJ: Fairleigh Dickinson Univ. Press, 1975), 133–
34; Charles DeBenedetti, *The Peace Reform in American History* (Bloomington: Indiana Univ. Press, 1980), 108–9. For a more detailed discussion

of the diversity within the peace movement, see Robert H. Ferrell, *Peace in their Time: The Origins of the Kellogg-Briand Pact* (New Haven, CT: Yale Univ. Press, 1952), 13–50; Charles Chatfield, *For Peace and Justice: Pacifism in America, 1914–1941* (Knoxville: Univ. of Tennessee Press, 1971); and Charles DeBenedetti, *Origins of the Modern American Peace Movement, 1915–1929* (Millwood, NY: KTO Press, 1978).

4. Much has been written about the meaning of internationalism in America and its diversity. I have chosen to ignore, for the most part, the transnational or "community" internationalists, for they had no power and influenced few during the interwar period. Instead this paper focuses on the mainstream "political" internationalists who came to dominate the American peace movement during the 1940s. I have also avoided, for the most part, the terms "liberal" and "conservative" in referring to internationalists. As pointed out by Warren F. Kuehl, the distinction presents as many problems as it solves; see Kuehl, *Biographical Dictionary of Internationalists* (Westport, CT: Greenwood, 1983), x. For a discussion of the varieties of internationalism, see Kuehl, "Concepts of Internationalism in History," *Peace and Change* 11, no. 2 (1986): 1–7; Sondra Herman, *Eleven Against War: Studies in American Internationalist Thought, 1898–1921* (Stanford, CA: Hoover Institution Press, 1969), 1–21; Gary B. Ostrower, "Historical Studies in American Internationalism," *International Organization* 25 (Autumn 1971): 899–916; and "Internationalism as a Current in the Peace Movement: A Symposium," in Charles Chatfield, ed., *Peace Movements in America* (New York: Schocken, 1973), 171–91.

5. Kuehl, *Biographical Dictionary of Internationalists,* passim.

6. Robert A. Divine, *Second Chance: The Triumph of Internationalism in America during World War II* (New York: Atheneum, 1967), 22–23; Robert E. Bowers, "The American Peace Movement, 1933–1941" (Ph.D. diss., University of Wisconsin–Madison, 1949), 227–28. The Carnegie Endowment for International Peace was headquartered in Washington, D.C.

7. Malcolm Davis, "The Reminiscences of Malcolm Davis," 1950, Oral History Research Office, Columbia University, 114–16.

8. Carnegie Endowment for International Peace, *Year Book: 1928,*19.

9. James T. Shotwell, "Are We at a Turning Point in the History of the World?" Carnegie Endowment for International Peace, *Year Book, 1927,* 106; George W. Egerton, "Collective Security as Political Myth: Liberal Internationalism and the League of Nations in Politics and History," *The International History Review* 5 (Nov., 1983): 503–5.

10. Quoted in Warren F. Kuehl, "Webs of Common Interest Revisited: Nationalism, Internationalism, and Historians of American Foreign Relations," *Diplomatic History* 10 (Spring 1986): 110.

11. Ibid., 108–11.

12. DeBenedetti, *Origins of the Modern American Peace Movement,* 14.

13. Ibid., 13; James T. Shotwell, "Locarno and After," *Association Men* 51 (Feb., 1926): 269–70.

14. James T. Shotwell, "Memorandum for the American Delegation to the Conference on World Economy," 2 Nov. 1935, I.F.2. #41236, Carnegie Endowment for International Peace Archives, Columbia University, New York City; James T. Shotwell, "Does Business Mean Peace? *Outlook and Independent* 151 (13 March 1929): 405–7, 436–37.

15. On the Outlawry of War, see Salmon O. Levinson, *A Plan to Outlaw War* (Chicago: American Committee for the Outlawry of War, 25 Dec. 1921); and Charles Clayton Morrison, *The Outlawry of War: A Constructive Policy for World Peace* (Chicago: Willett, Clark and Colby, 1927).

16. Warren F. Kuehl, "Internationalism," in Alexander DeConde, ed., *Encyclopedia of American Foreign Policy: Studies of the Principal Movements and Ideas,* vol. 2 (New York: Scribner's, 1978), 449.

17. DeBenedetti, *Origins of the Modern American Peace Movement,* 112.

18. James T. Shotwell, "Memorandum on the Draft Treaty of Mutual Assistance and Alternative Plans," 12 April 1924, Box 268, Tasker H. Bliss Papers, Library of Congress, Washington, D.C.; "Draft Treaty of Disarmament and Security," *International Conciliation,* 201 (Aug., 1924), 343–51.

19. Josephson, *James T. Shotwell,* 156–76; DeBenedetti, *Origins of the Modern American Peace Movement,* 183–216.

20. James T. Shotwell, *On the Rim of the Abyss* (New York: Macmillan, 1936), 177–79, 319–20; *New York Times,* 6 May 1934, sec. 8, pp. 3, 11.

21. "The Issue in the Crisis," *Survey Graphic* 24 (Nov., 1935): 522–23, 558.

22. James T. Shotwell, "A Way of Life," *New York Times,* 15 June 1938.

23. Devine, *Second Chance,* 40–41.

24. Ibid., 105.

25. Ibid., 68–69, 183, 252.

26. Quoted in ibid., 79.

27. Otto Nathan and Heinz Norden, eds., *Einstein on Peace* (New York: Schocken, 1960), 336.

28. Commission to Study the Organization of Peace, 5th Report, *Security and Disarmament Under the United Nations* (New York: Commission to Study the Organization of Peace, 1947).

29. Egerton, "Collective Security as Political Myth," 520–21.

30. Lawrence S. Wittner, *Rebels Against War: The American Peace Movement, 1933–1983* (Philadelphia: Temple Univ. Press, 1984), 178–80, 201–3.

31. Charles Chatfield, "Norman Thomas: Harmony of Word and Deed," in Charles DeBenedetti, ed., *Peace Heroes in Twentieth-Century America* (Bloomington: Indiana Univ. Press, 1986), 114–15.

32. Ibid., 115; Milton S. Katz, "Norman Cousins: Peace Advocate and

World Citizen," in ibid., 176–78; DeBenedetti, *Peace Reform in American History,* 150–56; Josephson, *James T. Shotwell,* 291–92.

33. Warren F. Kuehl, "The Principle of Responsibility for Peace and National Security, 1920–1973," *Peace and Change* 3, nos. 2–3 (Summer–Fall, 1975): 84–91.

34. Thomas L. Hughes, "The Twilight of Internationalism," *Foreign Policy* 61 (Winter, 1985–86): 25–26, 46.

35. Richard D. McKinzie in "Internationalism as a Current in the Peace Movement: A Symposium," in Chatfield, *Peace Movements in America,* 185–86.

CHARLES DEBENEDETTI

American Peace Activism, 1945–1985

THE MOST REMARKABLE FEATURE OF American peace activism
in the forty years following World War II has been the disparity between efforts invested and achievements effected. Operating in one
of the world's freest and most open societies, citizen peace activists
developed ideas, analyses, actions, and organizations that established
them as an irrepressible force. Nonetheless, they consistently failed
to convert their countless efforts into the kind of political effectiveness that might move them into the main currents of American life.
There were two reasons for this failure. The first was the disturbing
ambivalence that American peace-seekers felt toward the value and
purpose of United States power in the throes of Cold War rivalry.
The second was their overriding commitment to the peace of justice,
freedom, and liberation within a conservative political culture that
attached the highest value to notions of order, security, and stability.
Machiavelli once wrote that "the reason for the bad as well as good
fortune of men is to be found in the way in which their way of working fits the times."[1] American peace activists experienced more bad
than good fortune during these years, mainly because of a disincli-
nation to champion the political values most fitting to their times.

The story of American citizen peace efforts since 1945 is at once
heartening and demoralizing. Made up of only a small minority of
the population (estimates range from one-half to two percent of the
whole population), citizen peace activists initially worked from two
wings in their attempts to persuade the American people and their
government that the country's principal enemy was international war.

On the one hand, a small band of absolute pacifists struggled for
reasons of principle against war and violence. Inspired by figures
such as the longtime radical activist A. J. Muste, some of these radicals used their bodies in sustained campaigns of nonviolent direct

action against both the war system and domestic injustice. Organized in groups such as the War Resisters League (WRL), these radical pacifists felt a combined commitment to antiwar activism, as shown by their nonviolent attacks on U.S. nuclear test sites or missile installations, and to domestic justice, which they sought to advance by supporting black civil rights and women's liberation movements. Seeing themselves as a saving remnant, radical pacifists like WRL leader David McReynolds and Catholic priest Daniel Berrigan worked to change popular attitudes and national policies, but their first goal was a revolutionary adaptation of human thinking and action to the values of loving nonviolence.[2]

A second thrust came from internationalists who felt the need for a working world political system. They battled with declining influence in Cold War America to advance peace through institutionalized world order. Rallied at first by world federalists such as Grenville Clark and by atomic scientists like Albert Einstein, internationalists entered the postwar years heady with their success in establishing a new United Nations and eager to extend their achievements into the full-scale realization of a system empowered to achieve global security and national disarmament. Whether or not that aspiration was realistic, they were crushed into irrelevance between the pressures of right-wing nationalists and left-wing supporters of popular liberation movements. It was almost predictable. Having won victory for the United Nations through their support of the Allied cause during World War II, internationalists were unprepared to cope with the collapse of the Allied coalition and the Cold War effort. With the outbreak of war in Korea, most of those in the American Association for the UN and the United World Federalists threw their support behind the United States–United Nations military effort.[3]

Internationalists' support of the war effort in Korea briefly strengthened American popular enthusiasm for the UN, but any real hope of advancing world government fell apart as the war accelerated a resurgence of right-wing hypernationalist politics: McCarthyism. No matter how much public opinion polls indicated sympathy for the UN after 1950, the xenophobic politics of the Cold War overwhelmed designs for real world government and, in fact, effectively wrecked the country's fifty-year-old internationalist movement, which slipped into political sentimentalism and ineffectuality. Although some internationalists joined new single-issue organizations such as the National Committee for a Sane Nuclear Policy, few made any contribution to the domestic opposition to U.S. intervention in Vietnam, and most of them stood apart from the antinuclear and pro-disarmament protests of the late seventies and early eighties.[4] In fact, in a sorry testimonial to the internationalist decline, Thomas L. Hughes, president of the Carnegie Endowment for International Peace, recently wrote that the values and assumptions at the heart of the Endowment and modern internationalism "have pretty well exhausted themselves in mainstream American political life."[5] Even among its supporters, American internationalism is in an enfeebled if not comatose state, with a decidedly bad prognosis.

Gradually, a large and heterogeneous body of concerned liberals, leftists, and moderates emerged in organizations and operations of bewildering diversity. Joined only in common opposition to American Cold War policies, these peace activists first came forward in the mid-fifties in public protest against atmospheric nuclear testing and against the failure of the UN to extend world order and effective disarmament. These peace-seekers formed new organizations such as SANE and Women Strike for Peace. Although influenced by the New Left, they generally avoided any attempt to define themselves according to any coherent ideology or mode of action. Instead, they prided themselves on their heterogeneity, eclecticism, commitment to action, and common opposition to the prevailing militarized anti-communism and apathy about war in the nuclear age. Lacking a partisan focus, the new activists sought to establish themselves as an extrapartisan domestic opposition to U.S. armed interventionism and a force for multilateral peacekeeping and disarmament.[6]

The war in Vietnam provided, of course, the catalyst for this opposition movement.[7] Generated at first among absolute pacifists, radicals, and liberals, domestic opposition to U.S. intervention in Vietnam proliferated tremendously among a wide array of middle-class Americans between 1965 and 1971. Even when it declined, it left in place both the remembered experience and the functional networks required to rally Cold War critics later. Whether motivated by moral, ideological, or political concerns, the dissatisfied citizens who assembled and sustained organized opposition to Washington's bipartisan war effort made personal sacrifices in order to emphasize their common conviction that the government was terribly wrong and had to be put right. Inevitably, dissidents derived varying lessons from their experiences. In general, however, they shared one conclusion: millions of Americans could be mobilized against national war policy, and their voice would not go unheard among the decision-makers in Washington. The antiwar activists of the Vietnam era found that they could reach those policymakers who placed a particular definition of national interest above the forces of democratic politics. They learned that they could make history work for peace.

In the course of protesting the war in Vietnam, Cold War peace activists proliferated geographically and organizationally throughout the country, to embrace thereafter a variety of causes and concerns.[8] The major international peace organizations, including the Fellowship of Reconciliation and Women's International League for Peace and Freedom, continued to involve tens of thousands of people in their multi-issue activities. In addition, however, groups of people organized according to occupation, such as Physicians for Social Responsibility, concentrated on the nuclear arms race. At the same time, explicitly anti-interventionist organizations, such as the North American Congress on Latin America, emerged in opposition to U.S. intervention in the Third World, while a host of lobbying groups, such as the Council for a Livable World and the Center for Defense Information, developed impressive channels of influence in the media and foreign policy circles. Perhaps most important, the combination of civil rights activism, the opposition to the war in Vietnam, and the women's movement enlisted religious-minded people as everyday activists on the local level, in groups such as Sanctuary, to argue against armed interventionism, the arms race, and economic injustice.

Within the past quarter-century, citizen peace initiatives have proliferated with a breadth and power hitherto unknown in American history. Perversely, however, this burst of peace activism neither gained respectable political power within policymaking circles nor developed substantial lines of transnational contact, communication, and support. In part, this failure of American activists to expand their influence at home and abroad derives from the negative cast that has dogged the U.S. peace movement since World War II.

After failing to build a new world order through the United Nations, peace activists did not reassemble in a visible way until 1955; and then their concerns were defined by opposition to the arms race and the Soviet-American Cold War. Soon afterwards, peace activists provided the core of opposition to the U.S. war in Indochina. Then, after 1975, they lent vital support to domestic opposition to nuclear power and, early in the eighties, to the U.S. arms buildup. Always, it seemed, the peace movement was in opposition to something, its concerns less international than domestic. Ever it appeared to protest the deployment of American power.

Moreover, the failure of the American peace movement to advance both in U.S. politics and in transnational collaboration had roots in the peculiarly nationalistic bias of the American peace tradition. An America-First reform temperament informed recent peace-seeking in two respects: a traditional ambivalence toward American power, and a priority for justice and liberation over security.[9]

Domestic American reformers historically have felt ambivalent toward the scope and significance of American power. On the one hand, they have taken pride in the growth of American economic and military power as an expression of the rightfulness of the nation's democratic society. Out of this pride, American reformers have enthusiastically backed nearly every major U.S. war effort at the same time as they encouraged national leaders to seek more systematic international cooperation. On the other hand, American reformers have exhibited a healthy skepticism toward American power, partly because of its periodic misuse at home and abroad and partly because of their own discomfort over the very meaning and implications of power. Like all American reformers, the peace-seekers among them have generally assumed that people are basically good, capable of identifying their own self-interests, and prone toward right reasoning in the face of correct evidence. In the world of power relationships, however, these assumptions often are irrelevant if not wrong; and American peace-seekers, like most public figures, never have felt comfortable in confronting realities that contradict their guiding assumptions.

In addition, the America-First reform temperament at the heart of Cold War peace activism has driven peace-seekers to pursue promises of justice and liberation at the expense of the claims of order and security. After their post–World War II flirtation with world government, American peace advocates joined other reformers in emphasizing individual commitments to personal protest in the name of freedom and justice. For the past generation, U.S. peace-seekers have been among the principal practitioners of a peculiar public phenomenon that involves the "PERSONALIZATION of politics, the effort to translate one's heart-felt opinions and values directly into organizational forms, political expressions and public policies" for the sake of justice and liberation.[10] These values have merits — such modern American heroes as Martin Luther King, Jr., A. J. Muste, and Ella Baker preached, organized, and lived them — but they diverge fundamentally from the dominant preference within bourgeois America (as well as in western Europe) for the values of order and stability, security and coherence. America and its allies are conservative countries; and those who would alter the basic political values and practices of these countries — starting with their commitment to security through the prevailing international war system — must discover other ways of providing for the common defense through alternative power arrangements, globally conceived and internationally systematized.

We return to Machiavelli: "since new things disturb the minds of men, you should strive to see that these disturbing changes retain as much of the ancient regime as possible."[11] The prevailing international regime does possess things of value, beginning with various forms of state-maintained order that facilitate the pursuit of peaceable political struggle. American peace advocates must show how they would extend these things of demonstrated value to a supranational world authority that would protect the nations' established values from the threat of war.

In practice, this prescription implies that the American peace movement requires a double strategy. In the short term, American peaceseekers must seize upon all available means to change the foreign policies of the U.S. and its allies in ways that carry the great powers toward the negotiated settlement of the Cold War. In the long term, peace advocates must use political power to enlarge those plans and agencies capable of institutionalizing supranational security which the great powers must establish in the course of extinguishing the Cold War. Peace activists must realize that they cannot be satisfied with standing merely in opposition to U.S. Cold War policies or with questing for distant visions. They must advocate a new world order that is compelling because it is grounded in the wisdom of the past and responsive to the realities of the present. They must advocate a way that not only "fits the times" but also shapes them. They would most effectively proceed with a manifest respect for American power, trying to use it less in search of justice, freedom, and liberation and more for those things that matter to modern, industrial peoples: order, security, stability, and the globally-organized protection of a world of plural values without recourse to war.

NOTES

The essay was prepared for the Stadtschlaining conference, August 1986, and Professor DeBenedetti was unable to revise it before his death. Edited only for style, it reflects a prescriptive interpretation that derives from both his comprehensive study, notably *The Peace Reform in American History* (Bloomington: Indiana Univ. Press, 1980), and his intensive but uncompleted history of the peace movement in the Vietnam era.

Professor DeBenedetti worked from a wide array of primary published and archival sources, but he had documented this essay sparsely. The editors have provided references to secondary sources on which he was known to have drawn, in addition to his own citations (herein indicated by "CD" in brackets). He also indicated in a note to his paper the helpfulness of Charles Chatfield, "Concepts of Peace in History," *Peace and Change* 11, no. 2 (1986): 11-22.

1. "The Discourses," in Peter Bondanella and Mark Musa, eds., *The Portable Machiavelli* (New York: Penguin, 1979), 381.

2. The Berrigans and Muste are treated respectively in Anne Keljment, "The Berrigans: Revolutionary Christian Nonviolence," in Charles DeBenedetti, ed., *Peace Heroes in Twentieth-Century America* (Bloomington: Indiana Univ. Press, 1986), 227-54, and Jo Ann O. Robinson, "A. J. Muste: Prophet in the Wilderness of the Modern World," ibid., 147-67; but see also Robinson's *Abraham Went Out: A Biography of A. J. Muste* (Philadelphia: Temple Univ. Press, 1981 [CD]. Regarding pacifists in the postwar peace movement, see especially Lawrence S. Wittner, *Rebels Against War: The American Peace Movement, 1933-1983* (Philadelphia: Temple Univ. Press, 1984), chs. 7-10 [CD], and Neil H. Katz, "Radical Pacifism and the Contemporary American Peace Movement: The Committee for Nonviolent Action, 1957-1967" (Ph.D. diss., University of Maryland, 1974).

3. For recent studies of post-World War II internationalism, see Wittner, *Rebels Against War,* chs. 5-7; Paul S. Boyer, *By the Bomb's Early Light: American Thought and Culture at the Dawn of the Atomic Age* (New York: Pantheon, 1985), chs. 2-3; Robert D. Accinelli, "Pro-U.S. Internationalists and the Early Cold War: The American Association for the United Nations and U.S. Foreign Policy, 1947-1952," *Diplomatic History* 9, no. 4 (Fall 1985): 347-62; Charles Chatfield, "Norman Thomas: Harmony of Word and Deed," Harold Josephson, "Albert Einstein: The Search for World Order," and Milton S. Katz, "Norman Cousins: Peace Advocate and World Citizen," in DeBenedetti, *Peace Heroes,* pp. 85-121, 123-46, 169 97; and Harold Josephson, "The Search for Lasting Peace: Internationalism and American Foreign Policy, 1920-1950," in this volume [CD]. For Grenville Clark in this respect, see Alan Cranston, "Memoir of a Man," in Norman Cousins and J. Garry Clifford, eds., *Memoirs of a Man: Grenville Clark* (New York: Nor-

ton, 1975), and see also Jon A. Yoder, "The United World Federalists: Liberals for Law and Order," in Charles Chatfield, ed., *Peace Movements in America* (New York: Schocken, 1973), 95–115, and George T. Mazuzan, "America's UN Commitment, 1945–1953," *The Historian* 40, no. 2 (Feb. 1978): 309–30.

4. Regarding SANE, see Milton S. Katz, *Ban the Bomb: A History of the Committee for a Sane Nuclear Policy, 1957–1984* (Westport, CT: Greenwood, 1986) [CD].

5. "The Twilight of Internationalism," *Foreign Policy* 61 (Winter 1986), 26 [CD].

6. For overviews of this development see Wittner, *Rebels Against War,* 257–281, and DeBenedetti, *The Peace Reform,* ch. 8. The literature on the New Left is large: see especially George R. Vickers, *The Formation of the New Left: The Early Years* (Lexington, MA: Heath, 1975), Irwin Unger, *The Movement: A History of the American New Left, 1959–1972* (New York: Dodd, Mead, 1974), Edward J. Bacciocco, Jr., *The New Left in America: Reform to Revolution, 1950 to 1970* (Stanford, CA: Hoover Institution, 1974), and James Weinstein, *Ambiguous Legacy: The Left in American Politics* (New York: New Viewpoints, 1975).

7. See Nancy Zaroulis and Gerald Sullivan, *Who Spoke Up?: American Protest Against the War in Vietnam, 1963–1975* (Garden City, NY: Doubleday, 1984); Robert Cooney and Helen Michalowski, eds., *The Power of the People: Active Nonviolence in the United States* (Culver City, CA: People's Press, 1977); and Fred Halstead, *Out Now! A Participant's account of the American Movement Against the Vietnam War* (New York: Monad, 1978).

8. For two excellent guides to the breadth of modern U.S. peace activism, see Elizabeth Bernstein et al., *Peace Resource Book: A Comprehensive Guide to Issues, Groups, and Literature 1986* (Cambridge, MA: Ballinger, 1986), and Melinda Fine and Peter M. Steven, eds., *American Peace Directory 1984* (Cambridge, MA: Ballinger, 1984) [CD].

9. DeBenedetti initially explored the relationship of peace advocacy and American values in his "Afterthoughts" in *The Peace Reform,* 197–200, and his thinking was stimulated by Akira Iriye, "Culture and Power: International Relations as Intercultural Relations," *Diplomatic History* 3, no. 2 (Spring 1979): 115–28.

10. Harry C. Boyte and Sara M. Evans, "The Sources of Democratic Change," *Tikkun* 1, no. 1 (Summer 1986): 51 [emphasis in the original, CD].

11. "The Discourses," in Bondanella and Musa, eds., *The Portable Machiavelli,* 231 [CD].

THE NUCLEAR AGE

RALPH SUMMY

The Australian Peace Council
and the Anticommunist Milieu, 1949–1965

FOR TWENTY YEARS AFTER World War II, the Australian Peace
Council (APC) and its lineal descendants were linked with the World
Peace Council (WPC) to virtually constitute the Australian peace
movement. At the time, an intense and truculent anticommunism
pervaded the country. This was the most important factor determining the direction and impact of the major peace bodies. Criticism
of the movement came from nearly every established section of the
society, as well as from some highly virulent fringe groups on the
right. Although the accusations took many forms, they basically narrowed down to a single, unshakable belief: the peace movement was
serving the interests of international communism and, therefore,
gravely endangered Australia's cherished inheritance of capitalism,
Christianity, democracy, and freedom.

ORIGINS OF THE APC: DOMESTIC BACKGROUND

Despite the introduction of the world to a new, horrific form of human destruction with the dropping of the two A-bombs on Japan
in August 1945, the Australian peace movement passed through a
phase of relative quietism during the immediate postwar years. Only
the absolute pacifists, in contrast to the peace advocacy wing of the
movement, responded initially to the long-term implications of the
new weapon, but because their numbers were small, their resources
limited, and their activities unambitious, the absolute pacifists attracted little attention. The reaction of most Australians to the beginning of the atomic age was one of relief and thanksgiving. The
atomic bomb had pulverized Japanese militarism into submission
and, by bringing the war to a swift conclusion, saved thousands of

Allied lives. Little sympathy existed for the first victims of nuclear warfare.

If a less than purely pacifist wing of the movement were to emerge, it would have to have the support of liberal internationalists, socially-minded Christians, and radical socialists that had constituted the prewar International Peace Campaign. In due course the first two groups began to respond, placing their faith for an enduring peace in the effective operation of the United Nations. A few joined branches of the United Nations Association of Australia, but eventually their energies were absorbed in struggles against the takeover tactics of anticommunists from the political arm of Catholic Action known as The Movement, and in disgust they drifted away. Others merely gave their tacit support to the work of the Minister of External Affairs, Dr. Herbert Vere Evatt, who was attempting to strengthen the role of the middle-level powers at the UN. They also added their weight to the United States proposal to internationalize the control of atomic energy and weaponry, and criticized the counterproposal of the Soviet Union for its lack of a verification system. Outside the ambit of UN politics, an assortment of concerned intellectuals formed in 1948, during the Berlin blockade, the Peace Action Council (PAC), but its existence was short-lived as many of its members saw greater potential in working through the more widely based APC founded a year later.[1]

Meanwhile, domestic concerns preoccupied the radical socialists, as represented by a section of the trade union movement and some members of the Australian Labor Party (ALP) as well as the Communist Party of Australia (CPA). Since the ALP was so seldom in office, the left wing of the Party made its chief aim to promote and implement Prime Minister J.B. (Ben) Chifley's domestic programs and Evatt's foreign policies, not to venture off in mobilizing an independent peace movement. Similarly, the energies of the communists were channelled in other directions. Initially they elected their members to Parliament and then, renouncing the Browder policy of class collaboration, embarked on very militant tactics in the trade union movement and waged unremitting war against the ALP.

By early 1950, both the communist and noncommunist left had good cause to reassess their positions and build a strong, united peace movement. This revision of strategies stemmed primarily from a series of severe setbacks suffered by the entire political left as the Cold War heated up. The ALP had lost the December 1949 elections against an opposition that fanned the flames of anticommunism. Removal of the Labor Party from the government benches meant that its supporters were cut off from an important avenue for influencing peace policies, while inside the Party a polarization of ideologies had developed between the Catholic right and the socialist left that frustrated any dialogue on peace issues. Furthermore, outside the Party, the Evatt policy of a dynamic role for a collective international voice of all nations at the UN had been shattered by the complete dominance of the Great Powers acting through the Security Council or, what was considered worse, acting unilaterally outside the UN. The only way peace-minded members of the ALP could help even minimally to defuse the Cold War was to turn to an organization engaged in improving international relations on a people-to-people basis and, in particular, modifying the bellicose values and attitudes of ordinary Australians.

The communists were also beset with tribulations. By 1949 the Party's fortunes had plummeted dramatically from the sanguine days of 1945.[2] CPA membership had declined from about 20,000 to about 6,000; influence in the trade unions had been severely undermined by a Catholic-oriented, anticommunist trade union faction called the Groupers. Control of some of the country's biggest unions had been lost.[3] Not all setbacks could be attributed solely to the infiltration of the Groupers, because communist sectarianism had led to policies of class antagonism and adventurism that, in the existing conditions, spelled certain disaster.[4]

A campaign against the establishment of the Woomera Rocket Range in South Australia represented one of the few occasions prior to 1950 when the communists and other socialists became involved in what might be called a peace issue.[5] In the campaign, though, many pacifists expressed misgivings about working with the communists, so that on the rocket range issue they confined their cooperation to such groups as the Presbyterian Board of Missions and the Women's Christian Temperance Union.[6] Similarly, the communists showed little interest in developing a united front with bourgeois elements. They focused instead on the unions under their influence and distributed to workers a pamphlet which the government called subversive.

The Cold War persecution of communists reached unprecedented heights in the late 1940s. They were unmercifully shouted down if they dared to speak at public meetings. The police singled them out for arrest, often on [trumped-up?] charges.[7] In 1949 the Victorian state government set up a Royal Commission to investigate the allegations of a communist defector that the CPA was engaged in espionage, sabotage, and corrupt union practices.[8] Although the Lowe Commission (named after the Royal Commissioner) absolved the Party of almost all the specific charges, the acquittal so enraged the anticommunists that they redoubled their efforts to secure a Royal Commission into communism at the federal level. Despite resisting such pressures, the Chifley Labor government did prosecute individual communists for statements that allegedly promoted "feelings of ill-will and hostility between different classes of his majesty's subjects so as to endanger the peace, order or good government of the Commonwealth."[9] As a result, three leading party officials were given prison sentences.[10] It is reasonable to assume that none of the arrests and arraignments would have taken place had it not been for the anticommunist hysteria sweeping the nation. In this respect, the *coup de grâce,* as far as the communists were concerned, occurred when the Liberal–Country party coalition came to power in December 1949 and, honoring its election pledge, introduced legislation to ban the CPA. The Party prepared to go underground.

In this extremely hostile atmosphere, the communists became involved in setting up in the second half of 1949 the postwar peace advocacy section of the peace movement. They were interested in mollifying Cold War attitudes, and they sought to do this by forging an alliance with various noncommunist elements who were also alarmed at the doctrinaire course domestic and international events were taking. However, the communist decision to reinvolve itself in a widely based peace movement was not solely a simple, expedient defensive response. It emerged as a natural outcome of policies that had been evolving in world communist thinking for at least three years.

ORIGINS OF THE APC: FOREIGN LINKS

At a conference in early 1947, communist parties of the British Empire affirmed that aggressive U.S. imperialism, ably assisted by junior imperialist partner Great Britain, endangered world peace and security. Responsibility existed at the local level to work for the disengagement of their country from this ominous alliance. Such an analysis was developed further in the first pronouncement of the newly formed Cominform, in September 1947, calling for "the Communist Parties . . . [to] take the lead in resisting the plans of imperialist expansion and aggression . . . and rally around themselves all the democratic and patriotic forces in their respective nations."[11] Because the peace-loving peoples if united were stronger than all the warmongering imperialists, they could prevent World War III by effecting bans on atomic weapons and war preparations and by forcing the withdrawal of troops which were crushing anticolonial movements.

The Cominform's analysis and call for action appeared to be taken very seriously at the first postwar Congress of Australian communists held in Sydney in May 1948. The Congress condemned the alleged Anglo-American imperialists, and specifically resolved that it was the "duty of communists to lead the resistance to the warmongers and to organize peace-lovers around a broad program of peaceful cooperation among the nations."[12] Meeting in Hungary in October 1949, the Cominform declared: "Organization and uniting of the forces for peace . . . must at this time become the center of all the activity of the Communist parties."[13]

With these and other official statements encouraging the establishment of a mass, widely-based peace organization, the APC was founded on 1 July 1949. Although the majority of its founding members were noncommunists, the critical role played by the communists is indisputable. A number of factors had brought their formal resolutions to fruition. In the first place, rapidly deteriorating international and domestic circumstances created the need for allies; secondly, strong pressures existed from intellectuals within the Party for an alliance of peace forces; and thirdly, a series of significant international peace congresses and peace committees had been organized that greatly influenced local communist thinking.

The first of the overseas peace events was the World Congress of Intellectuals for Peace, held in Wrocław, Poland, in August 1948. Called by a combined group of Polish and French intellectuals, the Wrocław Congress attracted over 500 delegates from 44 countries.[14] Its proceedings received the lavish praise of the Cominform. One of its decisions was to set up a continuing committee called the International Liaison Committee of Intellectuals in Defense of Peace, with headquarters in Paris, and this Committee was instrumental in organizing the first World Peace Congress, held in Paris, 20–25 April 1949. Since some of the delegates were denied entry into France, a

simultaneous meeting was held in Prague which kept in telephonic
communication with the Paris Congress.[15] Out of these joint meetings a permanent committee emerged which in time became known
as the World Peace Council. That both the Paris and earlier
Wrocław conferences greatly influenced thinking within the CPA —
and hence galvanized communists behind the formation of the APC —
is suggested by or openly admitted in the statements of many leading
Australian communists.[16]

Despite the CPA emphasis on peace work, there were constant
complaints from its intellectual members that the actual support did
not match the rhetoric.[17] They wanted a greater commitment from
the Party's hierarchy and its trade union wing. In reality, they were
probably fortunate these sections held back, because an effective
peace movement strategy required a restrained communist presence
that would merely facilitate the more conspicuous peace work of the
Christians and other noncommunists. Such a strategy did unfold at
the launching of the APC, when the movement was *least* broadly
based and *most* dependent on communist support.

LAUNCHING OF THE APC

During the early years of the APC, a contingent of religious peace
advocates — clergy and laity alike — played a key role in the peace
movement's history. These were individuals (not churches) who were
generally alarmed at the unchristian bellicosity associated with Cold
War attitudes and, in particular, discerned a discrepancy between
Christian morality and the society's immorality in such positions as
the condoning of the atomic testing on the Monte Bello Islands, the
serious contemplation of an attack on the Chinese mainland, the fa-
talistic resignation to World War III's inevitability, and the West's
apparent inflexibility at the disarmament table. Together with an assortment of atheistic humanitarians, disillusioned members of the
Labor Party, civil libertarians and, of course, the communists, they
trace their involvement in postwar peace politics to a meeting at the
Melbourne Town Hall on 23 February 1949, which never took place!
The occasion was to be a public address by John Rodgers, the Director of Australia-Soviet House, who had recently visited the Soviet
Union. At the eleventh hour the Melbourne City Councillors denied

him the use of the hall. This action provoked an outcry from people who not only thought it important for Australians to hear the Soviet Union's version of the Cold War but considered the action a blatant denial of the democratic right of free speech. An organization quickly formed to reverse the decision. Called the Democratic Rights Council (DRC), with Doris Blackburn, a member of the House of Representatives, elected chairperson, and the Reverend Frank Hartley, a Methodist minister, the secretary, it waged a spirited campaign, bringing together people who shared an interest in reversing the escalation of the Cold War as well as in restoring free speech. A popular slogan expressed by the chairperson was that "freedom and peace go hand in hand."[18]

Commensurate with this theme, a meeting was held at the home of a Unitarian minister, the Reverend Victor James, on 1 July 1949 to form the APC and define its aims. About twelve persons attended, each of whom was associated in one way or another with the DRC, and some with close ties to PAC as well.[19] Besides the Reverend Mssrs. James and Hartley, a third minister, the Reverend Alfred M. Dickie (Presbyterian), completed the trio later dubbed "the three peace parsons."[20] The meeting elected an executive of six, comprising the Reverend Mssrs. Dickie (chairperson and honorary treasurer), Hartley and James (joint honorary secretaries); Dr. James F. Cairns (then a university lecturer, later to lead the anti-Vietnam campaign, and eventually to become Deputy Prime Minister of Australia); John Rodgers (a CPA member); and Heather Wakefield (of the Student Christian Movement).[21] A list of twenty-four "original or foundation members" was released, together with a broad statement of objectives.[22]

When branches of the ALP later banned the APC to its members because it putatively constituted "a communist front organization," the three peace parsons were moved to reply publicly: "We swear . . . that the Communist Party did not establish the Australian Peace Council, does not control its policy or activities, and cannot use it for ends other than advancing world peace."[23]

In the meantime the DRC had won its campaign to open Melbourne Town Hall to persons of all political persuasions. John Rodgers finally delivered his address six months after his scheduled appearance. A measure of the vitriolic anticommunism permeating the community can be gleaned from the way it was reported in a major

Melbourne daily, which referred to "the snow of Moscow ha[ving] melted off John Rodgers' boots" since he came "back from his rouble-subsidized mission to Moscow."[24]

As part of the APC's campaign to curb such "aggressive propaganda," it launched in the same Town Hall its first public rally on 7 September 1949.[25] At the meeting, chaired by Dr. Cairns and reportedly attended by 3,000 people, three main projects were identified: a huge propaganda campaign, a national peace ballot, and a national peace congress. The object was to change attitudes as a necessary precondition for the changing of policies.

THE DOUR DECADE

These three types of activities formed the basic pattern of peace campaigning during the next decade. While the second and third areas of activity were specific at the outset, the idea of a huge propaganda campaign came to mean: (1) arranging visits of prominent overseas guests to Australia and sending Australian delegations to international peace gatherings in Europe and Asia that were usually sponsored by the WPC; (2) distributing large quantities of antiwar literature, particularly among trade unionists; and (3) holding suburban and regional film showings and discussion sessions.

The first organizational task was to set up local peace bodies and integrate them into a national association. After a Victorian Peace Council was set up, a Queensland counterpart was formed at the end of September 1949 at a conference convened by the left-wing Queensland Legion of Ex-Servicemen and Women. A few weeks later, about 350 persons at the Sydney Radio Theatre sanctioned the formation of a New South Wales branch of APC, appointing as chairperson Lady Jessie Street, an Australian delegate to the drawing up of the UN Charter in San Francisco, and as honorary secretary Nell Simpson, a local ALP official. Similar branches were soon started in Adelaide and Perth. By November, the APC claimed over 150 peace auxiliaries in localities and workplaces operating under the aegis of the state peace branches.[26] The national executive, now extended to ten persons, included Ian Turner of the CPA, who assumed the full-time job of national organizing secretary.[27] The executive now consisted of six practicing Christians, three communists, and one ALP socialist.

In the course of the decade, the APC conducted or was involved in three major peace petitions, four national peace congresses, numerous tours for foreign visitors, and the sending overseas of Australian delegations almost every year to WPC-sponsored or initiated conferences. The theme of all the peace petitions centered on a total ban of all atomic weapons and the establishment of international controls to ensure the ban's implementation. At the end of 1949, the APC launched the initial Ban the Bomb petition (which it called a "Peace Ballot"). While over 200,000 signatures were collected in Australia for what subsequently became known as "the Stockholm Appeal," many respondents would not sign, as one canvasser recalled, "due to a fear that their signatures on the petition would be misused. Others questioned the petition's effectiveness, and many thought that such a ban would disarm the West and allow the Soviet Union to gain in the atomic race."[28]

The "Peace Ballot" aroused the unrestrained antipathy of the nation's media, non-Labor parties, and the right wing of the ALP. The New South Wales and Victorian Executives of the ALP queried the APC's genuine concern for peace, and in February and March of 1950 declared it to be a proscribed organization.[29] This was followed a year later by the Federal Party's Australia-wide ban on the ground that the APC "is a subsidiary organization to the Communist Party."[30] Among Labor parliamentarians only Senator William Morrow stood publicly by the APC and its policies at this time and, for his commitment, he was denied re-endorsement as candidate for the 1953 Senate election by his Party's state branch.[31] Subsequently he worked full-time as secretary of the New South Wales Peace Council and its successor, the New South Wales Peace Committee — both groups affiliated with the APC.

Condemnation of the APC was not confined to the right-wing Grouper element in the ALP, the press, and non-Labor parties. Many absolute pacifists and dissenting proponents of peace, with long memories of what happened to the International Peace Campaign in the late 1930s after the Molotov-Ribbentrop Pact, expressed doubts about the sincerity of the new peace body and hesitated to join in its campaigns.[32] The APC suffered a further setback in June 1950 when three of its more prominent members announced their resignations, ostensibly because they objected to the way the APC persisted in blaming the origins of the Korean War solely on the Americans and South Koreans.

Nevertheless, despite these and a host of other problems, the APC managed to survive and even achieve a modicum of success. A second peace petition, entitled "The Pact of Peace Appeal," was circulated in 1952, and obtained 125,556 signatures.[33] Another petition, circulated in 1955 and 1956, achieved slightly better results. Labelled the "World-wide Appeal," it gained the support of some well-known Australians. Many ALP members signed, for after the ALP had purged itself of its more extreme anticommunists in the "great split" of 1955–56, the remaining members were generally free to participate in peace movement activities. Although the ALP Federal Conference at Hobart in March 1955 passed a resolution condemning the use of the communist "peace tactic," it failed to name any specific Australian peace bodies. Moreover, a congruency was emerging between the ALP and the peace movement on a range of foreign policies. The Hobart Conference adopted as official Labor Party policies, for instance, the withdrawal of Australian troops from Malaya and the recognition of the People's Republic of China. Both policies were high on the list of peace movement demands.

Because it enjoyed the ALP's tacit approval, the peace movement was able to attract 150 members of the Labor Party to its third postwar peace congress, the Australian Assembly for Peace, held in Sydney in September.[34] Evatt, the Party's parliamentary leader, even sent the Assembly his personal greetings, commending it for providing the public with a forum where "a free exchange of ideas will enable humanity to survive."[35] All this was in marked contrast to the hostility encountered by the movement at its first two congresses, neither of which secured the official endorsement of a single ALP politician.

The APC sponsored a first national peace congress in Melbourne, 16–19 April 1950. Featured as principal speaker was the Dean of Canterbury, Dr. Hewlett Johnson, better known to the public by his media sobriquet, "the Red Dean." The opening rally at Melbourne's Exhibition Hall attracted 14,000 persons according to the APC's reckoning, or 10,000 by the estimate of the critical Sydney *Morning Herald*.[36] By any count the rally was a thunderous success in generating enthusiasm. The four-day Congress was attended by 674 accredited delegates claiming to represent 336 organizations and 549,000 Australians in a population that numbered less than ten million.[37] It produced an "Australian Peace Manifesto," calling for actions to ban the A-bomb, promote general and universal disarmament, renounce conscription, establish diplomatic relations with China, oppose military propaganda, and prevent military intervention in Southeast Asia (Malaya being designated a particularly vulnerable spot).[38] For the most part, this very broad program became the staple diet of the peace movement throughout the next fifteen years.

Although the "Australian Peace Manifesto" was fervently acclaimed by about 10,000 persons at the closing rally, the 1950 Congress never succeeded in popularizing its message among the masses of Australian people. The Congress did help, however, to stimulate interest among some individual clergymen. About a year after the Congress, a group of Melbourne ministers decided to launch the Peace Quest Forum.[39] This body proceeded to conduct weekly public forums in Melbourne, at which they discussed a variety of peace-related subjects from varying points of view. Most of the ministers were connected in some way or another with branches of the APC; some, such as the Reverend Mssrs. Dickie, Hartley, Van Eerde, James, and Brand, travelled overseas to attend conferences of the WPC. For these associations and for their efforts at promoting debate that questioned established Western perceptions of political reality, the ministers quickly earned a reputation as "communist dupes." They especially aroused a storm of anticommunist protest when they became involved in organizing the second national peace congress — the Australian Convention on Peace and War, held in Sydney, 26–30 September 1953.

This congress, unlike the one in 1950 which was run from beginning to end by the APC, was initiated and managed by a group of Christian ministers with the APC acting in a supporting role. Yet the 1953 convention provoked even greater anticommunist criticism than its predecessor. Its detractors were headed by Prime Minister Robert Gordon Menzies, who delivered a lengthy statement in the House, asserting that "facts . . . give good cause for believing that both the Communist party and the Australian Peace Council laid the groundwork for the convention and that they continue to provide, behind the scenes, a considerable amount of direction and organization."[40] Although the ten sponsoring ministers had indicated that no resolutions were to be passed at the conference, the Prime Minister warned people attending that they "would find themselves subscribing to resolutions that were 'loaded' in favor of the Communists." Conferences like this one were designed to have a "softening up effect on the democratic world."[41] Opposition leader Evatt, ever mindful of the anticommunist ideologues within his own party, agreed, pointing out that any persons concerned about peace could make their contributions through branches of the United Nations Association (as previously noted, most of these groups had been taken over by the extreme right).[42]

The list of opponents and objectors to the Convention was seemingly endless. The New South Wales ALP issued another ban.[43] Leaders of the Australian Council of Churches privately expressed their doubts.[44] The popular press, in particular, evinced an obvious anticommunist bias in its reporting and in its advertising policy.[45]

The frenzy of anticommunism had been heightened by Australia's participation in the Korean War and by constant references of leading public figures, including Menzies, that a third world war was imminent.[46] Menzies even contended that in the forthcoming conflict the atomic bomb "is a no less legitimate instrument of warfare than other modern means of mass destruction."[47] War talk of this nature pervaded the country. To safeguard Australian security, it was the responsibility of patriots to expose the communist peace design and the various overseas connections through which it would be implemented in Australia. The pivotal figure behind the 1953 Convention was the Reverend Alan Brand. He had been financed by the New South Wales Peace Council to represent it at the WPC-controlled Vienna Peace Congress in December 1952. On returning home, the impressionable Mr. Brand had met with other equally naive ministers and together they had issued a call for a local variant of the Vienna Congress, thereby unwittingly carrying out a directive of Joseph Stalin.[48]

One minister, intimately involved in organizing the Convention, directly challenged this conspiratorial interpretation of the facts. To clear up any misunderstandings, the Reverend J. Eric Owen sought and received an interview with Prime Minister Menzies. Although the interview changed neither man's basic position, the Prime Minister later made available to the Reverend Mr. Owen the government's security files. Upon reviewing the evidence, the Reverend Mr. Owen reported that he saw no new startling fact to cause him to withdraw his sponsorship.[49] Indeed, his resolve seemed to be strengthened as he became the central figure dedicated to the Convention's success.

Despite the absence of ALP participation, the Convention attracted over a thousand delegates, representing a wide range of occupational groupings.[50] However, although the leadership had revolved chiefly around the ten Sydney clergymen initially responsible for calling the conference and the Peace Quest Forum in Melbourne, only nineteen ministers were officially listed as having attended. This reflects, to some degree, enormous pressures from a large majority of their parishioners. The official register also disclosed a large number of blue-collar workers (almost half the delegates) but only a few students (two percent). Another feature was the involvement of many absolute pacifists. Indeed, the Convention marked a watershed in the reforging of the alliance between absolute pacifists and peace advocates that continued, with minor fluctuating fortunes, until the former were swamped as an identifiable force during the anti-Vietnam mobilization.

For the second time a national peace conference was able to galvanize enthusiasm into continuing organizations. Both the New South Wales and South Australian organizing committees of the Convention decided to continue as permanent bodies. This meant that Sydney now had two major peace organizations: the old Peace Council, whose secretary was ex-Senator William Morrow (subsequently to be elected to the WPC Bureau and to receive the Lenin Peace Prize), and the new Peace Convention Committee, with the Reverend Norman St. Clair Anderson as chairperson. These two groups, along with the APC that operated out of Melbourne under the leadership of the three peace parsons and a communist organizing secretary, were equally instrumental in laying the groundwork for the third national peace congress in 1956. As already noted, the Australian Assembly for Peace proved to be significant because it represented the first time the Labor Party had *not* seen fit to ban a peace congress. Many ALP members and politicians thus registered as delegates. Also apparent was the increasing support of the absolute pacifists.[51] As in the case of preceding congresses, the greatest financial support and delegate strength continued to come from the left-wing trade unions.

Anticommunist attacks this time centered on the ALP's capitulation to "communist unity moves." The ALP was denounced for ignoring the evidence of communist manipulation. The origins of the Assembly could be traced to the WPC's role in organizing the 1955 World Assembly for Peace in Helsinki, where the idea of regional conferences was promoted. Many of the two dozen Australians who attended this meeting, as well as the WPC's later meeting in Stockholm, were the leading proponents of the Australian variant of the Helsinki Assembly.[52]

Despite these revelations, 928 Australians, representing 503 organizations, opted to participate in the Assembly's deliberations.[53] It largely conformed to the pattern of previous congresses, organizing into broad commissions that proposed equally broad solutions to basically international problems. However, there were some indications that the peace movement was turning to more specific and locally oriented issues, such as providing social and economic justice for the Aborigines and promoting peace values and modifying competition in Australian schools. In the area of nuclear weaponry, they demanded concrete actions: the "Federal Government [was] to use all its influence in the United Nations to achieve an international agreement to discontinue nuclear weapons tests immediately, and at the same time to prohibit such tests in Australia."[54]

That attention should focus on nuclear weapons issues stemmed from more than the deteriorating international situation in the control of nuclear testing and stockpiling of weapons. Australia itself was becoming increasingly involved as a host and potential victim of nuclear explosions.[55] Beginning in 1952, Britain tested weapons at Monte Bello Island and at Emu Plain and Maralinga in South Australia. The extension of the Woomera Range to Maralinga meant that, by 1957, one-third of South Australia was used for weapons and rocket testing.

In order to protest against past and anticipated testing at Maralinga, the South Australian Peace Convention sponsored a conference in Adelaide, in October 1957. With the APC's various offshoot groups leading the way, the "left" generally stood united in its denunciation of Australia's collaboration in nuclear weapons testing. The Australian Council of Trade Unions (ACTU), together with all its state branches, as well as the main trade union outside the ACTU — the relatively conservative Australian Workers Union (AWU) — registered strong antitesting protests. The Labor Party also expressed its opposition. At the ALP federal conference in 1957, Dr. Evatt charged that "absurd risks are being taken by all nations experimenting with nuclear weapons. . . . There must be an organized effort to stop it all."[56] By 1958, the ALP was sufficiently sensitized to the issue so that it approved a nation-wide demonstration against continued testing.

Opposition came also from a few organizations with middle-class backing, such as the Australian branch of the World Council of Churches and the Women's Christian Temperance Union. In addition, 360 Australian scientists signed the UN petition of Professor Linus Pauling calling for an end to tests, and under the leadership of Sir Mark Oliphant, who began to attend Pugwash conferences in 1958, local branches were set up in Australia which carefully monitored, analyzed and publicized the radiation data on tests.[57] Moreover, the universal significance of Hiroshima was beginning to penetrate public consciousness. Some APC intellectuals, working through the journals *Overland* and *Meanjin,* organized a national arts exhibition of the famous Hiroshima Panels. Their display in the art galleries of the capital city drew record-breaking crowds and high praise from the editorial writers of the major newspapers.[58] The impact of this increasing concern and activity was reflected in the public opinion polls. The Australian Gallup surveys showed that between 1952 and 1956 *support* for Britain's exploding of "experimental atomic bombs" in central Australia fell from 58 percent to 38 percent. Of even greater significance was the 1958 result, in which 62 percent of Australians, as against 25 percent, thought "Britain and America should agree with Russia to ban H-bomb tests."[59]

Nevertheless, the Government remained firm in its belief (expressed by External Affairs Minister Casey) that these antibomb sentiments were whipped up by protests that originated in Moscow or, at best, were the result of "innocents" playing inadvertently into the hands of Soviet military strategists.[60] This line of reasoning persisted in the face of intensified left-wing criticism over the Government's decision to grant Britain the use of Christmas Island for larger bomb tests.

The peace movement channelled its dissent through an array of new and old groups. The aftermath of the 1956 Assembly for Peace saw the state organizing committees in Sydney and Brisbane established on a permanent basis. In South Australia the Peace Convention Committee still existed, while in Victoria and Western Australia the state branches of the APC retained their leadership roles. The sixth state, Tasmania, continued to operate with a local APC representative. However, after the next triennial peace congress, in November 1959, the APC withdrew completely from the limelight, and the main peace bodies in every state except Western Australia stemmed from this fourth and last congress of the decade. Although afflicted with a cumbersome title, Australian New Zealand Congress for International Co-operation and Disarmament and the Festival of Arts, the ANZ Congress excelled its predecessors in all respects, including the opposition it generated, and marked a watershed in the peace movement's postwar history.[61] In retrospect, it can be seen to have produced the first stirrings of a transformed movement whose features became unmistakably clear only during the years of protest against the Vietnam War. Thus generically, although not chronologically, this Congress in late 1959 belongs more to the early wave of aggressive protest that characterized the 1960s than to the more sedate and defensive style associated with the dour decade.

Another significant type of peace activity during the 1950s was the travelling of various peace leaders to and from Australia. The attendance of Australians at overseas peace conferences began, of course, as far back as the 1949 World Peace Congress in Paris. Thereafter, delegations of Australians — mainly intellectuals, trade union officials, and church figures — were trekking periodically to international meetings, sometimes two or three times a year. The meetings were designed to coordinate activities internationally as well as to establish personal contacts and exchange knowledge and experiences, thereby stimulating the thinking of the delegates along a wide range of peace issues.

Unfortunately, the conferences sponsored by the WPC were frequently the lamentable victims of Cold War thinking from a Soviet perspective. Yet they served the important function of providing a minimal degree of nonofficial contact between peoples from the two hostile blocs of nations. Because the Australian Government perceived the conferences as little more than ill-disguised but highly dangerous propaganda exercises, it was greatly reluctant to permit its citizens to attend. Often the departures of prospective delegates would be thwarted by a denial of passports. Those Australians who did manage to escape this security screen would then find themselves, on their return, subjected to all kinds of harassment by customs and security officers. The mass media were inclined to report the visits and the follow-up meetings at home as actions bordering on treason.

Perhaps the most controversial — but by no means atypical — of these overseas conferences was the 1952 Asian and Pacific Peace Congress in Peking. The anticommunist reaction to this conference was exacerbated by the fact that Australian soldiers were fighting forces of the host nation in Korea, and because the delegation attending the preparatory meeting in China was headed by Dr. John Burton, a former Secretary of the External Affairs Department and a designated Labor Party candidate for the forthcoming election. Accordingly, the Menzies Government effectively used the incident to smear its political opponent, deepening the rift within the ALP that eventually brought on the major split of 1955-56.

The government also introduced a rigorous policy of censorship, particularly as it pertained to films that the peace movement sought to import from abroad. Even if a film did manage to gain admittance, it might be subjected to the censor's scissors. For example, the sound track of the film, *Shadows Over the World,* was cut at the point where the narrator asserted "the world peace movement was responsible for the A-bomb not being dropped in Korea." Despite protests from the movement that "this is a great and dangerous tendency, this presumption to gauge 'truth' for the Australian people," its pleas for free speech were either ignored or simply dismissed as communist-inspired.[62]

The censorship also applied to the granting of entrance visas. Visitors from behind the "Iron" or "Bamboo Curtains" (unless they happened to be defectors) were declared *personae non gratae,* as were Westerners with known heterodox views. It was thus extremely difficult for the movement to enlist foreign guests on speaking tours around Australia. With the exception of the Dean of Canterbury, the American basso Paul Robeson, and the theologian Joseph Hromadka of Czechoslovakia, the guests permitted into the country tended to be either absolute pacifists like the British crystallographer Kathleen Lonsdale or parliamentarians like Senator Jiichico Matsumoto of the Japanese House of Councillors. Only towards the end of the decade did the Government's restrictive policy begin to ease slightly.

MARSHALLING THE NEW WITHIN THE OLD (1960-65)

Marion Hartley made a critical distinction in her biography of her husband, the Reverend Frank Hartley: "The World Peace Council and the Australian Peace Council were each trying to create an organization broader than itself, which could become quite autonomous in controlling its own outreach."[63]

In achieving this strategy, the Melbourne Congress of November 1959 was far more successful than its predecessors, although not in ways its organizers always approved or might have anticipated. Its sheer size — well over 10,000 delegates, official observers, and casual attenders — generated an enthusiasm that augured well for the future.[64] In terms of age, occupation, and political affiliation, the delegates covered a wide spectrum, including a group of dissident, critical intellectuals who vigorously upheld the "right to hold independent political views and insist[ed] that this right shall be accorded to all participants."[65] Some delegates were disaffected members of the CPA who had left the Party after the 1956 events in Hungary and Khrushchev's famous Twentieth Congress speech. Others came from a generation whose formative experiences lay outside the genesis of the Cold War. The large number of new recruits reflected the growing worldwide concern about the effects of nuclear testing, but they were also drawn to this peace congress because it represented the focal point of all left-wing political activity in Australia at this moment. A great deal of the credit must go to the organizers for staging what was clearly the most professionally run of the APC-related congresses. Overseas guests included such luminaries as the British writers J. B. Priestley and Jacquetta Hawkes and the American Nobel Prize laureate Linus Pauling. Local support came from a long list of outstanding Australians — prominent academics, writers, artists, politicians, trade unionists, church people, sport stars, and even a retired air vice-marshal. Nonetheless, the response of the Government and the media was, once again, to depict the Congress as a communist-directed plot. The publicity set off a wide-scale debate that, in turn, produced more publicity, thereby creating an atmosphere that guaranteed the immediate success of the Congress.

However, a few years elapsed before the enthusiasm and propaganda generated by the Congress were visibly transformed into a wider-based and more dynamic movement. From 1960 through much of 1962, the movement was still confined to a small, solid, and dedicated core of stalwarts. As before, the main support was based in the radical trade unions (whose workers often imposed levies on themselves, thereby providing the movement with the bulk of its finance), the CPA, the left wing of the ALP, and a scattering of highly committed clergy and lay pacifists. Accordingly, the sum total of participants represented a group of only minor influence, certainly not one that threatened establishment policies or approached anything like the massive scale of the CND movement in Britain.

During the heyday of the first British CND and the beginnings of the civil rights and peace movements in the United States, the Australian movement engaged mainly in unobtrusive and innocuous activities, whose only function seemed to be the reinforcement of the existing membership's views. Apparently the Cold War animus had not abated sufficiently that the movement's leaders were emboldened to resort to militant tactics, harboring as they did memories of suppressions. Other than staging the occasional police-sanctioned open-air rally or march, peace officials never ventured from the established routine of conferences, petitions, overseas trips, job-site meetings, film screenings, raffles, and the like. Such routine behavior was becoming an end in its own right. As attention centered on the *ritual* of keeping the faith, the original goal of *achieving* peace through socialism correspondingly receded from view.

A pattern also existed as to the type of policies being advocated. Continuing into the early sixties, solutions tended to be not only sweeping in nature but related to highly general and/or distant issues. Featured were such concerns as peaceful coexistence, universal disarmament, abolition of all nuclear testing, Cuba, Algeria, Berlin, the Congo, U-2 flights, and Japanese and German rearmament — policies and issues which must have seemed geographically and politically remote to most Australians, who traditionally have been concerned chiefly with incremental bread-and-butter politics and have left the grander global problems to the Mother Country or to Uncle Sam. Only the small band of ideologues on the right and a few opportunistic politicians bothered to reply to the general and remote matters raised by the peace groups.

Even when the movement turned to issues closer to home and directly affecting Australia, such as SEATO and the U.S. radio base in Western Australia, it tended to reject piecemeal and proximate solutions in favor of distant and inclusive goals. Thus the issue of colonialism demanded "immediate action to encourage . . . the emancipation of the New Guinea and Aboriginal peoples of Australia." Similarly, the movement's foreign policy stipulated "withdrawal from existing pacts and alliances" such as SEATO.[66] Since none of these sorts of "advanced" objectives were explained in terms meaningful to most Australians or were set out with intermediate strategies, the movement not surprisingly registered little impact on the political scene.

Notwithstanding this failure to make any apparent headway, there were signs of significant changes in the offing. The 1959 ANZ Congress had released nascent New Left forces that, in conjunction with external events, altered the complexion and direction of the movement. In 1960, a Victorian Campaign for Nuclear Disarmament

(VCND) was formed in Melbourne by a group of young intellectual dissenters inspired by the British unilateralists. These dissenters condemned the way in which peace politics was conducted in the ANZ Congress. Their central criticisms focused on the ANZ's bipolar projection of the world and the organization's use as a personal machine for a few individuals whose political biases were scarcely disguised, but they also denounced the ANZ Congress for its moderate tactics, which they contrasted unfavorably with the acts of confrontation and civil disobedience committed by the expanding CND movement in Britain. Although the Australian CND'ers could not call upon their government to relinquish nuclear weapons that it did not possess, they did join their British counterparts in stressing the importance of nonalignment for their country in the nuclear age. They wanted Australia to renounce any involvement in nuclear strategy, to pursue a more active role in the attainment of a universal test ban treaty, and never to undertake to develop an independent nuclear force.[67]

At Sydney a CND with similar aims was founded in March 1962 and, together with the VCND and the CND groups formed in 1962 in Western Australia and Queensland, it gave Australia a preview of the political flamboyance that was to become a trademark of dissenting politics from mid-decade onward. Drawing its support mainly from humanitarian and intellectual dissenters, with a large component of youth, the CND stressed mass direct action and a politics of personal commitment. Its supporters marched and sang. They developed a special subculture of defiance symbolized by the famous logo of the drooping cross and by an unconventionality in hair and dress styles. Even in the midst of fellow peace demonstrators, the CND'ers stood out as a fringe group. In Australia they always remained outside the mainstream of the peace movement, though they greatly shaped its course and were the stylistic forerunners of an important faction to take up the Vietnam and conscription issues. In fact, they were also organizational forerunners of this faction because in 1965 both the Victorian and Sydney CNDs dissolved into major anti-Vietnam bodies.

As the continuing committees of the 1959 Melbourne Congress progressed through the sixties, they showed an ability to amalgamate the new forces and to adopt or even co-opt the new styles. In particular, the leadership of the New South Wales Peace Committee and its successor, the Association for International Co-operation

and Disarmament (AICD), which evolved out of the last of the national congresses in Sydney in October 1964, seemed quick to recognize the potential of a movement based upon the moral zeal of the
middle class and the enthusiasm of youth for its drive, especially
when this was combined with the traditional forces of the left and
Christian pacifism. Thus, as early as mid 1961, when the peace committees in the three eastern mainland states were approached by the
British Committee of 100 (Lord Russell's breakaway group from
CND) for assistance in staging "a world-wide movement of resistance which will make it impossible for any government, East or
West, to have nuclear bombs or bases," the New South Wales leadership advocated a positive response.[68] According to its joint secretary,
"unless we take some initiatives about this type of activity, it will,
before very long, be initiated independently of our movement."[69]

Responding to the British appeal for action, the Australian peace
committees conducted a motorcade *cum* relay march to Canberra,
where selected participants then called on members of Parliament
and made the rounds of the embassies. It was a very tame-cat demonstration compared to some of the militant tactics adopted later, but
this small step nonetheless showed the leadership's appreciation of
the new militancy popularized abroad and emerging at home and the
need to incorporate it into the development of a viable, broadly based,
Australian movement. Beginning in 1962 and continuing annually until 1965, the established groups participated in joint Aldermaston-
type marches on the Easter weekends in those capital cities where
CND was based.

Because the old guard had the organizational advantage of a developed infrastructure, plus long experience and some financial resources, it was able to act as a core group in the three most populous
states. Its influence remained dominant as long as it showed flexibil-
ity and sensitivity to the needs of the new groups, which, besides the
CND chapters, now included opponents of the French nuclear tests
at Mururoa Atoll and some reconstituted WILPF branches. As viewed
by the AICD's secretary, the movement's diversification represented
its greatest strength. He called on the various core groups descended
from APC to encourage "independent and coordinated initiatives . . .
without in any way submerging the identity of the component parts"
of the movement.[70]

For the most part, this strategy prevailed. Moreover, the APC's
lineal descendants changed in another important respect. Gradually,

after late 1962, they began to discard peace abstractions and distant goals for the tackling of specific, local issues. This shift in policy orientation was probably due not so much to a deliberate, strategic choice as to a series of fortuitous, outside events forcing the movement into new areas of concern. The crisis in West Irian, the general worsening of Australia's relations with Sukarno's Indonesia due to the confrontation with Malaysia and the rise in power of the PKI communist party, the Opposition Leader's advocacy of a nuclear-free zone in the Southern Hemisphere, the decision of the French Government to test nuclear weapons in the Pacific, the palliative effect of the signing of the 1963 partial nuclear test ban treaty on the general disarmament question—all these events and others compelled the movement to concentrate on more specific issues of a local nature. When the Australian Government announced, in April 1965, that it was sending a small contingent of combat troops to Vietnam, all these issues became subordinate to the life and death issues of Vietnam and conscription.

EMERGENT THEMES

Several interrelated themes and questions emerge from the postwar history of the Australian peace movement. First, the period was marked by extreme anticommunism, mitigated only slightly towards the end. The abatement was not sufficient to prevent Australia's entry into the Vietnam War, which was seen as necessary to help check the "downward thrust" of Asian communism spearheaded by China and to encourage a strong military presence of the United States in the area. Thus from beginning to end, fear of communism and pro-Americanism were the chief obstacles confronting the peace movement. It defined its task mainly in the negative terms of offsetting or trying to break down an entrenched orthodoxy.

Second, as a corollary, in attempting to loosen the viselike grip of the consensus, the peace movement's supporters assumed the same bipolar model as their anticommunist antagonists, except that they turned it on its head. Not until some new forces joined the movement after the 1959 ANZ Congress was bipolarism really challenged. Previously, for the most part, the world was depicted as being divided into the militaristic monolith of Western capitalism counterpoised by the solidarity of the peace-loving socialist camp. Within that framework peace efforts were largely directed at exposing the perfidy of the "capitalist warmongers."

Third, the mainstream peace activists adopted a "united front from below" strategy and engaged in moderate tactics, assuming a role that would least offend and would enable the APC and its offspring to act as core bodies, ever widening the circle of supporters. Besides opting for nonprovocative and conventional activities, these core bodies deliberately propounded the movement's lowest common denominator regarding issues and policies, and in the process often exposed themselves to charges of promulgating peace banalities.

Fourth, the period witnessed an evolutionary broadening of the movement's socioeconomic base from a dependency on the left-wing trade unions to a greater involvement from the middle class. The movement became much more diverse in a number of areas: in occupational groupings, in the political affiliations of its supporters, in the increased participation of women, and in the upsurge of a volatile younger generation in the 1960s. Disappointing from the leadership's point of view was the tapering off of support from rank-and-file trade unionists.

Fifth, towards the end of this period, the strategy of involving new forces posed a threat to the movement. The dominance of the established organizations was challenged by the CND groups, whose popularity among young people siphoned off new recruits. Without the restraint of experienced leaders, it was feared, the "young turks" and their militant tactics would give anticommunists an excuse to invoke reprisals that would destroy the whole movement. Moreover, there were tensions over policy differences. The CND'ers focused almost exclusively on the nuclear issue and on the goal of unilateral renouncing of nuclear weaponry, whereas the descendants of the APC took up a wide range of issues and advocated universal, complete, and verifiable disarmament. Thus there was a potential threat to the carefully wrought strategy of enlisting respectable middle-class support while continuing to mobilize within the trade unions.

A sixth theme concerns the relationship of the movement to the Labor Party. Virtually at its inception, the movement as represented by the APC was outlawed to members of the ALP. However, after the 1955 split, the left-wing Labor members began to drift back into the movement. Henceforth, while the movement seldom attempted to pressure the ALP directly, it assiduously courted some of its leaders so that they would participate in movement activities, especially the periodic national congresses. Their involvement was considered to give the movement added publicity and prestige, thus contributing to the general strategy that targeted on the extraparliamentary politics of changing the society's values and attitudes. Success in this area, it was believed, would extend to the ALP, which in response to the dictates of *vox populi* or at least electoral pragmatism would become the instrumental agent for transforming the movement's demands into concrete peace policies.

In conclusion, what about the persistent questions that hounded the movement? Was it, as claimed by its opponents, secretly controlled by the Communist Party? Were there close ties that could be traced all the way back to the communist-run WPC? Were the communists holding key positions within the local bodies that enabled them to exploit the movement for their own purposes? Did the APC and its various offshoots merely ape the Soviet line on the critical peace issues? The answers to these questions are complex and require a subtlety of thought that unfortunately was lacking in most of the anticommunist critiques.

CPA members working in the peace movement certainly were not secretive about their political background. While no one went about broadcasting party allegiance, membership in the CPA was a matter of general knowledge within the movement. The one possible exception was Sam Goldbloom, the fourth of the APC's national organizing secretaries and the driving force behind the ANZ Congress.[71] The row about his credentials, however, occurred outside the movement; within, there was general adherence to the APC's principle of "discrimination against none, exclusion of none, and domination by none."[72] This view, prevailing among the noncommunists, was exemplified in a remark by a leading Australian scientist, Sir Mark Oliphant, that, although the communists might follow the USSR point of view too closely, they had the best of motives in their desire to promote peace, and "I'm all with them."[73]

Nor could it be alleged that the Party itself concealed its support for the peace movement, though that endorsement was less than complete. Reports and resolutions of CPA central committee meetings and conferences, as well as statements from party officials, were published openly in party publications such as *Communist Review* and *Tribune*. In fact, most of the evidence amassed to substantiate the charge of communist control was based on publicly distributed material.

With regard to the matter of control — or, rather, of influence — there is room for debate. Without any doubt the Party exercised influence. The question is the matter of degree. Moreover, its role did not remain static: as the years progressed, with the state organizing committees of the various congresses forming into permanent peace bodies, the extent of communist influence waned. During the latter years there were fewer communists occupying key positions, and there was frequently a divergence between the policies advocated by the peace movement and those of the CPA. Even at the beginning, the communists did not have it all their own way. Although in 1950 they held three of the ten positions on the APC's executive (one of them being the ex officio position of national organizing secretary), they did not exercise decisive control, as the political scientist Alastair Davidson points out.[74] For one thing, they could not count on the full commitment of their fellow communists, whose attention was directed elsewhere: in fighting against the Industrial Groupers to retain control of some important trade unions and in mobilizing public opinion against the government's Communist Party Dissolution Bill. The work of the peace movement was left to a few party intellectuals who did not hold top positions in the Party. The CPA's highest officials, such as its secretary and president, never were intimately involved in peace affairs.

The influence of the communists tended to be, as Sullivan-Talty asserts, "of the kind exerted by communists working as individuals rather than in strict accordance with any party directive."[75] There was no unanimity within the party hierarchy as to what the communist role should be.[76] Not until 1953 was the issue even partly resolved with the negative policy that the CPA should *not* try to lead as this would sow discord, hinder growth, and perhaps destroy the movement.[77] The CPA's president saw the need to keep the Party separate in its tasks and slogans from the peace movement which, to be effective, must represent a heterogeneous coalition composed of people with varying ideological viewpoints.[78] Thus, towards the end of the decade, the CPA's role in the peace movement was aptly summed up by a leading peace and communist figure as a striving for the following delicate balance: "We understand our task in the broad peace movement as sharing in this great struggle without either dominating or standing aside from it."[79]

How this relationship worked out in practice is explained by an ex-communist who for many years served as the APC's national organizing secretary:

> In short, the Peace Council, in Victoria and in Australia, was more than just a communist front. The parsons and others who worked with us accepted the fact that, unless the Left, and the politically organized Left, did do the donkey-work and did give leadership, behind the scenes in all sorts of ways, then there would be no peace movement and no challenge to the policies of the Menzies government. Only we had the experience, the apparatus and the contacts with the unions and other mass organizations. As far as I can see this was a perfectly realistic point of view.[80]

Such fine distinctions tended to escape the thinking of most anticommunists. Menzies even argued that the menace of communism increased in proportion to its restraint. As the date of the 1953 Peace Convention approached, he warned his fellow parliamentarians: "'Peace' propaganda and 'peace' conferences are even more effective if the measures of communist control or support is concealed or minimized."[81]

Usually the anticommunist case rested on the less specious ground that the peace movement slavishly followed the CPA's pro-Soviet line on major issues. In the early years there certainly was a close parallel, but it is difficult to distinguish communist influence from a concern to counterbalance the crude Cold War attitudes permeating the society. In any case, it is clear that by the mid-fifties the positions of the peace movement and the CPA began to diverge. The 1956 Australian Assembly for Peace expressed outright disapproval of Soviet intervention in Hungary.[82] While the APC Chairman, the Reverend Mr. Dickie initially professed skepticism about the probity of Western journalism and criticized Radio Free Europe for falsely raising the hopes of the Hungarians, he unequivocally went on record as being opposed to the use of force in Hungary.[83] The execution of Premier Imre Nagy in 1958 evoked an indignant public outcry from numerous peace leaders.[84] The CPA, in contrast, defended the USSR's actions. In 1957, the New South Wales Peace Council, but not the CPA, called for cessation of H-bomb testing by the United States, Britain, *and* the Soviet Union.[85] Again, in 1961, peace movement protests against the Soviet Union for breaking a moratorium on nuclear testing were not matched in CPA circles.[86] There were other departures from the communist position on specific issues and, more important, the 1959 peace congress broke with the standard communist doctrine of attributing war solely to capitalism, proclaiming that "responsibility for war is never one-sided."[87] Despite all the evidence, however, the charge persisted that the peace movement was subsumed by a communist monolith emanating from the Kremlin.

Undeniably there had been close associations with the WPC which, in turn, enjoyed the Cominform's blessing. The founding of the APC owed much to the Wrocław and Paris conferences. Some of the early nationwide petitions were formulated overseas, and the decisions to hold the 1950 and 1959 national congresses were greatly influenced by the Paris and Stockholm conferences respectively. Throughout the 1950s and even into the early 1960s, the size of an Australian delegation to a WPC-sponsored conference could number as high as twenty or more. The return of delegates carrying messages of international solidarity for peace helped local activists to overcome their sense of isolation in the face of ubiquitous anticommunism.

Although the influence of the WPC association cannot be discounted, such a one-dimensional view gravely distorts the total picture. As the years unfolded, the ties with international communism became attenuated; the sociopolitical base of the movement broadened. Even at the beginning there existed a significant pluralism. A symbiotic relationship characterized the different forces at work: the communists needed the clergy and other peace-minded people as much as the latter needed the communists. Perhaps the communists' dependency was greater, for one can readily imagine that sooner or later the birth of an Australian movement would have occurred without the midwifery of the communists. The extreme anticommunism that plagued the peace movement says more about the spirit of the times than the state of the movement.

NOTES

The following abbreviations are used for Australian names: ANU for Australian National University, Qld. for Queensland, and N. S. W. for New South Wales [Eds.].

1. See Lynne Strahan, *Just City and the Mirrors: Meanjin Quarterly*

and the Intellectual Front, 1940–1965 (Melbourne: Oxford Univ. Press, 1984), 126.

2. For figures and accounts of this decline see Alan Barcan, *The Socialist Left in Australia,* 1949–1959 (Sydney: Australian Political Studies Assn., Occasional Monograph No. 2, 1960), 23; John Playford, "Doctrinal and Strategic Problems of the CPA, 1945–1962" (Ph.D. diss., ANU, 1962), 43–45, 56–62; Robin Gollan, *Revolutionaries and Reformists: Communism and the Australian Labour Movement 1920–1955* (Canberra: ANU Press, 1975), 171; and Alastair Davidson, *The Communist Party of Australia: A Short History* (Stanford: Hoover Institution Press, 1969), 93, 120. The latter gives conflicting membership figures of 23,000 and 16,000 for the Party at the peak of its popularity.

3. Critical defeats were sustained in the Clerk's Union, the Federated Ironworkers' Association, and the Amalgamated Engineering Union.

4. See Robin Gollan, *The Coal Miners of New South Wales: A History of the Union, 1860–1960* (Melbourne: Melbourne Univ. Press, 1963), 232ff; L. F. Crisp, *Ben Chifley* (London: Longmans, 1963), 362–63; Playford, "Doctrinal and Strategic Problems of the CPA," 86–98; and Davidson, *The Communist Party of Australia,* 134–37.

5. Davidson, *The Communist Party of Australia,* 107–8.

6. Eleanor M. Moore, *The Quest for Peace: As I Have Known It in Australia* (Melbourne: Wilke & Co., 1949), 152.

7. Cf. Ralph Gibson, *My Years in the Communist Party* (Melbourne: International Bookshop, 1966), 136–43.

8. For an excellent analysis of this Royal Commission, see Vicky Rastrick, "The Victorian Royal Commission on Communism, 1949–50" (M.A. thesis, ANU, 1973).

9. *Crimes Act* (Commonwealth of Australia, 1914), Sec. 24 (A) (1).

10. For details of all three cases, see *A Public Remonstrance,* pamphlet (Melbourne: Australian Council for Civil Liberties, 1950).

11. "Declaration of the Cominform, September 23, 1947," quoted in Victor S. Mamatey, *Soviet Russian Imperialism* (Princeton, NJ: Van Nostrand, 1964), 159–60.

12. Cited in Davidson, *The Communist Party of Australia,* 103.

13. Cited in *Communist Review* 102 (Feb. 1950).

14. J. P. Forrester, *Fifteen Years of Peace Fronts* (Sydney: McHugh Printery, 1964), 2. Cf. House Committee on Un-American Activities, *Report on the Communist 'Peace' Offensive,* 82nd Cong., 1st Sess., 1 April 1951, Report 378.

15. The manifesto issued by the Congress was reported in full in *Communist Review* 94 (June 1949).

16. Cf. L. L. Sharkey, *Communist Review* 95 (July 1949); William Gollan, "The Peace Movement in Australia" (MS kindly supplied by author,

n.d.); Alec Robertson, "CPA in the Anti-War Movement," *Australian Left Review* 27 (Oct./Nov. 1970): 39–40; and Ian Turner, quoted in Davidson, *The Communist Party of Australia,* 122n.

17. For example, J. D. Blake, a CPA official contended that the Party "should *lead* and be the most active force in struggle for peace," complaining about the lack of interest. "Australian Communist Party Central Committee Meeting, July 1950: Report on the Tasks of the Party in the Struggle for Peace," *Communist Review* 109 (Sept. 1950): 643–52.

18. S. Murray-Smith memo, Stephen Murray-Smith Collection, ANU Archives, Canberra.

19. There seems to be considerable confusion about the number and identity of persons at the foundation meeting. Peter Kelly in a critical article in *The Bulletin* (23 June 1962) inferred that the radical scholar and activist Brian Fitzpatrick, an original member of the APC, had attended. Fitzpatrick denied this in a "Letter to the Editor," *The Bulletin* (7 July 1962) and claimed that a check with the Reverend Mr. James confirmed that the three "peace parsons" alone were present. Some other original members of the APC indicated to me, however, that about twelve persons were present, but not Fitzpatrick. Participants reflected a wide spectrum of ideological positions, thus tending to refute the claim of Kelly and others of a highly manipulated communist plot.

20. See entries for Alfred Matthew Dickie and Frank John Hartley in Harold Josephson, ed., *Biographical Dictionary of Modern Peace Leaders* (Westport, CT: Greenwood, 1985), and Marion Hartley's biography of her husband, *The Truth Shall Prevail* (Melbourne: Spectrum Publications, 1982).

21. *Peace* (journal of APC) 1, no. 1 (April 1950): 2.

22. Ibid.

23. *You Can't Ban Peace!* (APC pamphlet), Ian Turner Collection, ANU Archives, Canberra.

24. *Melbourne Herald,* 26 Aug. 1949.

25. *Peace* 1, no. 1 (April 1950): 15, 10.

26. Ibid., 10.

27. His successors, Alec Robertson and Stephen Murray-Smith, were also communists. After six years, Murray-Smith was followed by Sam Goldbloom who was accused of having covert CPA membership. For an analysis casting doubt on this, see Ralph Summy, "A Reply to Fred Wells," in R. Forward and R. Reece, eds., *Conscription in Australia* (St. Lucia, Qld.: Qld. Univ. Press, 1968), 210–12.

28. Keith McEwan, *Once a Jolly Comrade* (Brisbane: Jacaranda Press, 1966), 21.

29. *Sydney Morning Herald,* 18 Feb. and 20 March 1950.

30. Australian Labor Party, *Official Report of Proceedings,* 19th Commonwealth Triennial Conference, Canberra, 1 March 1951, p. 11.

31. See Audrey Johnson, *Fly a Rebel Flag: Bill Morrow 1888–1980* (Melbourne: Penguin, 1986), 203–17, and the entry for William Robert Morrow in Josephson, *Biographical Dictionary.*

32. For details of the debate among absolute pacifists, see their journal *Peacemaker,* issues June 1950–June 1953. Gradually during the 1950s these pacifists modified their outlook towards the APC and its affiliates. For an explanation, see Malcolm Saunders and Ralph Summy, *The Australian Peace Movement: A Short History* (Canberra: Peace Research Centre, ANU, 1986), 33.

33. *Tribune* (CPA newspaper), 5 March 1952.

34. Ibid., 19 Sept. 1956.

35. *Peace Bulletin* (news sheet of the Australian Assembly for Peace), Oct. 1956; and *Tribune,* 12 Sept. 1956.

36. *Sydney Morning Herald,* 17 April 1950; and *Peace* 1, no. 2 (June 1950): 6.

37. Ibid.

38. "Australian Peace Manifesto," in ibid., 4; cf. APC pamphlet, *The Dean of Canterbury's Message to Australia,* ca. May 1950, Ralph Gibson Collection, Melbourne Univ. Archives.

39. See Barbara Carter, "The Peace Movement in the 1950s," in Ann Curthos and John Merritt, eds., *Better Dead Than Red: Australia's First Cold War, 1945–1959,* 2 vols. (Sydney: Allen & Unwin, 1986), vol. 2: 64–65.

40. *Commonwealth Parliamentary Debates, House of Representatives,* 1 (16 Sept., 1953), 258. Hereinafter cited as *CPD, HR.*

41. Ibid., 257.

42. *Canberra Times,* 17 Sept. 1953.

43. *Sunday Telegraph* (Sydney), 27 Sept. 1953.

44. J. E. Owen, *The Road to Peace* (Melbourne: Hawthorn Press, 1954), 43.

45. See ibid.

46. For instance, the Prime Minister justified the government's Defence Preparations Bill on the need to prepare Australia for a major war by the end of 1953. *Sydney Morning Herald,* 7 July 1951.

47. Quoted in ibid., 2 Dec. 1950.

48. For this anticommunist line of argument, see Forrester, *Fifteen Years of Peace Fronts,* 26–27; and H. Colebatch, "An Examination of the Sources, Ideologies, and Political Importance of Peace Movements in Australia from Approximately 1950 to Approximately 1965" (M.A. thesis, Univ. of Western Australia, 1974), 97–99, 112–15.

49. Owen, *Road to Peace,* 199–20.

50. *Record of the Australian Convention on Peace and War* (Glebe, N.S.W.: Liberty Press, 1953), 2.

51. See *Peacemaker,* Dec., 1955 and June, Aug.-Sept., and Oct., 1956. The two editors of this journal of the Federal Pacifist Council, W. J. Latona and Rev. E. E. Collocott, proselytized for greater cooperation with nonpacifists and were active in both wings of the movement.

52. See Colebatch, "An Examination of the Sources," 124-25; and Forrester, *Fifteen Years of Peace Fronts,* 34.

53. *Tribune,* 19 Sept. 1956.

54. *Australian Peace Review* 3 (Melbourne: APC, Oct. 1956).

55. For a detailed account of these tests, see Adrian Tame and F.P.J. Robotham, *British A-Bomb: Australian Legacy* (Melbourne: Fontana/Collins, 1982), esp. chap. 4.

56. Australian Labor Party, *Official Report of Proceedings,* 21st Commonwealth Triennial Conference, Brisbane, 11-15 March 1957, p. 41.

57. Harry Redner and Jill Redner, *Anatomy of the World: The Impact of the Atom on Australia and the World* (Melbourne: Fontana/Collins, 1983), 273-74.

58. Ibid., 272.

59. David Campbell, *Australian Public Opinion on National Security Issues* (Canberra: Peace Research Center, ANU, 1986), 20, 52.

60. *CPD, HR* 15 (2 May 1957), 985.

61. See Ralph Summy and Malcolm Saunders, "The 1959 Melbourne Peace Congress: Culmination of Anti-Communism in Australia in the 1950s," in *Better Dead Than Red,* 75-95.

62. APC letter to Prime Minister Menzies, 14 Nov. 1953, Murray-Smith Collection.

63. Hartley, *The Truth Shall Prevail,* 163.

64. A. G. Platt, "A Report to the President and Members of the N.S.W. State Executive of the ALP on the ANZ Congress for International Cooperation and Disarmament," *Peace Action* (journal of N.S.W. Peace Committee) 6, no. 2 (March 1964). Cf. editorial, *The Socialist* 1, no. 5 (Dec. 1959), and also the *Sun* (Melbourne), 14 Nov. 1959.

65. Platt, "A Report to the President . . . ," editorial, *Outlook* 3, no. 5 (Oct. 1959).

66. "Interstate Peace Committee Resolutions of 18 Feb. 1961," *Peace Action* 2, no. 2 (March 1961).

67. Victorian Campaign for Nuclear Disarmament circular (Aug. 1963).

68. Michael Randle, Secretary of British Committee of 100, to William Morrow, Joint Secretary of N.S.W. Peace Committee (copy), 13 July 1961. Qld. Peace Committee files, Brisbane.

69. G. R. Anderson, Joint Secretary of N.S.W. Peace Committee, to Norma Chalmers, Secretary of Qld. Peace Committee, 11 Aug. 1961. Qld. Peace Committee files.

70. G. R. Anderson, *Secretary's 1965 Report to Annual General Meeting of Association for International Co-operation and Disarmament* (AICD formed after 1964 Sydney Congress), 26 May 1966, p. 7.

71. The Accusation was spelled out in Harold Crouch, James Leon Glezer, and Peter Samuel, eds., *The Peace Movement* 2nd ed. (Melbourne: Dissent Publications, 1964), 5, and in Peter Kelly, "Peace Movements in Australia," *The Bulletin* (23 June 1962), 14.

72. Hartley, *The Truth Shall Prevail,* 71.

73. Sir Mark Oliphant on the Australian Broadcasting Commission's "Four Corners Progamme" about the peace movement, 3 August 1963, quoted in J. Sullivan-Talty, "The Australian Peace Movement, 1949-1964: A Study in Social Protest with Specific Reference to the Australian Peace Council" (B. A. thesis, University of Wollogong, 1982), 59.

74. Davidson, *The Communist Party of Australia,* 105.

75. Sullivan-Talty, "The Australian Peace Movement, 1949-1964," 44.

76. See, for instance, the different views of L. L. Sharkey, the Party's secretary, and J. D. Blake, a member of the Central Committee, in *Communist Review,* 98 (Oct. 1949) and 109 (Sept. 1950).

77. Ibid., 140 (Aug. 1953).

78. R. Dixon, in ibid., 133 (Jan. 1953).

79. William Gollan, in ibid., 198 (June 1958).

80. Stephen Murray-Smith to Ralph Summy, 6 Oct. 1966.

81. *CPD, HR* 1 (16 Sept. 1953), 258. The same line of argument appears in Fred Wells, "A Comment on Mr. Guyatt's Chapter," in *Conscription in Australia,* 194-95.

82. See *Tribune,* 7 Nov. 1956.

83. Statements of APC in Melbourne daily, *The Age,* Nov. 1956. For the range of opinions within the WPC regarding Hungary, see *Tribune,* 4 July 1958.

84. Letters in *The Age,* 10 July 1958, and in *Sydney Morning Herald,* 4 July 1958.

85. *Peace Bulletin* 1, no. 4 (May 1957).

86. Failure of the media to report the New South Wales Peace Committee's press release criticizing the Soviet Union's action prompted a bitter denunciation. See *Peace Action* 2, no. 10 (Nov. 1961).

87. CPA president Dixon pointed out this fundamental difference but did not regard it as an obstacle to cooperation between the Party and the peace movement (*Communist Review* 217 [Jan. 1960]).

LAWRENCE S. WITTNER

The Transnational Movement against Nuclear Weapons, 1945–1986: A Preliminary Survey

ONE OF THE LARGEST, most turbulent movements of modern times has been the transnational crusade against nuclear weapons. For more than four decades, this campaign has mobilized millions of people around the globe. Sometimes it has taken on mythic dimensions — of life against death, of resistance and revolt. The nuclear disarmament symbol figured prominently in the vast funeral procession for the murdered Greek parliamentary deputy, Grigoris Lambrakis; it was scrawled defiantly on the walls of Prague during the Soviet invasion of 1968; 7,000 protestors against the Vietnam War, imprisoned in a Washington stadium, formed it with their bodies.[1] And yet, unlike other peace movements, the nuclear disarmament struggle has sought to ban a particular kind of weapon and, thereby, avert a particular kind of war. This approach has provided it with its own distinctive strengths and weaknesses.

I

The first wave of nuclear disarmament sentiment was generated by the U.S. atomic bombing of Hiroshima and Nagasaki in August 1945, and continued in strength until approximately 1949.

As the world's first people to develop nuclear weapons and to wage nuclear war, Americans were especially obsessed with them. Even before the bombs fell on Japan, a small group of atomic scientists had sought to prevent their use. Although moved by moral concerns, they emphasized to higher officials the more "practical" consideration of preventing a postwar nuclear arms race. Higher officials, however, remained unimpressed. Nor did many Americans disagree with the use made of the bombs. A poll on 8 August 1945 found that 85 percent of Americans supported the atomic bombing of Japanese cities, while only 10 percent opposed it. The most outspoken critics of the bomb's use were pacifists and Catholic and liberal Protestant church leaders.[2]

American fascination with the bomb was based less upon guilt than upon fear. By September 1945, pollsters contended that 83 percent of Americans believed that, in the event of another world war, there was a genuine danger of the destruction of urban civilization by atomic bombs. Large numbers thought that the way to avoid nuclear catastrophe was to strengthen international authority. The atomic scientists' movement rallied behind the ill-fated Baruch Plan for United Nations control of atomic energy. Many of their leaders, like Albert Einstein, also threw their prestige behind the emerging world government movement.[3]

Naturally, antinuclear sentiment also ran very strong among the first victims of nuclear warfare, the Japanese. The terrible devastation of the war, the postwar exposure of militarist deceptions, and the nightmare of the atomic bombings led the Japanese toward pacifism and, particularly, rejection of nuclear weapons. New rallying cries of "No More Hiroshimas!" and "No More War!" became staples of Japanese life. Article 9 of Japan's new postwar constitution renounced "war . . . and the threat or use of force as a means of settling international disputes."[4] Although this provision appears to have been imposed by the American occupation authorities, it had the solid backing of Japanese public opinion.[5]

In Great Britain, a country indirectly linked to the Hiroshima bombing, the response was less dramatic. As in the United States, overwhelming support for use of the bomb against Japan was accompanied by a brooding sense that survival itself was now at stake. Nevertheless, antinuclear protest was slow to develop. In April 1948, pacifists did manage to stage a public meeting on the question of the new weaponry. And the following year, after the establishment of NATO, a group of prominent Britons published an open letter calling on their governments not to manufacture or borrow atomic bombs and to close American bases that housed them. In 1950, shortly after U.S. President Harry Truman announced his decision to develop a hydrogen bomb, one hundred Cambridge University scientists urged the British government to assume world leadership by rejecting the American initiative.[6]

Among nations that had no contact with events at Hiroshima, the reaction was more restrained. In nonaligned Sweden, world government advocacy grew. In France, where grass-roots pacifism was weak and political parties strong, the socialists took an ambiguous stand on nuclear weapons, and the communists condemned nuclear weapons only after it became clear that the U.S. atomic bombs threatened the Soviet Union. Although small in numbers and influence, Australian pacifists focused their energies upon a critique of atomic warfare. Third World nations — generally remote from the nuclear arms race and preoccupied with their own issues of national independence, economic growth, and social and economic equality — remained even more detached from nuclear disarmament concerns.[7]

These and other antinuclear stirrings of 1945–49 — never pulled together into a formal nuclear disarmament campaign, but nonetheless substantial in scope — faded rapidly with the intensification of the Cold War. In part, of course, the decline of nuclear concern reflected the passage of time. Alarmed by the bomb after events at Hiroshima, many people gradually became accustomed to it. Doubtless, much initial fear of the bomb was also repressed by individuals, allayed by skillful government and mass media programs, and displaced onto foreign "enemies" of the nation. After all, one possible response to the heightened anxiety engendered by the Soviet development of an atomic bomb — a feat accomplished by late 1949 — was to build a bigger one.[8]

The growing commitment to the Cold War had a direct impact upon the critics of nuclear weapons. In Japan, peace groups were thrown on the defensive as the conservative Japanese government, in response to U.S. pressure, flouted the "peace constitution" by developing national armed forces and signed the U.S.-Japan Security Treaty. In Hungary and Czechoslovakia, the advent of communist governments led to the dissolution of pacifist groups. Recognizing the deteriorating international situation, Australian pacifists changed their emphasis to improving Soviet-American relations, but without much effect upon public opinion. In Turkey, the nation's first peace group was suppressed almost immediately.[9]

The impact of the Cold War was particularly severe in the United States. The last stand of the once-feisty atomic scientists' movement came in October 1949, when the General Advisory Committee of the U.S. Atomic Energy Commission unanimously opposed the development of the hydrogen bomb. Thereafter, as the president gave the go-ahead for the H-bomb project and the Cold War lurched forward, the militant wing of the scientists' movement formally dissolved, while the moderate wing continued its existence in a cautious, muted form. The world government movement also crumbled. Membership declined, state legislatures rescinded their supporting resolutions, and self-proclaimed patriots violently denounced "one-worlders."[10]

The decline of the nuclear disarmament movement accelerated when, under pressure from the Soviet Union, the world communist movement seized on the nuclear weapons issue as the focus of its own peace campaign. In August 1948, the Polish government had hosted a World Congress of Intellectuals for Peace, and this led, the following April, to the organization of a World Peace Congress in Paris, directed by French communist leaders. Impressed by the potentialities of this campaign, the Cominform directed all communist parties to make the peace movement the "pivot of [their] entire activity."[11] In March 1950, when the communist-dominated World Peace Committee met in Stockholm to denounce Western military measures, it initiated a mass petition campaign calling for a ban on the atomic bomb. By the end of the year, the organizers of this Stockholm Peace Appeal claimed to have garnered 500 million signatures. Substantial numbers came from Western countries, but the vast majority were drawn from communist nations.[12]

Of course, it was not pacifism that led communist leaders to champion the Stockholm petition. By mobilizing public opinion against atomic weapons, the new venture had the potential of neutralizing the U.S. military advantage in this area, disrupting NATO before it could become an effective military alliance, and facilitating communist party recruitment among peace-minded citizens of Western nations. At the same time, the Soviet Union could move forward with the development of its own atomic weapons and seize the initiative from the suspiciously independent peace movements of Western nations.[13]

The self-serving nature of the communist-led peace campaign became increasingly evident after the beginning of the Korean War. At the Warsaw congress, in November 1950, delegates planned another mass signature campaign, the Warsaw Appeal. This downgraded the importance of nuclear disarmament and developed new themes, most notably an immediate end to the Korean War and an investigation of American war crimes. The World Peace Committee became the World Peace Council (WPC), which soon claimed 562 million signatures (90 percent of them from communist nations) on the Warsaw Appeal. In August 1951, the WPC began publicizing alleged U.S. atrocities in Korea, a campaign which peaked the following spring with denunciations of alleged germ warfare by the United States. Nuclear disarmament continued to decline on its scale of priorities.[14]

The communist peace movement enjoyed its greatest popularity in France, a country which had an unusually large Communist party (PCF) and a substantial reservoir of sympathy for the Soviet Union. At the behest of the Cominform, PCF leaders joined Partisans of Liberty, a non-communist organization infused with the aura of the wartime resistance, and took command. Renamed Partisans of Peace, it organized a national peace congress in November 1948. At the Paris conference of April 1949, the French group was reorganized as the Movement for Peace (MDP), chaired by Charles Tillon, a prominent PCF leader. Tillon was a very independent and open-minded Communist and, initially at least, the MDP could point to substantial non-communist participation and to 14 million signatures on the Stockholm Appeal. Nevertheless, it gradually became a creature of PCF policy and lost credibility.[15]

The same pattern emerged in North America. A small group of communists and communist sympathizers launched the Canadian Peace Congress (CPC) in 1947. With Canadian communists doing most of the CPC's work circulating the Stockholm petition, the organization acquired a very unpopular "Red" image — an image confirmed in 1952, when the CPC endorsed germ warfare charges against the United States and its leader was awarded the Stalin Peace Prize. The communist-led peace campaign made its debut in the United States in March 1949, when a Cultural and Scientific Conference for World Peace opened in New York City. The following year, the prominent black intellectual (and communist), W. E. B. Du Bois, helped to establish the Peace Information Center in New York City. Issuing "Peacegrams" and circulating the Stockholm Appeal (to which it claimed 2.5 million signatures), the Center aroused the ire of the U.S. government, which indicted Du Bois and its other officers for failure to register as foreign agents. The courts dismissed the charges, but the communist peace campaign made little headway among the public or among nonaligned peace groups.[16]

Although less isolated elsewhere, the communist peace campaign could hardly be judged a success. In Scandinavia, it generated some initial enthusiasm but eventually deteriorated. In Great Britain, the communist-dominated British Peace Committee received a very chilly reception from most Britons and the Labour party, which placed the Committee on its list of proscribed organizations. The Australian Peace Council, established in July 1949, leaned heavily upon the Communist party for support and inspired considerable antipathy during its campaigns. Naturally, in the Soviet bloc nations of Eastern Europe, the World Peace Council and the Stockholm Appeal received an enormously friendly welcome. Nevertheless, as the WPC's "peace struggle" became a euphemism for military preparations and Soviet foreign policy, it created widespread cynicism among the peoples of Eastern Europe. Here, as elsewhere, the communist-led peace campaign did little more than discredit the cause that it claimed to represent.[17]

II

A second and considerably more powerful wave of antinuclear sentiment began developing in the mid-1950s. Generated by the escalation of the nuclear arms race, as symbolized by hydrogen bomb testing and the spread of nuclear weapons to additional nations, it crested between 1957 and 1963.

The most prominent of the nuclear disarmament groups, Britain's Campaign for Nuclear Disarmament (CND), was launched at an exceptionally large, enthusiastic public meeting in February 1958. Unilateralist rather than pacifist, CND called upon Great Britain to renounce possession of the bomb, regardless of what other nations might do. The first CND Easter march began that year, with thousands of demonstrators bearing the nuclear disarmament symbol, designed for the event, from London to the atomic weapons research facility at Aldermaston. These annual Aldermaston marches, with the route reversed in subsequent years, drew large and enthusiastic crowds behind the banners of CND regions, universities, Labour party branches, and church groups. Combined with changes in trade union leadership, the grass-roots nuclear disarmament fervor made a substantial impact upon British politics. Meeting in 1960 for its annual conference, the Labour party adopted a resolution supporting unilateral nuclear disarmament.[18]

In the next few years, however, the British movement suffered some serious reverses. At the insistence of Labour party leader Hugh

Gaitskell, the unilateralist resolution was scrapped at the party's 1961 conference. Furthermore, from CND's inception, some activists had been impatient with the legal, electoral route to nuclear disarmament championed by its chair, Canon John Collins. In September 1960, assisted by CND's president, Bertrand Russell, they broke away from CND to form the Committee of 100, which fostered acts of mass civil disobedience. As a result, the British movement not only dissipated much energy in a nasty dispute between the two groups, but also came to be perceived by the general public as a pretty strange bunch. Opinion polls found support for British nuclear disarmament dropping from 33 to 22 percent.[19]

Whatever its problems in Great Britain, however, the CND model enjoyed considerable popularity elsewhere. CND groups sprang up after 1960 in the Australian cities of Melbourne, Sydney, Brisbane, and Perth, drawing upon an overwhelmingly youthful, middle-class constituency. With an eye to Aldermaston, CND'ers developed yearly Easter marches. They also engaged in occasional acts of civil disobedience. As the yearly marches gathered momentum, the older, established peace movement threw its support behind them. This added to their effectiveness but also stirred some degree of rivalry as well as disputes over unilateralism and the exclusive focus on nuclear weapons.[20]

In Canada, opposition to nuclear weapons testing crystallized in 1959, when an Edmonton group formed what became the first branch of a national organization, the Canadian Committee for the Control of Radiation Hazards. With the nuclear arms race blossoming as a topic of discussion in Canada, the Committee circulated a petition which urged the Canadian government to reject acquisition of nuclear weapons. At a February 1962 convention, the Committee changed its name to the Canadian Campaign for Nuclear Disarmament and absorbed peace groups in various cities as its branches. Bowing to antinuclear protest, the Conservative Prime Minister, John Diefenbaker, promised not to install nuclear weapons in peacetime. But the powerful Liberal party supported acquisition of nuclear weapons and, after its 1963 election victory, arranged for their installation in Canada.[21]

The antinuclear movement experienced greater success in Scandinavia. Danish participants in Britain's Aldermaston march brought the movement back to their own country, where an antinuclear march and demonstration were first held in October 1960. The following month, Norway's nuclear disarmament movement was launched with a public meeting and an appeal signed by "The 13," a diverse group of Norwegians who protested the inhumanity of the new weapons and sought to prevent their installation in Norway. They staged a number of demonstrations, obtained 225,000 signatures on their petitions, and in April 1961 secured the agreement of the governing Labor party to maintain its earlier decision not to install nuclear weapons on Norwegian territory in peacetime. In neutral Sweden, when the possibility of producing a Swedish atomic bomb was publicly broached in the mid-1950s, the result was the immediate development of an antinuclear weapons movement. Established by about thirty prominent intellectuals, it organized rallies, demonstrations, and debates. Between 1957 and 1961, opposition to the bomb rose to 56 percent of the Swedish population. Even the military finally spoke out against the weapons, arguing that it would be too expensive and would undermine the effectiveness of conventional military forces. As a result, Sweden did not build a bomb, and traditional peace groups integrated many antinuclear activists into their ranks.[22]

The nuclear disarmament movement also made considerable headway in Japan. In March 1954, when a U.S. hydrogen bomb test at Bikini showered a Japanese fishing boat, the *Lucky Dragon,* with radioactive fallout, a furor erupted in that antinuclear nation. A group of Tokyo housewives began a petition drive against atomic and hydrogen bombs which eventually attracted 32 million signatures. The following year, on August 6, the first World Conference Against Atomic and Hydrogen Bombs convened in Hiroshima, attended by 50,000 people. Sensitive to public opinion, the Japanese government appealed for a global ban on the manufacture and testing of nuclear weapons, a position which polls found to be supported by 89 percent of the population.[23]

Events in West Germany proved considerably less satisfactory to antinuclear activists. In February 1958, General Lauris Norstad, NATO's commander, had declared that it was "absolutely essential" to arm West German military forces with atomic weapons,[24] a position quickly embraced by the ruling Christian Democrats. This inspired the formation of the Campaign Against Atomic Weapons and the Struggle Against Atomic Death, supported by the opposition Social Democrats and the German trade union federation. In July 1958, more than 300,000 people took part in antinuclear demonstrations. The issue set off a passionate debate and near schism within the Protestant Church, although the Catholic Church solidly supported German nuclear armament. But, in 1960, in hopes of entering the government, the Social Democrats and their union allies ended their participation in the antinuclear campaign. Thereafter, Easter marches similar to those in Great Britain attracted dwindling numbers, and calls for nuclear disarmament were confined to prominent individuals and fringe groups.[25]

In Greece, another NATO nation, the nuclear disarmament question became caught up in the bitter antagonisms of national politics. Grigoris Lambrakis, an immensely popular former athlete and left-wing member of parliament, had helped to develop a large, non-aligned peace movement in Greece. Returning from the British Aldermaston march in 1963, he planned a similar trek from Marathon to Athens for late April. With that march likely to attract a very large and radical turnout, the rightist government banned the event and arrested about a thousand prospective marchers, beating them up and then releasing them without charges. Lambrakis had parliamentary immunity, however, and made the march himself. About a month later, as he sought to address a political meeting in his home district of Salonika, he was set upon and murdered by right-wing thugs, mobilized for the occasion by top officers of the Greek armed forces. At his funeral, on May 28, an estimated half-million people thronged the streets of Athens, bringing the city to a standstill. They carried enormous wreaths of flowers, in the shape of the nuclear disarmament symbol, a symbol which appeared everywhere at the vast Marathon marches of 1965 and 1966, as well as on the plain gray stone that marked the grave of Lambrakis.[26]

In these same years, the composition of the peace movement shifted substantially in France. The Cuban missile crisis, the entreaties of independent peace groups, and a revolt against the communist monopoly on "peace" led to the establishment in 1962 of the nonaligned Movement Against Atomic Armament (MCAA). As the conservative government of Charles de Gaulle embarked upon a program to develop French nuclear weapons, the MCAA joined with the communist-controlled MDP to establish a broad umbrella organization, the Committee Against the Force de Frappe. This brought together the major unions, student groups, and left-wing parties, as well as a large number of other organizations, for massive demonstrations against French nuclear weapons and those of other nations.[27]

The nuclear disarmament movement made even greater headway in the United States. Ever since the Bikini bomb tests of 1954, public controversy had swirled over the practice of nuclear testing. With large numbers of scientists warning of the health hazards of radioactive fallout, several dozen prominent pacifists and peace-minded Americans met in 1957 to chart a campaign to end nuclear testing. By the following year their National Committee for a Sane Nuclear Policy (SANE) had 25,000 members. As SANE began its work of education, marches, and lobbying, a more militant group—the Committee for Nonviolent Action (CNVA)—also formed in 1957, sponsored dramatic acts of civil disobedience. Within a short time, SANE and CNVA had catalyzed a very visible campaign, not only against nuclear testing, but against nuclear weapons themselves.[28]

Given their relative remoteness from the nuclear arms race, Third World nations continued to evince considerably less grassroots support for nuclear disarmament. Although remarkable nonviolent activism cropped up during the postwar years in Brazil, Nyasaland, South Africa, Namibia, India, Ghana, Algeria, Mozambique, and Zambia, none of these ventures focused upon an international peace issue. By the mid-1960s, the various pacifist internationals claimed branches in only a few Third World nations.[29] Even so, some of their rulers did play very important roles in softening Cold War confrontations and fostering policies of nonalignment and peace. The danger of relying on national leaders without disarmament movements was illustrated in 1962, however, when the Gandhi Peace Foundation held an Anti–Nuclear Arms convention in New Delhi. At the meeting, major Indian leaders supported unilateral disarmament, but only four months later many recanted when a serious border clash developed between India and China.[30]

Nevertheless, as the great powers brought the nuclear arms race to the Third World, it encountered growing resistance. During the summer of 1959, the French government announced that it would conduct an atomic bomb test in the Sahara desert and began removing local Algerians from the area. In response, prominent activists from the nuclear disarmament campaigns in Great Britain and the United States traveled to Ghana to help organize a nonviolent invasion of the test site. Inside Ghana, the Sahara protest team addressed numerous mass meetings and official gatherings. And beginning in December, the small team—international in composition, but with a Ghanaian majority—commenced the first of three fruitless attempts to reach the test site. Meanwhile, demonstrations or official protests against the tests erupted around the world. Although French West African nations, then negotiating for independence from France, kept their distance from the protest, some 500 African students from French Community nations were arrested in Paris as they sought to present an antitesting petition to the French premier.[31]

The success of Anglo-American nuclear disarmament activists in sparking an international furor over the French bomb tests raised pacifist prestige considerably in Africa. At their suggestion, Kwame Nkrumah called together an All-African Conference on Positive Action for the Peace and Security of Africa in April 1960. Although the Accra conference called for larger-scale measures against French bomb tests and the establishment of African centers for training in nonviolent resistance, no provision was made for funding the non-violence training centers, and the Sahara team leaders were forced to fall back on Nkrumah for assistance. Distracted by other issues, international and domestic, he seemed to lose interest in the nuclear testing question. Discouraged, the Sahara team decided to disband. Even so, at the suggestion of British CND, Nkrumah did host and fund an Accra Assembly of nonaligned peace groups in June 1962. And, in later years, Western pacifists also worked closely with Kenneth Kaunda of Zambia and Julius Nyerere of Tanzania, although not on antinuclear projects.[32]

The international nature of the movement in Africa reflected the closer relationships developing among nonaligned nuclear disarmament organizations. In January 1959, in response to an initiative by the British and West German groups, the European Federation Against Nuclear Arms was established at a meeting in London. Although the European Federation brought together groups in Switzerland, Sweden, Holland, West Germany, and Great Britain, it remained a rather weak and ineffectual body. Under pressure from numerous quarters to form a new, nonaligned international, the European Federation organized a meeting for this purpose in January 1963, at Oxford, England. In a final, stormy session, delegates overcame their national, political, and ideological divisions and voted to establish the International Confederation for Disarmament and Peace. By the beginning of the following year, it could point to member groups in nearly thirty countries.[33]

Naturally, relations between the nonaligned nuclear disarmament movement and the communist-led peace movement were strained.

When a number of nonaligned nuclear disarmament groups attended the July 1962 World Peace Council meeting in Moscow, they proved a considerable embarrassment to their hosts. Not only did the nonaligned groups from Britain and France issue a minority report, but some nonaligned delegations turned up with leaflets opposing the possession of nuclear weaons by *all* countries. Forbidden to distribute the leaflets outside the conference confines, a nonaligned contingent promptly began handing out thousands of them at a public demonstration they staged in Red Square. This act of *lèse majesté* enraged communist-dominated peace delegations and seriously irked the Soviet government as well.[34]

Divisions between nonaligned and aligned groups took a particularly nasty form in Japan. Within the Japan Council Against Atomic and Hydrogen Bombs, conflict between socialist and communist factions heightened. At its ninth World Conference, in 1963, the communist faction, under the influence of China, drew a distinction between the nuclear bomb tests of capitalist and communist nations, while the socialists insisted on opposing all nuclear tests. This caused the antibomb movement to split into *Gensuikyo* (allied with the Communist party) and *Gensuikin* (allied with the Socialist party and Sohyo, the trade union federation) and seriously eroded its nonpartisan appeal.[35]

Despite such problems, the second wave of nuclear disarmament activism met with some success. Admittedly, nuclear testing did not end, nuclear weapons proliferated, and the nuclear arms race continued. Nonetheless, popular awareness of nuclear dangers increased substantially. Moreover, government leaders, chastened by the global uproar, did show signs of drawing back from nuclear confrontation, certainly after the Cuban missile crisis of 1962. In this sense, it can be said that the nuclear disarmament movement laid the groundwork for the atmospheric test ban treaty of 1963, the nuclear nonproliferation treaty of 1968, the strategic arms limitation treaty of 1972, and the Soviet-American détente of the 1970s. Under intense popular pressure, a number of governments quite capable of developing nuclear weapons chose not to do so. In December 1967, the Japanese prime minister announced his government's intention not to possess, manufacture, or introduce nuclear weapons into Japan.[36] Other nations, such as Norway and Denmark, banned nuclear weapons from their territory in peacetime. As the 1960s progressed, nuclear war seemed less and less likely.

This perception of dwindling danger contributed to the rapid decline of the antinuclear movement after 1963 and to its virtual disappearance by the end of the decade. With the signing of the partial test ban treaty in 1963, the movement rapidly ebbed in Norway, Sweden, Canada, and Holland. In Great Britain, CND waned quickly after 1963, and, in elections the next year, nuclear disarmament was not a major issue. The test ban treaty also had a substantial impact upon the American peace movement and upon public opinion. Between 1959 and 1964, the percentage of Americans listing nuclear war as the nation's most urgent problem dropped from 64 to 16 percent. Soon, in fact, the issue disappeared from the surveys. In France, the antinuclear positions of the Socialist and Communist parties had a similarly soothing effect; all the antinuclear forces had to do, it seemed, was to wait for an electoral victory of the Left.[37]

In addition, however, nuclear disarmament activism ebbed because the nuclear danger was preempted by other concerns—in this case, the Vietnam War. In France, Britain, West Germany—indeed, in much of the world—the peace constituency rapidly jettisoned antinuclear efforts in an attempt to bring the brutal Vietnam conflict to an end. Beginning in the mid-1960s, a widespread anti–Vietnam War campaign surged across Japan, drawing upon students, unions, women's groups, citizens' organizations, and the Left parties. The Swedish Peace and Arbitration Society, which had played an important part in the movement against nuclear weapons, organized a Committee for Peace in Vietnam that became a magnet for political parties, the peace movement, and youthful antiwar protestors. In Australia, the government's decision to send combat troops to Vietnam led the peace movement to focus exclusively on the issues of Vietnam and conscription. Similarly, in Canada, local anti–Vietnam War committees replaced CND groups, while the student magazine *Our Generation Against Nuclear War* became simply *Our Generation*. The result was a substantial lull in antinuclear activism.[38]

III

A third wave of nuclear disarmament sentiment began to develop in the late 1970s, achieved enormous momentum from 1980 to 1983, and declined thereafter. As before, the major stimulus was a surge in the nuclear arms race, symbolized this time by the deterioration of Soviet-American détente; the deployment of Soviet SS-20 missiles in Eastern Europe; the NATO decision (of December 1979) to install cruise and Pershing missiles in Western Europe; and the advent in Washington of the Reagan administration, with its loose talk about fighting and winning a nuclear war. These factors heightened the popular perception of danger and revived the dormant nuclear disarmament movement.[39]

Unlike past surges of nuclear disarmament activism, however, this one began with a strong transnational emphasis. In early 1980, a small group of British CND stalwarts decided to launch a movement to remove all nuclear weapons from Europe. The result was an Appeal for European Nuclear Disarmament (END), drafted by the British historian E. P. Thompson. Issued in April 1980, the Appeal condemned the political leaders of East and West for their "aggressive actions," called upon peace groups to "free Europe from confrontation," and proclaimed an ultimate goal of dissolving "both great power alliances." END urged not great power negotiations, but rather (in Thompson's words) "the regeneration of internationalism," the "resistance of peoples inside each bloc."[40] Consequently, END sought to develop a transnational alliance of peoples that would take unilateral initiatives toward multilateral disarmament. With the upsurge of nuclear disarmament activism in the following years, END's goals began to appear a real possibility. Annual END conventions brought together most of the nonaligned peace groups and sympathetic forces in Europe — part of what an END pamphlet enthusiastically called "the biggest mass movement in modern history."[41]

The revival of the British movement was particularly dramatic. Between 1979 and 1984, CND's national membership jumped from 4,267 to 90,000, while local membership soared to 250,000. CND rallies attracted unprecedented numbers of people, including an estimated 400,000 in 1983. As before, CND drew very heavily upon the educated middle class and, once again with the assistance of the unions, prevailed upon the Labour party (in opposition) to support unilateral nuclear disarmament. Polls never found more than 31 percent of the population in favor of unilateral nuclear disarmament, but they did report that most Britons opposed the installation of cruise missiles. This provided support for the daring (and controversial) women's actions at the U.S. air force base at Greenham Common, a site for missile installation.[42]

Although the Dutch movement had different origins than the

British, it was soon heading in a similar direction. In 1966, the major Protestant and Catholic churches in the Netherlands had founded the Inter-Church Peace Council (IKV) to foster reflection on problems of war and peace. A decade later, appalled by the lack of progress in halting the nuclear arms race, IKV embarked upon a campaign to "help rid the world of nuclear weapons, starting in the Netherlands." IKV led the battle against deployment of cruise missiles, sparked unprecedented demonstrations, and hoped to pull together a parliamentary majority. But although the social democrats and the small Left parties voted solidly against deployment, the Christian Democrats proved more hawkish than expected.[43]

The situation was quite similar in neighboring West Germany. Here, too, the NATO missile decision and the hawkishness of the Reagan administration generated a very large and dynamic nuclear disarmament movement. Polls found that four out of ten respondents sympathized with the peace movement and that a majority opposed the installation of cruise and Pershing missiles. The West German Protestant Church played a crucial role in these developments. Young people provided another key nuclear disarmament constituency. Many were drawn from church youth groups, but still others were attracted to the countercultural movement that had persisted since the 1970s. This movement secured provincial representation in 1982 and parliamentary representation in 1983 through small victories by the new Green party. Out of power after 1982, the Social Democrats, along with their union allies, joined the Greens and the rest of the peace movement in campaigning vigorously against deployment of the missiles.[44]

A somewhat different pattern emerged in Italy, where the communists for some time had been behaving like cautious social democrats and the tiny Radical party had taken the lead in pacifist ventures. Although Catholic antimilitarism had been growing ever since the 1960s, the Catholic Church formally supported nuclear deterrence, as did its major political expression, the ruling Christian Democratic party. In 1979, when the NATO missile announcement was made, the Radicals were in the vanguard of the opposition, along with other prominent figures of the independent Left. Initially vague, the position of the small Socialist party hardened in 1981 in favor of the missiles. That August, when the Italian government declared that cruise missiles would be installed at Comiso, Sicily, there was an upsurge of protest. A march of half a million people several months later in Rome owed much to demonstrations elsewhere and to the organizing efforts of the Communist party, which was determined not to lose ground to the mushrooming forces on its Left.[45]

In other Mediterranean nations, antinuclear activism was also on the ascendant. Freed at last of Franco's right-wing dictatorship, a large Spanish peace movement developed, pressing both for rejection of NATO membership and a nuclear-free Spain. In Greece, the 1981 electoral victory of Andreas Papandreou's Pan-Hellenic Socialist Movement also opened up antinuclear prospects. And, in fact, Papandreou promptly opposed missile deployment and supported the creation of a nuclear-free zone in the Balkans — both stands favored by Greek public opinion. Perhaps the most surprising development in the region was the formation, in 1977, of the Turkish Peace Association. Founded during a period of the democratization of Turkish public life, the Peace Association campaigned for nuclear disarmament and against proposals to site the neutron bomb, cruise, and Pershing missiles in Turkey. The Peace Association evoked an enthusiastic public response and, with the formation of a social democratic government in 1978, it acquired considerable respect within policymaking circles as well.[46]

Only in France did the growing alliance between the social democratic Left and the nuclear disarmament movement become unhinged. Ironically, the 1981 election victory of the socialist-communist coalition provided the occasion. Like much of the public, both left-wing parties had come to accept French nuclear weapons as a guarantor of foreign policy independence. Nevertheless, nuclear disarmament activism grew at the grassroots. The communist-led MDP and a somewhat more independent Appeal of the 100 staged massive demonstrations behind vaguely worded peace declarations. At the same time, representatives of twenty-seven nonaligned peace, women's, and ecological organizations met in late 1981 and formed the Committee for Nuclear Disarmament in Europe (CODENE). Taking a moderate approach, CODENE called for a freeze on all French nuclear weapons systems and testing and for international action toward creating a nuclear-free Europe — a position quite in line with public sentiment.[47]

As before, the nuclear disarmament movement showed particular strength in the Nordic countries. Launched as a spontaneous protest in October 1979, the Norwegian No to Nuclear Weapons campaign sharply assailed plans for cruise and Pershing missiles and the deployment of Soviet SS-20s. A Danish No to Nuclear Weapons campaign, with a similar orientation, followed in January 1980. The idea of a nuclear-weapon-free zone, suggested by government leaders in Sweden and Finland in the early 1960s, became exceptionally popular in 1981 and 1982, when more than 2.5 million citizens of Finland, Sweden, Norway, and Denmark signed petitions calling upon their governments to implement it and vast demonstrations around the issue erupted in Sweden and Finland. Such campaigns drew the enthusiastic support of the major nonaligned peace movements in the region.[48]

Japan, too, resumed antinuclear efforts on a remarkable scale. The immediate occasion was the United Nations' second Special Session on Disarmament, which inspired a coalition effort that brought together not only Gensuikyo and Gensuikin but also national labor federations, women's groups, youth associations, and religious groups. By 1982, 28.8 million signatures had been gathered on a petition urging the United Nations and the Japanese government to publicize the effects of nuclear weapons, adopt an international convention outlawing their use, expand nuclear-free zones, and draft an overall treaty for disarmament. Furthermore, numerous municipalities passed resolutions declaring themselves nuclear-free zones, vast antinuclear rallies occurred in Hiroshima and Tokyo, and polls found that 76 percent of the population reacted favorably to antinuclear movements. Although the ruling conservatives looked askance at these developments, they continued to give their verbal support to Japan's "three non-nuclear principles."[49]

Elsewhere in the Pacific, antinuclear sentiment attained unprecedented dimensions. In Australia, nuclear disarmament activism began to resume in the late 1970s, in large part as a response to that country's mining of uranium for nuclear power and weapons. Thereafter, the revival of the Cold War and of the nuclear disarmament movement elsewhere led to enormous antinuclear rallies, as well as to heightened protests by church groups, doctors, scientists, and academics. In New Zealand, antinuclear sentiment intensified in the late 1970s, as doubts grew about the rationality of U.S. foreign policy and as the conservative government began to welcome visits by U.S. nuclear-powered and -armed warships to New Zealand ports. With anxiety spreading that New Zealand would become a nuclear target, the very fragmented peace groups banded together in 1981 into Peace Movement New Zealand.[50]

Indeed, support grew rapidly for a nuclear-free Pacific. When the Pacific Conference of Churches organized a 1975 conference in Fiji to discuss French nuclear testing in the area, Pacific islanders established the Nuclear Free and Independent Pacific movement. A decade later, it was comprised of 185 organizations and could point to some impressive achievements: stopping the Japanese government from dumping nuclear waste in the Pacific, mobilizing Pacific nations against French nuclear testing, and securing agreement of nine out of ten South Pacific countries to a treaty for a nuclear-free zone. A number of small nations—including Vanuatu, Papua New Guinea, the Solomon Islands, and Belau—adopted nuclear-free constitutions.[51]

Antinuclear sentiment also reached unprecedented levels in the United States. In the late 1970s and early 1980s, groups such as Mobilization for Survival and Physicians for Social Responsibility publicized the effects of nuclear war, while radical Christians carried out acts of civil disobedience at weapons sites. These stirrings turned into a mass movement with the advent, in 1980, of the campaign for a Nuclear Freeze—a bilateral agreement to halt nuclear testing, production, and deployment of nuclear weapons. More than 70 percent of the public supported a Freeze, all polls indicated. In June 1982, nearly a million Americans participated in an antinuclear rally in New York City—the largest demonstration in U.S. history. That fall, a majority of voters backed the Freeze in nine of the ten states where it appeared on the ballot. Older peace groups like SANE and the Council for a Livable World grew substantially, and were joined in their critique of the nuclear arms race by mainline Protestant and Catholic churches and, for the first time, by major unions.[52]

The newest and most courageous antinuclear activism appeared in the nations of Eastern Europe. Deeply suspicious of autonomous ventures, and particularly of those raising questions about official policy, the authorities viewed these independent peace efforts with considerable apprehension. Furthermore, it was easy enough for the population to focus on other problems—such as shortages of housing and consumer goods—which were both more immediate and more acceptable as topics of conversation. Nevertheless, disturbed by the accelerating nuclear arms race and encouraged by nonaligned peace activism in the West, independent peace movements did emerge in Eastern Europe. Occupying a marginal place in the political culture, however, they lacked the formal membership, well-publicized campaigns, and mass demonstrations of their Western counterparts.[53]

The independent antinuclear movement was particularly vigorous in East Germany. Here, the growing fear of nuclear war (with Germany as the battleground), the high level of militarization, the example of Western peace demonstrations, and the sanction afforded by the powerful Evangelical Church combined to stir unprecedented demands. Official church bodies initiated proposals in the early 1980s for the creation of a "peace service" as an alternative to conscription, for "peace studies" courses in the schools, and for the renunciation of nuclear deterrence and nuclear war. In November 1980, the Evangelical Church began its first Peace Week under the slogan "Make Peace Without Weapons." As enthusiasm grew, the churches repeated their peace sermons and discussions the following year, adding "peace festivals" of poetry, music, and song. Young people, particularly, flocked to these events. Meanwhile, in early 1982, one of the GDR's best-known independent Marxists, Robert Havemann, and a prominent youth pastor, Rainer Eppelmann, issued the "Berlin Appeal," calling for the removal of nuclear weapons from both Germanies and the abandonment of assorted military measures. Distributed in schools, factories, and churches, the Appeal was signed by thousands of East Germans and additional West Germans.[54]

In Hungary, a somewhat more tolerant government and official Peace Council helped compensate for the absence of a peace-oriented church hierarchy. One key constituency of the new peace movement consisted of the 300 religious "base communities," organized in Hungary during the 1960s. Formed around the radical Catholic Eucharist movement of Father Gyorgy Bulanyi, these communities campaigned for nonviolence and the right to conscientious objection. In January 1982, their Committee for Human Dignity issued a statement opposing nuclear weapons in either bloc. Meanwhile, in late 1981, students at Budapest University proposed a peace march condemning American and Soviet nuclear weapons. Although authorities frustrated this plan, the following spring, high school students revived the idea and established a Hungarian Anti-Nuclear Campaign. Student antinuclear activism spread rapidly in secondary and trade schools, with leaflets, posters and buttons. University activism, largely confined to a few arts universities, crystallized around the Peace Group for Dialogue.[55]

Nonaligned peace activism also flared up in other Warsaw Pact nations. Despite the imposition of martial law in Poland, underground periodicals debated missile deployment and the impact of military spending on the economy, while the Committee for Social Resistance issued statements calling for opposition to the deployment of U.S. and Soviet missiles. In Czechoslovakia, the human rights group Charter 77 published a letter of solidarity with the East German peace movement, carried on a friendly dialogue with the Western peace movement, and distributed leaflets protesting deployment of nuclear missiles in its own country. The Protestant Church in Czechoslovakia spoke out strongly against missile installation, student antinuclear protests erupted, and petitions against missile deployment were circulated successfully in a number of large industrial plants.[56]

Independent peace activism emerged even in the Soviet Union. In June 1982, the Group to Establish Trust Between the US and the USSR held a press conference in Moscow. Disavowing any thought of political opposition, the Trust Group proposed a ban on nuclear testing, the establishment of nuclear-free zones, and creative measures to promote a direct exchange between Russians and Americans. They organized discussions in private apartments, corresponded with Western peace activists, collected signatures on the street, handprinted a peace journal, and held art exhibits in people's homes. Trust Groups appeared in about a dozen cities of the Soviet Union and drew upon perhaps 2,000 activists, many of them young, countercultural, pacifist types.[57]

Despite the enormous upsurge from 1980 to 1983, the world antinuclear movement usually proved unable to translate popular support for its positions into public policy. Euromissile deployment, opposed by majority sentiment in each of the five countries scheduled for it, eventually secured parliamentary majorities and was implemented in all of them. In the United States, the federal government rejected a Freeze, scrapped the SALT II treaty, and moved forward with plans to militarize space. Social democratic parties opposing missile deployment lost elections in the Netherlands (1982 and 1986), West Germany (1983), and Great Britain (1983), while the pro-Freeze Democrats suffered an electoral debacle in the United States in 1984. Elsewhere, too, antinuclear parties proved unable to win the majorities necessary to govern (as in Japan and Italy). In large part, this reflected the difficulty of diverting governments from their Cold War fixations and of mobilizing most voters around the antinuclear issue, particularly when other matters seemed of more immediate relevance to them. Even peace activists were often distracted from the nuclear question by other foreign policy crises: repression in Poland, the Falklands war, the struggle in South Africa, conflict in the Middle East, the war in Afghanistan, and U.S. intervention in Central America.[58] Once again, there arose the difficulty of isolating the nuclear issue from other elements of public and governmental concern.

This was all the more true where governments, obsessed with the Cold War, also had a limited tolerance for dissent. In Turkey, a right-wing military coup in 1980 led to the silencing of the Turkish Peace Association and the imprisonment of eighteen of its leaders by military tribunals. In Czechoslovakia and Poland, frightened governments also clapped peace activists into prison.[59] In East Germany, during 1983, the authorities expelled twenty young peace activists, charged two leaders of Women for Peace with "treason" for providing news of their activities to a British peace worker, and arrested young activists in Weimar for their graffiti campaign ("SS-20 — No thanks!"). As harassment, detention, and fines accelerated in Hungary, the Dialogue group voted to dissolve; one fragment turned to closer work with the official Peace Council and the other chose the risks of illegal autonomy. Repression was at its fiercest in the Soviet Union. Members of the Trust Group were imprisoned, sent to labor camps, placed in psychiatric institutions, expelled from universities, beaten up, sent threatening letters, and deported.[60]

As an organ of Soviet diplomacy, the World Peace Council also remained a prisoner of the Cold War. Although it could claim affiliates in 141 nations by the mid-1980s, only a few of these had any influence in the West. Publications of the WPC sharply contrasted Moscow's work "towards promoting peace and security in the world" with Washington's "maniacal space militarization program," "global war plans," and "drive towards a global apocalypse."[61] Unable to control or even influence the nonaligned nuclear disarmament movement, the WPC eventually turned savagely against it. Yuri Zhukov, president of the Soviet Peace Committee, claimed that the "true objective" of nonaligned groups like END was to "split the anti-war movement," "infiltrate cold war elements into it," and "conceal and justify an aggressive militarist policy of the USA and NATO."[62] Naturally, nonaligned peace groups found it very difficult to deal with the WPC and its affiliates.

Despite these problems, the third round of nuclear disarmament activism did produce some victories. In Spain, voters approved a referendum that, while providing for continued membership in NATO, banned nuclear weapons from Spanish soil. In India, now nuclear-capable, no nuclear arsenal was constructed. In New Zealand, where the Labour Party campaigned vigorously against admitting nuclear-powered or -armed ships, it swept to victory in 1984, ousted the ruling conservatives, mobilized other nations behind a nuclear-free Pacific, and bravely defied the U.S. government. Furthermore, having won the support of most social democratic parties, antinuclear forces looked forward to policy changes in numerous Western countries where they were serious contenders for power. At the same time, nonaligned peace movements in Eastern bloc countries seemed to have taken root, even though they remained beleaguered. Nor, despite a lull in mass demonstrations, was the nuclear issue dead. In January 1985, the leaders of Argentina, Greece, India, Mexico, Sweden, and Tanzania called for a halt to the testing, production, and deployment of nuclear weapons, followed by substantial reductions in nuclear arsenals. The following October, they renewed this "five continents' peace initiative."[63]

Not least among the antinuclear movement's accomplishments was the creation of a new and broader peace movement international. The International Confederation for Disarmament and Peace had failed to flourish, in part for financial reasons, while END and the International Peace Communication and Coordination Center (organized by IKV in 1981) remained oriented toward Europe and opposed to building "bureaucratic" organizations. In order to accommodate the new array of nonaligned nuclear disarmament groups, leaders of the International Confederation and of the International Peace Bureau (founded in 1892) met at Gothenburg, Sweden, in September 1983, voted to merge, and adopted the name of the latter. Although the International Peace Bureau remained considerably weaker than many of its constituent organizations, by 1986 it had drawn together 41 of the major nonaligned groups from Europe, North America, and Asia. In the words of its secretary, it worked "against nuclear weapons, for a nuclear test ban, to strengthen international law, and to increase the impact of the peace movement on the official disarmament machinery."[64]

IV

What are we to conclude from this survey of the forty-one-year history of the world antinuclear movement? First, the movement has ebbed and flowed in response to the perceived dangers of nuclear war. Divisions on national, political, and bloc interest lines have been overcome to some degree in proportion to the apparent likelihood of nuclear destruction. Second, the movement, in turn, has heightened public consciousness about the implications of nuclear weapons and brought significant pressure to bear upon political leaders. In this fashion, it has served as a brake on the nuclear arms race. Without the eruption of a mass antinuclear movement, nuclear testing would almost certainly have been more common, nuclear proliferation greater, and nuclear war more likely. Third, despite the popularity of unilateral nuclear disarmament among a substantial minority[65] and of proposals to block new missile deployment or freeze the arms race (i.e. to maintain the status quo) among a majority, the antinuclear movement has failed to stop the nuclear arms race — much less secure nuclear *dis*armament. In short, the antinuclear weapons movement has slowed but not halted the nuclear arms race. Whether one views this as a success or as a failure, it is certainly not what the nuclear disarmament movement intended to accomplish.

How should one account for this? It appears that both the strength and the weakness of the nuclear disarmament movement are inherent in its emphasis on weapons. The strength of the movement lies in the fact that it focuses narrowly upon eliminating a weapon which most people consider odious, even suicidal. Therefore, the nuclear disarmament movement has the potential for overcoming political, national, and ideological divisions and for mobilizing considerably larger numbers of people than does traditional pacifism, with its more fundamental critique of violence, nationalism, and warfare. On the other hand, weapons are a symptom — and not the cause — of the problem: the problem of violent competition among nations. Thus, as Einstein wrote in 1949, "so long as security is sought through national armament, no country is likely to renounce any weapon that seems to promise it victory in war."[66] Weapons, in short, cannot be divorced from the international conflicts that inspire their development and use. Certainly this is the tragic backdrop to the relentless nature of the nuclear arms race. It explains why so many national leaders are not serious about nuclear arms negotiations and why average citizens are so easily sidetracked from the cause of nuclear disarmament. To confront the problem (and not merely the symptom) does not require accepting the existence of nuclear weapons and the prospect of nuclear holocaust. But this study suggests that it does require a recognition that the bomb probably cannot be banned if nations remain free to go about their traditional business of waging war. If this is correct, avoiding nuclear catastrophe may mean—as some peace leaders have recently argued—that peace movements around the world must tunnel under the nation-state to secure "détente from below." Or it may mean—as many internationalists have argued—that transnational authority at the top should be strengthened to the point that nations lose the ability to opt for war. Perhaps it means some combination of the two. In any case, nuclear disarmament seems unlikely without constraints upon the right to violence of the nation state. The real lesson of Hiroshima is that there must be no more war.

NOTES

1. Peggy Duff, *Left, Left, Left* (London: Allison & Busby, 1971), 117, 271.

2. Hadley Cantril, ed., *Public Opinion, 1935–1946* (Princeton, NJ: Princeton Univ. Press, 1951), 20; Lawrence S. Wittner, *Rebels Against War: The American Peace Movement, 1933–1983* (Philadelphia: Temple Univ. Press, 1984), 126–29; Paul Boyer, *By the Bomb's Early Light* (New York: Pantheon, 1985), 202–203.

3. Wittner, *Rebels Against War*, 130–50, 165–81; Charles DeBenedetti, *The Peace Reform in American History* (Bloomington: Indiana Univ. Press, 1980), 146–50; Boyer, *By the Bomb's Early Light*, 13–45.

4. Nobuya Bamba and John F. Howes, eds., *Pacifism in Japan: The Christian and Socialist Tradition* (Vancouver: Univ. of British Columbia Press, 1978), 31–32, 269–70; Kazuko Tsurumi, *Social Change and the Individual: Japan Before and After Defeat in World War II* (Princeton, NJ: Princeton Univ. Press, 1970), 258–59, 263–65, 271–73, 280–83; Nobuya Bamba, "Peace Movement at a Standstill: Roots of the Crisis," *Bulletin of Peace Proposals* 13 (1982): 39.

5. Bamba and Howes, *Pacifism in Japan*, 31–32.

6. Christopher Driver, *The Disarmers: A Study in Protest* (London:

Hodder and Stoughton, 1964), 16–21, 98; L. John Collins, *Faith Under Fire* (London: Leslie Frewin, 1966), 267–68.

7. Jan Andersson and Kent Lindkvist, "The Peace Movement in Sweden," in Werner Kaltefleiter and Robert L. Pfaltzgraff, eds., *The Peace Movements in Europe and the United States* (London: Croom Helm, 1985), 11; Jolyon Howorth, *France: The Politics of Peace* (London: Merlin Press, 1984), 14–16, 22–24, 34–37; Malcolm Saunders and Ralph Summy, "One Hundred Years of an Australian Peace Movement, 1885–1984: Part II: From the Second World War to Vietnam and Beyond," *Peace and Change* 10 (Fall/Winter 1984): 59.

8. Boyer, *By the Bomb's Early Light*, 291–339. "Psychic numbing" and the embrace of nuclear weapons as a cure for anxieties are discussed in Robert J. Lifton, *Boundaries: Psychological Man in Revolution* (New York: Random House, 1970), 26–34.

9. Hitoshi Ohnishi, "The Peace Movement in Japan," *International Peace Research Newsletter* 21 (1983): 32; Gertrude Bussey and Margaret Tims, *Women's International League for Peace and Freedom* (London: Allen & Unwin, 1965), 195–96; Saunders and Summy, "One Hundred Years," 59; Jean Furtado, ed., *Turkey: Peace on Trial* (London: END and Merlin Press, 1983), 9.

10. Wittner, *Rebels Against War*, 188–90, 199–201, 208–10; "Taking Bearings," *Common Cause* 4 (April 1951): 449–50; "This Critical Hour," *Common Cause* 4 (June 1951): 613.

11. Marshall D. Shulman, *Stalin's Foreign Policy Reappraised* (New York: Atheneum, 1966), 85–132.

12. Ibid., 132–33.

13. Ibid., 80–81, 100, 133. For the lengths to which a communist-dominated peace conference went to avoid sympathetic remarks about world government by Albert Einstein, see Otto Nathan and Heinz Norden, eds., *Einstein on Peace* (New York: Schocken, 1968), 492–93.

14. Shulman, *Stalin's Foreign Policy*, 155, 188, 202; Ilya Ehrenburg, *Post-War Years, 1945–54* (Cleveland: World, 1967), 180–81, 187.

15. Howorth, *France*, 18, 25–27; Shulman, *Stalin's Foreign Policy*, 85, 88–91; Joel-Francois Dumont, "The Peace Movement in France," in Kaltefleiter and Pfaltzgraff, *The Peace Movement*, 134.

16. Gary Moffatt, *History of the Canadian Peace Movement Until 1969* (St. Catharines, Ontario: Grapevine Press, 1969), 68–74, 77; Wittner, *Rebels Against War*, 203–206; W. E. B. Du Bois, *The Autobiography of W. E. B. Du Bois* (New York: International Publishers, 1969), 349, 356–57, 364–65, 385–86; Fellowship of Reconciliation, "Peace Fronts Today" (May 1951), Fellowship of Reconciliation records, Swarthmore College Peace Collection.

17. Andersson and Lindkvist, "The Peace Movement in Sweden," 11–12; Bussey and Tims, *Women's International League*, 196, 214; John Min-

nion and Philip Bolsover, eds., *The CND Story* (London: Allison & Busby, 1983), 11; Saunders and Summy, "One Hundred Years," 59–61; Ferenc Köszegi and Istvan Szent-Ivanyi, "A Struggle Around an Idea: The Peace Movement in Hungary," *New Society* 62 (21 Oct. 1982): 117.

18. Frank Parkin, *Middle Class Radicalism: The Social Bases of the British Campaign for Nuclear Disarmament* (Manchester: Manchester Univ. Press, 1968), 60–87, 168–87; Collins, *Faith Under Fire,* 297, 307–18; Driver, *The Disarmers,* 47; Duff, *Left, Left, Left,* 115, 122–28, 160.

19. Driver, *The Disarmers,* 49–51, 95–99, 106–22, 148–54; Bertrand Russell, *The Final Years: 1944–1969,* vol. 3 of *The Autobiography of Bertrand Russell* (New York: Bantam, 1970), 144–62; Collins, *Faith Under Fire,* 318–34; Duff, *Left, Left, Left,* 169–81, 191–97, 215–16; Parkin, *Middle Class Radicalism,* 4–5, 126–39.

20. Saunders and Summy, "One Hundred Years," 61–62, 72; Ralph V. Summy, "Militancy and the Australian Peace Movement, 1960–67," *Politics* 5 (Nov. 1970): 149–50, 153.

21. Moffatt, *History of the Canadian Peace Movement,* 41–43, 88–92.

22. Sten Sparre Nilson, "The Peace Movement in Norway," in Kaltefleiter and Pfaltzgraff, *The Peace Movements,* 35–37; Andersson and Lindkvist, "The Peace Movement in Sweden," 12, 29–30.

23. Sunao Suzuki, "Japanese Attitudes Toward Nuclear Issues," in Japan Peace Research Group, ed., *Peace Research in Japan* (1974–75): 103, 114; Bamba, "Peace Movement at a Standstill," 40.

24. Driver, *The Disarmers,* 76.

25. Peter H. Merkl, "Pacifism in West Germany," *SAIS Review* 4 (Summer 1982): 87; Diana Johnstone, *The Politics of Euromissiles: Europe's Role in America's World* (London: Verso, 1984), 46, 61–64; Bernd W. Kubbig and Thomas Risse-Kappen, "Living Up to the Ethical Dimensions of Nuclear Armament," *Bulletin of Peace Proposals* 15, no. 1 (1984): 72, 74.

26. Duff, *Left, Left, Left,* 245–47, 254. The Lambrakis case is portrayed in the film *Z* .

27. Howorth, *France,* 27–29; Claude Bourdet, "The Rebirth of a Peace Movement," in Jolyon Howorth and Patricia Chilton, eds., *Defence and Dissent in Contemporary France* (London: Croom Helm, 1984), 193–94.

28. Boyer, *By the Bomb's Early Light,* 352–53; Wittner, *Rebels Against War,* 240–78.

29. Marjorie Hope and James Young, *The Struggle for Humanity: Agents of Nonviolent Change in a Violent World* (Maryknoll, NY: Orbis Books, 1977), 109–44; M. Aram, "Peace in Nagaland," and Narayan Desai, "Intervention in Riots in India," in A. Paul Hare and Herbert H. Blumberg, ed., *Liberation Without Violence* (London: Rex Collings, 1977), 74–91, 208–19; Charles G. Walker, "Nonviolence in Africa," in Severyn T. Bruyn and Paula M. Rayman, eds., *Nonviolent Action and Social Change* (New York: Irving-

ton, 1979), 186–88; War Resisters League, *Peace Calendar* (1967); Bussey and Tims, *Women's International League*, 245.

30. Peter Brock, *Twentieth-Century Pacifism* (New York: Van Nostrand, 1970), 220–23; Jo Ann Robinson, *Abraham Went Out: A Biography of A. J. Muste* (Philadelphia: Temple Univ. Press, 1981), 181–82.

31. April Carter, "The Sahara Protest Team," in Hare and Blumberg, *Liberation without Violence*, 126–40; Robinson, *Abraham Went Out*, 171–73; A. J. Muste, "Africa Against the Bomb (I)," *Liberation* 4 (Jan. 1960): 4–7, and "Africa Against the Bomb (II)," *Liberation* 4 (Feb. 1960): 11–14.

32. Carter, "The Sahara Protest Team," 140–43; Robinson, *Abraham Went Out*, 173–80; Duff, *Left, Left, Left*, 233–36; Collins, *Faith Under Fire*, 342; Walker, "Nonviolence in Africa," 190–210.

33. Collins, *Faith Under Fire*, 311, 337–38; Duff, *Left, Left, Left*, 226–43; Driver, *The Disarmers*, 134.

34. Duff, *Left, Left, Left*, 237–39; Driver, *The Disarmers*, 136–39.

35. Bamba, "Peace Movement at a Standstill," 40; Glenn D. Hook, "The Ban the Bomb Movement in Japan," *Social Alternatives* 3 (March 1983): 35.

36. Tsuneo Akaha, "Japan's Three Nonnuclear Principles: A Coming Demise?" *Peace and Change* 11 (Spring 1985): 75.

37. Andersson and Lindkvist, "The Peace Movement in Sweden," 12; Nilson, "The Peace Movement in Norway," 37; Ben ter Veer, "The New Peace Movements in Western Europe," *International Peace Research Newsletter* 21, no. 3 (1983): 10; Moffatt, *History of the Canadian Peace Movement*, 94–95; Peter Byrd, "The Development of the Peace Movement in Britain," in Kaltefleiter and Pfaltzgraff, *The Peace Movements*, 64–65; Paul Boyer, "From Activism to Apathy: The American People and Nuclear Weapons, 1963–1980," *Journal of American History* 70 (March 1984): 825–30; Bourdet, "The Rebirth of a Peace Movement," 194.

38. Howorth, *France*, 29; Parkin, *Middle Class Radicalism*, 40; Duff, *Left, Left, Left*, 268; Merkl, "Pacifism in West Germany," 87; Yoshiyuki Tsurumi, "Beheiran," *Japan Quarterly* 16 (Oct.–Dec. 1969): 444–48; Andersson and Lindkvist, "The Peace Movement in Sweden," 12; Saunders and Summy, "One Hundred Years," 62; Moffatt, *History of the Canadian Peace Movement*, 91, 93; Wittner, *Rebels Against War*, 281–92; Boyer, "From Activism to Apathy," 835–37.

39. See, for example, Armand Clesse, "The Peace Movements and the Future of West European Security," in Peter van den Dungen, ed., *West European Pacifism and the Strategy for Peace* (London: Macmillan, 1985), 53–54; Byrd, "The Development of the Peace Movement in Britain," 65.

40. E. P. Thompson, *Double Exposure* (London: Merlin Press, 1985), 10, 27; E. P. Thompson, "Notes on Exterminism, the Last Stage of Civilization," in New Left Review, ed., *Exterminism and Cold War* (London: Verso, 1982), 28–29.

41. E. P. Thompson, *Beyond the Cold War* (New York: Pantheon, 1982), 121; Ferenc Köszegi and E. P. Thompson, *The New Hungarian Peace Movement* (London: Merlin Press, 1982), inside cover.

42. Byrd, "The Development of the Peace Movement in Britain," 66–99; Barbara Harford and Sarah Hopkins, ed., *Greenham Common: Women at the Wire* (London: The Women's Press, 1984), passim.

43. Philip P. Everts, "Reviving Unilateralism: Report on a Campaign for Nuclear Disarmament in the Netherlands," *Bulletin of Peace Proposals* 11, no. 1 (1980): 43–50; ter Veer, "The New Peace Movements," 10; N. H. Serry, "The Peace Movement in the Netherlands," in Kaltefleiter and Pfaltzgraff, *The Peace Movements,* 49–58.

44. Merkl, "Pacifism in West Germany," 81–89; Hartmut Grewe, "The West German Peace Movement: A Profile," in Kaltefleiter and Pfaltzgraff, *The Peace Movements,* 106–31; Johnstone, *The Politics of Euromissiles,* 48–56; Kubbig and Risse-Kappen, "Living Up to the Ethical Dimensions," 72–76.

45. Sergio A. Rossi and Virgilio Ilari, "The Peace Movement in Italy," in Kaltefleiter and Pfaltzgraff, *The Peace Movements,* 141–61; Johnstone, *The Politics of Euromissiles,* 142–45; Nigel Young, "The Contemporary European Anti-Nuclear Movement," *Peace and Change* 9 (Spring 1983): 6.

46. Young, "The Contemporary European Anti-Nuclear Movement," 7; Johnstone, *The Politics of Euromissiles,* 177–78; Furtado, *Turkey,* 5–12.

47. Howorth, *France,* 4–17, 37–47, 55–83; Christian Mellon, "Peace Organizations in France Today," and Vladimir Claude Fisera, "The New Left and Defence: Out of the Ghetto?" in Howorth and Chilton, *Defence and Dissent,* 202–16, 242.

48. Jon Grepstad, "The Peace Movement in the Nordic Countries," *International Peace Research Newsletter* 20, no. 4 (1982): 10–15; Nilson, "The Peace Movement in Norway," 36–47; Andersson and Lindkvist, "The Peace Movement in Sweden," 12–13, 24, 30–32.

49. Ohnishi, "The Peace Movement in Japan," 26–33; Hook, "The Ban the Bomb Movement in Japan," 35–39; Bamba, "Peace Movement at a Standstill," 40.

50. Saunders and Summy, "One Hundred Years," 68–71; Kevin P. Clements, "New Zealand's Relations with the UK, the US, and the Pacific," *Alternatives* 10 (1985): 592–97; Wayne Robinson, "Current Peace Research and Activism in New Zealand," *International Peace Research Newsletter* 21, no. 3 (1983): 34–35.

51. Roman Bedor, "Protecting the Source of Life," *Mobilizer* 5 (Winter 1986): 8–9.

52. Wittner, *Rebels Against War,* 293–98; Michael Kazin, "The Freeze: From Strategy to Social Movement," in Paul Joseph and Simon Rosenblum, eds., *Search for Sanity* (Boston: South End Press, 1984), 445–61; Jim Cas-

telli, *The Bishops and the Bomb: Waging Peace in the Nuclear Age* (New York: Doubleday, 1983), passim; "Nuclear Arms," *Gallup Report* 208 (Jan. 1983): 10.

53. Köszegi and Szent-Ivanyi, "A Struggle Around an Idea," 117, 120, 163; John Sandford, *The Sword and the Plowshare: Autonomous Peace Initiatives in East Germany* (London: Merlin Press and END, 1983), 22–23.

54. Sandford, *The Sword and the Plowshare*, 13, 27–77, 89–96, 107–108; Ronald D. Asmus, "Is There a Peace Movement in the GDR?" *Orbis* 27 (Summer 1983), 301–16; Suzanne Gordon, "From the Other Shore: Movements for Nuclear Disarmament in Eastern Europe," *Working Papers* 10 (March–April 1983): 34–35, 39–40.

55. Köszegi and Thompson, *The New Hungarian Peace Movement*, 3–4, 11–13, 24–25, 32–33; Köszegi and Szent-Ivanyi, "A Struggle Around An Idea," 164; "Hungarian Leadership Reacts to Independent Peace Groups and Initiatives," *Peace and Democracy News* 1 (Winter 1984–85): 6.

56. Cathy Fitzpatrick, "Update: Independent Peace Groups in the Eastern Bloc," *Peace and Democracy News* 1 (Spring 1984): 3, 12; Gordon, "From the Other Shore," 38; A. W. Jackson, "Eastern European Peace Activists Face New Repression," *WRL News* 241 (March–April 1984): 6, 8; "An Open Letter from Charter 77 to the Western Peace Movement," *Peace and Democracy News* 1 (Winter 1984–85): 14–17.

57. Fitzpatrick, "Update," 12; "The Independent Soviet Peace Movement: An Interview with Two Founding Members," *Peace and Democracy News* 2 (Summer–Fall 1985), 14–18; Jackson, "Eastern European Peace Activists," 8; Yuri Medvekov, "Time for Some Trust Building," *END Journal,* 21 (April–May 1986): 23.

58. Thompson, *Double Exposure,* 93–94, 141–42; ter Veer, "The New Peace Movements," 14; Akaha, "Japan's Three Nonnuclear Principles," 84, 86; Everts, "Reviving Unilateralism," 50.

59. Furtado, *Turkey,* 13, 26–27, 44; Mehmet Demir, "Turkey: Thousands of Political Prisoners Still in Jail," *Peace and Democracy News* 1 (Spring 1984): 6; "An Open Letter from Charter 77," 15; "Polish Peace Activists Arrested," *Nonviolent Activist* 3 (April–May 1986): 13.

60. Jackson, "Eastern European Peace Activists," 6; Fitzpatrick, "Update," 3, 12; "Hungarian Leadership Reacts," 6–7, 22; Thompson, *Double Exposure,* 72–73; "The Independent Soviet Peace Movement," 15–18; "Crackdown on 'Moscow Trust Group,'" *Nonviolent Activist* 3 (April–May 1986): 14; "Trust Group Under Pressure," *END Journal* 21 (April–May 1986): 5.

61. *World Peace Council: List of Members, 1983–1986* (Helsinki: Information Centre of the World Peace Council, n.d.), 170–74; Thompson, *Double Exposure,* 51–54; World Peace Council, *The U.S. Space Offensive: Road to Nuclear Annihilation* (Helsinki: Information Centre of the World Peace Council, 1985), 3, 17; *Peace Courier,* 2–3/1986.

62. Thompson, *Double Exposure,* 1, 27, 39–40, 56.

63. "Referendum Confirms NATO Membership," *Socialist Affairs* 1, no. 86 (1986): 71; Jonathan Schell, *The Abolition* (New York: Knopf, 1984), 147; Clements, "New Zealand's Relations," 597–603; Thompson, *Double Exposure,* 141–43; "The Prague Appeal," *Peace and Democracy News* 2 (Summer–Fall 1985): 10–11; "Polish Peaceniks Held," *END Journal* 21 (April–May 1986): 3; "World Leaders Offer Third-Party Verification of Test Ban," *Socialist Affairs* 4, no. 85 (1985): 6.

64. Wim Bartels, "Clarification of the IPCC-network of peace movements 2" (7–9 Oct. 1983), Sheila Cooper to "Friend" (ca. June 1983); Rainer Santi and Margie Graf to friends and members of IPB, 19 Feb. 1986, and Ranier Santi to Mobilization for Survival, 27 May 1986, Mobilization for Survival records, New York City.

65. According to a Louis Harris poll in November 1983, unilateral nuclear disarmament was favored by 35 percent of the Italians, 25 percent of the Dutch, 23 percent of the West Germans, 17 percent of the Britons and 16 percent of the French (Johnstone, *The Politics of Euromissiles,* 110).

66. Einstein to Jacques Hadamard, 29 Dec. 1949, in Nathan and Norden, *Einstein on Peace,* 516.

Notes on Authors and Organizations

Authors

CHARLES CHATFIELD earned his Ph.D. from Vanderbilt University and took postdoctoral study at the University of Chicago. Professor of History at Wittenberg University, he has been active in international education and in the Council on Peace Research in History (CPRH), of which he was a president. During 1981–82 he coedited the journal *Peace and Change*. In addition to numerous articles and chapters, he has authored *For Peace and Justice: Pacifism in America, 1914–1941* (1971), edited *Peace Movements in America* (1973), and compiled and edited several books in the Garland Library of War and Peace, a reprint series of which he was a coeditor. Currently he is preparing an analytical study of peace movements in the United States and is researching international Protestant-Catholic collaboration on world issues in the seventies.

ROGER CHICKERING earned his Ph.D. at Stanford University and has been a Visiting Research Fellow at historical institutes of the Ludwig-Maximilian University in Munich and the Free University of Berlin. Currently he is Professor of History at the University of Oregon. Active in professional associations in history and international exchange, and the recipient of several research fellowships, he is the author of *Imperial Germany and a World Without War: The Peace Movement and German Society, 1892–1914* (1975), *We Men Who Feel Most German: A Cultural Study of the Pan-German League, 1886–1914* (1984), and numerous articles and chapters of books. He currently has in progress a work on Karl Lamprecht (1856–1915).

CHARLES DEBENEDETTI died on 27 January 1987, forty-four years from the day of his birth. A prolific scholar, he received his B.S.

from Loyola University of Chicago and his M.A. and Ph.D. from the University of Illinois. Professor of History at the University of Toledo, he was active in the Society of Historians of American Foreign Relations and in the CPRH, of which he served as president from 1979 to 1981. He was the author of *Origins of the Modern American Peace Movement, 1915–1929* (1978), *The Peace Reform in American History* (1980), and cocompiler of *Kirby Page: Writings on Peace and Justice* (1977), and editor of *Peace Heroes in Twentieth-Century America* (1986). For nearly a decade before his death he had been working on a history of the antiwar movement in the Vietnam Era.

JOST DÜLFFER is Professor of Modern History at the University of Cologne. He is the author of books including *Weimar, Hitler und die Marine. Reichspolitik und Flottenbau 1920–1939* (1973) and *Regeln gegen den Krieg? Die Haager Friedenskonferenzen 1899 und 1907 in der internationalen Politik* (1981), and is coauthor and coeditor of *Hitlers Städte. Baupolitik im Dritten Reich* (1978), coauthor of *Inseln als Brennpunkte internationaler Politik. Konflikbewältigung im Wandel des internationalen Systems: Kreta, Korfu, Zypern 1890–1914* (1986), and coeditor of *Bereit zum Krieg: Kriegsmentalität im wilhelminischen Deutschland 1890–1914* (1986). He has also authored numerous articles and contributions on contemporary German history, international relations in the nineteenth and twentieth centuries, and historical peace research.

ELLY HERMON earned his Ph.D. in history at the Paris-Sorbonne University and has taught at the Sherbrooke, Quebec at Chicoutimi, and Laval Universities in Canada. He has published articles on interwar European history of international relations and especially on peace education and international intellectual cooperation in the interwar period, many of which have been based on research sponsored by the Social Sciences and Humanities Research Council of Canada.

KARL HOLL is Professor of Contemporary German History at the University of Bremen and has been a member of the State Legislature of Bremen. He earned his Ph.D. from the University of Mainz. A leader in the German Working Group on Historical Peace Research (*Arbeitskreis Historische Friedensforschung*), he has edited

Der deutsche Pazifismus während des Weltkrieges 1914–1918. Aus dem Nachlass Ludwig Quiddes (1979) and coedited *Pazifismus in der Weimarer Republik* (1981), *Die Friedensbewegung.* Organisierter Pazifismus in Deutschland, Österreich und in der Schweiz (1983), and *Bereit zum Krieg: Kriegsmentalität im wilhelminischen Deutschland 1890–1914* (1986). Currently he is writing a history of exiled German pacifists in the thirties.

NORMAN INGRAM is a Killam Fellow at the University of Alberta in Canada. He earned his Ph.D. at the University of Edinburgh as a Commonwealth Scholar, writing his thesis, "The Politics of Dissent: Pacifism in France, 1919–1939," under the supervision of Professor Maurice Larkin. He earned his M.A. at the University of Toronto, and has presented formal papers and lectures on his field of study in Canada and Britain.

HAROLD JOSEPHSON received his Ph.D. at the University of Wisconsin-Madison and has published widely on the history of the peace movement in the United States. He is author of *James T. Shotwell and the Rise of Internationalism in America* (1975) and editor of the *Biographical Dictionary of Modern Peace Leaders* (1985), which won the 1985–86 Warren F. Kuehl prize for a work in the history of internationalism and/or peace movements. Currently Professor of History and Director of the Center for International Studies at the University of North Carolina at Charlotte, he is working on a book-length study of ex-communist witnesses and the Cold War.

NADINE LUBELSKI-BERNARD received her Ph.D. in Political Science at the Institut de Sociologie, Université Libre de Bruxelles, where she now serves as chief research assistant. Her dissertation, "Les mouvements et les idéologies pacifistes en Belgique (1830–1914)" focused her scholarly interest in the Belgian and European peace movement.

DAVID S. PATTERSON is Chief of the Operations Staff, Office of the Historian of the United States Department of State. He earned his Ph.D. at the University of California, Berkeley. Active in the CPRH, he is currently its president. In addition to articles on diplomatic history, including a study of Woodrow Wilson and the mediation movement, he has written on the peace movement, notably

Toward a Warless World: The Travail of the American Peace Movement, 1887–1914 (1976). He is preparing a history of Eisenhower and the arms race.

MARIA ANTONIETTA SARACINO is a lecturer in English literature at the University of Rome. She earned her M.A. at Sheffield University in the field of contemporary African literature in English. She has published essays, articles, and translations in this field as well as in nineteenth-century English literature.

WERNER SIMON is an archivist at the Library of the United Nations, Geneva. He earned his Ph.D. at Wiesbaden with the thesis "Die Britische Militärpolitik in Indien, 1878–1910" (1974), and undertook studies in modern history at the South Asia Institute, Heidelberg University. His works have included essays on Bertha von Suttner and on the historical archives of the UN Library at Geneva. Currently he is researching the history of the International Peace Bureau.

RALPH SUMMY is a graduate of Harvard University, has an M.A. from the University of Sydney, and is a Lecturer in Government at the University of Queensland. He has written articles on the Australian peace movement and is editor of *Social Alternatives*. Presently he is coauthoring a history of the Australian peace movement.

PETER VAN DEN DUNGEN is a Lecturer in Peace Studies in the School of Peace Studies at the University of Bradford in England. He received a Ph.D. in War Studies from the University of London. His publications on peace history and peace research include *Foundations of Peace Research* (1980), *The Hidden History of a Peace 'Classic': Emeric Crucé's Le Nouveau Cynée* (1980), and *The Making of Peace: Jean de Bloch and the First Hague Peace Conference* (1983). He serves as a coordinating secretary for the European Working Group, and his current work includes a survey of the resources for peace research in history in European archives.

JO VELLACOTT holds a B.A. and M.A. from Oxford University, an M.A. from the University of Toronto, and a Ph.D. from McMaster University. She is an Adjunct Fellow at the Simone de Beauvoir Institute, Concordia University, in Montreal, Canada, and is also currently a Friend-in-Residence at Woodbrooke College, UK. The author of *Bertrand Russell and the Pacifists in the First World War* (1980), she has recently coedited (with Margaret Kamester) writings from the First World War by Mary Sargant Florence, Catherine Marshall, and C. K. Ogden (*Militarism Versus Feminism*, 1987). Currently she is writing a biography of Catherine Marshall.

SOLOMON WANK received his Ph.D. from Columbia University. The author of many articles on Austro-Hungarian and Central European history, he is the editor of *Doves and Diplomats: Foreign Offices and Peace Movements in Europe and America in the Twentieth Century* (1978) and *The Mirror of History: Essays in Honor of Fritz Fellner* (1988), and associate editor of the *Biographical Dictionary of Modern Peace Leaders* (1985). He is currently preparing a biography of the Austro-Hungarian diplomat and foreign minister, Count Alois Lexa von Aerenthal. A member of the Council of the CPRH, he is Professor of History at Franklin and Marshall College.

LAWRENCE WITTNER received his Ph.D. in history from Columbia University. He is the author of *Rebels Against War: The American Peace Movement, 1933–1983* (1984), *Cold War America: From Hiroshima to Watergate* (1974, 1978), and *American Intervention in Greece, 1943–1949* (1982), as well as of other books and numerous articles and reviews. He is an associate editor of the *Biographical Dictionary of Modern Peace Leaders* (1985). A former president of the CPRH, he has also served as co-executive editor of *Peace and Change*. He has taught at Hampton Institute, at Vassar College, and at Japanese universities under the Fulbright program, and currently he is Professor of History at the State University of New York/ Albany. He is preparing a comprehensive history of the international movement against nuclear arms.

Organizations

THE COUNCIL ON PEACE RESEARCH IN HISTORY (CPRH) was founded in 1963–64 in order to encourage, support, and coordinate peace research in history and social science. In the aftermath of the assassination of President John F. Kennedy and amidst the dimly seen beginnings of the Indochina war, a sizable group of historians organized in the realization that little effort had been made in their field to study the cause of peace. Subsequently, the CPRH became an affiliated society of the American Historical Association and achieved Non-Governmental Organization status at the United Nations. Prior to November 1986 it was known as the Conference on Peace Research in History.

The CPRH has contributed scholarly panels to meetings of professional organizations, notably the American Historical Association and the Organization of American Historians. It has sponsored conferences of its own on subjects such as Peace and Sovereignty, Wars and Society, Peace Research and Its Impact on the Curriculum, and The Multinational Corporation as an Historical Phenomenon. It also has held joint conferences with the Society of Historians of American Foreign Relations and the American Military Institute. Since 1972, the CPRH has published the scholarly journal, *Peace and Change* (now copublished with the Consortium on Peace Research, Education, and Development), which is explicitly interdisciplinary and international, and it distributes a quarterly newsletter to its members with information on the organization and also news of scholarly conferences, new publications, research announcements, and current programs at colleges and universities.

In association with the CPRH, individual historians have collaborated to produce significant contributions to scholarship, notably: Blanche Wiesen Cook, *Bibliography on Peace Research in History*

(1969); Blanche Wiesen Cook, Sandi Cooper, and Charles Chatfield, eds., *The Garland Library of War and Peace* (1972–77), a 350-title collection of reprints with new introductions; Solomon Wank, ed., *Doves and Diplomats, Foreign Offices and Peace Movements in the Twentieth Century* (1978), Harold Josephson, ed., *Biographical Dictionary of Modern Peace Leaders* (1985), Charles F. Howlett and Glenn Zeitzer, *The American Peace Movement: History and Historiography* (1985); and Charles DeBenedetti, *Peace Heroes in Twentieth Century America* (1986).

The members of the CPRH include diplomatic historians, analysts of military policy, chroniclers of movements for peace and social justice, and those interested in their work. They include researchers, teachers, students, peace activists, and members of the general public. Increasingly the organization has drawn members from around the world, and it encourages the formation of comparable regional associations.

THE EUROPEAN WORKING GROUP ON PEACE RESEARCH IN HISTORY was formed at the conclusion of the Stadtschlaining Conference, August 1986, as an informal network linking European historians in peace research. That had been, in fact, one of the aims of the European-American Consultation on Peace Research in History. The need for such a network had become increasingly obvious when, in the 1970s and 1980s, the peace ideas, institutions, and movements of the past became subjects of scholarly research in various European countries, thereby opening up sometimes virtually untapped primary sources. The achievements of the CPRH in the United States provided a stimulus and model for the creation of a similar European organization.

Its founding had been suggested during the August 1985 Stuttgart conference of the International Association of European Contemporary History (*Association Internationale d'Histoire Contemporaine de l'Europe*, AIHCE). On the initiative of the president and the secretary-general of AIHCE, Professor Jacques Bariéty of the Sorbonne and Professor Antoine Fleury of the University Institute of Advanced International Studies, Geneva, the conference devoted a special session to initiatives for international peace, from the mid-nineteenth century to the Briand-Kellogg Pact. On this occasion, a working group was set up to facilitate contacts between historical peace researchers, with Dr. Werner Simon of the United Nations

Library, Geneva, as secretary. By this time, there existed a cohesive German Working Group on Historical Peace Research (*Arbeitskreis Historische Friedensforschung*), coordinated by Professor Karl Holl of the University of Bremen, which provided a model of national organization, and also the nascent Peace Movements Study Group of the International Peace Research Association, coordinated by Professor Nigel Young of Colgate University, New York, for the comparative study of historical and contemporary peace movements.

The European delegates at the Stadtschlaining meeting agreed to develop an informal network which should work with existing international groups and also encourage national organization on the model of the German Working Group. Since the search for peace commonly has been pursued from an internationalist perspective, attempts to identify, describe, analyze, and compare peace endeavors similarly must transcend national frameworks. In this respect, the existence of a network enables researchers to draw on a common pool of information, exchanging data and views, and coordinate their work in progress with that of others. One of the first aims of the European Working Group is the preparation of an inventory and assessment of European archival resources, for which Peter van den Dungen, University of Bradford, has taken the initiative.

Index

Peace Movements and Political Cultures was designed by Sheila Hart; composed by Lithocraft, Inc., Grundy Center, Iowa; and printed and bound by Braun-Brumfield, Inc., Ann Arbor, Michigan. The book was set in 10/12 Times Roman with Caledonia display and printed on 60-lb. Glatfelter.